ACTS OF COURAGE

❧c ꝏ❧

Václav Havel's Life in the Theater

Carol Rocamora

SMITH AND KRAUS

Published by
Smith and Kraus, Inc.
177 Lyme Road, Hanover, NH 03755
www.smithkraus.com

First edition: March 2005
9 8 7 6 5 4 3 2 1

Cover and text design by Julia Gignoux
Freedom Hill Design, Reading, Vermont

Library of Congress Cataloging-in-Publication Data
Rocamora, Carol.
Acts of courage ; Václav Havel's life in the theater ; a biography /
by Carol Rocamora. — 1st ed.
p. cm. — (Art of theater book)
Includes bibliographical references and index.
ISBN 1-57525-344-5 (cloth) — ISBN 1-57525-325-9 (pbk.)
1. Havel, Václav. 2. Dramatists, Czech — 20th century — Biography. I. Title: Václav Havel's life in the theater ; a biography. II. Title. III. Art of theater series.

PG5039.18.A9Z87 2003
891.8'6254—dc22
[B]
2003044258

For Tomáš, Thea, Jiří
and all my Czech friends,
who have been a
"light on a landscape."

All the world's a stage,
And all the men and women merely players.
They have their exits and their entrances;
And one man in his time plays many parts . . .

As You Like It, Act II, scene vii

Contents

PART III
THE SEVENTIES: THE PLAYWRIGHT AT A CROSSROADS

PART IV
THE EIGHTIES: FAR FROM THE THEATER

PART V
THE NINETIES AND BEYOND:
POLITICS AND THEATER AS ONE

PART VI
EPILOGUE

PART VII
CURTAIN CALL

Preface

I n the fall of 2000, while visiting Prague, I attended a production of *The Beggar's Opera*. It was not John Gay's, it was Václav Havel's, who was not only the playwright but also the president of his country at the time. The play was being performed at a small but celebrated theater called Jára Cimrman, known for its original comedic work. The theater was tucked away on a quiet tree-lined side street near the center of Prague. The performance was produced by DAMU (Academy of the Dramatic Arts), our equivalent of the Juilliard School, and in the lobby we were greeted by eager young people who were passing out tickets and brightly colored hand-printed programs. Inside the auditorium, students in their early twenties acted out the familiar roles of Macheath and Polly Peachum with all their hearts. At first I missed the accompanying musical score, but the passion of the youthful performers and the wit and irony of the version provided a music of its own.

The Beggar's Opera wasn't the only theatrical performance by Havel in Prague at the time. Across the river, looming high above the other bank of the Vltava, the majestic Prague Castle had been transformed into the setting for his newest production. Forum 2000, a three-day international symposium on globalization, was then in its fourth season of dialogues on issues of universal concern, including human rights, world hunger, education, spiritual values, and culture. This time, his cast wasn't amateur; it was all-star and international, featuring prime ministers, heads of states, Nobel Peace Prize–winners, and other luminaries ranging from the religious (the Dalai Lama) to the popular (rock star Peter Gabriel) to the literary (Nigerian playwright Wole Soyinka and Rumanian-born writer Elie Wiesel).

Back to Havel on the smaller stage. I thought about those young students at DAMU and wondered what it must feel like for them to live in a culture in which their president is a playwright and they were performing his play. Utopia, certainly. (I was envious. I teach playwriting students at New York University's Tisch School of the Arts and imagined how they might feel under such circumstances). I approached one of my

Czech colleagues at the New York University program in Prague, where I had been teaching. Utopia? Not exactly, he replied. It's a long story.

Later, I heard the beginnings of that story. DAMU, the prestigious theater conservatory that had performed the production of *The Beggar's Opera*, had repeatedly rejected Havel as a student years ago for reasons pertaining to his class status (under Communism, he was labeled a "bourgeois"). Furthermore, while *The Beggar's Opera* has been performed frequently since the Velvet Revolution, it had been banned before that, as were all of Havel's plays, for over two decades. After *The Beggar's Opera* was first written, there was an illegal performance in 1975, and many of those who appeared in and attended the production were punished with arrests, imprisonment, and other severe sanctions.

The beginnings of a long story, indeed. I started questioning colleagues in the theater community in Prague and learned that behind the drama written by Havel was a far greater human drama, one not widely known in the West. Ever since the Velvet Revolution in 1989, Havel's presidency has eclipsed his playwriting; yet he is an author of a rich and significant dramatic œuvre, one of great consequence to his country's culture and its history.

Back in America, I did a preliminary survey of the literature about Havel. I was surprised to find that while Havel the human rights activist and president is a world celebrity, Havel the playwright is more obscure. Yes, of course, all my colleagues knew he was a dramatist, but some were hard pressed to name a title of one of his plays. (The majority cited *The Memorandum*, remembering a production directed by Joseph Papp in 1968, in his first season at the Public Theater.) While Havel is celebrated in the West as a world leader, his plays have been overlooked in favor of his political profile.

Then I delved deeper and started to learn the extraordinary story of Václav Havel's life in the theater. It was a story that was not his alone, a story that involved many people and numerous theater companies, a story that involved risks and sacrifices, lives and livelihoods. A story that reflected his country's history, and a story that shaped it. A thrilling story. And one that, amazingly and inexplicably, hasn't yet been told fully in English.

Marisa Smith and Eric Kraus, the American play publishers, who share my admiration for Havel's plays, were encouraging. "He's been a hero of ours for years," they said. "Write a book about him."

As someone who teaches dramatic literature to young playwrights at the Tisch School, I have strived for years to convey to them the importance of theater — what it means, what it can mean. I am grateful to have found a story to tell them, one that can set an example, one that can inspire, one that can change the way we see the theater and the world.

It is a story wherein writing, directing, performing, and even attending a play constitute an extraordinary act of courage.

Acknowledgments

M y profoundest thanks go to the New York University in Prague, under the direction of Jiří Pehe and Thea Favaloro. Ever since May 2000, when I went there to teach theater in the Tisch School of the Arts International Program, it has become my "home" in Prague where I could conduct research for this book. Thanks to their resources, their endless assistance, and the tireless support of their staff including Marta Štecová and Martina Faltová, I have had access to many contacts and sources in the community that would otherwise not have been available to me.

Thanks also to my other two research bases in Prague — the Theatre Institute (Divadelní ústav) (Helena Albertová, Andrea Landovská, and Jiřina Šormová) and the Theatre on the Balustrade (Ivana Slámová, Marie Fišerová, Martina Musilová, and their kind, attentive staff) who opened their archives to me and provided invaluable help.

Finding and assembling the source material for Havel's life in the theater has been a major challenge. Much of it is scattered, hidden, misplaced, lost, or not yet translated. Other information has not even been recorded. In the process of researching this book, I am hugely indebted to many generous, kind, and patient colleagues without whose help I could not have written it.

First, there are the plays themselves. Havel's collected plays have been published in Czech in volume II of *Spisy* (Writings), published in Prague by Torst in 1999. (The four coauthored one-act plays from the late 1950s and early 1960s are not, however, included in that collection.) Most but not all the plays have been translated into English. My thanks to Aurapont, the Czech writers' agency, for permitting me to see archival copies of some of these shorter, unpublished works. My further thanks to the Theatre on the Balustrade, for permitting me to see archival copies of the early drafts of some of Havel's plays. As for productions of Havel's plays themselves, my very special thanks to the Theatre Institute in Prague (Divadelní ústav) and especially to Helena Albertová, for her kind assistance in permitting me to borrow all the videotaped productions in Czech of Havel's plays from the institute's excellent video archives.

Second, there are Havel's writings about the theater, including essays, articles, and letters. They have not yet been collected. Some have not been published; others haven't even been translated. Still others are hidden away in private archives. (I even found one original letter framed on the wall of director Andrej Krob's cottage!) Now that Havel's presidency is over, it is hoped that there will be an effort to collect, publish, and translate all these important writings about the theater. Of what has been translated and published to date, the most valuable, primary sources have been *Disturbing the Peace* (the closest we have to an autobiography by Havel) and the collected *Letters to Olga*, which was written while he was in prison from 1979 to 1983. Both contain rich and illuminating passages about his life in the theater, and both have been beautifully translated by Paul Wilson, who has also translated many of Havel's essays and speeches. My special thanks also to Miloš Forman, Gail Papp, Andrej Krob, and Klaus Juncker for taking the time to locate and to provide me with some of the unpublished correspondence between Havel and others. These letters are treasures.

Third, there are video-archival sources about Havel's life in the theater and in politics. For these secondary source materials, I am most grateful to the efforts of Marta Štecová at New York University in Prague; thanks to her efforts, Martin Vidlák at the Prague Castle provided me with access to the castle video archives and the Czech Television archives during Havel's presidency. Thanks also to Andrej Krob and Aleš Kisil for access to their video collections about the Theatre on the Road and to Jan Grossman.

Fourth, there is access to the playwright himself. Thanks to the introduction by Jiří Pehe and the arrangements by Anna Freimanová, President Havel's secretary at the Prague Castle, I was able to begin a correspondence with the playwright/president in October 2001, and later to have a personal interview at the castle in March 2002. Thanks also to Klaus Juncker, Havel's dedicated and devoted agent/publisher in Reinbek, Germany, who, despite ill health, opened his files to me and provided invaluable archival materials and information. Both Anna and Klaus have been patient and available in answering an endless flow of questions.

Fifth, there are the stories and personal reminiscences. In researching this book, I have found that much of Havel's life in the theater, particularly in the 1970s and 1980s when his work was banned, is still in the realm of oral history. So I conducted interviews with numerous Czech theater artists — playwrights, directors, dramaturgs, actors, critics, biographers — interviews that have provided the most illuminating and moving material. My heartfelt thanks for the time, patience, and reminiscences of those who provided so much. In the Czech Republic: Helena Albertová, Alexandra Brabcová, Jan Burian, Vlasta Chramostová, Anna Freimanová, Vlasta Gallerová, Ivan Havel, Zdeněk Hořínek, Vladimír Just, Jan Kačer, Ivan Klíma, Aleš Kisil, Ladislav Klepal, Eda Kriseová, Andrej Krob, Karel Kříž, Andrea Landovská, Pavel Landovský, Marie Málková, Josef Mlejnek, Martina Musilová, Jiří Ornest, Petr Oslzlý, Jiří Paukert/Kuběna, Jiří Pehe, Vilém Prečan, Jiřina Šormová, Jiřina Šiklová, Ivana Slámová, Martin Švejda, Ivan Vodička, Tomáš Vrba, and Ivan Vyskočil. In the West: Edward Albee, Achim Benning, Michael Billington, Olympia Dukakis, Miloš Forman, Mel Gussow, Klaus Juncker, Jeri Laber, Wendy and William Luers, Roger Michell, Gail Papp, Harold Pinter, Michael Simmons, Tom Stoppard, Sam Walters, and Erika Zabrsa.

There are moments from those interviews that are unforgettable, like the time spent with Havel's close friend, the actor Pavel Landovský, at his dacha in Kytín outside Prague. We sat around his swimming pool one June afternoon talking about the traumatic events of the 1970s and 1980s while his son Jakub, a young attorney who now works in the Castle, showed me where the cow had fallen into the water a few days before in pursuit of a bobbing apple — a tranquil, bucolic setting in contrast to his father's dramatic stories. I also recall the interview with Jiřina Šiklová, the eminent Czech professor of sociology and former organizer of a ring to smuggle dissident literature outside Czechoslovakia. After sitting in her Prague apartment that served as the clearinghouse for smuggled manuscripts for over a decade, and hearing about her year in prison, she showed me the lacy party frock that her five-year-old granddaughter was to wear that evening to meet President Havel on his last Independence Day Celebration (October 27, 2002) at the Castle.

There was the moment when Ivan Havel showed me the tiny room behind the kitchen in the family apartment, affectionately called the *pelech* (meaning "den" or "lair") where his older brother Václav wrote his first play at the age of twenty-three and where the two brothers made up the language of Ptydepe which served as the foundation of his play, *The Memorandum*. And the visit to Andrej Krob's cottage at Hrádeček in the Czech countryside, when he showed me the props stored above the corner armoire that came from that legendary production of *The Beggar's Opera* in 1975. And the moment Klaus Juncker, Havel's dedicated agent/publisher dug into his files in his sun-filled study in Reinbek, Germany, to find an original, unpublished letter from Beckett to Havel. And the hours that Helena Albertová spent cutting photos off her carefully assembled international exhibit on Havel's plays so that they might be included in this book. For all their generosity, time, efforts, and heart, I am endlessly grateful. Theirs was a labor of love for the playwright and for the theater he created.

For resources and support here in New York, I offer thanks to Mary Schmidt Campbell, the dean of the Tisch School of the Arts, and to the vice dean, Randy Martin, for supporting my research; to my chairmen Mark Dickerman and Richard Wesley for supporting my leave of absence to complete this book; to my colleague Janet Neipris for inviting me to teach with her at New York University in Prague in 2000; to Andrew Mc-Caldon for his fine research assistance, and to my former student Beth Bigler for her additional support. My thanks also to Troy Pugmire for helping me translate the German transcription of the interview with Klaus Juncker, Havel's agent. Thanks also to the continuing efforts of my literary agent, Diana Tyler, of MBA Literary Agency in London and her associate Dana Ondrejmiskova. Additional thanks to Alan Hirsig and Michael Simmons, for their efforts in identifying some valuable source material.

For the idea of the book, the resources, and the encouragement, I am, above all, deeply indebted and grateful to my publishers Marisa Smith and Eric Kraus. Their love of theater and admiration for Havel prompted them to suggest that I write this book. Thanks also to their fine staff, and especially to Julia Gignoux and Kate Mueller for their production and editorial services.

For editorial guidance, my heartfelt thanks to Constance Rosenblum, who read and edited the manuscript and has given so generously and endlessly of her time, expertise, and friendship.

There is a special category of acknowledgment for my research assistant, the playwright and novelist Tomáš Rychetský, who sat with me at every interview and translated from Czech to English, who drove me all over the Czech Republic and back in pursuit of every story of Havel's life in the theater, who searched everywhere for books and tapes, who poured over the dozens of reviews and articles, who carried piles of books hither and yon, who hunted down photographs, and who translated almost everything we could find that up to now hasn't been translated about Havel's life in the theater (which is a considerable amount). He has been more than an interpreter/translator. He has been a dedicated and gifted guide through this rich, complicated, often impenetrable culture—its history, its politics, and its literature. His insights into the complexities of his country and to Havel's plays have been invaluable. He has been, to use Havel's phrase, "a light on the landscape." With gratitude, I dedicate this book to him and to all the Czech colleagues and friends who have been my companions and guides on this journey through Václav Havel's fascinating and unique life in the theater.

For additional translation assistance, thanks also to Renata Tumlířová in Prague for all her efforts and to Nicole Potenec in New York.

For photographs, my heartfelt appreciation to Helena Albertová for her time and patience in opening the photo archive of the Divadelní ústav exhibition on Havel's plays, which is the fruit of her tireless efforts. Thanks also to Ivan Havel for his permission to use some photos from the private family archive; to the Theatre on the Balustrade, Činoherní Klub, and Vinohrady Theater for permission to use their production photos; and to the photographers Jaroslav Kořan, Viktor Krombauer, Alan Pajer, Hana Rysová, and Oldřich Škácha. Heartfelt appreciation again to Thea Favaloro, for her endless patience and efforts in helping to assemble these photos.

A special acknowledgment is offered regarding scholarship on Havel's life and work. There are two existing biographies: Eda Kriseová's *Václav Havel: An Authorized Biography* (1993) and the British journalist John Keane's *Václav Havel: A Political Tragedy in Six Acts* (2000). While both focus on his life in politics, they also offer important information about his life in the theater. Then there is *Disturbing the Peace* (1986), the long-distance interview with Havel conducted by the journalist Karel Hvížďala and translated by Paul Wilson. It is in a special category all its own. Although it is in question/answer format, it is the closest we have to an autobiography by Havel, and it contains many rich, deep, and personal passages about Havel's feelings about the theater and his plays. I could not have written this book without the biographical information included in these three works.

As for literary criticism, there is surprisingly little written about Havel's plays and his life in the theater, the reasons for which shall be offered throughout this book. What exists, however, is of very high quality. Markéta Goetz-Stankiewicz, professor emerita of Germanic studies and comparative literature at the University of British Columbia and a Czech emigré, is the leading scholar of Havel's dramatic works. She kept a focus on his plays beginning in the late 1970s and throughout the 1980s, when they were banned in his own country. Her chapter on Havel's plays of the

1960s and 1970s in *The Silenced Theatre* (1979) and her introductions to *Drama Contemporary: Czechoslovakia* (1985), *The Vaněk Plays* (1987) and *Good-bye Samizdat* (1992) have provided commentary that was extremely informative. Her edited *Critical Essays on Václav Havel* (1999) has been helpful in showcasing the scholarship of others. It is hoped that her work and that of the others will continue in the future to illuminate Havel's dramatic literature.

As for theater criticism of Havel's plays, a collection of Czech reviews and commentaries on Havel's plays have not yet been translated into English, to my knowledge. The individual reviews and commentaries that I have quoted in this book have all been translated from the original by Tomáš Rychetský (unless otherwise noted).

Finally, there is Václav Havel himself. During the time that I was researching and writing this book, he was the president of his country. In the midst of his inhumanly demanding schedule, he graciously made time to talk about the theater and answer my questions. For this opportunity, I am deeply honored and grateful. He has an unforgettable way of speaking — soft-spoken and low-voiced. His thoughtfully shaped sentences and sculpted paragraphs flow. He speaks as beautifully as he writes. He is gentle, wise, modest, kind, and very funny. In short, he is a great man, and he has my most profound admiration. From him I have learned what the theater can mean.

I hope that this book will do justice to the story of his life in the theater.

A WORD ABOUT TRANSLATIONS

Quotations from Havel's translated plays, essays, letters, and poems are in English; in each case, I have acknowledged the translator in the footnotes. The names of Havel's plays and the names of Czech theaters are also in English. Names of Czech newpapers, magazines, journals, and other publications are in Czech (with their English names in parentheses).

I am not Czech, and though I speak fluent Russian, French, and German, my Czech is minimal. Several of my Czech colleagues told me that it would be hard for an outsider to tell this story, that only those who lived through those strange and difficult decades under Communism, with all its paradoxes and absurdities, can comprehend it. "It was complicated here," they warned me. "Our story is hard to understand."

For all those nuances or subtleties that I may not have grasped: mea culpa. Perhaps I have rushed in where angels fear to tread, in attempting to tell a broad and deep story that may be beyond the capabilities of an outsider. Nevertheless, since I live in a culture where the role and the identity of the playwright are still evolving, I am filled with admiration for the story of Havel's life in the theater. For me, it has set an example. It is a hope that his acts of courage will ignite the imagination and hearts of others.

One day, perhaps, the theater will matter in our culture the way it has in his.

Special thanks go to Václav Havel for permission to quote from his writings (plays, essays, interviews, poetry). Quotations from Havel's *Selected Plays 1963–1983* and *1984–1987* (see bibliography for various translators) are made with permission of Faber & Faber and Grove Press. Quotations from Havel's *The Beggar's Opera* (translated by Paul Wilson) are made with permission of Cornell University Press. Quotations from *Letters to Olga* (translated by Paul Wilson) are made with permission of Faber & Faber and Alfred A. Knopf, a division of Random House, Inc. Quotations from *Disturbing the Peace* (translated by Paul Wilson) are made with permission of Alfred A. Knopf. Quotations from Arthur Miller's *The Crucible* are made with permission of Viking Penguin, a division of the Penguin Group, Inc. (USA). Quotations from Arthur Miller's *I think about you a great deal* are made with permission of International Creative Management, Inc. Quotations from *The Vaněk Plays* are made with permission of the University of British Columbia Press.

❧c Prologue ᴐ❧

Not long ago in Prague, a seven-volume collection of writings, bound in green, was published in Czech. It contained most of the work written over a forty-six-year period by Václav Havel, a man who was also his country's president at the time. The modesty of the simple title, *Spisy* (Writings), belies its contents. It is a prodigious collection of more than seven thousand pages, including over two volumes of essays on a broad range of philosophical, political, and ethical topics written from 1953 to 1989; two volumes of political speeches written during his presidency from 1990 to 1999; a volume of poetry written from the early 1950s (while in his teens) until the late 1970s; and a volume of 144 letters to his wife, Olga, written while he was in prison from 1979 to 1983.

This significant literary event went by largely unnoticed, eclipsed by the author's celebrated public life. That is hardly surprising. Havel, who was born in 1936, is known the world over as a great man of the twentieth century. He is admired for his heroic struggle for human rights in Czechoslovakia for three decades under Communism and for leading his country out of darkness in the Velvet Revolution of 1989. He is recognized for his enlightened presidency of a new democracy and for his visionary efforts in globalization at the millennium. The events in his political life had been a daily front-page focus in papers all over the world for decades. In the weeks before his departure as president, the *New York Times* described his image abroad "as a kind of living saint."[1]

Still, the publication of the collection is a reminder that the president of his country and the humanist admired universally for his accomplishments is, fundamentally, a writer. And that while his presidency could not last, his writings will, and with them the ideas that he has lived and worked for, ideas that have made his country and the world a better place.

In that collection of writings, there is also a volume entitled *Hry* (Plays). It includes ten full-length plays, five one-acts, and one television and one radio play (four other coauthored one-act plays are not included).

A major body of dramatic work, it has been largely overlooked during the past three decades, except for some diligent scholarship on the part of a dedicated few, upstaged by the traumatic events unfolding in Czechoslovakia in which Havel himself played the leading role. The reasons are clear: In his own country, Havel's plays could neither be produced nor openly discussed for years. And abroad, interest in Havel as a human rights activist and subsequently as a head of state was stronger than interest in his dramatic work. Yet Havel's plays constitute a significant body of work spanning the period from 1959 to 1988, a crucial dramatization of human existence in a crucial era.

In February 2003, Havel stepped down from his thirteen-year term as president of the Czech Republic. With the conclusion to the story of his life in the presidency, it is now possible to turn our attention to this compelling body of dramatic work and what lies behind it, a remarkable story of a life in the theater largely unknown outside his country. It is a story waiting to be told.

What is the value of telling it? The story of Havel's life in the theater illuminates the man, the work, and the times in which his plays were written. Havel is a man of many identities — philosopher, playwright, essayist, editor, poet, human rights activist, ethicist, dissident, prisoner, politician, president, world statesman — all of which have been celebrated. Now there is an opportunity to focus on his identity as a playwright. The work? A rich and complex oeuvre with universal themes and a unique voice, it has a special place in twentieth-century dramatic literature, one that is yet to be claimed. The times? An era that must not be forgotten, lest we are ever again in peril of losing our identity and our human rights — above all, the right to write.

Together, the plays themselves and the drama behind the drama are worthy of recognition. For they are illuminating to those who want to better understand the turbulent events of the twentieth century and to those who value the theater, its powers, and its historical significance.

Václav Havel's life in the theater divides itself clearly into five decades, paralleling his country's history in a striking way. That makes it an easier story to tell. It is an inspiring story, one unlike any other in recent theater history. And it is not Václav Havel's alone; it involves a large cast of characters, playing significant roles in a variety of settings. Moreover, it is a story that is still evolving. Once a president, but always a playwright.

The question, then, is how to tell it. In speaking about his life in politics, Václav Havel has often said ruefully that it has been likened to a fairy tale. During a speech entitled "A Farewell to Politics" given in September 2002 at CUNY (City University of New York), on the occasion of his last official visit to the United States as president of the Czech Republic, he remarked:

> In the past, when I would receive honorary degrees and listen to the laudatory speeches made on those occasions, I often had to smile to myself at how, in so many of those tributes, I came across as a fairy-tale hero, a boy who, in the name of the good, beat his head against the wall of a castle inhabited by evil kings, until the wall fell down and he himself became king and then went on to rule wisely for many long years.[2]

Like Havel's life in the presidency, his life in the theater is no fairy tale, either. It is more like a drama, but one with fairy-tale elements. Theatrical and thrilling. Suspenseful and extreme. There is good and there is evil. It may not have a happy ending, but that is because it has no ending. The curtain may go down, but there is still the larger theater, the one of the playwright's vision that can be played on any conceivable stage.

It does have a moral, though.

It shows us, in the special context of that extraordinary time, what theater can mean and what being a playwright can mean, if one acts and writes with courage.

So, chronologically, then —

Once, in a land ruled by dark and invisible forces, there lived a young writer . . .

The Fifties

The Education of a Writer

I'd been writing ever since they taught me the alphabet . . .[1]
— Havel, *Disturbing the Peace*

SCENE ONE

"Wake up, Vašek! It's way past eleven! They're here!"

A bright fall morning in 1952. His mother stood anxiously over the bed in the tiny back room overlooking the courtyard. A tousled, golden, sixteen-year-old head peered out from under the bedcovers at the embarrassed young faces clustered at the door. So began another meeting of the 36ers, a remarkable circle of teenage literati whose fate it was to be born bourgeois in a country that would fall under totalitarian rule and deny them formal education. And a remarkable circle it was, because it would spawn a young writer who would one day lead his country out of that totalitarian darkness into the light.

But first, that would-be leader had to put on his clothes. There were the good-byes said to Božena Havlová,[1] his mother, as she stood in the high-ceilinged drawing room of the family's elegant Art Nouveau apartment, with sweeping views of the Vltava River and the majestic sixteenth-century castle beyond it. Then, closing the huge doors behind them, the group forsook the elevator and bounded down five flights of the majestic mansion that was once inhabited by the Havel family. (Václav's grandfather had built it in 1905, but under Communism Václav's parents eventually were allocated the fifth floor only.)[2] Outside, a brisk October day in Prague awaited them. They crossed the embankment of the churning Vltava and ran five blocks along the river to Národní Street. On the corner, opposite the stately National Theater, stood their destination, the

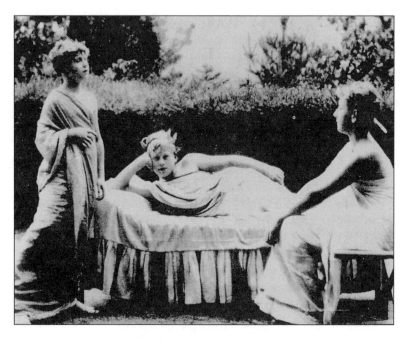

Václav (center) at play, Havlov, summer 1949
(from the Havel family archive)

Café Slavia, haven for the intelligentsia during that severe Stalinist era. A warm, welcoming light emanated from the broad glass windows, through which they could see marble-topped tables and inviting red banquettes. They entered eagerly through the grand double doors and took their seats in a place they would later call their university.

1951–1955: THE EDUCATION OF AN OUTSIDER

> My childhood feeling of exclusion . . . could not but have an influence on the way I viewed the world — a view which is in fact a key to my plays. It is a view "from below," a view from the "outside."[1]
>
> — Havel, *Disturbing the Peace*

Obtaining a classical education in Czechoslovakia was a perilous affair in the 1950s, especially if you were a child of privilege. For young Václav Havel, born in 1936 into one of Prague's "grand bourgeois families," it was an obstacle course.

Consider the prominence of his family. Václav's paternal grandfather, one of Prague's first capitalists, was a self-made man, a eminent architect and contractor who built Lucerna Palace, the city's first steel-and-concrete building. Václav's father (also called Václav) followed in his footsteps and became the builder who developed the fashionable Barrandov district — one of the most beautiful in all Prague. Václav's uncle Miloš, who built Barrandov Film Studios, was a leading force of Czech cinema.

But all that splendor ended in 1948 when the Communists came to power, confiscating the family property and banishing the bourgeoisie from Prague. Overnight, the family, eminent and wealthy on both his father's and mother's sides, became outsiders. As Vera Blackwell, one of the first translators of Havel's plays into English, put it in the 1960s: "If Czechoslovakia had remained primarily a capitalist society, Václav Havel would be today just about the richest young man in the country."[2]

Václav's mother was prepared. Daughter of a famous journalist, diplomat, and politician, Božena Havlová was a cultured, confident woman with high standards, and the education of her children was the first priority. Like other affluent Czechs, ever since the assassination of Reinhard Heydrich (the Nazi ruler of Czechoslovakia) by the Czech underground in 1942, she sensed that Prague would be a dangerous place in which to raise her two small sons, Václav, age six, and Ivan, age four. So the Havels retreated to the safe haven of the family country estate, Havlov, deep in the Moravian forests. The house was grand and spacious, built from wood at the turn of the century. It featured a large living room and dining room, ten guest rooms, and a half-moon-shaped swimming pool, a rare amenity at the time. The house itself sat atop a hill overlooking the Bobrůvka River and the gently sloping Moravian hills. Behind it was a garden, and beyond, pine trees, woods, and fields. It was lovely. The family spent most of the war and the early postwar period in the beauty and safety of their rural retreat.[3]

In 1942, Božena enrolled Václav, age six, in the local village school in Žďárec, within walking distance from Havlov. The school had three classrooms with two to three grades clustered in each and roughly fifty children in all. Every day until age eleven, Václav and his brother walked to the local elementary school, through the fields and along the country roads. So life went on, with a semblance of normality that Božena tried valiantly to maintain.

While a haven from the hostilities in Prague, it was also a life of paradoxes. Even in the countryside, young Václav was aware of a world in peril. There were air raids in the nearby village of Žďárec. On May 9, 1945, the day after the Nazis were defeated in Europe, the eight-year-old Václav wrote in his schoolbook (alongside crayon sketches of fighter planes) of how the village was being bombed because German troops were still there and how afraid the villagers were. There was also the discomfort over his life of privilege as "a gentleman's son."[4] His parent's household included a governess, a maid, a gardener, a cook, and a chauffeur. As a result, young Václav was painfully aware of the social barrier between him and his fellow students. Reflecting on his childhood years later, he wrote:

> I was ashamed of my advantages, my perks; I pleaded to be relieved of them and I longed for equality with others, not because I was some kind of childhood social revolutionary, but simply because I felt separate and excluded, because I felt around me a certain mistrust, a certain distance . . . because I knew that between me and those around me there was an an invisible wall, and because behind that wall — and this may seem paradoxical — I felt alone, inferior, lost, ridiculed. . . . In short, I felt "outside," excluded, humbled by my "higher status."[5]

Then there was the endless teasing he suffered at school for being overweight or, as he put it, "a well-fed piglet."[6] This only compounded his feelings as an outsider, as he interpreted the ridicule of his peers as an act of unconscious social revenge. Of his parents, Havel wrote forgivingly, saying they always did what they thought best and were simply unaware that their protectiveness and pampering might provoke such an adverse outcome.

From another perspective, his early years at Havlov were idyllic. He was enveloped by the warmth of family life and the wealth of their possessions, richest of all being their books. While his younger brother Ivan played outside on the family estate, swam in the pool, and wandered through the woods, ten-year-old Václav sat indoors, blissfully reading through the family library. He devoured volumes of poetry, literature, and philosophy. He read works of Karel Čapek, the Czech playwright, and Tomáš Masaryk, the father of Czech democracy. Family friends such as the eminent Czech philosopher Josef Šafařík came to visit, and the children were encouraged to converse with them.

A few months before the Communist takeover of February 1948, Václav's mother transferred him to a small private boarding school in Poděbrady, thirty miles east of Prague in Bohemia. Founded after the war for orphans, the school soon became a place where affluent Czechs sent their children as well. As one of its other former students, Miloš Forman, describes it: "The student body consisted of one-half orphans and one-half pampered kids of Communists and capitalists."[7] Modeled after the renowned British school Eton, it was located in a sixteenth-century castle. "The walls were three feet thick," says Forman, "with lots of secret corridors where we found cannonballs from centuries past. The classrooms were cold." Forman, who was fifteen at the time, supervised a group of younger boys that included Václav, who was eleven. "We became friends, although there was an age difference," Forman recalls. "He was just as he is today, extremely polite, tactful, shy, but if you jabbed him, you reached an inner core of steel." Boarding-school life was severe, and included rigorous academics and whippings. But during his two and a half years at the school, Václav had some pleasures, including his friendship with Forman and an introduction to drama, which became his favorite extracurricular activity. (His brother Ivan recalls how he once came home from school, bursting with news about a production of *Hadrian*, a Czech adaptation of the Roman play that had thrilled him.)

While Václav was at Poděbrady, things got worse for the Havel family. In March 1949, Václav's father was arrested, interrogated, and accused of trying to help his father-in-law to leave Czechoslovakia. He was held in prison for three months, and though eventually he was acquitted and released, the episode took a toll on Václav's mother. Václav's paternal grandfather was also brought to trial and later acquitted. His uncle Miloš was imprisoned for two years at Plzeň-Bory (a place that would reappear in Havel's own adult life) for trying to cross the border illegally, and his property was confiscated.

The school at Poděbrady was ultimately closed by the Communists for "class bias." In 1950, when the secret police had begun weeding out the more privileged, Václav was one of the first to go. (Forman, by contrast, was expelled "for political reasons." As he describes it, he had played a prank on a higher Communist official. But the headmaster was compassionate. "Here's your diploma," he said. "Now run for your life!")

Back to Prague the Havel family went, to the stately mansion on the embankment. The years 1950 to 1951 were lost years in Václav's education. He tried to finished his compulsory schooling in the state system, but was expelled because of his class status. Discouraged, the fifteen-year-old Václav lost interest and spent time sitting around in cafés with a friend who was suffering the same fate. Since he was out of school, he was required to work and served for a while as an apprentice carpenter. Then, through his parents, he found a job as an apprentice laboratory assistant at the Institute of Chemical Technology in Prague. Meanwhile, his parents encouraged him to apply to night school in Štěpánská Street just off Wenceslas Square, so he could finish his formal education. The night school had been established for working-class managers to broaden their education, rather than for bourgeois children who were expelled from day school. Years later, Havel wondered how he managed it — eight hours of work in the laboratory on the other side of Prague, then four hours at night school. On top of that there were dancing lessons (at his mother's insistence) and endless reading. But at least at night school, he found a peer to whom he could relate, a youth named Radim Kopecký whose father, the Czech ambassador to Switzerland, was in jail for anti-Socialist behavior. Together, the boys talked philosophy and politics and prowled through secondhand bookstores.

The years 1951 to 1953 were dark ones in Prague. The Stalinist purges were in high gear, and a prolonged period of terror descended on the city that would last until 1956. The weeklong public trial in November 1952 of Rudolf Slánský, general secretary of the Czech Communist Party, and thirteen high-ranking Communist codefendants was, as Havel's political biographer John Keane called it, "a bizarre exercise of totalitarian power."[8] It ended horrifically. Slánský and ten others were hanged and then cremated, their ashes scattered on a road outside Prague. After Stalin's death in March 1953, these "show trials" in Czechoslovakia continued, with further arrests, imprisonments, and executions. More than one hundred Czech political leaders were purged and murdered; tens of thousands were jailed or deported. These were tense, fearful times for the Havels; there were repeated efforts to entrap them by the secret police.

The year 1952 was an especially traumatic year for the family. Václav's father finally had to leave Lucerna Palace, the building he and his family had constructed. He had been allowed to stay on and work there since the government had confiscated it in 1949, but eventually he was forced to leave. He went to work for a physical fitness organization as manager of its transportation department. Meanwhile, the state tried to confiscate the Havel's family mansion; when Havel's maternal grandfather heard about it, he became so upset that he suffered a fatal stroke. Václav's maternal grandmother died soon after. Nothing was left of all the family wealth. In the end, Václav's family was forced to move to the top floor of the building, where one apartment was left. Václav was given the small room behind the kitchen overlooking the courtyard. As a result of that move, his mother sent the family china, paintings, and sculpture to various museums in Prague to be stored; according to Havel's Czech biographer Edá Kriseová, the family later lost these items, along with all their real estate. The state even tried to seal up the Havlov estate, an action that Václav's father fought as best he could and even delayed for a while. But by the end of the 1950s, all the family's considerable wealth, property, and belongings on both sides were gone.[9]

Despite it all, Božena was determined not to lose heart and focused instead on continuing her eldest son's education. She seized on the idea of an intellectual circle centered around Václav and Radim, his new friend, and quickly encouraged its formation.

During the autumn of 1952, a remarkable literary circle emerged. Radim named them the 36ers, after their common year of birth. They had other things in common: their privileged status and the persecution of their parents by the state. In addition to Radim and Václav, both of whose fathers had been imprisoned, the group included Miloš Dus, whose industrialist father had suffered the same fate. There was a third point of commonality, their intellect and creativity. The group included would-be philosophers, writers, and musicians, including the essayist Pavel Švanda, the poet Jiří Paukert/Kuběna, the pianist Petr Wurm, and the poetess Viola Fischerová. A number of them lived in Brno, but they made the long journey to Prague eagerly, especially for the gatherings at the Café Slavia. United by a shared enthusiasm for literature, philosophy, art, and ideas, the group organized swiftly. All through the winter of 1952 to 1953, insulated from the political storm raging around them by their passion and enthusiasm, they walked home from night school in the snow, engaged in lively philosophical debates. Every Saturday, they gathered at noon at their "headquarters" at the Café Slavia; on Sundays, they favored long walks through the winding, narrow lanes of Malá Strana, where Kafka had wandered before them. They debated philosophy and poetry; they poured over forbidden books such as Kafka's *The Castle*; they discussed theater (Shakespeare and Molière — the 36ers preferred the latter); they read Masaryk and the memoirs of Eduard Beneš, the Czech leader overthrown by the Communists in 1948; they discussed Nietzsche and Marx's *Das Kapital*. They had their own standards, drawing up lists of eminent writers and poets and ranking them. They avidly followed French and American literary trends, scoured secondhand shops, and circulated library books amongst themselves.

Quickly, Václav became the circle's driving force. He organized group visits to gurus like the Nobel prize–winning poet Jaroslav Seifert and the eccentric poet Vladimír Holan, who lived in a little house in Kampa, tucked away behind the Charles bridge. Miloš Forman remembers accompanying Havel on one of those visits to Holan. "We brought him our attempts on poetry; he talked at length about Václav's, and hardly said a word about mine."[10] He initiated the "publication" of a 36er poetry review, with contributions by Václav, typed by Václav, and designed by his mother. A 36er literary journal, including essays and literary criticism, soon followed. Václav kept diligent minutes of each meeting (twenty "official" meetings were held in the first year), issued assignments, and even organized a 36er syllabus. At the end of the first year, he produced a formal twenty-eight-page report, entitled "After a Year of Sculptural Work," laced with political and ethical theory, calling for a standard of participation, and even chiding some members for "Czech Schweikian behavior" (a reference to the protagonist in Jaroslav Hašek's famous novel, *The Good Soldier Schweik*, who feigned conformity while actually subverting authority).[11] Amusing as that serious-minded, fanatically ordered report by a sixteen-year-old seems, in retrospect it clearly bore the stamp of the astute political leader of the future.

He organized symposia, and there was even a weeklong 36er congress at the Havlov estate in August 1954 organized by Božena Havlová, featuring discussions, photography, and poetry competitions in between dips in the swimming pool.

But the core activity of the 36ers were the Saturday afternoon gatherings at their own table at the Café Slavia, whose atmosphere they adored. The café had a long and rich tradition. Dating from the early 1900s, the L-shaped space looks today very much as it did when the 36ers frequented it: a stylish Art Nouveau décor with high ceilings, mirror-lined walls, mahogany paneling, marble floors, and long rows of windows. To the south, they face Národní (National) Street and the imposing stone arcade of the National Theater. To the west, they look directly onto a dramatic view of the Vltava River, and high above it, on a steep, hill, the Prague Castle. Whether on the bleakest day or the brightest, the view is stunning.

One enters through double doors off Národní Street and turns left from the lobby into a long main room. A shiny glass pastry case stands to the side, topped with stacks of white espresso cups. Crimson carpet runners stretch lengthwise along the marble floors; round wooden tables, some with marble bases and tops, are set throughout the room. Overhead, stylish steel conical shapes shine brightly, and in the center glows a circular green neon lighting fixture. According to the regulars, the main room of the Café Slavia was where foreign visitors and "respectable Praguers" would sit, scattered at tables for two and four. Then the room turns right, offering a sweeping view of the river. Along the back walls of this portion there are a row of tables and banquettes. Some are large, accommodating six to eight people. It was at the second one to the right that Václav and his young friends sat. They could look out onto the river, or at the other eager young Czechs around them, clustered in animated conversation about art, philosophy, literature, and poetry. The tables were never empty in this part of the café, where the artists and intellectuals sat. What cachet it had for those aspiring young writers, with its smoke-filled surroundings and faded grandeur!

But what the 36ers longed for most was to meet their idols, the "forbidden" writers of the older generation, as exemplified by the poet/artist Jiří Kolář. Creator of photographic poetry collages, "rollages," "crumplages," and other objets d'art, Kolář's work was banned because his avant-garde aesthetic was in opposition to Socialist Realism, the official art. As such, he represented those writers in their forties whom the young 36ers, then seventeen, revered for their vision and their uncompromising standards in art and literature. Kolář and his contemporaries belonged to the so-called Group 42, a circle of writers, painters, poets, critics, and professors who gathered in 1942 and were active until the Communist takeover in 1948, when their work was banned. They continued to meet and exchange their creations in handwritten or typewritten form called *samizdat* (meaning the unofficial reproduction of unpublished manuscripts). They even had their own artistic manifesto, in which they declared themselves surrealists. Young Havel had read all the books Kolář had published before 1948, as well as his underground publications from the early 1950s. How the 36ers longed to meet the members of this visionary Group 42, whom they idolized! They could talk of nothing else. Little did they know that the Group 42 had its own table at the Café Slavia; it was, in fact, the table right next to theirs. The idols they had been waiting to meet had been sitting alongside them all that time.

Even after the 36ers disbanded in 1954, Havel kept his table at the Café Slavia, with frequent visits from Jiří Paukert/Kuběna and Miloš Forman, Václav's friend from Poděbrady, who stopped by regularly before and after his classes at the film school. "It was wonderful just to sit there and look out at the castle and the river," recalls Forman. "We met there to share our discoveries — Kafka, Ionesco, Beckett. That was the only way under Communism to disseminate information. And the coffee was so cheap!" There were other new faces at Václav's table, too, including the young playwright Josef Topol and an aspiring actress named Olga Šplíchalová, who first came to the Café Slavia in 1953. There they sat for hours, smoking, laughing, engaged in deep, intense conversation, ordering nothing because they had no money. The waiter would finally come to the table and say gently: "Mr. Havel. You should consume something." "Of course," Havel replied, with unfailing politeness. "One mineral water, please."[12]

Forman recalls another activity they shared. "Václav and I would sit there, dreaming about making a movie together," he said. Václav had been reading Max Brod's book on Kafka, which spoke of a village called

Siřem-Zurau in the Sudetenland, where Kafka's sister lived and where Kafka visited her in the summer. According to the book, the village had a castle, after which Kafka had modeled *The Castle*. So the two friends decided to write a screenplay of Kafka's novel. Armed with the book, they journeyed together to Siřem to conduct their research. "We arrived there to find no castle, only a silo on the hill, which Kafka probably imagined to be a castle," recalls Forman. Next, they set out to find the little house where Kafka's sister had lived. They asked people they saw in the street, but no one could answer because, as Forman explains, Sirem was in the Sudetenland; all the Czechs there had been expelled at the beginning of the war and replaced by newcomers. They were advised to go to the town hall, where the mayor let them look at the archives. Still, they found no indication that Kafka's sister had lived there. Finally, Havel opened Brod's book and showed one of the Communist officials a photo of the village of Sirem. As Forman describes it, the official examined the book and pointed to the picture of Kafka on the cover. "What a pretty face he has!" the official said. Václav and Forman explained that Kafka had had tuberculosis, a disease that gave him an ethereal look. "So that's why I'm so ugly — it's because I'm healthy!" the official exclaimed. The two young men laughed and left, returning to Prague and the Café Slavia. "We never found out where Kafka's sister lived," Forman said. They never made the film either. "I think we had a nice concept of how to do the film," Forman added, "but when I eventually approached the studio, they said 'No way' because it was about Kafka."

By the mid-fifties, the Café Slavia had become the so-called Parnasse of Czech intellectuals.[13] Around the corner stood the philosophy department of Charles University; close by were the classrooms of the film institute; across the street was the National Theater. The café was the meeting place of faculty, students, and artists alike, and the mixture of the younger generation with the older made the place resemble a beehive where ideas were busily cross-pollinating. As such, it was the site of many legendary literary and artistic moments. The story goes, for example, that one afternoon Kolář was sitting at his table with his fellow forbidden writers, holding a photograph of Božena Němcová, the first Czech female novelist. Taking a pair of scissors, he cut the picture into long strips and pasted them onto another page, thereby creating the first collage.[14]

Eventually, Václav and his young companions were invited to sit at Kolář's table. This was the opportunity they had been waiting for, an entrance into what Václav called the "second culture."[15] It was at Kolář's table that the new horizons of modern art were discussed and a whole new world was revealed. For Václav, those discussions were, as he put it, a "kind of university of writer's morality."[16] It was at Kolář's table that he obtained an invaluable education in ethics from the older generation of forbidden writers, one that he couldn't have gotten in any Czech philosophy department at the time. The idea of a moral dimension in literature, the idea of self-publishing rather than conforming to official standards — these are the values Václav learned from his "faculty" at the "University Café Slavia," values that became his foundation. As he said years later in *Disturbing the Peace*, his life as a writer "would be unimaginable without [Kolář's] initial lesson in a writer's responsibility."[17]

The early fifties were vibrant years for Václav and his fellow intellectuals, despite the grayness of the world around them. Through the dark years of Stalinism, with its terrible trials and their chilling aftermath, Václav and his friends stayed tucked away in relative safety behind a cloud of smoke at the Café Slavia, talking, arguing, learning, laughing. Inspired by it all, he would return home, sequester himself in his room overlooking the courtyard (soon dubbed the *pelech* by his family, meaning "den" or "lair" in Czech, because of the hours he spent burrowed in there) and write and write. Some of what he wrote would become part of his first collection of poetry, published in 1957, as well as a book of philosophy called *A First Look at the World*. In short, this unusual education had served him well.

Above all, it was the moral and ethical education at the "University" Café Slavia that he received from his mentors, plus the dignity and tenacity they displayed as banned authors, that taught Václav what it meant to be a writer. In his view, it was because of the type of education he received as an outsider rather than despite it that he became the sort of writer he did.

> I should be thankful for my bourgeois origins . . . the feeling of being excluded through no fault of my own, both in childhood and later, when I was actively persecuted, turned out in the end to be productive. Sometimes I even wonder whether the original reason I began writing, or why I try to anything at all, was simply to overcome this fundamental experience of not belonging, of embarrassment, of fitting in nowhere, of absurdity — or, rather, to learn how to live with it.[18]

In those years, as they sat at the Café Slavia, Václav and his friends gazed through its broad glass windows and across Národní Street onto the great façade of the National Theater, cold and imposing. Though it was built on a bedrock of idealism in the late nineteenth century (it was the first theater dedicated to perform Czech dramatic literature in the Czech language), this "stone theater," as it is called by the Czechs, had no allure for the young intellectuals. In the fifties, the National presented only "official theater," meaning Socialist Realism, and official culture held no interest to them.[19] In the early fifties, the theater had not entered into young Václav's life. Not yet.

1956: A YOUNG WRITER MAKES HIS DEBUT

> My entry into public literary life, then, had a whiff of rebellion about it.[1]
>
> — Havel, *Disturbing the Peace*

The year 1956 was significant for the young writer Havel, and for his country, too. As he remembers it:

> I was twenty in 1956. . . . Historically, it was a fascinating period; for the first time in our part of the world the merry-go-round of hope and disappointment, of half-baked remedies and their half-baked liquidation, of renewed ideals and their renewed betrayal, began to turn.[2]

It was the year of the thaw in the Soviet Union, the year Nikita Khrushchev denounced Stalin and his cult of personality. It was the year of the Hungarian uprising against totalitarianism. Still, the Czech Communist Party remained as implacable as the stern stone statue of Stalin that had been erected on the banks of the Vltava the year before. So it was also the year of the new Czech Five Year Plan, allowing no liberalization of social institutions. Indeed, that word wasn't permitted to be used.

There were, however, signs that the ice might be cracking. At the second congress of the Czechoslovak Writers' Union in Prague in 1956, the poet Jaroslav Seifert, one of Havel's idols, courageously spoke out against the government's policies for the first time. He referred to those writers who had been imprisoned and whose work had been purged from the

Czech literary canons. At the same time, during student May Day festivities, the first criticisms of the 1950 Stalin show trials were tentatively articulated. The razor-sharp lines between the official and the "second" cultures were blurring, and there was hope at the writer's congress that some of the banned books might be published. Something was happening, but it was too early to tell exactly what.

After graduating from night school in 1954, Havel submitted applications to various university humanities programs, including one to study art history and philosophy and another to attend the film school of AMU (Academy of Arts). Again, he was rejected. Party profile was a determining factor in the admissions process, and his parents were not members of the Communist Party. Meanwhile, the threat of the draft loomed large. So in 1955, out of desperation, he applied to the economics faculty of the Czechoslovak University of Technology, to which admission was easy. He was accepted in, of all places, the department of public transport. He enrolled, trying to convince himself that economics would somehow bring him closer to the social sciences.

Undeterred, Havel continued to write, contributing to a number of underground literary periodicals. Then in 1956, the official Writers' Congress founded a new magazine for the younger generation of writers, called *Květen* (May). Although it was an establishment publication, its purpose was to promote writings about everyday life, which until that time had been absent in official literature. The magazine immediately attracted both Havel's attention and his criticism. Boldly, he fired off a letter to its editor expressing his concerns over the inconsistencies of its mission and challenging the magazine to recognize Group 42, which, in his opinion, had already opened poetry up to modern life. To his astonishment, *Květen* published his letter, which in turn provoked a dialogue on its editorial pages. Its editors, all graduates of the establishment Charles University, clearly knew nothing about Group 42, but were willing to engage in a dialogue about the issues of official and suppressed literature. As a result, young Havel found his name on a list of neophyte authors invited to the official three-day conference of young writers in Dobříš, approximately twenty miles southwest of Prague.

Dobříš was the site of an impressive castle, where the official Writers' Union held its conferences. Members of the union had the privilege of using its facilities, which included accommodations and the splendid gardens. Havel went with decided misgivings. What was he doing, he wondered, at an establishment writers' conference, a complete unknown among so many renowned figures? On the other hand, the invitation to be a guest for three days in an eighteenth-century chateau offered allure, as well as opportunity.

Dressed soberly in a suit and tie, seemingly undaunted by the famous writers present (all of whom were members of the party and the Writers' Union), this twenty-year-old unknown shocked the establishment with a daring speech challenging the status quo and its belief that art must be faithful to Socialist Realism. He also confronted the issue of official and suppressed literature head on. Why did the editors not recognize the writers of Group 42 and the great poet Kolář? Why did they not recognize the esteemed Czech dramatist Karel Čapek? Did the editors secretly believe that modern art was bourgeois? Or were the editors silent because deep down they could no longer agree about Socialist Realism's hold over art and yet were simply too afraid to say so? His comments provoked a wildly divergent reaction ranging from spontaneous praise ("daringly critical," "courageous") to outright hostility ("a rebellious bohemian"). Havel's response to the attacks from the floor? "I didn't understand how they [the Czech writing establishment] could hold a costly conference on poetry when it was forbidden to talk about Czech poets."[3]

In retrospect, this response simply reflected the uncertainty of the times. Stalin had fallen in the Soviet Union, Wladyslaw Gomulka had been brought from jail back into power in Poland, and there was even talk that Rudolf Slánský, whose hanging some of the writers present had witnessed only a few years before, might be rehabilitated posthumously. Indeed, while Havel gave his address at Dobříš on that chilly November day in 1956, Hungarian youths were fighting against Soviet tanks with their bare hands on the streets of Budapest.

And so, Havel made his debut at Dobříš in the role of the controversial writer. It was the role in which he cast himself and the role he found himself playing from then on, whether he intended to or not. Looking back on the event, Havel noted with irony that many of the establishment writers who argued with him far into the night subsequently found themselves in the same (banned) boat as he did years later.

The year 1956 was significant for Havel in another aspect. It was the year he started dating Olga Šplíchalová.

The two met at the Café Slavia in 1953 when he was seventeen and she was twenty, but it had taken Havel three years to summon enough courage to ask her out. This was largely because Olga was from Žižkov, a rough working-class neighborhood in Prague of which his mother was quite wary. Olga's father had left the family when she was young, and she lived with her mother and an older sister, whose five children she cared for. From an early age, Olga had to bear responsibility for others. She received no formal education. When she was fifteen, she enrolled in a trade school for factory work, determined to become independent. While learning to operate a shoe-manufacturing machine, she had an accident and lost several fingers on her left hand. There was a toughness and a resilience about her that Havel found alluring.

It was an attraction of opposites, according to Pavel Kosatík, Olga's biographer. Olga, who came from Prague's roughest working-class neighborhood, was rebellious, outspoken, and gruff, while Havel had his mother's genteel manners. Olga found his blond, boyish looks charming and his educated and refined manner pleasing. As Kosatík describes Havel at the time when they met: "He was seventeen years old, three years younger than Olga, and he looked even younger. He was a bit chubby and he seemed vulnerable. Everyone who met him had the feeling that they should take care of him."[4] Havel represented a world that was exciting to Olga, the world of literature and, even more thrilling, of "forbidden" literature. Although he looked younger, he acted like a sophisticated intellectual, and his astute and articulate comments about other writers and their work dazzled her. If Olga ever dreamed about escaping from the practical demands of everyday life, Havel's abstract world of ideas offered it to her. In return, she felt she might give him something, a bridge to reality.

For Havel, the mature and charismatic Olga was the symbol of a different world, forbidden and exotic. But Havel didn't pursue her actively. They simply fell into a pattern of dating, coming to the Café Slavia as a couple; at night, he accompanied her home to Žižkov. Afterward, he would return to his parent's apartment and write love poems, inspired by those nocturnal visits to that other, fascinating world. In Havel's poems, which were published in Kolář's underground journal, Olga became Žižkov, and he, a wanderer through it. Take, for example the following:

Your Soul Is on the Outskirts (1956)[5]

Your mind is urban
Full of smoky and dusty roads
Graveyards and pubs
Full of life dramas
Full of people living somewhere on the edge . . .
You read poems, you want to become an actress, and
    you say that you are cruel
I walk through your mind, an alien, an atheist tourist,
And slowly recognize where those dusty roads lead
And what is buried in those graveyards
As slowly, I start to recognize, to understand this cruel
    landscape.

According to Kosatík, the love between Havel and Olga was romantic and rebellious. Havel's mother had great aspirations with respect to her son's education and social status. When he began his "education" among the 36ers at the Slavia, she approved. But when the circle widened to include young people like Olga, she became concerned. Olga was rough and uneducated, and Božena Havlová was alarmed by this liaison and by what she thought to be her son's growing "bohemian lifestyle."[6]

Olga had one great passion — the theater, which she had loved since childhood. She even took private acting lessons, for which she paid 200 crowns a month (roughly seven dollars today), an extravagance in those times. When she and Havel began dating, she was already studying acting and attending the theater regularly, and soon made her stage debut in a children's theater production at the Vinohrady Theater (Vinohradské divadlo), another stone theater in Prague.

At the time, it was a young relationship, as much a friendship as a romance. But the couple's lives would join together significantly a few years later when Havel fell in love with the theater, too.

1957–1959: A SOLDIER PLAYS

It's very important that Vašek did time in the service, because all his
life he mixed in circles of prominent fools.[1]

— Pavel Landovský

One of the many ironies of Václav Havel's life in the theater is that it began in such an unlikely place as the military. After two years of courses in road construction and the nature of gravel and sand, Havel found himself no closer to the social sciences or the arts than when he had begun. So he decided once again to try to transfer to the film faculty of AMU. The writer Milan Kundera, a teacher there, did his best to help, but again Havel was rejected. Finally, in 1957, deeply frustrated, Havel succumbed to the inevitable and, along with his brother, enlisted in the army. He was to be stationed near a town called České Budějovice in southern Bohemia.

The day Havel departed for service, Olga came to say good-bye at the train station in Prague. Among the other departing soldiers that day was one named Andrej Krob (who would one day play a major role in Havel's life in the theater). Krob remembers seeing the couple standing together on the platform. Who were they? he wondered. He made a mental note of the striking young woman with her natural beauty, her full head of wavy hair and her confident stance. Though they were actually the same height, she seemed to tower over the short, stocky blond fellow standing with her, dressed meticulously in his uniform.

It was in the army that Havel first came into active contact with the theater. At first, he was assigned to the unit of society's least desirables (the bourgeoisie and prisoners), the troops who performed manual labor like building bridges and digging ditches. Though they could not shirk these duties, Havel and his friend Karel Brynda, a fellow officer who shared his interest in literature, were nonetheless desperate to avoid drills and skirmishes. At the time, the army supported cultural activities, and the eager young duo seized the opportunity to form a regimental theater company as a way of escaping unpleasant assignments. The army, not surprisingly, favored plays about army life, so for their first production the two performed in *September Nights* by Pavel Kohout, a young Czech playwright. Havel played an officer who aspired to be a commander; offstage, he and Brynda proudly paraded around the camp wearing artificial beards and the costumes of higher ranking officers, while other soldiers saluted them. Havel's performance, however, disturbed his true-to-life commanding officer, who feared that his acting revealed his true ambitions, and he demoted him to a mere foot soldier. This delighted Havel because it helped him to accomplish his goal and relieved him of the task of carrying a bazooka.

In 1958, during Havel's second year of service, an all-army theater festival was held in the town of Mariánské Lázně. Havel and Brynda decided to write an original play "just for the fun of it," as Havel put it.[2] And so they did, huddled in a corner of the infirmary, where their fellow soldier Andrej Krob found them one day laughing and plotting. The result was a clever little morality play about rank-and-file soldiers, called *The Life Ahead* (Život před sebou). In it, a young private named Maršík falls asleep while on duty one night. He is awakened by a gunshot. By mistake, an intruder has been shot with Maršík's rifle by another officer on duty. Horrified, both men agree on a cover-up. Meanwhile, Maršík is awarded for the deed, promoted, and then asked to join the Communist Party. A jealous friend threatens to expose him, but Maršík wants to accept Party membership, following his commanding officer's advice that his whole life is before him and he shouldn't needlessly stand up in support of false morality. During his induction speech, however, he breaks down, and refuses the temptation by revealing the truth. His future in the army is ruined, but his life is indeed before him in the way he will choose to live it, in truth.

Havel and Brynda provided roles for their friends and had enormous fun performing the play. It was a great success in the early stages of the competition. But when the time came to take the play to the finals in Mariánské Lázně and it seemed it might actually win, officials took a closer look at Havel and Brynda's files and concluded that the army was being made fun of by the two soldier playwrights. Ultimately, a military tribunal condemned the play as antiarmy; it could not condone a work in which a Czech soldier falls asleep on duty.

Still, Havel and Brynda found the incident amusing and were delighted to have a week off in Mariánské with no army responsibilities. More important, behind the façade of what Brynda called "this ridiculous little play"[3] lay the seminal seeds of Havel's great themes of living in truth and betrayal, which would be articulated in his plays of the 1970s, at a time when informing and telling the truth had become matters of survival.

And that was young Havel's first experience in the theater, at the age of twenty-two.

above Olga and Havel at the Café Slavia, 1958 (Havel family archive)

left Private Václav Havel (left) and Sergeant Ivan Havel, 1958 (Havel family archive)

❦ PART II ❧
The Sixties
Enter Václav Havel

There was something happening, and throughout the sixties, this created extraordinarily favorable conditions for my writing: I knew why I was writing, and whom I was writing for . . .[1]
— Havel, "Second Wind"

1960: LEARNING THE ABCs

It was there I came to understand . . . that theater doesn't have to be just a factory for the production of plays . . . it must be something more.[1]
— Havel, *Disturbing the Peace*

While in the army, his interest piqued by his theatrical experiences there, Havel applied once again to AMU, this time to the theater faculty. He was rejected, and when he was discharged in 1959, he had no place to go.

Meantime, the Havels' difficulties increased. The family was forced to leave Havlov. They lost the furniture in their Prague mansion, although they managed to hold on to the top-floor apartment. Meanwhile, there was no hope of Havel studying the humanities at university. He had no desire to return to technical studies, and no job interested him. He had no idea what he was going to do. Then his father appealed on behalf of his son to an old friend, Jan Werich, who ran a small theater on a side street off Wenceslas Square in Prague. So, in late 1959, Václav found himself working as a stagehand at the ABC Theater.

The ABC's 1959–1960 season was inspiring. It gave Havel an education in the theater, this time from the inside. Jan Werich was part of Voskovec/Werich, the celebrated comedy acting team famous in the

The playwright at his debut, *The Garden Party,* 1963
(Rafael Sedlaček, Prague Theater Institute archive)

1920s. Their stand-up routine, a combination of clowning, practical joking, and improvisation reminiscent of the Marx Brothers or Laurel and Hardy, was legendary. Every evening Havel stood in the wings, thrilled, watching Werich and his new partner, Miroslav Horníček, perform their revues in front of the curtain during intermission. The audience knew the routines by heart, as did the musicians, who stayed in the pit to watch them rather than retreat to their dressing rooms. After all, Werich and his partner were part of the Czech theatrical heritage of vaudeville, a vibrant and entertaining contrast to the somber Socialist Realism fare playing at the official stone theaters like the National. As Havel wrote, years later, in *Disturbing the Peace*:

> What was it that enthralled everyone time and time again? It was something difficult to describe, perhaps even mysterious. Nevertheless, it was intrinsically theatrical, and it convinced me that theater made sense. The electrifying atmosphere of an intellectual and emotional understanding between the audience and the stage, that special magnetic field that comes into existence around the theater — these were things I had not known until then, and they fascinated me.[2]

As part of his education in the theater during this formative year, Havel also had a chance to assist on a production of *A Swedish Match,* an adaptation of a Chekhov short story. The director was Alfred Radok, considered by European critics to be one of the great Czech directors of the twentieth century. An intense, hardworking director, versatile in theater and film, Radok was known mostly for his epic and historical productions. This was Havel's introduction to Radok and his work, and he was in awe of his rigor and meticulousness. At the same time, he was intimidated by Radok's method of working with actors, which tended to be provocative and confrontational. A few years later, in 1962, he wrote a twenty-five-page essay about Radok's work, entitled "Some Notes on *A Swedish Match*." "One never knows what is going to happen next," he said about rehearsals. "It has led me to another discovery. Many valuable and concrete moments in the theater may be born from discussion and dialogue only."[3] Looking back on the apprenticeship with Radok in that essay, it taught Havel about professionalism and the grandeur of the theater tradition. But it also turned him toward a different style of working in the theater, one based on collaboration.

All through that year, Havel lived and breathed the atmosphere of working theater, and it stimulated his own writing. He wrote numerous reviews and theoretical articles for *Divadlo* (Theater), a theater magazine. And for the first time, he made a solo effort at playwriting. The result was his first one-act called *An Evening with the Family* (Rodinný večer), written in 1960 and subtitled *A Tragedy in One Act*. A realistic drama, Havel called it "a small study on the banality of life" in his commentary to the play written in the same year. (Writing commentary was a practice Havel would follow with many of his plays, at first to give voice to the work's philosophical content, and later for other, more urgent reasons.)

An Evening with the Family focuses on the life of the Pokornýs, who are meant to represent a typical Czech family. A *babička* (Granny) is at home in the family apartment playing solitaire (she has played cards for thirty years, and that's fine because, as she says, everyone should have a hobby). She sits with her middle-aged daughter at the kitchen table. They chat about what they're serving for Sunday dinner (Granny has bought a goose), about Felix the canary, who has just died, about where they should bury him, about whether they should buy another one ("Why bother? It's going to die, anyway . . . that's life"). The doorbell rings, and the young daughter and son-in-law enter. They chat about shopping, about cigarette brands, about what's healthy to cook with (butter or goose fat), about plans for the holidays. The young woman wants to go to the sea by train; the young man wants to go to Slovakia by car. (The parents never went anywhere by car because they couldn't afford to have one). They want to watch television, but the television is broken. Meanwhile, snippets from the radio interrupt their banal banter with equally banal reports of a Socialist Realist nature. Eventually, one by one, the family members nod off.

Though the scene is realistic, there are telling touches of the absurd: the young people's shopping list, for example, includes everything beginning with a *sh* sound. In the end, as the family members sit around the kitchen table, drooping in sleep, we hear the radio: "And now we dedicate the next song to different workers of different Socialist companies." The list drones on and on, with names of institutions and factories, as the lights fade on a scene of a sleeping family with a birdcage and a dead canary.

Although Havel refers to it as a "somewhat Ionescan one-acter,"[4] it is far more Pinteresque in its barren, chilly landscape of family life. In his commentary, Havel earnestly describes his intent to show the banality of daily life in Communist Czechoslovakia despite the government's vigorous attempts to purge its bourgeois residue (an ironic observation, given that Havel's family and others were cruelly persecuted for their bourgeois origins). The younger generation may "work for today" (a Communist phrase) but they live very narrow, conscribed lives, nonetheless.

With its realistic kitchen-table scene, the play stands alone as a curiosity in the canon of Havel's plays in the 1960s. The subtitle, *A Tragedy in One Act,* is of interest, too. It was Havel's only play in that genre to be subtitled, and one senses that Havel's youthful intention was ironic. Yet, *An Evening with the Family* offers glimmerings of the themes in plays to come, such as materialism and its effect on the soul, suffocating it like the dead canary (miners traditionally used canaries to check for poison gas in the mines; if the canary died, they knew they had to leave immediately). One senses the absurd encroaching inexorably on that benign tableau, like sleep slowly enveloping the family and society itself.

An Evening with the Family was not performed at the ABC Theater that year. As Havel put it, at that point he was writing plays "only for myself, of course."[5] But clearly, he was becoming fascinated with playwriting. There was another early effort in this important apprenticeship year, a rough first draft of a full-length play. Although he put it aside, five years later it would metamorphose into a play called *The Memorandum* (Vyrozumění).

Clearly, it was a year of discovery. At the tiny ABC, Havel had a first vision of what theater really is: "a living spiritual and intellectual focus, a place for social self-awareness, a vanishing point where all the lines of force of the age meet, a seismograph of the times, a space, and area of freedom, an instrument of human liberation."[5]

1960: THE PLAYWRIGHT FINDS A HOME

> That period was extremely important for me, not only because those eight years in the Theatre on the Balustrade were in fact the only period when I was able to devote myself fully to theater, to the only kind of theater that interested me, but also because it formed me as a playwright.[1]
>
> — Havel, *Disturbing the Peace*

Sitting at the Café Slavia throughout the 1950s, Havel and his friends used to gaze at the huge National Theater across the street, filling the café windows with its imposing façade. One of the so-called stone theaters, along with Estates Theater (Stavovské Divadlo) and the Vinohrady, those large official institutions played the classics and the satire of Socialist Realism.

It did not interest Havel and the other young writers at the Café Slavia, however. The kind of theater that excited them was one of new ideas, new forms, new modes of expression. They sat at their table, eagerly awaiting news of trends from the West, like the work of the existential philosophers Kierkegaard, Sartre, and Camus. Absurdism was in the air, and the plays of Ionesco, Beckett, and Anouihl were being translated for the first time in Czech magazines like the monthly *Světová literatura* (World Literature) and the smaller *Svět a divadlo* (World and Theater). Copies were eagerly passed around the Café Slavia tables. But these playwrights and their plays had no hope of finding a stage in the stone theaters of Prague.

There had been, however, a tradition of small theaters and cabaret in Prague. In the 1920s, theaters like Dada, Werich's Liberated Theater, and others defined this tradition, but after 1948, they disappeared. The only vestige of this tradition was the ABC. But in the late 1950s, while Havel was serving in the army, there began a renaissance of small theaters in Prague. It started at the tiny Reduta, which held only sixty people and was jammed every night with eager young Czechs who came to hear the Akord Klub, one of the first Czech rock bands. The atmosphere was marvelous; as Havel described it, there was a "very special conspiratorial sense of togetherness that to me is what makes theater. That was where it all began."[2]

By 1960, while Havel was at the ABC, the small theater movement was in full swing, paralleling what was happening in Greenwich Village in New York and at the Royal Court in London. Theaters were mushrooming everywhere, in alleys, on tiny cobblestone streets, in basements, in abandoned buildings — lively new spaces with colorful names like Semafor and Rokoko. They were run by eager young Czechs who performed revues, cabaret, and improvisational comedy drawn from the Czech vaudeville tradition with a fresh new energy and interpretation.

Meanwhile, while he was working at the ABC, the magazine *Kultura 60* invited Havel to write about this new cultural phenomenon. In this article, he described how the young Prague theaters were not only pockets of entertainment, but also the vanguard of a new aesthetic, a particular sense of absurd humor akin to a new kind of modern art. Inspired by this article, the editors of *Kultura 60* arranged for a round table of representatives from these small theaters, to which Havel was invited. It was there that he met Ivan Vyskočil, artistic director of a small new theater called Theatre on the Balustrade (Divadlo na zábradlí). Vyskočil was a talented, eccentric young comedic actor/director with a broad face, a quirky smile, and a mischievous twinkle in his eye. They liked each other immediately. Havel lent Vyskočil a copy of *An Evening with the Family*, and as a result, the director offered him a job as a stagehand at the Balustrade. According to Vyskočil, Havel was actually offered the choice of being an actor or a stagehand; the shy Havel chose the latter. The members of the Balustrade company were closer to Havel's own age and were not concerned with reviving works from the past; rather, they were searching for new forms. The young playwright felt he might have a better chance to make a contribution there than at the ABC. In the summer of 1960, he wrote a letter of resignation to Werich, thanking him for the opportunity, and began work at the theater that would become his artistic home.

A jewel among Prague's small theaters, the Theatre on the Balustrade was tucked away in the tiny cobblestone square called Annenské náměsti in the Old Town, just steps from the Vltava River and the Charles bridge. Its upper floors once served as a youth hostel for young Catholics from the countryside, while the ground floor was a former warehouse and metalworks. The building was in disrepair; there was no entrance save through the yard and no foyer. Next to the auditorium was a laundry with a window, so that when the space was converted into a theater, people could be seated in the laundry room. In the auditorium, the chairs were attached to one another; if one were moved the entire row would collapse. An old coal heater spewed soot and fog all over the walls.

The theater had been founded in 1958 with money from the local municipal cultural budget allocated for dancing and cooking lessons. In 1959, after Havel was discharged from the army, he had seen its first production, called *If a Thousand Clarinets*. The play had been written by the theater's founders — Jiří Suchý, an actor/composer from the Reduta Theater, and Ivan Vyskočil.

Havel immediately fell in love with the atmosphere of this charming place, with the old coal stove burning in the corner of the auditorium and the old-fashioned lamps flickering on the walls. The auditorium was so tiny that patrons had to squeeze down the one aisle sideways and literally slither to their seats, if indeed they were lucky enough to obtain one.

Many of the audience stood on the balcony in the courtyard, watching through the window. For Havel, the place had the atmosphere of a nightclub, with a exciting tinge of adventure and an exotic seediness. He was captivated by the energy and sense of freedom. Above all, he delighted in the fact that here was theater that didn't take itself too seriously. Here was something new, he felt. Here was something to be part of.

Havel threw himself into the life of the theater, by his own account, with an almost preposterous enthusiasm. "I began as a kind of working stiff at the Theatre on the Balustrade, someone who lived only for his work in the theater."[3] He was there from morning till night, working every job imaginable — stagehand, lighting technician, secretary, script reader, even tour guide. He built scenery and made props with Olga Šplíchalová, the fascinating young woman from his Café Slavia days, who was now working there as an usher and a ticket taker. At the family's apartment, when he had the time to go home and sleep, he even turned his little den into an office where he kept records for the theater. Vyskočil marveled at Havel's passion for structure, his organizational skills, and the way he tried to make order of this colorful, chaotic place.

From the time of the theater's founding in 1958 until he left in 1962, Vyskočil himself was responsible for its creative energy, as well as (by his own admission) its disorganization. Two troupes inhabited it — the theatrical one, headed by Vyskočil, and the mime troupe, headed by a talented and eccentric artist called Fialka (of the first generation of Czech mimes, educated by Marcel Marceau). *Sad Christmas* was the first Vyskočil production on which Havel assisted when he arrived in 1960, scurrying around backstage day and night, hammer in hand. Based entirely on Vyskočil 's special brand of improvisation, it had no script. Havel helped build the set and operated the lighting board. Afterwards, Vyskočil performed his famous "text appeals," a mixed genre of satirical storytelling, improvisation, and pastiche. He performed them standing up, cabaret-style, in front of the curtain. These works delighted Havel, and he watched them nightly following each performance till four in the morning, along with an enthralled audience composed primarily of students. *Sad Christmas* baffled the critics. They described it as modern or existential or used other nebulous terms; the word *absurd* had not yet entered the critical vocabulary.

Havel admired Vyskočil 's brand of theater enormously. Drawing from the tradition of stand-up Czech comedy that Werich and Voskovec had established in the 1920s, Vyskočil created theater based on collaborative playwriting, improvisation, and audience interaction, seeking to engage the spectator's intellect and imagination through spontaneous dialogue.

His form was that of the revue, or a series of short vignettes, characterized by an intellectual humor, an original imagination, a satirical wit, a sophistication (Vyskočil had a degree in philosophy and psychology), a sense of the absurd and, above all, an unconventional spontaneity. His spirit was inquisitive and his aesthetic playful. Havel greatly admired his risk-taking theatrical spirit and his love of experimentation and exploration.

Knowing of Havel's ambitions to become a playwright, Vyskočil invited him to collaborate on a theater project called *Hitchhiking* (Autostop). Written in five scenes, it was a mixed genre of text appeals, revue, and storytelling. The idea was Vyskočil 's — an absurdist satire about the contemporary mania for the automobile, and it bears the mark of his wry, playful, satirical humor. In it, a narrator lectures the audience about a deadly new disease that is causing people to turn into cars. It is called "motorismus," and there is neither treatment nor cure. He introduces a professor who has seen a number of cases and reports a connection between a man's I.Q. and the size of the car's engine into which he is transformed. He then introduces a young girl named Félinka who has been transformed into a Felicie, a type of Czech car. She drives herself onstage, making noises like a motor. The professor inquires about her health. She replies that she has problems with her brakes. In the final scene, the disease spreads like an epidemic, and all the people who have been transformed into cars drive off happily.

Vyskočil himself wrote three of the five scenes, and invited Havel to write the third scene, called "Motomorphosis" (Motomorfóza). In it, a club called "The Enemies of Cars" holds a meeting and invites the narrator (whom Havel calls an inaugurator) and a professor of science to lecture on this new disease of epidemic proportions. As the club members listen, they start transforming into cars themselves.

Havel wrote the role of the professor expressly for Vyskočil. In this scene, Havel uses the technique of audience involvement he learned from Vyskočil's "text appeals," by having the narrator address the audience directly and involve them in the scene. But there were problems in rehearsal, and in the end, Vyskočil transformed the work into a one-man show, which he himself performed.

Although it was not performed exactly as written, the charming and quirky vignette called "Motomorphosis" is noteworthy in Havel's development as a playwright. Its title, a play on the word *metamorphosis*, indicates Havel's exposure to Kafka. Moreover, it reflects the influence of Ionesco, for whom both Vyskočil and Havel shared a passion. Havel had read a translation of *The Chairs* published in the magazine *Divadlo*, which came into his hands "by some miracle,"[4] as he put it, at the army. Subsequently, he read a translation of *The Bald Soprano* and recalls a reading of Beckett and Ionesco plays held at the Mannes Gallery in the Old Town of Prague around 1960, at which he himself gave an enthusiastic talk on the two playwrights.

One audience member — a critic named Jan Grossman — was captivated by the vignette that Havel had written. Grossman subsequently wrote an article on the production, one that prompted Vyskočil to invite him to work at the Theatre on the Balustrade:

> The most consequent part of *Hitchhiking* is the demonstration named "Motomorphosis." . . . *I* don't think that it is necessary to speak about Ionesco and Kafka's inspiration, because "Motomorphosis" is both very original and very Czech. Compared with Ionesco's *épatage*, Havel goes deeper into the reality. Havel is more complicated; he holds up a mirror, reflecting true contemporary human types.[5]

Grossman went on to praise Vyskočil 's performance in the role of the professor. However, he found fault with the scenes in *Hitchhiking* other than the one by Havel, saying while they were comedically inspired, they were too improvisational. Ultimately, Grossman recognized the original comedic muse of this young theater company, while at the same time noting that it needed more definition, more discipline. It was a judgment Grossman himself would soon have a major role in correcting.

> The Theatre on the Balustrade is mainly the theater of comedy; but even the art of nonsense has its own laws and its own style. The comedy of Hašek, Jarry, Mack Sennet, Chaplin has at the heart of its absurdity a very strong and strict structure and system which help the audience to understand the play. But [because it is too chaotic in this production] the audience often misses the comedy at the Balustrade . . . [6]

Hitchhiking marked the beginning of artistic tensions between the eccentric artistic director and his methodical young playwright-in-residence. On the one hand, Havel greatly admired Vyskočil 's aesthetic, but on the other, he was frustrated by his lack of practical sense. He felt Vyskočil was disorganized as an administrator and unpredictable in his planning. There were constant scheduling problems, inconsistent casting judgment, and uneven preparation for rehearsals. On stage and off, Vyskočil 's spontaneity and need for freedom proved incompatible with Havel's passion for order and structure.[7]

Still, both men greatly admired each other's qualities. Vyskočil was, undisputably, an original, and — with his unique "text appeals" and his quirky creativity — he earned Havel's praise as "one of the godfathers" of the small theater movement.[8] Moreover, he had a great influence on Havel during his formative years as a playwright, stimulating the younger man's innate sensibility of the absurd and teaching him that the theater could be a place of spontaneity and creativity, that the purpose of text was to "appeal" to the audience, to engage and involve them, to make them think and feel.

The Vyskočil era (1958–1962) may have been hectic and chaotic, but it was rich, colorful, uninhibited, and creative. And it taught Havel a great deal about what actually happens in performance.

Havel's life in the theater blossomed in those formative years at the ABC and under Vyskočil at the Theatre on the Balustrade. It was a time of growth and experimentation as a playwright, and he explored many tones and forms, from realism in *An Evening with the Family* to the absurd in *Hitchhiking* and the first draft of his first full-length play, *The Memorandum*, to a cabaret-style revue he coauthored at the Balustrade in 1962. Vyskočil had asked Havel and the dramaturg Miloš Macourek to write a popular cabaret revue to attract audiences and bring in revenue. Entitled *The Best Rock Years of Mrs. Hermanová* (Nejlepší rocky paní Hermanové), the program of songs, gags, and jokes was written for a swing singer named Ljuba Hermanová, who had been the rage in the 1930s but was banned during the 1950s. This was to be her comeback. The title in Czech contains a play on words — rocky meaning both "rock" and years" — and it was written purely for entertainment purposes. At the same time, as with *An Evening with the Family*, it gave Havel a chance to experiment:

> *The Best Rock Years of Mrs. Hermanová* was a sort of cabaret, but at that time of all the productions in Prague it was the one that the audience loved the most. And in *The Best Rock Years* I invented a trick

which I used in my later work. It consisted of reversing the order of questions so that the answer was out before the question was articulated. It took some time and effort for the actors to learn and to play it in a way that was understandable to the audience.[9]

In the volume of dramatic works including in *Spisy* (Writings), published in 1999, the texts of *Hitchhiking* and *The Best Rock Years of Mrs. Hermanová* are not included. Nor is the poetic revue called *The Demented Dove* (Vyšinutá hrdlička), for which Havel also wrote several scenes. According to Vyskočil, the latter was hastily thrown together in early 1962 at a time when there were no new texts to perform at the theater, and meanwhile there was pressure on the company to inspire serious new work. The cabaret-style revue consisted of poetry, songs, and some short scenes wherein a dramaturg was advising a playwright about how to write new plays. In this playful spoof about the creative process, there are also satirical hints at the problems young writers faced in the Czech theater, given the prevalent threat of censorship. Yes, the times are changing, and yes, a new generation with fresh creative energy is eager to write, but what will be allowed? What will be tolerated?

Havel did not take these collaborative works seriously and does not consider them an important part of his oeuvre. But in those formative years from 1959 to 1962, Havel discovered that the theater could be a place of fun, spontaneity, and communication between artists and audience. He enjoyed the experience of collaboration and the feeling of freedom that experimentation provides. Furthermore, he learned that the absurd — his own brand of it — was an aesthetic that suited him well. Not only does the absurd entertain, he found, but it also is a convenient smoke screen for a new kind of satire.

Above all, these early collaborations gave him confidence and a sense that he was ready to write on his own. But first he needed the opportunity and the encouragement. Then late in 1961, while *Hitchhiking* was still being performed in the repertoire, a new artistic force appeared at the Balustrade.

In his usual informal fashion, Vyskočil had issued an open invitation to the critic Jan Grossman to come to the Balustrade as a dramaturg, "just to be around," as he put it. Planning for the 1961–1962 season was already underway, but the Balustrade was in financial straits and suffering from administrative disarray. Fialka's mime troupe, which shared space on the season's program, continued with its program. But the dramatic ensemble was dissolving, and the repertoire lacked energy and new ideas. Vyskočil felt that it needed new inspiration.

Grossman, who arrived on the scene in 1961, was in every way the antithesis of Vyskočil. An eminent theater critic, dramaturg, and director, he was a worldly man with a European sensibility, sophistication, and enormous charm. Tall, sleek, dark-haired, a multilingual bon vivant and an expert on Brecht, Grossman was a renaissance man of the theater. "He was a great thinker in twentieth-century theater, a guru," says Zdeněk Hořínek, the Czech theater critic.[10] He had tremendous charisma, and according to Hořínek and Marie Málková (a young actress in the company who eventually became Grossman's wife), everyone who had contact with him was influenced by him.

The day Grossman met the company, he stood up on the stage of the Balustrade, as Málková recalls, and said: "I promise you that I will do everything in my power to use this small stage as a field for big and provocative questions."[11] The actors were charmed. Grossman's style of working with them was gentle; he was focused, articulate, and polite. Havel, stagehand and aspiring young playwright, was thrilled. Grossman had been a kind of guru of the Café Slavia group in the 1950s; everyone at Havel's table had been familiar with the dozens of articles Grossman had written on theater theory and criticism, and knew his work as a translator, editor, and cofounder of the newspaper *Mladá fronta* (Young Front). Here, thought Havel, was someone who could mentor him and who could challenge him intellectually and aesthetically.

The year 1962 became a definitive one for the Theatre on the Balustrade. Under the new leadership of Grossman, who became the unofficial artistic director in the spring of 1962, the theater's philosophy of dramaturgy changed. In the Vyskočil years, there had been "open dramaturgy," which involved collaboration, improvisation, and ensemble development of text. Grossman insisted on a stricter, more classical system in which a playwright generated a text in conjunction with a dramaturg. His idea was to transform an essentially free and fluid theater community into a more structured form. He wanted to attract prestigious artists to the Balustrade like Otomar Krejča of the National Theater, whom he invited to direct the first production under his artistic leadership, *Heroes Do Not Live in Thebes*, a modern version of *Antigone*, in November 1962. The adaptor recast the story to the present day, and the new artistic ensemble put on a impressive, critically acclaimed production.

Grossman also invited Alfred Radok to direct *The Best Rock Years of Mrs. Hermanová* in November, but when Radok declined, Havel and Grossman directed it together. Grossman helped Havel and Macourek shape the script, and the result was a great popular success, which toured all over Czechoslovakia. So began a close working relationship between Grossman and Havel that would last six years, consisting of intense daily contact and mutual respect and admiration between mentor and disciple.

Vyskočil ultimately left the Theatre on the Balustrade in 1962, several months after Grossman arrived, but not before making a final, and significant, contribution. One night that year, shortly after Grossman arrived, Vyskočil and Havel were sitting in a wine bar, as they often did after a performance. The company was seeking new material for their current season, and Havel had showed him a copy of *The Memorandum*, his first attempt at a full-length play. Vyskočil felt that a satire about power and language was too risky at that time. Instead, he suggested that Havel write something safer from the point of view of the authorities.

As Havel remembers it, Vyskočil challenged him to tackle a number of themes and ideas. As Vyskočil remembers it, he suggested that Havel write about a man in search of his identity who loses his way, comes home, and doesn't recognize himself. "The fact is," Havel writes about Vyskočil, "that he never, at least not in those days, turned any of his ideas into plays, but he did have a bottomless supply of them, and they'd always be different, because he'd be making them up as he was talking."[12] So while the actual genesis of the idea will remain a mystery, there is mutual acknowledgment that Vyskočil's suggestions and provocations contributed to the genesis of Havel's first produced full-length play, *The Garden Party* (Zahradní slavnost).

With Grossman now at the artistic helm of the Balustrade, Havel was proud to be promoted to assistant dramaturg and became Grossman's closest artistic colleague and collaborator. Together they worked side by side daily on every facet of the theater's operation. "We did everything together," Havel remembers. "We chose the actors, the plays, the directors. We sorted out the everyday working problems of the theater. If Ivan Vyskočil founded the Theatre on the Balustrade and established its character, Grossman took that initial investment and turned it into the theater that left its mark on the era."[13]

And while the author of those words was too modest to say so himself, the theater's greatest legacy was the nurturing of Václav Havel, dramatist, and the production of his first three major plays. "It formed me as a playwright," Havel said of the Theatre on the Balustrade.[14]

1963: *THE GARDEN PARTY*

Difficult times — Must try and hold out![1]
— Havel, *The Garden Party*

Totally immersed in his life in the theater (the pursuit of a formal education abandoned, to his mother's displeasure), young Havel threw himself headlong into the writing of his first produced full-length play.

As in the case of many groundbreaking works in the theater, much legend surrounds the writing and producing of *The Garden Party*. Havel himself cannot recall how many drafts he produced; scholars mention five or six. There is one very early draft that can be found in the archives of the Theatre on the Balustrade, a dog-eared, undated, typewritten copy called *His Day* (Jeho Den). It is written in a style similar to *An Evening with the Family*, but (with the exception of several characters) it is markedly different from the final version, suggesting that there were indeed multiple drafts and that the input of Grossman, who served as dramaturg, was considerable.

Havel worked on the drafts all spring of 1963. Some time over the summer, Havel's father arranged for a retreat in the Krkonoše Mountains for his son and Grossman. At the time, his father was employed as an economist by a physical fitness organization, and he was able to obtain rooms for his son and his collaborator at a country hotel in Harrachov for athletes in training. The location was kept a tight secret to ensure their privacy. Away from the demands of their bustling theater, Havel and Grossman sequestered themselves in neighboring rooms. Havel would work all through the night and shove his pages under Grossman's door the next morning. By day, Grossman would read the scenes and offer comments. And so it went for three weeks straight. There is an amusing anecdote that Grossman remembers about their stay. Evidently, Havel had loaned the hotel chambermaid a copy of Kafka's *The Trial* (Grossman was writing a dramatization of it at the time). When she returned it to Havel, she complimented him on his writing.[2]

There is another story, too, about a surprise visit from a persistent young actor who was so determined to work with Grossman and Havel at the Balustrade that he found out where they were sequestered, hitch-hiked into the mountains, and showed up at the hotel uninvited. (He ended up playing a few rounds of chess with Havel, and then left.) The visitor was Pavel Landovský, a flamboyant, exuberant, larger-than-life actor with the physique of John Goodman, the audacity of John Belushi, and the heart of Zero Mostel, who would become one of his country's best-known and beloved stage and screen character actors. Landovský was born in Bohemia in 1936, the same year as Havel. (His father came from Russia; he claims that his grand-uncle, a musician, knew Chekhov and used to walk home with him after performances at the Moscow Art Theater.) The theater was Landovský's first love. As a teenager, he started working as as an extra in Shakespearean productions at a theater in Teplice, a remote Czech border town, while forced to earn his livelihood by smuggling needles from East Germany for a local factory and digging coal and selling it illegally. He got his first screen-acting opportunity in Teplice, in a film directed by Alfred Radok. After he left the army in 1959, the same year Havel left, he moved to Prague and fell in love with the Theatre on the Balustrade, where he hounded Grossman and Havel, unsuccessfully, for acting opportunities.

Havel loved Landák, as he called him, but Grossman was intimidated by the man, perhaps because of his unorthodox ways of getting attention. The same year Landovský turned up uninvited at the country hotel, he used another extreme tactic to get attention. He literally grabbed Havel one day, sat him down on the seat of his motorcycle, drove him out to a remote provincial theater in Klatovy, and forced him to sit through a play in which Landovský was performing, to prove to Havel that he was a good actor. Nothing came of the attempt, but it would not be the last time the paths of the two men crossed.

Having rid themselves of Landovský, at least for the time being, Havel and Grossman continued to work on *The Garden Party*. Grossman watched the developing script with pride. Its originality and magnetism reminded him of *The Seagull*, the first of Chekhov's great plays. Like Chekhov, he thought, Havel was finding his own voice, as well as the freedom to create "new forms" for the theater. Sensing the power of the script, Grossman invited the prestigious Otomar Krejča to direct it.

Although at the time Krejča was in rehearsal for *Romeo and Juliet* at the National Theater, he accepted, attracted by the unusual script. He brought with him the National's equally prestigious stage designer Josef

Svoboda. Grossman served as the dramaturg, and Havel as assistant to the director. Colorful stories about the rehearsal period abound. One deals with the schedule itself: in the morning, Krejča would direct the company and then leave for his rehearsals of *Romeo and Juliet* at the National Theater. During the rest of the rehearsal day, Grossman and Havel would redirect the company according to their own interpretation.

Another story is offered by Andrej Krob, Havel's acquaintance from the army. Krob was a tall, lanky, affable young man with an earnest, open face and a self-effacing sense of humor. He, too, loved the theater. During a few unfocused years following military service, he tried different occupations, but nothing appealed to him. A friend suggested he try working at the Balustrade. As Krob tells the story, when he knocked on the theater door, it was opened by Mr. Grossman and Mr. Havel. "When I saw those two geniuses, I began to shake and ran away," Krob says. "After ten days and fifteen beers, I came back and became an artist."[3] Krob remembers with pride the moment when he was hired. "I felt like Jack London's gold-digger in Alaska who accidentally appeared among New York bankers. Finally, because I liked my job and because I was reliable and hard-working, those gentlemen — Grossman, Havel and Fára [the Balustrade's set and costume designer] — accepted me and appointed me production manager."[4]

By 1963, Krob was at the Balustrade, working as the technical director and production manager. *The Garden Party* was to be his first production, and he was in awe of Havel, Grossman, and the rest of the artistic team. It was Krob's responsibility to build the set, and eager to make a good impression, he had it constructed and finished weeks in advance. To the entire company's astonishment, the completed set stood waiting for them on the first day of rehearsal.

The set consisted of huge mirrors and did not entirely please Havel and Grossman. One night, just two weeks before the production, someone slipped into the hall — rumor has it that it might even have been the playwright and director — and smashed the mirrors to pieces. Krob, who discovered the destruction the following morning, found himself in a pool of tears mixed with broken glass. As Krob tells the story, he even called the police, thinking it was the work of outsiders, until he heard a rumor that the act had been committed "for artistic reasons." The collaborators held an emergency meeting. Svoboda pulled out a piece of paper and sketched a series of spheres with connecting rods resembling the atomium (a sphere-like construction) he had seen at the 1958 Brussels World's Fair. Here, he said to Krob: build fifty spheres. Krob dutifully toiled away, and built the new set by hand himself. The day before opening, Svoboda surveyed his new design and instructed Krob to remove twenty of the spheres and paint the remaining thirty white. On opening night, the actors were warned not to touch the set, for fear of getting fresh paint on their costumes.

The sense of anticipation was keen. "Everyone knew we were working on something very important, very special," Krob said, "like Americans flying to the moon." Grossman said the same to his wife-to-be, actress Marie Málková. In fact, *The Garden Party* was published in *Divadlo* magazine prior to the opening, in case the censors would refuse to give the theater permission to produce it. Later, in an interview in *Mladý svět* (Young World), Havel recalls the ironic circumstances under which the censors finally approved *The Garden Party*. It was at the time of the Cuban missile crisis. The play had been at the censorship office for several months. But one day in the morning the censors read in the newspapers that Khrushchev admitted that Russian missiles were stationed in Cuba. The censors panicked, thinking that the world was on the verge of collapse. On that day, according to Havel, they approved every submission they had in the office, including *The Garden Party*.[5]

In fact, *The Garden Party* was something very new indeed. A bizarre, quirky, contemporary parable, it tells the story of one Hugo Pludek, a pleasant young indolent who lives in his parents' middle-class home, contentedly doing nothing except playing chess against himself. "Such a player," his mother says proudly, "will always stay in the game."[6] His parents recite a barrage of garbled proverbs and clichés in an attempt to educate him and rouse him out of his apathetic state, to no avail. So his father, frustrated by Hugo's lethargy and eager for his son to get ahead in the bureaucratic establishment, uses his connections to get him a job in a Kafkaesque government agency called the Liquidation Office. The plan is for Hugo to meet his father's contact at an office garden party. Hugo arrives on the scene, only to find officials decked out in papier-mâché clown noses and engrossed in a convoluted discussion of the regulation size of the dance floor. Posing as a fellow bureaucrat, Hugo deftly insinuates himself into the conversation, and soon he is speaking the language of the Liquidation Office fluently, peppered with his own chess-speak.

Secretary: Large Dance Floor A is indeed large! . . .
Hugo: Excuse me, but in direct proportion to the amount by which
   Large Dance Floor A is larger than Small Dance Floor C is the
   number of employees who can entertain themselves with funny
   noses at one and the same time . . . Check!"[7]

Quickly, Hugo wheedles himself into the good graces of Mr. Falk,
chief officer of the rival Inauguration Service. When a secretary and a
clerk become embroiled in a dialectic about art and technology, Hugo
impresses Falk with his mastery of the art of saying nothing:

Hugo: In fact, they were both sort of right and sort of wrong — or
   rather, on the contrary — both were wrong and both were right,
   weren't they? I mean they were, were they not? Yes, I agree, they
   were not, though I don't think they were . . .
Falk: I like the way you speak. In a human sort of way. And you're
   with it! I like you, you know! You're a born inaugurator!"[8]

By Act II, Hugo has infiltrated the bureaucratic infrastructure by
looking, sounding, and acting like everyone else. The next scene takes
place in the office of the Liquidation Office, where the director sits at a
desk piled with a mountain of paper, conversing with a secretary who is
carrying out the business of liquidation by stamping documents with
rubber stamps. (In the National Theater's 1990 production, the director
is clad only in his underwear, a choice that invites no comment throughout the scene.) Enter Hugo, now a clone of Falk, complete with papier-
mâché nose, talking institutional jargon fluently, playing institutional
chess, making all the right moves, fooling everyone into thinking he is
part of the establishment. No one with whom he speaks knows who
Hugo Pludek is, but they assume that he must be somebody important
and that he must know something they don't.

Now embarked on a meteoric rise up the bureaucratic ladder, he effectively takes over, and begins a campaign to liquidate the Liquidation Office
as well. Meanwhile, he learns the party line on dissent: "We mustn't be
afraid of contrary opinions. Everybody who's honestly interested in our
common cause ought to have from one to three contrary opinions . . ."[9]
From that point on, the absurdities escalate. It is decided that the rival Inauguration Service must be liquidated too. But there is a conundrum. Who
should inaugurate the liquidation, an inaugurator or a liquidator? How

could anyone inaugurate that which he has already liquidated? Conversely, how could a liquidator be capable of inaugurating? The answer: Hugo can.

Hugo: Best if both trainings were organized at the same time. Inaugurators will be training liquidation officers, while liquidation officers will be training inaugurators.

Director: And will it then be inaugurated by a liquidation officer trained by an inaugurator, or by an inaugurator trained by a liquidation officer?

Hugo: Another training will have to be organized. Inaugurationally trained liquidation officers training liquidationally trained inaugurators, and liquidationally trained inaugurators training inaugurationally trained liquidation officers.

Director: And will it then be inaugurated by a liquidationally trained inaugurator trained by an inaugurationally trained liquidation officer, or by an inaugurationally trained liquidation officer trained by a liquidationally trained inaugurator?

Hugo: By the latter of course![10]

Like his Kafkan predecessor, Gregor Samsa, Hugo undergoes a metamorphosis; only in his case, instead of turning into an insect, Hugo becomes the quintessential bureaucrat (an insect of another kind), adapting to the impersonal world around him. Hugo succeeds in this world by learning how to become all things to all people. As a result, he loses his identity. And if identity goes, so goes language, degenerating into a jumble of distorted, meaningless words and phrases. And once language goes, so does any articulation of the truth.

At the play's end, Hugo returns home, where his parents have received three telegrams. The first announces that their son has been appointed head of the Liquidation Office. The second announces that he has been appointed the head of the Inauguration Service. The third announces that he has been appointed head of a new institution, a Central Commission for Inauguration and Liquidation. But they cannot share the good news with him because they no longer recognize him. At the play's end, he unravels in a final outburst of unintelligible rage against his loss of identity:

Pludek (father): Listen, who are you, in fact?
Hugo: Me! You mean who I am? Now look here, I don't like this one-sided way of putting questions, I really don't! You think one can ask in this simplified way? No matter how one answers this

sort of question, one can never encompass the whole truth, but only one of its many limited parts. What a rich thing is man, how complicated, changeable, and multiform . . . In man there's nothing permanent, eternal, absolute; man is a continuous change — a change with a proud ring to it, of course! Today the time of static and unchangeable categories is past, the time when A was only A, and B always only B is gone; today we all know very well that A may be often B as well as A; that B may just as well be A; that B may be B, but equally it may be A and C; just as C may be not, only C, but also A, B, and D; and in certain circumstances even F may become Q, Y, and perhaps also H . . . Truth is just as complicated and multiform as everything else in the world — the magnet, the telephone, Impressionism, the magnet — and we all are a little bit what we were yesterday and a little bit what we are today; and also a little bit we're not these things. Anyway, we all are a little bit all the time and all the time we are not a little bit; some of us are more and some of us are more not; some only are, some are only, and some only are not; so that none of us entirely is and at the same time each one of us is not entirely . . ."[11]

And on and on he raves, as Havel's nonhero unravels before our eyes. "What a rich thing is man" is Havel's version of Hamlet's "What a piece of work is a man"[12] Only Havel's Hugo isn't a man — he's any man at all.

What was so remarkably new and fresh about this play, besides its central idea and quirky sense of humor, was its young author's use of dramatic language. Inspired by the repetitive, meaningless conversations of the couples in *The Bald Soprano*, Havel set out to put Ionesco's dialogue into Czech to illustrate his own reality. Hugo's parents' recitations of proverbs and homilies are twisted, distorted, even demented: "He who fusses about a mosquito net can never hope to dance with a goat," or "Not even the Hussars of Cologne would go to the woods without a clamp," or "He who knows where the bumblebee hides his stinger never rolls up his leggings."[13] If traditional wisdom is so garbled and distorted, what does that say about the value of tradition?

In the bureaucratic jargon of the Liquidation Office, the audiences instantly recognized the double-talk of Communist slogans to which they themselves have been subjected, slogans that were not only confusing and misleading, but also dangerous if believed. Consider the Khrushchevian platitudes from the 1950s that Falk utters: "Today we must discuss! And while we're doing it, we mustn't be afraid of contrary opinions."[14] Or the

Director's declaration that the Inauguration Service "is an outworn vestige of the past," and his reference to "imprudent excesses,"[15] political jargon of the day that referred to the political trials of the 1950s. Onstage,
this language was both funny and startling. After all, the audience had
never heard it in a theater before. At the same time, it was sinister. No
wonder, on opening night, there was laughter of shock and recognition.
This is the life we lead, the audience saw, and language is the weapon of
the totalitarian system, a weapon that is denying us our identity, making
us unrecognizable. We no longer know ourselves.

Jiří Paukert/Kuběna, poet and 36er friend, recalls the atmosphere on
opening night, December 3, 1963:

> *The Garden Party* was a big surprise to us. It was a brilliant analysis
> of the social and political issues of the times, and at the same time
> it was avant-garde. The chemistry between the actors and audience
> was incredible. The audience went wild.[16]

Miloš Forman was there, too.

> *The Garden Party* was wonderful, intelligent, witty, unlike anything
> else ever produced in Czech dramatic literature. What a revelation
> it was! Out of the blue, here was something so original, so new, like
> nothing before it. As thrilled as we were, we couldn't let the excite-
> ment show too much because the Communists might smell danger.
> Still, after the curtain fell, we all crowded into the bar; we were so
> excited we didn't want to leave.[17]

And Havel's brother Ivan, who was also in the audience, said:

> There was strong word-of-mouth in advance of the play. The audi-
> ence was packed with intellectuals who were very sensitive to any
> political innuendo. There were outbursts of laughter in many
> places, and long stretches of applause. The reason people laughed
> was that they felt a release of their fear. The censor came to dress re-
> hearsal; it would have been dangerous for them to have discovered
> it beforehand.[18]

Vladimír Vodička, the theater's managing director, recalls the tremendous response at the premiere. In the audience, there were two rows
of seats reserved for the Communist authorities; the rest of the audience

were members of Prague's elite, including intellectuals, artists, and writers. "I had the difficult task of explaining to the Communists that this is a Socialist play, while at the same time begging the intellectuals to be quiet and not tell the officials what this play was really about," Vodička said.[19] Because the officials perceived it as a play about bureaucracy, he added, they simply did not perceive it as a play against totalitarianism and its dehumanizing influences, an allegory of institutional life in present-day Czechoslovakia, and a bitter exposé of Socialist institutions. "It was easier to have Communists approve this play than bankers," he said.

Jiří Ornest, a young actor (who, over three decades later, would become a coartistic director at the Balustrade), was also in the opening-night audience:

> It sent chills up our spines. *The Garden Party* was a landmark play. It was fantastic because it was different; there was nothing to compare it with. It was Havel's own specific style, not Beckett, not Ionesco, not Pinter, but Havel. Yes, *The Garden Party* was absurdist, but it was Havel's own Czech sense of the absurd.[20]

Then there were the critics. Even in 1963, coming off the cruelly restrictive era of the 1950s, the freeze on cultural life hadn't completely thawed. But the heat emanating from this breakthrough play certainly sped the process along. The critics, who had been reviewing Socialist Realism for a decade, were caught off guard and found themselves provoked to write without inhibition. Almost unanimously, from the more enlightened ones to the Stalinists, they praised the production. It was as if the floodgates of repression were opening, and a wave of enthusiasm poured forth. From the leading papers like *Rudé právo* (Red Law), there was praise: "Different, original . . . *The Garden Party* shines with humanism."[21] From the esteemed critic Sergej Machonin in *Literární noviny* (Literary News): "An author with excellent talent."[22] Machonin, who entitled his review "Satire at the Crossroads" added: "If an audience member wants to see satire which deserves its name and which forces us to think about this drama genre on a higher level, he must go to the Theatre on the Balustrade." From *Mladá fronta*: "*The Garden Party* is our first absurd drama."[23] "The first Czech antidrama," wrote Eva Uhlířová in *Divadelní noviny* (Theater News).[24] From *Smena* (Exchange): "*The Garden Party* is the first satire which deserves the name 'satire' . . . It is the strongest play about 'us' that we've ever seen."[25] Even the hard-line critics were positive, thinking that Havel was helping Communism by attacking bureaucracy.

Clearly, this clever new play was something new in genre, tone, and content, provoking both audience and critic alike to perceive the theater in new ways. Who are the influences? Čapek, Kafka, Ionesco? What is the genre? Satire? Antidrama? Theater of the absurd? Who is Hugo Pludek? A Czech everyman? Candide? And what about the world of the play? A "through the looking glass" journey into an absurdist bureaucratic fantasyland? To the Czech audience on opening night, that wasn't an absurd world, that was Czech realism. They scrambled to define what they saw and to describe the new voice that they heard.

But Havel did not fit into any pattern or mold. Here was a determined new young playwright who was apprenticed in the tradition of Czech satirical comedy, guided by a dramaturg with classical European sensibilities, inspired by new existential trends, with his own perceptions of the systems in his society and an innate sense of the absurd. It was a unique and original combination, and it set a daring new tone for the Czech theater.

The play remained in the Balustrade repertoire for five years and was sold out every performance, according to Andrej Krob, the production manager. The British critic Kenneth Tynan, visiting in 1967, saw a performance, called Havel "the star turn at the Balustrade," and called the play "an acid comment on bureaucracy and the hopes raised by de-Stalinization."[26] Then came 1968, and the events that would change Havel's life in the theater irreversibly.

Meanwhile, for everyone in that packed opening-night audience, the reality of the life they were leading under a totalitarian system was being dramatized for the very first time on the stage. Yes, it was in the form of a parable; yes, it was funny and entertaining; but there it was, nonetheless, the truth about the world as they saw it. As Grossman put it in an essay on *The Garden Party*:

> Great theater does not only reveal itself and its own story. It also reveals the audience's story, and through that, the audience's urgent need to compare their own experience — their own "subject matter" — with the subject matter offered them on stage.[27]

No Czech author under Communism had ever tested the contemporary theater with such boldness. In its own clever way, *The Garden Party* represented an act of courage and cunning on the part of both its author and its performers.

Writing about *The Garden Party* today, scholar Paul Trensky says: "It is perhaps the greatest satirical play exposing the bureaucratization of life and the deformation of intellect by a totalitarian social system that has ever come from the pen of a European dramatist."[28]

And that, at the age of twenty-seven, was Havel's debut as a serious playwright.

1963–1964 IN PRAGUE: A CULTURAL AWAKENING

It was a global explosion of creativity.[1]

— Olga Havlová

In 1963, in Prague, *The Garden Party* was the right play written at the right time. What, then, were those times like?

When one asks the Czechs today about the sixties, they talk about that period with a special tone of reverence in their voices. Quite simply, the 1960s were a phenomenon, a golden era in which music, art, film, criticism, and literature blossomed and thrived. After the cold, fearful decade of the 1950s, with the harsh, punitive rule of Communism and the dark shadow of Stalin cast overhead, the 1960s were a verdant oasis, a ray of sunlight. Beginning in the mid- to late 1950s, fresh new cultural ideas and influences from the West were slowly seeping into Czechoslovakia through cracks in the Iron Curtain: existentialism, absurdism, modern art, popular culture, rock music. By the 1960s, they were taking hold. "It was a period of weakening, of release of the strong grip of Communism and the police," says Ivan Havel. "In culture, we felt the changes."[2]

In 1963, information on the terrible purge trials of the early 1950s was released and became public knowledge. As theater historian Jarka Burian describes it: "Other absurdities of the regime revealed themselves, chiefly its use of bureaucracy to control, if not suppress, creativity and critical thinking."[3] The abuses of the Stalinist period were openly discussed in writers' meetings. As a result, the changes Ivan Havel speaks of began to transform cultural life.

Literary magazines were sprouting as fast as writers could produce articles and translations, cramming their pages with heretofore forbidden works, both Czech and foreign, to accommodate their readers' interests. Kafka and Čapek were removed from the banned list. In 1963, the first Kafka conference ever to be held on Czech soil took place in Liblice, in a castle belonging to the Academy of Sciences. For the first time ever, Kafka's works were officially translated into Czech. (Kafka, of course, wrote in German, another irony of Czech literary history.) Journals like *Světová literatura* offered European literature in translation, including the existentialists and the absurdists. Between 1963 and 1965, a number of Beckett's plays — *Waiting for Godot, Play Without Words, Endgame, Happy Days, Krapp's Last Tape* — were published in Czech. So were Ionesco's *The Bald Soprano* and *Rhinoceros*. Novels critical of life since 1948 were published in increasing numbers. Magazines carried photos of modern Western art, like the works of Jackson Pollack.

In *Disturbing the Peace* (a written interview conducted by Karel Hvížďala in 1986), Havel reminisced about the explosion of cultural life in the 1960s. He spoke of the New Wave movement in film, in the visual arts, in classical and popular music, and in experimental poetry. In film, he cited directors like Miloš Forman, Jan Němec, Věra Chytilová, and Pavel Juráček. (There were also Jan Kádár and Emar Klos, whose *Shop on Main Street* won an Academy Award in 1965.) In the visual arts, he mentioned Medek, Koblasa, the Šmidras group, and younger artists who were beginning to exhibit and were challenging the official art of the times. In classical music, he spoke of the New Music group; in popular music, he spoke of the arrival of Czech "big-beat." In poetry, he cited the works of Věra Linhartová, Bohumil Hrabal, and Josef Škvorecký. In scholarship, too, he referred to a freeing from the "rigid dogmatic straitjackets."[4]

In short, it was a pancultural renaissance, an across-the-board blossoming. The atmosphere was vibrant; the spirit, fantastic. Prague was becoming part of that Western phenomenon called the 1960s. Looking back on it decades later, Olga Havlová would say: "We were all so young and influenced by all those wonderful new things coming at us, from the movie theaters, from art, everything. It was a global explosion of creativity."[5]

At the vanguard of this cultural explosion was the small theater movement. In addition to the first flourishing of small theaters around 1960 like the Semafor, the Reduta, and the Rokoko, there were the new additions such as Krejča's Theater Beyond the Gate (Divadlo za branou) and Vostrý and Kačer's Činoherní Klub (Drama Club). They all celebrated the small form — anecdotes, song, poetry, mime, and "text appeals." By the end of the decade, the critic Martin Esslin would describe the 1960s as an era in which "the Czechoslovak theater was, without doubt, the most exciting theater in Europe — its designers, directors, playwrights and actors led the world."[6]

And at the Theatre on the Balustrade, the young playwright in residence, Václav Havel, had just written a breakthrough play, *The Garden Party*, which placed his theater center stage of the small theater movement. It was Havel who had the instinct, the vision, and the ability to synthesize new trends and influences with existing traditions, and to articulate them in a coded way so his play could be appreciated by the establishment and the intellectual vanguard alike. It was he who took the absurdist influence and translated it into Czech reality, which, as any Czech of that era will tell us, is absurd to begin with. In short, he gave his culture absurdism on its own terms and in its own language.

1964: A SEASON OF THE ABSURD AT THE THEATRE ON THE BALUSTRADE

If absurd theater had not existed before me, I would have had to invent it.[1]

—Havel, *Disturbing the Peace*

With the spotlight now fixed on Theatre on the Balustrade, Grossman and Havel launched their 1964 season with a daring program of absurdist French masterpieces. For the first time, Czech audiences saw professional productions of *The Bald Soprano* and *Waiting for Godot*. In this so-called absurdist season, Grossman also staged an outstanding production of *Ubu Roi* by Alfred Jarry, whose critical acclaim confirmed his reputation as one of Prague's finest stage directors. These plays were enormously popular with an audience that recognized in them the quality of their own existence as well. And the performing of these plays and the applauding of them became, in a sense, an act of existential freedom.

The artistic success of the 1964 season, which included *The Garden Party* now in its repertoire, earned a European-wide reputation for the Theatre on the Balustrade as the showcase for the theater of the absurd, both foreign and domestic. The production of *Ubu Roi* and, later, Kafka's *The Trial* (both directed by Grossman) toured in Europe throughout the 1960s, earning accolades from the critics, who called the troupe "those devils from the East."[2]

At the time it was known as "the absurdist season," but looking back on it, Havel challenges that categorization:

> [A]bsurd theater as such — that is, as a tendency in dramatic literature — was not an explicit part of the artistic program of any of the small theaters in Prague in the 1960s, not even in the Theatre on the Balustrade, which came the closest to it of any. And yet the experience of absurdity did exist somewhere in the bowels of all those theaters. It was not merely transmitted through particular artistic influences; it was, above all, something that was "in the air."[3]

As the theater's dramaturg, Havel found himself in charge of preparing *The Bald Soprano* and *Waiting for Godot* for production. Havel had already read Ionesco's *The Chairs* in the late 1950s, when it was first published in the journal *Světová literatura*. "I was struck by Ionesco, a sudden touch of something that I found was very close to my heart," he recalls.[4]

So he flung himself into the task with great excitement and a sense of responsibility, too. He and Grossman had commissioned new translations, but Havel wasn't entirely satisfied with them. Looking back on the work today, he says: "We made a number of amendments and perhaps in my work on the text [of *The Bald Soprano*] you may find an imprint of my theatrical invention. At the end of *The Bald Soprano* there's a loose incoherence, and the translators tried to translate it literally. It made no sense, so I more or less actually wrote it myself."[5]

The Bald Soprano — with its changing characters, repetitions, and cyclical structure — had stylistic features that greatly appealed to Havel. He eagerly incorporated them into his next two plays at the Balustrade, *The Memorandum* and *Increased Difficulty of Concentration*. Clearly, Havel learned even more about playwriting during this successful 1964 season. However, it is important to note that the writing of *The Garden Party* predates his work on the absurdist season; as Havel pointed out, it was already "in the air" and part of his own innate aesthetic. His exposure to the French absurdists only brought it to the surface.

In that year, the Balustrade was at the height of its popularity. Every night, scores of young people would queue up for hours at the box office for tickets, and every night, the theater was packed with a vibrant, eager crowd. The authorities, in effect, left the theater alone, assuming that the youthful audience was no threat to the regime. As a result, there was an almost euphoric atmosphere of freedom. Before the show and during intermission, the tiny courtyard was packed with young people, a glass in one hand and a hand-printed program (which Havel had written) in the other. The Balustrade followed the European system of a rotating repertoire, so each night in that sensational season there was a different play, for example, *The Garden Party*, followed by *Ubu Roi, The Bald Soprano,* and *Waiting for Godot.* The postperformance mood in the long, narrow smoke-filled buffet with its colorful theater posters was vibrant. People stood three deep at the tiny bar, laughing and talking and arguing about Beckett and Ionesco and Havel. Deep into the night, the gaslights burned, as they discussed new ideas, new forms. There was a sense of excitement, of freedom, of possibility.

That 1964 season was one of feverish activity for Havel — the premiere of his own full-length play, the preparation of the "absurdist" season, and the myriads of tasks it all entailed. He loved every minute of it. He was at the theater from morning till night, correcting new translations of the foreign texts, attending rehearsals, writing the programs. He even found time to play a nonspeaking role in *Ubu Roi,* which Grossman created especially for him. It was of Villibald, an English tourist. When Havel played the part, he carried a camera he borrowed from Andrej Krob. After the opening, he and Krob alternated in the role. He barely had time to go back to his little den in the family apartment any more.

Totally immersed in his fascination for the absurd and preparation for the 1964 season, Havel also found the time just after *The Garden Party* to write a short essay entitled "The Anatomy of the Gag" (Anatomie gagu). In this serious-minded, theoretical study about the connection between humor and the absurd, he dissects the act of comedic performance, which he has learned through observation:

> When somebody cries because of the death of his wife, it is not a gag. When someone shakes a gin fizz, it's not a gag either. But if Chaplin receives the message that his wife has died, he turns his back to us and starts to shake and cry and then he slowly turns his face to us again and we see that he didn't shake because he was crying but because he was shaking a gin fizz.[6]

Havel then launches into a highly intellectualized discussion, offering a theory of the dialectic of humor, tying it to the challenge of performing the gag, and arriving at the purpose of the gag itself: exposure of the truth. What is significant in this little essay is the fusion of so many aspects of Havel's education in the theater thus far: the powerful theoretical influences of Grossman, the exposure to the theater of the absurd, the knowledge of Western influences from Dadaism to Charlie Chaplin, as well as all those hours of watching Werich at the ABC and Vyskočil at the Balustrade perform their comedic sketches. He was absorbing and integrating all the influences around him, and he loved to theorize about it.

Meanwhile, news of *The Garden Party* had traveled abroad, too. Among those who heard of it was Klaus Juncker, a sophisticated young German literary agent, who was working at the the Rowohlt Verlag publishing house in the Hamburg suburb of Reinbek. At the time, all the well-known British and German writers were already represented — the roster of writers at Juncker's publishing house included Harold Pinter, Tom Stoppard, Samuel Beckett, and Lawrence Durrell — and Juncker wanted to scout for new voices in the theater. He had gone in Berlin in 1963 to attend the premiere of one of Pinter's plays at the Schillertheater. There, the artistic director Boleslav Barlog told Junker that he had heard of a new theater called the Balustrade in Prague where a young writer named Václav Havel, assistant to the esteemed director Jan Grossman, had written an exciting new play. In response, Juncker asked the head of his publishing house to subsidize his trip to Prague. "I said to Mr. Rowohlt: 'You've already lost one famous Czech writer named Franz Kafka to another publishing house. Perhaps I can find you a new one to replace him.'"[7]

Juncker went to Prague on November 7, 1964. When he arrived at the Balustrade's tiny box office, which consisted of a closet with a half-open door, he was greeted by an attractive young woman who left her post and led him personally to his seat. (Juncker later learned that she was Olga Šplíchalová, who had a special relationship with the playwright.) Juncker recalls that night vividly:

> I still remember the seat number: row 2 seat 16. . . . The play went well — I could tell by the reaction of the audience, even though I didn't speak any Czech — one gets the feeling for these things when one works in the theatre. In the lighting booth at the back sat a young blond man, 30 years old or so. He was watching me, and af-

terwards he came up to me and said (in English): "Why didn't you laugh?'" I replied: "I couldn't laugh because I don't speak Czech."[8]

The young man was Václav Havel. After the play, he invited Juncker back to his family's apartment, where the literary agent met the playwright's parents.

We got along famously from the first minute, because Václav's grandfather was Counsel General in Hamburg and his mother had spent her early life there. Now they had no money; Václav's mother was a translator and his father had to work for a sports organization near Prague. Ivan Havel showed me his brother's study. "Vašek keeps me up all night typing, just to annoy me," Ivan told me. "Imagine — he thinks someone might actually be interested in what he's writing!"[9]

Juncker wasn't the only guest that evening. The apartment was packed with actors, directors, and writers. As Juncker describes it, all Prague's theater world seemed to be there. Because there weren't enough chairs, people were sitting everywhere, on the floor, even on the tables.

Jan Grossman was there, so was Alfred Radok [the esteemed director whom Havel had assisted at ABC]. On the worktable in Havel's little "den" in the back of the flat there were books by Brecht, Dürrenmatt and Ionesco. Everyone was talking to me at once, asking me what they should put into the repertoire at the Balustrade, what did I know about this play and that play and so on. Never before and never again did I have to answer so many questions in such a short time.[10]

The next morning, Juncker offered Havel a contract on behalf of Rowohlt Verlag.

1964: MARRIAGE

We both feel that we are probably inseparable.[1]

— Havel, Introduction to *Letters to Olga*

It was clear that Havel was wedded to his life in the theater, in earnest. He was soon to be wedded to another, as well — Olga Šplíchalová, the aspiring young actress who had sat at Havel's table at the Café Slavia through the 1950s, the object of his first love poems. In contrast to his mother, who was keenly disappointed that he had not yet finished his higher education, Olga avidly supported Havel life in the theater. In fact, she shared it, working every night as an usherette at the Balustrade and helping Havel with his various tasks from program collating to set building.

It was no surprise that Olga and Havel's mother did not particularly get along. According to Keane's biography, for years Božena Havlová had been upset about her older son's lifestyle, his staying out late and socializing with friends of a "questionable social background" like the "tough-minded, chimney-smoking, spirit-drinking girl from working-class Prague."2 Olga had her own strong views on situations and people. One such opinion was about Pavel Landovský, with whom Havel went pub-crawling after performances so the two men could talk passionately about theater and politics. Landovský corroborates it:

> As for Olga, we became fast enemies. She hated me immediately. When a performance would finish at the Balustrade, Olga had to stay a few minutes longer to straighten up; so before she finished, I would kidnap Havel and take him to bars.3

Olga was the one to propose marriage to Havel, and he accepted despite his mother's views. After all, they shared so much — the Café Slavia, the Theatre on the Balustrade, the excitement of the 1960s with its heady influx of Western culture. They loved parties, exhibitions, movies. As Olga said: "We both fell in love with Fellini and Polanski. We didn't like Godard, but we really adored Bergman."4 Above all, they shared a life together in the theater.

They were married in secret on the morning of July 9, 1964, at the Žižkov Town Hall, in the district of Prague where Olga was born. It was two days before Olga's thirty-first birthday; Havel was not yet twenty-eight. It was a simple, unsentimental wedding; the bride carried no flowers, wore no veil, and no rings were exchanged. There were but two official witnesses, the director Jan Grossman and Libor Fára, the theater's set and costume designer. After lunch at the Moskva pub in Žižkov, the newlyweds returned to the Balustrade to work at the evening performance. It was just another day of a life in the theater. After a week, they told everyone. Looking back on that event years later, under the most adverse of circumstances, Havel would write to Olga:

Not only was our marriage (a hundred years ago) an act, among other things, signifying my definitive emancipation from dependence on my mother and through her, on the social milieu of my family, but when we began to "go out" together (two hundred years ago) it marked the moment when I (perhaps) overcame the "fat boy" stereotype. Such things may be superficial, but they symbolize far more.[5]

Looking back on their marriage during those later, adverse times, too, Olga said in her direct, laconic style:

Our wedding was a secret. I was 31, Vašek [Václav] was 28 . . . We liked the same things. Paintings, for example. We both liked a good meal. And we had friends in common. When I married, my friends became Vašek's, and his became mine. We were together all the time. Sometimes I'd even tell Vašek: "Go there alone, don't let us be like Siamese twins." . . . Perhaps it was because of me that he started going to the theater. . . . We did everything together.[6]

1964: *ANTICODES*

[Writing poetry] was all the more adventurous for an eager young man searching for the "second culture."[1]

— Havel, *Disturbing the Peace*

With all the activities of that hectic year, it was remarkable that Havel had time to get married at all. Even so, he also found time to complete a collection of typograms entitled *Antikódy* (Anticodes). He had been writing them since the early 1960s, in fact, just to amuse himself and friends.

Havel had been exposed to the art of typogrammy while sitting around Jiří Kolář's table at the Café Slavia in the late 1950s. A new aesthetic, typogrammy was an attempt to release poetry from its traditional form. As such, it was consistent with the search for new forms in all the arts during the 1960s. Practiced only by a handful of poets, among them Jiří Kolář, Ladislav Novák, and Havel, it was based on visual messages and the relationship between form and content. In his preface to Havel's collection, Josef Hiršal describes them as "constellations":

It is a group of words linked together vertically or horizontally which have a very close connection to each other. The constellation must be short and exact, and it's easy to remember it as a picture. It is international but it is not translatable. You just have to provide a helpful key.[2]

Havel's typograms covered topics ranging from love to war to politics to philosophy and expressed his relish for structure, experimentation and ideas. They were specific and provocative. His poem "Vpřed"[3] (Ahead), for example, was a satirical riff on Communist sloganeering:

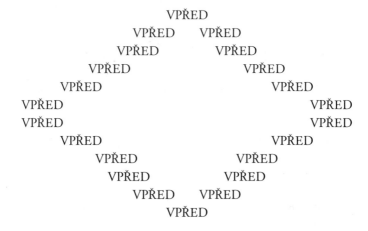

His poem entitled "Filozof" (Philosopher) avoided words altogether:[4]

```
!!!!!!!!!!!!!!!!!!!!!!!!!
!!!!!!!!!!!!!!!!!!!!!!!!!
!!!!!!!!!!!!!!!!!!!!!!!!!
!!!!!!!!!!!!!!!!!!!!!!!!!
!!!!!!!!!!!!!!!!!!!!!!!!!
!!!!!!!!!!!!!!!!!?!!!!!!
!!!!!!!!!!!!!!!!!!!!!!!!!
```

These would be published in 1966 in a literary magazine called *Podoby* (Forms). A second collection of a pointed political nature appeared in the autumn of 1968 after the Communist invasion; they were published in a two-volume collection in 1993 entitled *Antikódy*.

Typogrammy was not Havel's main creative interest, but he clearly enjoyed writing typograms at the same time that he wrote his plays. They were an expression of his fascination with form and with the Beckettian notion of how form expresses content. At the same time, they provided him with a complementary way of articulating his plays' themes — such as "man in the system" and "man and identity." Said Hiršal in his preface: "All Havel's texts in 'Anticodes' are very specific messages, almost like appeals or provocations."[5]

In 1964, Havel's life in the theater was blossoming. He was at the vortex, center stage of a theater that in turn was center stage of a culture in flux. All this rich creative activity around him stimulated his own writer's productivity. And he was only just getting started as a playwright.

1965: *THE MEMORANDUM*

> Death to all artificial languages! Long live natural human speech!
> Long live man![1]
>
> — Havel, *The Memorandum*

Inspired by his work on *The Bald Soprano,* flourishing from his rich collaborative relationship with Grossman, stimulated by the success of the 1964 season, Havel plunged into work on his next full-length play.

His brother Ivan recalls the play's genesis. One day in 1959, while working at ABC, the twenty-three-year-old Havel was sitting in the family apartment, having yet another conversation about philosophy and ideas with his twenty-one-year-old brother Ivan, who was now a mathematician and a philosopher. Václav had recently read Ionesco's *The Chairs* in *Světová literatura* and was marveling at the playwright's bizarre and hilarious use of language.

"Why not make up a language and write a play about it," Ivan suggested. "What shall we call the language?" his brother asked. Ivan suggested "Ptydepe," a nonsense name that sprang into his mind. "Be more specific," ordered Václav, who was intrigued by the idea and respected the disciplined mind of his younger brother. In response, Ivan gave him a short text of nonsensical dialogue in Ptydepe. Then, in between stagehand duties at ABC and writing theoretical essays about the theater, Václav took a stab at a first draft of a full-length play. Once at the Balustrade, he showed it to Vyskočil, who suggested he put it aside and work instead on another idea, about identity. The result was *The Garden Party.*[2]

Now Havel applied himself anew to the draft of *The Memorandum,* profiting from all he had learned at the Balustrade. Fortified by the relationship with the brilliant Grossman, who this time was serving as both dramaturg and director, they worked closely and intensely together. "Havel was writing *The Memorandum* and Grossman was looking over his shoulder," reports Andrej Krob. Today, Havel recalls three or four drafts, though in other accounts he mentions six or seven. Speaking of Havel's method of playwriting, Olga later said: "Every time Vašek writes a play, it takes him a long time. He always produces several versions. Sometimes he wakes me up in the night and reads me the part he has just written."[3] He dedicated the play to the Balustrade, thereby expressing his abiding commitment. "He even named his characters after members of the Balustrade ensemble," recalls Marie Málková, Grossman's wife, who played the role of Marie.

Following on the heels of *The Garden Party*'s success, the stakes for Havel were high, and he felt the pressure. To test audience response, he and Grossman held a reading of the play at the public library before rehearsals started. "The reaction was fantastic," recalls Andrej Krob, who attended. Rehearsals began with high hopes. Having worked through the season of 1964, the ensemble had exposure to the absurd aesthetic and approached the text with confidence, ready for rewrites if necessary. Krob, the technical director, stood at the back of the rehearsal room, watching raptly. The process was fascinating, Krob recalls, and he attended every single rehearsal. By his account, Grossman and Havel were at their best, collaborating and creating. Grossman taught and analyzed as he directed. "Grossman inspired the actors," Krob recalls, "and made them feel that they were in the virtual reality of the world of Václav Havel."[4]

Like *The Garden Party*, *The Memorandum*, a play in twelve scenes, is set in the labyrinthine world of bureaucracy, once again in a nameless organization whose purpose is never articulated. Mr. Gross, its managing director, arrives at work one morning and is surprised to find on his desk an incomprehensible memorandum written in a strange, unfamiliar language. He is further unnerved to find that all his subordinates are aware of this language's existence. It is called Ptydepe, and, unbeknownst to Gross, it has been declared the official language of the organization. In fact, all the employees are enrolled in compulsory Ptydepe classes to learn it. In the meantime, a Ptydepe Translation Center has been created, as well.

Gross, bewildered, investigates the source of this change and discovers that his own deputy, Mr. Baláš, together with his silent, Golem-like sidekick have been plotting behind his back. Baláš's goal, in introducing this strange new language, is to improve communication and hence the organization's effectiveness — or, as he puts it, "to make office communications more accurate and introduce precision and order into their terminology."[5] This newly fabricated language, he further asserts, is built on a scientific basis and is free of any ambiguity and emotionality. Gross, a self-described humanist, is appalled:

> Gross: My concept of directing this organization derives from the idea that every single member of the staff is human and must become more and more human. If we take from him his human language, created by the centuries-old tradition of national culture, we shall have prevented him from becoming fully human and plunge him straight into the jaws of self-alienation. I'm not against precision in official communications, but I'm for it only insofar as it humanizes Man.[6]

Angered and alarmed, Gross orders Baláš to cancel the introduction of Ptydepe. However, classes continue. In the next scene, we watch as the professor of Ptydepe, explains the basics of the new language to a classroom of stunned employees, who are struggling to grasp its linguistic principles. Built on a strictly scientific basis according to mathematically conceived laws, the language boasts an extensive vocabulary and a "rational" grammar. The purpose: to eliminate similarities between words by using the least probable combination of letters, as well as to promote clarity and efficiency. For example, the most infrequently used words are the ones with the most letters: such as *wombat*, which in Ptydepe has 319 letters. Conversely, the more common the meaning, the shorter the word. For example, the most commonly used word, *whatever*, is rendered in Ptydepe by the word *gh*. And there is even a shorter word in Ptydepe, *f*, although as of now it has no meaning; it is being held in reserve in case a word more commonly used than *whatever* is discovered.

The precision of this language is demonstrated in a lesson on the most common Ptydepe interjections.

> Lear: Well then, our "ah" becomes "zukyba," our "ouch!" becomes "byku," our "oh!" become "hayf dy doretob," English "pish!" becomes "bolypak juz," the interjection of surprise "well!" becomes "zyk"; however, our "well,well!" is not "zykzyk," as some students erroneously say, but "zykzym" — "aow!" becomes "varylaguf yb de solas," or sometimes, though much more rarely, "borybaf"; "bang!" as the symbol of a shot or explosion becomes "hetegyx

ujhoby"; "bang" as a colloquial expression for sudden surprise is "maluz rog." Our "eek!" becomes "hatum."

Thumb: *(Raises his hand.)* Sir —

Lear: What is it?

Thumb: *(Gets up.)* Would you mind telling us how one says "oops" in Ptydepe?

Lear: "Mykl."

Thumb: Thank you. *(Sits down.)*

Lear: "Psst!" becomes "cetudap"; "mmnn" becomes "vamly," the poetic "oh!" is rendered in Ptydepe by "hrulugyp." The "hoooo" of a ghost is translated mostly as "lymr," although I'd prefer the expansion "myrb uputr." Our very important "hurrah!" becomes in Ptydepe "frnygko jefr dabux altep dy savarub goz texeres."[7]

In fact, according to Baláš, the ultimate goal of Ptydepe is to eliminate the need for communication entirely, for "the good of Man," of course.

The plot thickens, along with the indecipherable language. Gross seeks out the Translation Office in his organization and tries to have his memo translated there. But he is told by the secretary that he needs an authorization for such a translation, and the form is in Ptydepe. In other words, as Gross says: "The only way to know what is in one's memo is to know it already."[8] (She wouldn't listen to his pleas, anyway, since her boss is always sending her on shopping trips for lemons and melons.) When Gross tries to issue an order cancelling Ptydepe as the organization's official language, his deputy, the treacherous Baláš, says he cannot issue an order to cancel it because he never issued an order to introduce it in the first place.

Soon the bewildered Gross finds that he has lost any ability to communicate with his staff members regarding changes that are being instituted without his knowledge.

Gross: Why did you actually need the personal registration documents?

Savant: Well, it's like this, you see . . . How shall I put it? I'm sorry, Mr. Gross. You see, I'm used to speaking in Ptydepe and so it's rather difficult for me to find the right words in a natural language.

Gross: Please go on.

Savant: In Ptydepe one would say axajores. My colleagues sometimes ylud kaboz pady el too much, and at the same time they keep forgetting that etrokaj zenig ajte ge byvoz.

Stroll: Abdy hez fajut gabob nyp orka?

Savant: Kavej hafiz okuby ryzal.

Stroll: Ryzal! Ryzal! ryzal! Varuk bado di ryzal? Kabyzach? Mahog? Hajbam? . . .

Gross: Wouldn't it be enough if a chap just told you himself everything you want to know about him?

Savant: That wouldn't guarantee that everything was hutput.

Gross: I beg your pardon?

Savant: Hutput. Quite exact . . .

Gross: I understand — (Jokingly.) I've a completely hutput zexdohyt of it.

Savant: Zexdohyttet! You've forgotten that every noun preceded by the adjective hutput takes on the suffix "tet" — [9].

Unable to get a straight answer from any of his subordinates, let alone a cigarette, the increasingly desperate Gross appeals to George, the staff watcher, whose job it is to spy on everyone in the organization.

Gross: Mr. Watcher — (Pause.) Mr. Watcher — (Pause.) Listen, Mr. Watcher, can you hear me? Have you got a cigarette? (Pause.) He must have fallen asleep. (Carefully opens the box.)

George: (Offstage.) What do you mean — fallen asleep!

Gross: (Jerks away from the box.) Well, why didn't you answer me?

George: (Offstage.) I wanted to test you.

Gross: I beg your pardon! Do you realize who I am? The Managing Director!

George: (Offstage.) Habuk bulugan.

Gross: I beg your pardon?

George: (Offstage.) Habuk bulugan, avrator.

Gross: What did you mean by that?

George: (Offstage.) Nutuput!

Gross: (Looks at his watch, then walks quickly to the back door; turns by the door.) I won't put up with any abuse from you! I expect you to come to me and apologize. (Exits by the back door.)

George: (Offstage.) Gotroch![10]

Ultimately, Baláš insists on taking over the organization — a move that Gross does not resist ("I can at least salvage this and that"). Gross is demoted to the position of "Watcher," the unseen worker who sits in a small airless cubicle and spies on all employees. There Gross languishes until an interesting change occurs. Reports begin to circulate that

Ptydepe is beginning to show the symptoms of all languages, including imprecisions, vagueness, and emotionality. Furthermore, it is utterly unteachable; only one student in the class, the steady Mr. Thumb, ever gets its gist, while the rest are lost. Meanwhile, the Head of the Translation Center himself admits that the language is so difficult for him that he is only on his second translation.

Gradually, a reversal occurs. Gross confronts Baláš, whose power is slipping under the degeneration of Ptydepe. Baláš admits defeat, Gross returns to his position as director with Baláš once again as his deputy, and Ptydepe is liquidated as the organization's official language. In the final classroom scene, however, we are, Ionesco style, back at the beginning. A new language, Chorukor, is being introduced as the organization's official language, whose purpose it is to intensify, rather than eliminate, the similarity between words. Already, Lear is at work teaching the employees:

> Lear: . . . Chorukor is very easy to learn. Often it is enough to know only one word from within a certain radius of meaning in order to guess many other words of that group. We can do that unaided and without any further study . . . Monday becomes in Chorukor "ilopagar," Tuesday "ilopager," Wednesday "ilopagur," Thursday "ilopagir," Friday "ilopageur," Saturday "ilopagoor." Now, what do you think Sunday is? Well? *(Only Thumb raises his hand.)* Well, Mr. Thumb?
> Thumb: *(Gets up.)* Ilopagor. *(Sits down.)*
> Lear: Correct, Mr. Thumb. You get an A. It's easy, isn't it?[11]

Gross, the quintessential organization man, is there to institute Chorukor and to work with Baláš once more. Again the refrain: "There was nothing else I could do. Any open conflict would have meant that I'd be finished. This way, as the Managing Director, I can at least salvage this and that."[12] His parting words are to Marie, the young secretary who was fired by Baláš for having translated the memorandum for Gross even though Ptydepe is now obsolete ("A rule is a rule"). Marie begs Gross to reverse Baláš 's decision, which he says he cannot do:

> Gross: Dear Marie! We're living in a strange, complex epoch. As Hamlet says, our "time is out of joint." Just think, we're reaching for the moon and yet it's increasingly hard for us to reach ourselves; we're able to split the atom, but unable to prevent the splitting of our personality; we build superb communications

between the continents, and yet communication between man and man is increasingly difficult . . . Like Sisyphus, we roll the boulder of our life up the hill of its illusory meaning, only for it to roll down again into the valley of its own absurdity. Never before has Man lived projected so near to the very brink of insoluble conflict between the subjective will of his moral self and the objective possibility of its ethical realization. Manipulated, automated, made into a fetish, Man loses the experience of his own totality; horrified, he stares as a stranger at himself, unable not to be what he is not, nor to be what he is . . . I am in fact totally alienated from myself.[13]

In *The Memorandum* as in *The Garden Party*, once again there is a "through the looking glass" quality, as we are catapulted into a world in which everything seems off-kilter. We don't know the organization's purpose, but we do know there are fire extinguishers on every door and knives and forks in every employee's desk drawer and that interoffice communications are all about coffee breaks and canteen-related issues. And the business of the day seems to be shopping for lemons and melons, or preparing birthday parties.

In *The Memorandum* as in *The Garden Party*, once again one feels the collision of Kafka's world with that of Ionesco. Havel's office reminds us of the same bureaucratic machinery found in Kafka's novels — the same anonymity, mystery, and unpredictability. In *The Memorandum*, there is not even a clue as to the office's real function. All we know are the rules, the procedures, and the conferences concerning one issue: Ptydepe. Language is all they talk about in *The Memorandum*, which is ironic, because the purpose of language is to make communication clear and effective. By the end of the play, the former teacher of Ptydepe, now a teacher of Chorukor, criticizes Ptydepe using the same arguments that at the beginning of the play he used to praise it. The story arrives at the point where it started. The only difference is that one artificial language based on absurd principles has been exchanged for another.

Like the language of Ionesco's "Orator," who speaks in gibberish, Ptydepe is completely nonsensical. So, too, is the communication in the totalitarian system in which Havel and his fellow Czechs live. "For us, the language which the Communists created was so hollow," said Miloš Forman. "The words had no meaning; they were hybrids."[14] Just like Ptydepe. But after all, since absolute power needs no justification or explanation, what need is there for communication? Ptydepe becomes the antithesis of language; it becomes antilanguage, just as Ionesco calls his plays "anti-plays," based on his belief that in a senseless universe there is no communication, and therefore plays are not meant to communicate or be understandable. *The Memorandum* is both a hilarious and a harrowing view of man in the system, a victim of the manipulation of the one thing essential to communal human existence — language.

The Memorandum was the first new production to follow the Balustrade's celebrated 1964 absurdist season, and critics were eager with anticipation. Answering questions in a preopening interview, Havel sounded somewhat like a character in his own play:

> Question: What can the audience expect from *The Memorandum*?
> Havel: 17,832 words in Czech, and 347 words in the Ptydepe language, which I invented.
> Question: What can the audience not expect from *The Memorandum*?
> Havel: An easy ride.[15]

The premiere took place on July 26, 1965, and the reviews were adulatory: "A step forward from *The Garden Party*"[16] (*Rudé právo*); "the event of our theater season"[17] (*Svobodné slovo* [Free Word]); "the production of Havel's satire is an honorable act"[18] (*Pravda* [Truth]).

As for the leading critics, Zdeněk Hořínek, in his article "From Ptydepe to Chorukor" in *Host do domu* (A Guest of the House), pays Havel the ultimate tribute. He says, in essence, that Havel's plays are changing society by satirizing the slogan-like phrases of the Communist Party and demonstrating how incomprehensible and meaningless they really are.[19] Sergej Machonin of *Literární noviny* echoes this judgment:

> Our past is a history of personal adaptations, which signify the loss of reason, character, dignity and honor. Havel has the brilliant talent and intellect to generalize events and to recognize their cause. Such an artist helps society to understand itself and to straighten itself out.[20]

Meanwhile, the daily business of life in the theater continued. All throughout that year, even with the intense preparation of *The Memorandum* — writing, rewriting, rehearsing — Havel diligently tended to his responsibilities at the Balustrade. He and Grossman would alternate nights attending performances, and Havel would prepare meticulously detailed reports in his clear, round handwriting. As these notes suggest, the ubiquitous role of dramaturg at the Balustrade, as played by Havel, involved much broader responsibilities, including stage manager, house manager, even lighting board operator. And Havel played all the facets of his role earnestly.

February 21, 1965:
Waiting for Godot: A lady in the audience has fainted. Havel.

March 6, 1965:
The Garden Party: 1) Mr. Viktora [the lighting board operator] didn't come in the afternoon to the rehearsals, and it wasn't clear if he'd come to the evening performance either. So it was necessary to call Mr. Rada to substitute for Mr. Viktora. Mr. Viktora finally came, but we had to pay a fee to Mr. Rada anyway. 2) On the balcony all throughout the performance there was an open window. 3) Somebody forgot to switch off the intercom, so all through the second half of the performance on the stage, you could hear the intercom from the cloakroom. 4) The children in the audience were too young to understand the performance, but I must admit that they were at least disciplined. Havel.

April 7, 1965:
The Garden Party: Mr. Viktora didn't come to the afternoon performance. So it was necessary to break open the door to the lighting booth and I had to operate the lighting board myself. Mr. Viktora came at the interval. During the evening performance, Mr. Viktora fell asleep by the end of Act III, so he missed the cue at the end of Act III. It is necessary to solve this problem and come to some kind of resolution. P.S. Libíček [the heavyset actor who played Chief of Inaugurators] is asking for a new T-shirt. Havel.

May 10, 1965:
The Bald Soprano: The wig wasn't ready. So the intermission had to be prolonged. Havel.

June 19, 1965:
Waiting for Godot: Sloup [an actor] was "indisposed" during the performance [Sloup hrál "indisponovaný": The word *indisponovaný* in Czech means "drunk."] Havel.

Nov. 3, 1965
The Memorandum: There were no fire extinguisher and cigars on the stage, which seriously marred the entire performance. The actors got nervous, etc. It is necessary to solve the prop problem definitively, and without delay. Havel.

(No date)
Jaroslav Vízner left the theater during the performance to shoot a scene in a movie, although he hadn't been given permission to do it. He came back on time [to make his entrance] but he was so distracted that he made a serious mistake on the stage: he said goodbye in a scene where he wasn't supposed to say it. I suggested to Mr. Grossman to give to Mr. Vízner a penalty. Havel.

(At the bottom of the page) "Penalty, 50 crowns. Grossman."[21]

And so it went in those golden years of 1963 to 1966 at the Balustrade, those exciting times called the Grossman/Havel era, when the ensemble spirit ran high, with no jealousy or rivalry among those young workers who were all at the beginning of their lives in the theater. A secretary at the Balustrade recalls those years:

> What impressed me about Venoušek [Václav Havel] was what a decent, modest person he was. Just to avoid taking a bow, he would hide in the attic, in the bathroom, or run from the building altogether. With Venoušek and with Mr. Grossman — they were my favorites — there was no difference between the crew and the actors. They ran things differently there than in other theaters. The secretary's office was something like a confessional, and I don't remember anyone being jealous or saying things behind each other's backs . . . in the 1960s everyone stuck together.[22]

Much later in the 1970s, after the golden 1960s seemed an unreality, after Havel became the enemy of the Soviet-ruled government, and after the persecution of Havel and all the other human rights activists, a few staff members from the Balustrade were interviewed on television and asked who Havel was. They answered: "Was there somebody with that name here? Oh yes, I think he was a stagehand who also wrote plays."[23]

1965–1968: FROM THE BALUSTRADE TO THE THEATER OF POLITICS

> This attempt to devote oneself to literature alone is a most deceptive thing, and . . . often, paradoxically, it is literature that suffers for it.[1]
> — Havel, *Disturbing the Peace*

In Havel's life in the theater all through that hectic year of 1965, there must have been more than twenty-four hours in a day.

In addition to working on the production of his new play, Havel found time to go to Reinbek, Germany, to visit Klaus Juncker, his publisher/agent. "It is as beautiful here as in Pushkin's poetry," reads the entry in Juncker's guest book written by the visiting young playwright, who sported a stylish 1960s leather jacket. Juncker drove Havel to visit theaters at Gottingen and Bochum, eager to have his new author attend productions of his plays that Juncker had arranged.

Somehow, with all his duties at the Balustrade that year, Havel also found time to join the editorial board of the Writers' Union's literary monthly, *Tvář*, a publication for young writers. Its purpose was severalfold: to be a bridge between the older and newer generation of writers, to publish new young voices, and to establish a new literary criticism. There, at the age of twenty-nine, Havel found an arena in which he could exert the leadership skills he had practiced in the 36ers years and at the Writers' Conference in Dobříš in 1956. "It was my private school of politics," he said in retrospect.[2]

The fact that such a publication could be established officially was a sign that conditions for writers were becoming freer. Still, at first, Havel kept himself aloof from *Tvář*. Its founders were slightly younger than he was and had grown up in a different time. Consequently, they had the opportunity to go to high school and university, to study philosophy at Charles University, and to work in publishing houses and magazines — in short, all those opportunities that Havel had longed for but had been denied him. They were insiders, and Havel felt slightly envious of them although he had no special ax to grind and in fact submitted some of his typograms to *Tvář*, which published them. Feeling like an outsider nonetheless, he kept his distance.

Then there came a changeover on the editorial board, and Havel was invited to join. In doing so, he was caught up in the young journal's struggle for survival. "It was also the beginning of my 'rebellious' involvement with the Writers' Union, also lasting several years," he wrote in *Disturbing the Peace*. "At the same time, it was the beginning of something deeper — my involvement in cultural and civic politics — and it ultimately led to my becoming a 'dissident.'"[3]

At that time, the Writers' Union was an arena of interaction between writers of the old-guard Communists and the "new cultural establishment," as Havel called it, a softer Communist constituency called the "anti-dogmatics." But *Tvář* was different. It had no establishment ties, no political identity, no ideological point of view. Somehow, it stood apart, just as the small theaters and New Wave film did. It was a part of a younger generation, with no clear political profile. Its editorial board made choices that were independent of any ideology. This made the union hostile to its own publication, like a parent hostile to an independent offspring it cannot control.

At the union's summer conference of 1965, Havel again made a bold and inflammatory speech (as he did at the conference nine years earlier) against the group's intolerance and bureaucracy and its continued banning of many wonderful authors. In response, the union decided to change the makeup of the editorial board. Havel and his new colleagues immediately circulated a petition in protest, and Havel went to great personal lengths to collect signatures from writers all over the country; on one occasion, he broke through a physical blockade to prevent him from boarding a train. The Communist Party also threatened to close the Balustrade because, as they put it, that troublemaker Havel was its dramaturg. Recognizing Havel as a "dangerous fellow," the union ultimately succeeded in closing the journal in 1967, by order of the Communist Party's Central Committee. (It was revived briefly in 1968 with Havel as the chairman of the editorial board and closed for good in June 1969.) His name was also removed from the list of candidates for the union's Central Committee, along with the names of the writers Ivan Klíma, Pavel Kohout, and Ludvík Vaculík.

The whole episode was a vital part of Havel's education in "political theater," a rehearsal, in effect, for greater performances to come. It also created an alliance among writers against a common cause, an ensemble that would be put to its ultimate and dramatic use a decade later.

Havel, the political rebel, threw himself into the writers' political arena as energetically as he did into the theater, describing it as "a fierce, stubborn, and often inept attempt to do things differently."[4] It was here among the various warring factions of the Writers' Union that Havel, a "non-communist," received an invaluable political education. He learned about the difficulties of circulating a petition and how to do it effectively. He experienced his first police harassment. He met with criticism in the local media from the Communist Party's Central Committee. He learned the dangers of intrigue; at one point he was offered a chance to start his own journal, only to realize it was a trap being set for him. He learned the responsibilities of leadership, as the chairman of the Young Person's Action Group within the union. He had his first crack at mediating between opposing factions; in this instance, between the editorial board and the Writers' Union. He developed a personal style characterized by a combination of hard work, speaking out with conviction, and a wariness of intrigue. He also learned the lesson of defeat; despite all his efforts, *Tvář* closed in 1967. The last issue included a contribution from Jan Patočka, the eminent Czech philosopher.

But despite *Tvář*'s eventual demise, its benefit to Havel were enormous. Through his involvement, Havel acquired skills and forged relationships that would help determine his political future. The experience also broadened his worldview and provided him with invaluable educational experience as a writer.

1965–1968: *THE INCREASED DIFFICULTY OF CONCENTRATION*

> When I returned to Prague recently, the theater was full of ideas and optimism. "Just now, it's a garden of Eden," a young playwright told me. "But winter might come at any time. . . . The next year or so will be the test. The important thing is not to praise us for reasons that might be used against us."[1]
>
> — Kenneth Tynan, *The New Yorker*

As the title of his next play (and the final one of his decade at the Balustrade) suggests, the late 1960s found Havel torn in many directions.

With each year, his life became more multilayered and complex. While 1960 to 1965 were years of living and breathing theater and only theater, from 1965 to 1968 he found himself involved in a myriad of activities. At long last, after a decade of attempts, he was finally admitted to the drama faculty at AMU, where he was enrolled from 1966 to 1967. Even so, during this time, his involvement in the political arena of the Writers' Union intensified.

And there was continued recognition for his writing. In 1966, his first book, *Minutes* (Protokoly), was published by *Mladá fronta* in Prague. It contained two plays, *The Garden Party* and *The Memorandum*; his collection of typograms, *Anticodes* (1964); and two theoretical essays, "The Anatomy of the Gag" (1963) and "On Dialectical Metaphysics" (1964).

In 1967, the British critic Kenneth Tynan visited Prague, a city he called "the theater capital of Europe."[2] He was captivated by it, and by its leading young playwright, whom he described as driving around "in a dashing little Renault bought with the royalties from his plays," wearing "smart but conservative clothes, being a dandy in the classic rather than the romantic mode. . . . He both walked and talked with purposeful briskness and elegance."[3] Tynan found Havel to be completely affable, and at the same time stylish and self-assured; "in a well-kept way, he exudes integrity and moral resilience."[4] In another publication, Tynan called Havel "an extraordinary, bullet-headed little genius, absolutely fearless, who turns out plays that use the technique of Ionesco, but puts it to a social and political purpose."[5]

The thirty-one-year-old Havel was now his country's leading playwright, and gaining an international reputation. His plays were produced all over Europe — in Berlin, Rome, Belgrade, Paris. When critics like Tynan visited Prague, it was Havel they wanted to meet — the most important Czech voice in the theater and the first to achieve international recognition since Karel Čapek with his *RUR* (1920) and *The Insect Comedy* (1921).

Tynan found Prague's theaters thriving, with steady, productive young playwrights like Havel, Ivan Klíma, Pavel Kohout, Ladislav Smoček, Josef Topol, and Milan Uhde; world-class directors like Jan Grossman, Alfred Radok, and Otomar Krejča; a small army of gifted young actors; a flourishing cluster of experimental theaters (there were nineteen "legitimate" theaters at the time, subsidized by the state or the municipality); and the most influential stage designers in Europe, above all, Josef Svoboda. If Prague were the theater capital of Europe, as Tynan called it, then Havel was enjoying a center-stage role.

At the Balustrade, Havel continued his affiliation, but his involvement in the daily operations was less intense. Grossman was on tour with various productions, most recently John Gay's *The Beggar's Opera* in Munich. Both men were drifting away from the everyday life of the theater. Meanwhile, Havel was also deeply immersed in writing his dissertation project for AMU. Entitled "Commentary on *Eduard*," it was a lengthy (approximately fifty pages) and intense analysis of a new full-length play he was writing. The idea for the play, he explained, came to him from the reaction of audience members who had seen *The Garden Party* and *The Memorandum* at the Balustrade.

People come to me and ask me: "How do you know my boss, my secretary, my manager! They say exactly the same thing, using the same words!" They ask me if I were there, because I know these people perfectly. It started to matter to me, this concreteness; it wasn't my intention to make an image of some concrete director, boss or secretary. On the contrary, I wanted to create a "hook" upon which to hang an idea.[6]

Eager not to repeat himself, Havel was searching for a new challenge. He had already made his mark as a young writer who was ahead of his time. In *The Garden Party*, he had helped his audience understand the need to look at the system and what it does to man. He gave voice to what the audience felt and sensed. He had helped to set change in motion, and now, in the later 1960s, everyone was talking about society and the need to humanize it. After *The Memorandum* in 1965, people were optimistic, enthusiastic. They felt better able to criticize Communism and the system; they felt freer. So now Havel plunged into a new work on a new theme.

Taking his cue from the Western existentialists he so admired, Havel turned inward, to private life as opposed to life "in the system," and set out to explore the notion of what he called "self-mystification." His friend Andrej Krob, who had had difficulties with the Balustrade management, was working as a caretaker of Březnice, a castle in Pribram, southwest of Prague, in the gentle Bohemian hills. Krob invited Havel to the castle to work on his new play. The beauty of the setting, with its lakes and natural life, offered a welcome retreat. Havel sequestered himself there with the rough draft of a new play.

Using his AMU assignment as an opportunity to experiment with form and content, Havel tried, once again, to illustrate Beckett's theory about their interrelation. If he were writing about man's fragmented existence, why not experiment with a fragmented structure? He plunged into a new playwriting process. Using the same technique he had learned at Kolář's table at the Café Slavia, he filled the pages of his commentary with charts of the play's scenes and themes. Then, as he describes it: "I made graphs, cut strips of paper, changed the order of the scenes, and reassembled them. So in the end you have a continuous story which is cut into 33 pieces and repasted together in a new order."[7]

The play, originally titled *Eduard* and then renamed *The Increased Difficulty of Concentration* (Ztížená možnost soustředění), tells of one day in the life of Dr. Eduard Huml, social scientist and writer, who is trying to write a lecture on the search for human happiness. In Act I, we find him disheveled, distracted, and pajama-clad in his Prague apartment, pondering the meaning of life and preparing for the day. What follows is a series of recurring scenes. There is breakfast with his wife Vlasta, who searches for the honeypot for his rolls, prepares the stew for lunch, inquires about dinner, and advises him on how to deal with the demands of his mistress, Renata. There is lunch with Renata, who wears Vlasta's apron to serve him the stew, romps around the room in Vlasta's dressing gown, and then demands that Huml leave his wife. There is a visit from his secretary, Blanka, who takes dictation from Huml and wards off his advances. "Remember the Dolomites!" he croons to each woman, changing the mountain range to suit the fantasy, as he tried to placate and pacify.

The book Huml is writing is on human potential and the search for human happiness. He dictates:

> Huml: There exist situations — for example in some advanced western countries — in which all basic human needs have been satisfied and still people are not happy — they experience feelings of depression, boredom, frustration, etc. — full stop. In these situations man begins to desire that which in fact he perhaps does not need at all — he simply persuades himself he has certain needs which he does not have - or he vaguely desires something which he cannot specify and thus cannot strive for — full stop. Hence, as soon as man has satisfied one need— i.e. achieved happiness — another so far unsatisfied need is born in him so that every happiness is always simultaneously a negation of happiness . . .[8]

To top it off, there is a visit from a group of scientists who have somehow invaded Dr. Huml's home to study his behavior patterns. They explain that he has been selected in a random sample because his name begins with an H and because his house has an odd number. For this purpose, they have brought along a computer named Puzuk, which they have programmed to function like a person. The machine's assignment is to collect data from Huml's environment as part of an experiment to create the unique personality of the future. During the course of the day, Puzuk gradually turns into a sweet, whimpering child with emotions and feelings (the metamorphosis theme again), who speaks in a baby voice and responds to temperature, pressure, and humidity.

As Huml ponders the meaning of existence, the various women and the scientists in his life enter and exit through the four upstage revolving doors like characters in a French farce, while Huml follows after them, changing from pajamas to trousers and back again. The scenes of Huml's day replay over and over again in repetitive, nonchronological order, accelerating at a rapid rate. In the center of this cycle stands Puzuk, the computer, whose light finally turns from red to green. Having lived in the Huml household and observed Huml's life, Puzuk is programmed at last. Now "he" is ready to collect the data that will determine the unique personality of the future. He articulates his questions in a child-like voice:

> Puzuk: Which is your favorite tunnel? Are you fond of musical instruments? How many times a year do you air the square? Where did you bury the dog? Why didn't you pass on it? When did you lose the claim? Wherein lies the nucleus? Do you know where you're going and do you know who's going with you? Do you piss in public, or just now and then?[9]

At this point, according to Havel's stage directions, all the characters suddenly appear on stage, entering and exiting from one door to another, repeating with Puzuk all the questions he has been addressing to Huml. Their movements and their speech accelerate, their voices crescendo, their lines are cascade of nonsensical non sequiturs, their dialogue becomes a repetitive jumble. The result is chaos, with Huml rushing among the characters, seeking some order to the chaos.

> Mrs. Huml: You're not just trying to jolly along the fish, are you? You're not just trying to jolly along the fish, are you? *(Etc.)*
> Beck: Tomorrow I'm going carroting and that's that! Tomorrow I'm going carroting and that's that! *(Etc.)*
> Renata: Do you ever eat any jolly plums? Do you ever eat any jolly plums? *(Etc.)*

Machal: You should be ashamed of yourself, Dr. Huml! You should
be ashamed of yourself, Dr. Huml! *(Etc.)*
Blanka: Have you seen the safety bolt of the moisture meter? Have
you seen the safety bolt of the moisture meter? *(Etc.)*
Kriebl: Dr. Huml? Dr. Huml? *(Etc.)*
Miss Balcar: Give me your high-altitude plums! Give me your high-
altitude plums! *(Etc.)*
Puzuk: Which is your favorite tunnel? Are you fond of musical
instruments? *(Etc.)*[10]

Only the eruption of Puzuk's siren-like wail halts the growing chaos.
Huml has made his point. Science cannot define human personality. On
the contrary. Once again, as in his previous two plays, Havel ends this
work with a speech by the protagonist on human identity and the nature
of humanity.

Huml: The only key lies in man's complexity as a subject of human
togetherness, because the limitlessness of our own human nature
is so far the only thing capable of approaching — however im-
perfectly — the limitlessness of others . . . Hence, the fundamental key to man does not lie in his brain, but in his heart.[11]

In the finale, however, unable to chose or to change, Huml puts up
no resistance to this crescendoing chaos. His life continues in this meaningless, repetitive cycle; in fact, he evens adds a new woman to his retinue,
the scientist Miss Balcar. In the end, the Professor of Happiness is no
closer to his subject than when the play began.

Just as in 1963, when he audaciously put Communism on the stage
(in the guise of the system), so in 1968 Havel astutely sensed the opportunity to explore man's private domain. In doing so, he boldly experimented with an eclectic collage of absurdist, existential, and Kafkaesque
themes, illustrating how modern man is threatened by a menacing alliance between society and science. The result is absurdist science fiction
that combines random influences of the robot (Čapek's RUR) and metamorphosis (Kafka's Gregor Samsa), with a touch of the angst of existential man (Camus' Meursault) and the superfluous one, too (Chekhov's
spiritually empty "superfluous man," Ivanov). (Havel dedicated the play
to Josef Šafařík, an essayist and philosopher whose work he admired).

The Increased Difficulty of Concentration went into rehearsal at the
Balustrade in 1968. Havel was not as intimately involved with the pro-

duction as he had been with the first two. Grossman was abroad directing, and Havel was distracted by his increasing political involvement. The production was directed by Václav Hudeček, a Balustrade regular, who had directed *Hitchhiking, The Bald Soprano,* and *Waiting for Godot.* After the previous two comedies by Havel, the audience's response was one of surprise. They didn't laugh at the chilling and ironic humor of *The Increased Difficulty of Concentration* as they had at the more absurdist and satirical humor of *The Garden Party* or *The Memorandum.* This was a new tone for Havel.

Critics devoted less attention to *The Increased Difficulty of Concentration* than they had to his two previous plays. Perhaps this was because of the excitement generated by the dramatic political changes swirling around its opening in April 1968. Those who did pay attention found it a curious play and were intrigued by the newness of the subject matter as well as by its significance in the Havel oeuvre.

Vlasta Gallerová, writing in *Práce* (Labor), saw *The Increased Difficulty of Concentration* as part of a trilogy: "In all three plays he analyzes the situation of man in the modern world. It is a kind of human deformation."[12] Sergej Machonin, one of the leading critics of the day, described Dr. Huml as the "superfluous man of our time" in *Literární listy* (Literary Letters).[13] He also wrote about the unifying theme in Havel's trilogy of 1960s plays. In his first two plays (*The Garden Party* and *The Memorandum*), Machonin noted, Havel had described the dehumanizing effect of bureaucratic institutions. Now with *The Increased Difficulty of Concentration*, he continued, Havel goes a step farther and takes a broader view of how all these elements combined (science, psychology, as well as bureaucracy) to dehumanize man: "This monstrous product of modern civilization is so widespread, that it has become lethally dangerous for mankind and for his culture alike." Machonin also noted the duality of man and the machine (Huml and Puzuk) and pointed out how both were malfunctioning. Zdeněk Hořínek, another leading critic of the day, praised Havel's ambitious experimentation with form in *Divadlo*: "To understand the world means that a playwright must keep on creating newer and newer models of it."[14]

On the other hand, other critics found Havel even more pessimistic than Beckett. From *Svobodné slovo*:

> Beckett's *Waiting for Godot* gave us hope — theoretical and ambiguous — but hope all the same for the possibility of man's liber-

ation. . . . Now, Havel's new play brutally eliminates the last signs of hope. The devastating emptiness and cynical nothingness of his hero's life is not determined by any dark evil powers of any social mechanism but only by himself, by the absence of any real human motivations, needs and feelings. There is no chance for liberation, changes in the society will not help — in fact nothing can change our lives until we ourselves start to act freely in truth. . . . Havel's message is too cruel and cheerless, but then again today's world doesn't react to gentleness and tact.[15]

But in the program notes for the production at the Theatre on the Balustrade, the words of the philosopher Josef Šafařík — close family friend and mentor to Havel — express the humanism that is at the heart of the play:

What man needs is the sanctity of his home. But technology considers the home as a world it needs to conquer, to invade. No wonder our "home" is so spiritually empty. We need to fill it with something more than technology — like emotion and humanity.[16]

While his new play about the confusion in man's personal life was rehearsing during that spring of 1968, the air in Prague was filled with hope and optimism. It was a spirit that was hard to resist, and Havel found himself caught up in its euphoria, so much so that he was too busy to pay attention to his own opening. However, Havel was a writer who was both a participant in the moment and an observer on the outside. His new play reflects his ability to see the broader picture, one that both incorporates the political events of the day and transcends them. Despite the growing optimism in his country, in this play Havel was commenting on modern man's spiritual confusion in an uncertain and changing world.

In retrospect, *The Increased Difficulty of Concentration*, produced in a year of great change, resonates oddly as a personal play in an intensely political time. But Havel was always ahead of his times, a playwright of multiple concerns: personal, political, and philosophical. Harold Clurman, who saw the play the following year in a production by the Forum of the Repertory Theater of Lincoln Center (1969), sensed that strong personal message:

The central character declares his conviction that the truth of life cannot be measured by computers or bureaucratic dictates but only by the motivations of the human heart, is what Havel means his play to say. That is what gave it social force in his country. . . . Thus the play . . . becomes something vital to the Czech citizen forever under the vigilant and evil eye of who can say just what.[17]

In the canon of Havel's plays, this curious work stands as an early and prescient reminder that the deeper issues of the human soul transcend politics and lie in a broader, metaphysical sphere. They need to be addressed. So many demands are placed on modern man. Where is his clarity? As for Václav Havel, playwright and writer, it would be much later, through the trials of the terrible decades to follow, that he found that clarity, by taking a moral stand in an amoral universe, or as he was to call it, by "living in truth."

1968: *GUARDIAN ANGEL* AND *A BUTTERFLY ON THE ANTENNA*

> You write plays about the passivity of the Czech intelligentsia, and meanwhile this is what is happening in real life![1]
> — Havel, *A Butterfly on the Antenna*

In the first half of 1968, Havel also managed to find time to write two other dramatic works that expressed his sense of unease and uncertainty: a radio play called *Guardian Angel* (Anděl strážný) and a television play called *A Butterfly on the Antenna* (Motýl na anténě). Looking back on that period so filled with hope, it is telling that both the protagonists of these curious, almost surreal little plays are playwrights who are in peril of not hearing and seeing what is happening around them.

Guardian Angel was actually the expansion of a much shorter work that Havel had written in 1963 for *Divadelní noviny*, the literary magazine.[2] This subtle, jarring little two-character one-act concerns a playwright named Vavák. Successful, newly married, Vavák is in the process of writing a new play entitled *Guardian Angel*. One day, he is visited by a stranger, who introduces himself cheerfully as Machoň and insinuates himself into Vavák's living room, carrying a strange-looking suitcase. Machoň professes to have met Vavák. In fact, he knows all about Vavák's private life, has read all Vavák's plays, and has even attended all the opening nights. Acting like an intimate friend, Machoň asks for cigarettes and a glass of milk, chatting on and on while Vavák obligingly serves as his host. When Vavák politely questions Machoň's identity and the purpose of his visit, Machoň interrupts him sharply: not yet, he snaps. Eventually, Machoň urges Vavák to open the suitcase, saying that it contains a present for him. Vavák opens it and finds a strange device that Machoň enthusiastically describes is a "nuclear hair polishing kit" invented by his own brother. If used every two hours, he continues, it will render his hair shiny. Vavák demurs, saying he is unworthy of such an elaborate gift and that in any case he would not have time to use it. Machoň insists, and then comes to the real point of his visit. Vavák needs help, he says, and he has come to provide it. The true issue is Vavák's ears. They are too big, and that puts Vavák in danger. But isn't that the point of being a writer, Vavák asks, to have the ability to listen to people? Exactly, says Machoň, that's the problem, and that is why Machoň is here to help.

> Machoň: All I care about is your welfare. I'm sure that often when you write something or other, you don't actually mean it the way it comes out, but you know people — someone always pounces on it. It's no use provoking people. I understand the artistic mentality, I've been in close touch with you artists for donkey's years! So I realize how tempting it is to write down this or that which you've just overheard. But do try and think realistically — is there much point in going on with it? Is there? Let's face it, it's just a lot of baloney.
>
> Vavák: Well, how about cotton wool in the ears? Would that be all right?
>
> Machoň: *(Bursts out.)* Are you mad? You think that when, in a couple of hours your cotton wool begins to itch and you take it out for a moment and overhear something, and bang it down on a sheet of paper — I'll let myself be in trouble on your account? I do a lot for artists, but I'm not going to be your bloody martyr!
>
> Vavák: Well, what's your advice?
>
> Machoň: A radical measure. Then you'll be all right till the day you die![3]

Whereupon Machoň whips out a pair of "ear shears," and the last sound the audience hears is Vavák's screaming as Machoň cuts off his ears.

Guardian Angel not only expresses the battle that Havel and other writers had been fighting with censorship for the past eight years; it also expresses Havel's ironic view of censorship — that it is not threatening or angry, but rather ordinary, bureaucratic, seemingly benign, and even caring. Indeed, it has a mission: to protect the artist and the nation, hence the title *Guardian Angel*. It is also a play about "listening" — not only in the sense of the playwright as everyday observer, but also as a prophet who can "hear" the sound of what is to come. As such, this surrealistic little parable offers a chilling prophesy of what actually would happen later on in that crucial year of 1968.

The equally unsettling teleplay *A Butterfly on the Antenna* also features a playwright, one who is the process of writing a new play. Jeník is celebrating his thirtieth birthday with his wife and her mother. While their boarder, Mr. Bašta, sits sleeping on a recliner, and the mother-in-law knits, Jeník and Marie reminisce about the good old days, calling themselves the "first Czech beatniks" with a certain sense of self-satisfaction. Meanwhile, from the other room comes the sound of dripping water. The mother-in-law tries to warn them that the water might soon flood the apartment. She reminds them, helpfully, that their boarder, Mr. Bašta, happens to be a plumber, so it might be a good idea to enlist his aide. But rather than wake him up to do something about this impending threat, Jeník and Marie proceed instead to discuss and analyze the situation. Wouldn't this make a fine idea for a one-act play? asks Jeník excitedly — namely, a young writer who is celebrating his birthday while water is flooding his apartment. And wouldn't the dripping water, a symbol of time, make a fine metaphor? On and on they talk about the play, analyzing the water in scientific and philosophical terms, and discussing how well the metaphor will suit the play's message. While the mother-in-law tries to divert the conversation with absurd stories and remarks (maybe the sound of the dripping water is really a horse?), the son cannot stop discussing his play, and meanwhile the water is seeping into the living room where they are sitting. Jeník and Marie continue to intellectualize about the water, still not doing anything about it, until the option is introduced to wake up Mr. Bašta, the plumber. "A genius idea: I can't believe we didn't think about it before," exclaims Marie, and still they continue to discuss it. The "running joke" becomes one of the running water itself while they blithely discuss whether they should wake up the plumber.

Finally, they can ignore it no longer — the water is rising all around

them, and they must grab buckets and start bailing it out to one side of
the stage. Suddenly, Mr. Bašta cries out in his sleep: "Turn off the faucet!"
The mother-in-law, who is the bastion of reality and pragmatism, leaps up,
runs into the next room, turns the water off, and stalks out of the house,
leaving the amazed couple behind with their dazed boarder. Now awake,
the plumber tells them of his disturbing dream, which includes everything
that has just happened onstage. He expresses his panic that, with water rising everywhere, he might not have been able to save them (the intelligentsia) from impending disaster. Jeník and Marie listen, enrapt.

> Marie: Can you feel it, Jeník, how everything is connected?
> Jeník: This dream, this is an idea. Jesus. It would make a good play,
> this dream! . . . It will work! It's so symbolic. What a great symbol!
> Marie: A symbol of what?
> Jeník: I don't know, but it's great, for sure.
> Mr. Bašta: So, happy birthday! Many happy returns of the day![4]

Delighted, Jeník decides to incorporate Mr. Bašta's dream into his
play, too (making it a dream within a play within a play).

At the end, Mr. Bašta adds that he has forgotten one last detail from
his dream: high on the rooftop of the young couple's house was a long antenna and on it was perched a butterfly. End of dream.

A Butterfly on the Antenna is a wicked little satire on Havel's generation.
It satirizes the Czech literati and their tendency to analyze and philosophize
everything, rather than act. It satirizes Czech writers, who complain about
the passivity and the self-involvement of the Czech intelligentsia but meanwhile are incapable of taking matters into their own hands. It satirizes, in
particular, the pretentiousness of Czech writers, their passion for Western
writing, especially the theater of the absurd, and their obsession to convert
everything they see into literature, while reality is flooding the world
around them, dangerously. The plumber is asleep? "How Kafkaesque," says
Jeník. "How Ionescan," says Marie. The style of Jeník's play? Perhaps, says
Jeník, it will be a psychological drama à la Tennessee Williams. Literary allusions abound — from Kafka and Ionesco to Proust. They discuss the play
at length with relish, delighted to have the metaphor of the water, yet completely unaware of both its meaning and its consequence. The admonitions
of the mother-in-law, the voice of reality, go unheeded. After all, why
should the intelligentsia listen to the ordinary citizen?

Marie: Excellent! What a great metaphor!

Jeník: It could be a play about the passivity of the Czech intelligentsia —

Mother-in-law: Silence. Can you hear it? What is it?

(Everyone listens.)

Jeník: It's probably just the sound in your ear.

Marie: — unable to wake up the nation from the sleep when it is in danger.

Jeník: That's nice, but "they"[5] wouldn't allow it. The symbol is so specifically Czech. Aren't we really sleep-walking through this era, unable to awaken ourselves and to inspire ourselves into a great creative act?

Mother-in-law: Silence. Can you hear it? What is it?

(Everyone listens.)

Marie: Oh Mummy, you're wrong, it's nothing. What do you think, Jeník?

Jeník: I can't hear anything.

Marie: And do you know what the title should be? I've got it! The title should be "Who Is Afraid of Edward Albee?"

Jeník: They wouldn't allow it.

Marie: Why not?

Jeník: Anyway, you know that I have a different approach to drama from Edward's. I'm more focused on the representation of automatized psychology, while Edward is more focused on the representation of psychological automatism.

Marie: That's true, actually. And you work with dialogue in a different way, too.

Jeník: That's the point. It comes from my mentality. And from my generation and its background. The tragedy of our generation is that we came of age before we were able to realize ourselves, and at the same time we had to realize ourselves before we could come of age. And that is what all the Albees of the world can't understand . . .

Mother-in-law: Quiet! Can you hear it? What is it?

(Everyone listens.)

Marie: Oh Mummy, stop it! We told you already that we can't hear anything, so just stop it![6]

The water is finally turned off by the only realistic character in the play (the mother-in-law), but still Jeník and Marie don't understand. They can only perceive reality in literary terms, so much so that they end up sounding like characters in an Ionesco play themselves.

Jeník: She just turned the tap
Marie: The water stopped flowing —
Jeník: And then she left —
Marie: Jeník, isn't that absurd?
Jeník: Just like in Beckett!
Marie: She just turned the tap —
Jeník: The water stopped flowing —
Marie: And then she left —[7]

In this clever, ironic little play, Havel addresses the fundamental problem of the writer in his society, himself included. Yes, he can analyze his own situation, yes, he is self-aware, and yes, he is aware of his self-awareness — but what does that change? He does not, cannot, will not act. He is so obsessed with his creative world that he insists on making it his reality. No wonder he doesn't hear the water slowly seeping into it. Like Vavák, he has lost his hearing; but in Jeník's case, it's by his own hand.

Jeník: Of course, the typical behavior of intellectuals is characterized by a very high level of self-absorption. Those people are constantly observing themselves. They understand themselves as a literary theme, they distance themselves from everything they say and do, and thanks to this distance they can look at their behavior objectively. They know exactly what their own mistakes or weaknesses are. But they are unable to correct them. The creative approach to life requires that one jumps into life as into water without thinking, that is, if one's properly dressed to swim. Just when you start controlling yourself, you lose your ability to live naturally. Your own controlling eye is always faster than you are. You see your own action before it happens, in a critical light. And then you obviously never do it.[8]

A writer obsessed with self-analysis (Havel) analyzing a writer obsessed with self-analysis (his character, Jeník). As such, *A Butterfly on the Antenna* is also a tongue-in-cheek little piece of self-satire on his own penchant for intellectual pretentiousness, a reminder as well as a birthday gift to himself (Jeník turned thirty; Havel was soon to turn thirty-two). Hearing the droll dialogue, one can almost hear Havel and Olga sitting around their table at the Café Slavia, dropping names of Czech and Western writers with aplomb:

Jeník: I was reading my diary from those times today. It's a sort of Joycean montage/collage, it hasn't received a prize in literature yet, but for me it's a very interesting document. For example, the first night of our honeymoon, I made this note: "I can't make sense of my own life by day, but I can make sense of history by night." This note, it seems to me, in its Shaldan precision, describes the human condition of my generation.

Marie: And it also captures all that emotional atmosphere; we were hysterical, pathetic, superficial, self-aggrandizing. The first Czech beatniks.

Jeník: Yes, and yet we suffered in a slightly Sramekian way. Or rather, we were spastically overcomplicated in a Ludvikkunderabrnoesque way.

Mother-in-law: Wha-? I didn't get that —

Marie: Jeník said that our generation — Petr, him and me — are the first Czech beatniks. But spastically overcomplicated in a Ludvikkunderabrnoesque way.

Mother-in-law: I see. Now I understand. Isn't the water overflowing?[9]

A Butterfly on the Antenna may not have the threat of violence that the frightening conclusion of *Guardian Angel* does, and yet there is a strong admonition in its depiction of the writer trapped in his need to analyze and theorize at the expense of his sense of reality. It's as much Havel's admonition to himself as it is to others, the threat of an impending, self-fulling prophesy. If he continues to talk, and not act, the water will continue to rise till it engulfs everything around him. The butterfly atop the antenna on the roof remains as a reminder of promise of freedom — to write, to create, and to act — lest of course the water rises to engulf that, too.

As such, these two odd, unsettling little plays stand as strong warnings to the writer that he need be aware of the world around him. Danger is near. Consistent with the other ironies and absurdities of Havel's life in the theater, however, these warnings went unheeded. Indeed, the author himself was so busy during that hectic year of 1968 that he didn't even have time to hear the broadcast of his own play, *Guardian Angel*, when it was aired on Czech radio. Meanwhile, *A Butterfly on the Antenna* received a prize from the Czechoslovak Television, which was prepared to tape it. But the political events of August 1968 intervened, and the airing never took place. Ironically, *A Butterfly on the Antenna* was broadcast for the first time as a radio play years later by Norddeutscher Rundfunk in Western Germany in 1975, after it was too late. As Havel had predicted, the water had indeed been rising, and no one had turned off the faucet.

The playwrights Vavák and Jeník would reappear in his work years later in a new incarnation called Vaněk — a writer facing the dire consequences forecast in the frightening little play *Guardian Angel*, drowning in the flood of reality that *A Butterfly on the Antenna* prophesied.

But that was a long way to come. First there was the phenomenon of Prague Spring.

1968: PRAGUE SPRING

> I understand 1968 as the logical outcome and culmination of a long process, lasting for many years, in which, as I say, society gradually became aware of itself and liberated itself.[1]
>
> — Havel, *Disturbing the Peace*

While Havel was revising his draft of *Eduard*, significant political changes were occurring in his country — ones that had been developing for as many years as he had been writing. These changes bore fruit in the historic year of 1968.

The year 1968 was one of the most dramatic in modern Czech history, and Havel found himself onstage both at the Balustrade and in the broader political arena. Early that year, progressive Communists in the government, deciding that the time was ripe for political reform, had elected Alexander Dubček as secretary of the Communist Party. While the world watched with elation, Dubček ushered in a program of reform entitled "The Action Program," soon to be known as "socialism with a human face." It gave hope for democratization of the Czech Communist Party and independence from Moscow. A period of cultural freedom called "The Prague Spring" ensued.

It was an unusually warm spring that year, and the gaiety of the May Day parade in Wenceslas Square reflected a buoyant public spirit. Optimism about the future, as well as well as a fresh spring breeze, was in the air. As the happy crowds waved flags and chanted, Havel's spirits soared, too.

> Suddenly, you could breathe freely, people could associate freely, fear vanished, taboos were swept away, social conflicts could be openly

named and described, a wide variety of interests could be expressed, the mass media once again began to do their proper job, civic self-confidence grew: in short, the ice began to melt and the window began to open. It would have been hard not to be struck and fascinated by all this.

Of course it's also true that my delight was mixed with increasingly agonizing doubts and hesitations, but I was not alone in this either; it was a general phenomenon.[2]

Despite his reservations, Havel was caught up in the momentum of the Prague Spring and swam headlong with the tides of change. His intense involvement with the Writers' Union continued. In March, along with twenty others, he signed a proclamation to establish an Independent Writers' Circle within the union, the first entity of its kind whose members did not belong to the Communist Party. He was also named the group's chairman.

In April, Havel used the new organization to enter the broader political arena. His article "On the Subject of Opposition," published on April 4 in the weekly journal *Literární listy*, advocated a two-party system and the establishment of a democratic party based on Czech humanitarian traditions. It may have been the only article of the time to recommend openly the ending of single party rule. At that moment, merely suggesting such a thing would have been extremely daring, but Havel was already well rehearsed, thanks to his Writers' Union experience of 1965, and was now prepared to make his entrance onto the larger political stage.

The opening of *The Increased Difficulty of Concentration* on April 11, 1968, one week after publication of his article, went by relatively unnoticed. By the end of April, Havel had signed an open letter to the Communist Party's Central Committee in which 150 writers and cultural figures supported the "democratization progress" of the Dubček regime.

At the time of Prague Spring, the theme of man's spiritual void as expressed in *The Increased Difficulty of Concentration* hardly seem relevant. Nor did the danger of hearing what was going on in the world, as expressed in *Guardian Angel*.

In the spring of 1968, there was hope.

1968: NEW YORK SPRING

> I think New York is amazing, and am quite smitten with this city. I
> never cease to thank you with all my heart; without you, I would
> never had the chance to see it.[1]
>
> — Havel, letter to Joseph Papp, July 28, 1968

Riding the wave of the crest of change, Havel the playwright was carried
into the international arena. In May, he traveled to New York to attend
the American premiere of *The Memorandum* at the New York Shakespeare
Festival (also known as the Public Theater). Joseph Papp had been appointed artistic director of the Public the year before, and his first priority was a search for new work. In May 1966, Henry Popkin, critic of the
Times (London), had written to Papp in response to his inquiry, telling
him about a young writer named Václav Havel, dramaturg at the Theatre
on the Balustrade, whose new work, *The Memorandum*, might be of interest. The translator, Vera Blackwell, sent Papp a translated copy.

According to Papp's widow, Gail, the play appealed to him very
much. "Having lived through the McCarthy era, Joe responded to the
play very well," Gail Papp remembers. "He had no problem relating to it,
and understanding what it was about."[2] The notion of "Ptydepe," a fabricated language, was particularly intriguing. However, Vera Blackwell
wrote Papp a letter of caution:

> I don't know if I'd ever told you that Havel was in trouble with
> the regime. It started the time he was supposed to come to New
> York with me last June — when his passport was taken away from
> him — and it's been getting worse ever since. The Balustrade The-
> atre is cagey about renewing his contract. All his applications to go
> abroad (on business) are being turned down. He was investigated by
> the police for 48 hours nonstop — rather vigorously, I hear. So —
> in other words — all one can do for him in the way of publicity
> abroad may be more than just a natural reaction to the discovery
> of a young writer of considerable talent. It may prove to be — lit-
> erally — a life-saving endeavor.[3]

That was enough for Papp. He immediately wrote Havel asking his
permission to produce *The Memorandum* in the 1967 season and inviting

him to New York. It was to be Papp's very first season at the Public, and he himself would direct the play.

> We are very pleased that we will soon be reaching an agreement to present your fine play *The Memorandum*. . . . It would be of considerable value to us if some arrangement could be made to have you here during the final rehearsals and for the opening. In fact, we would hope that Jan Grossman could accompany you. We have heard a great deal about your excellent theater and would enjoy meeting the key artistic people connected with it. (January 26, 1967)[4]

Havel was delighted. He replied:

> I thank you very much for your letter. I was naturally very pleased to hear of your intention to present my play *The Memorandum*. I would love to attend the performance (as would Mr. Grossman) and to assist at your final rehearsals. If the play will really be put on the stage and if I shall be able to come, I shall certainly profit from the opportunity. Wishing you every success in your work and looking forward to your further news, I remain . . . (February 5, 1967)[5]

Thus began a lengthy and warm correspondence that would later to blossom into a friendship. Later that year, as Papp prepared for the production, he wrote to Havel:

> I am beginning to turn my thoughts to your play, *The Memorandum*, and it would be very helpful to me if you were able to send me a recording, either a tape or a record, of the way in which Ptydepe was spoken in your Czechoslovakian production. Naturally, I intend to use the Czechoslovakian only as a guide. I have my own ideas about it. . . . My thoughts at this moment lean toward the notion of trying to reproduce the Czechoslovakian scene rather than attempt to ignore that fact or to make it American. While we here in the United States certainly have no lack of bureaucratic procedure, the texture and tone and smell or your play are very, very special, and if we can recreate it in some way it would appeal to our audiences. I am really speaking of environment and stage setting, not acting behavior. I have been reading of your travails, and I hope that in spite of the difficulties you will be able to visit our theater and attend rehearsals of your play. (December 8, 1967)[6]

Havel responded with a mixture of enthusiasm, deference, and apologies:

> Ptydepe has to be pronounced in a manner that sounds like an existing language, but bears no resemblance to any particular language. It would by no means be good, if, for example, it resembled the Slavic languages. . . . Its pronunciation should present no difficulties to the actors; they should speak the language naturally and fluently, but nothing concrete ought to be associated with it. . . .
>
> Regarding this play, I can say in general that for the Czechoslovak audience it is not merely a satire on bureaucracy, but, as I intended, people find in it a metaphor of different events, problems and attitudes from our recent national history. This cannot, of course, be translated directly to the American experience; your audiences have quite a different reality. Nevertheless, I believe that it would be good if some wider and deeper analogy of the social problems in your country could be found; for example, in the betrayal of one's own convictions, in opportunism, etc. Ptydepe should not sound like a foolish idea of some pedantic bureaucrats, but rather as a symbol of all scientific/ideologic/phraseologic systems, which are meant to serve people, but which instead enslave and terrorize them.
>
> Regarding the staging of the play, from the various productions in Czechoslovakia and abroad that I have seen, I have learned that the best result is always obtained when the comedic elements are not being stressed, but rather when the piece is played quite earnestly, realistically, psychologically.
>
> I do hope that you will not take these few remarks as an intention to advise you — I have only mentioned some of my fundamental views and experiences. The essential thing is to produce the play according to your own feelings, instincts and enjoyment. It would definitely not help the matter if you took on other views — not even mine — if you don't fully share them.
>
> By this I do not mean, of course, that I would not deem it advantageous, if I could attend the rehearsals of your production. . . . There are, however, two problems: the first is the issue of time . . . the formalities connected with obtaining permission to travel, as well as the visa, take some time. . . .
>
> The second problem is a financial one: I cannot pay for my airplane tickets with my [foreign] royalties . . . and in our currency this surpasses my abilities. It is rather embarrassing for me to talk about this, but I am obliged to, as I do not know whether your invitation

includes the covering of expenses connected herewith. These are considerable amounts of money — Czechoslovakia is unfortunately very far from New York. I could accept your invitation only provided that some American institution pay my expenses; the situation is such that I can obtain my travel permission only if the invitation expressly states this. (January 14, 1968)[7]

A spirited correspondence continued through the late winter, with discussions of arrangements, airplane tickets, press nights, and so on. Papp inquired about the existence of a musical score from the Balustrade production of *The Memorandum*, as well as any recordings of Czech popular music. Havel congratulated him on the review of *Hamlet*, which Papp had directed in a modern version. *Hamlet* marked Papp's directorial debut at the Public; *The Memorandum* would be his second play. Papp wrote to Havel about speaking engagements he had arranged at New York University and Columbia University. "Dear Václav (and do please call me 'Joe' — I am not that old yet)"[8] he wrote, inquiring about arrangements for an interpreter for Havel's lectures. Havel replied in his meticulously polite manner, embarrassed and apologetic once again about his need to inquire about travel subsidy. Papp assured him that the Public Theater would pay his travel expenses. Havel was thrilled by the prospects of the upcoming journey.

In April, after the opening of *The Increased Difficulty of Concentration*, Havel and Olga set out for New York. On the way, they stopped over in Paris, spending a blissful week of freedom with members of the Czech émigré community. At that time, the West was in the throes of changes, and the Havels experienced them firsthand. The day they arrived in Paris, immigration barriers between the East and West had been relaxed, and meanwhile, Parisian universities were in the grips of student strikes.

Once in New York, Havel tasted the heady freedom of a culture he adored. The year 1968 was a turbulent one in America, one that saw the assassination of Martin Luther King, student demonstrations against the war in Vietnam, the flamboyant hippie culture, and the protest music of Bob Dylan. Havel walked the streets of New York enthralled, absorbing the turbulence of the times. He listened to his favorite 1960s music (Lou Reed and the Velvet Underground, the Rolling Stones, the Bee Gees), grew his blond curls long, wore an "Elect Bobby Kennedy" campaign button, and sported a peace sign on a leather strap around his neck.[9]

At the Public Theater, Joe Papp greeted the bell-bottomed, turtle-neck-clad writer with enthusiasm. "He wore light-color crew-neck sweaters, and there was a twinkle in his eye," Gail Papp remembers. Their first face-to-face meeting sparked a close friendship that would last for over two decades. As Helen Epstein, Papp's biographer, points out, they shared certain characteristics. Like Papp (whose early jobs included push-cart vendor, shoeshine boy, and shipping clerk), Havel had held a series of menial jobs as a young man. Like Papp, Havel "had become a theater person by doing theater."[10]

Under Papp's direction, the American premiere of *The Memorandum* took place on April 23, 1968. It starred Paul Stevens as Josef Gross and John Heffernan as Baláš, and the cast included Olympia Dukakis and Raul Julia. The set was by Douglas W. Schmidt; costumes were by Theoni W. Aldredge. Clive Barnes of the *New York Times* called the play "witty, funny and timely" and "light political satire." He praised the work for its use of artificial language as a metaphor, saying it "clearly represent polit-ical systems forced upon people without regard for human values."[11]

Barnes cited *The Memorandum*'s popularity in Czechoslovakia as a sign of positive change resulting from "the eastern bloc's ideological thaw." Above all, he recognized how Havel's brand of satire transcended national and political boundaries.

> The play's passionate concern for the individual, the human being, contains social criticism that at one time would not have been tol-erated, let alone welcomed. . . . Also we must not forget that *The Memorandum* has a message for us as well as for Eastern Europe, be-cause the concept that the human being is more valuable than any bureaucratic organization controlling him is not irrelevant to our own paternalistic corporation-structured society. *The Memorandum* works on more than one level.[12]

Havel made a deep impression among the artists at the Public The-ater. "Joe thought Havel was a great writer, an important writer," recalls actress Olympia Dukakis, a member of the cast of *The Memorandum*. He had tremendous respect for Havel." As for her own response: "He was handsome, charming, and shy," Dukakis remembers "his face shone with kindness." Dukakis and the cast were touched by his appreciation. "He was sweet and generous and encouraging. He was wonderful to our cast, and I'm not sure we deserved it."[13]

While in New York, Havel met up with Miloš Forman, who was, as he put it, "here pretending that I wanted to make a film."[14] Together they walked the streets of New York, frequented Greenwich Village cafés, hung around clubs in St. Marks Square (among their favorites were the Electric Circus and CBGB), and strolled through Central Park. "Those were wonderful days we spent together," Forman recalls. "He loved it."

Klaus Juncker, Havel's agent/publisher, also joined Havel in New York. "We celebrated Vašek's American success in New York in our very own way," Juncker recalls. "Every night we went to the theater: we saw the opening night of *Hair* and of Arthur Miller's *All My Sons*."[15] Havel's stay in New York lasted three weeks; Juncker stayed one. But a traumatic event that month altered their plans. Martin Luther King had been assassinated on April 4 in Tennessee. A demonstration of over 100,000 people was being organized in Central Park to support the fight for civil rights. "Of course we couldn't miss that event," recalls Juncker. He and Havel delayed their departure and joined other writers and theater people to participate in the march, which protested segregation and honored King's memory. Rolf Hochhuth, the German playwright who was in New York for the premiere of his plays *Soldiers*, joined them in the march. "For Václav, it was another world," Juncker remembers of this trip. "A much bigger one. It made a huge impression on him."

In May, Havel left New York for London and a BBC interview, where he forecast even more freedom for his country. Elated, he returned to Prague in late June, unaware that one day he would look back upon those weeks abroad as the freest of his life.

Shortly after in Prague, he wrote to Papp:

Dear Joe:

I was extremely sorry not be able to say good-bye to you in New York; I went to the theater before my departure to see you, but you were out, and after that I have been so busy trying to prolong my stay, for which I kept hoping in vain to obtain permission. So I had to finish all sorts of arrangements and leave. After my return home, I found myself in a whirlwind of all sorts of trouble, work and political activities, so that only now, during my vacation, I have time to write letters which I wanted to write long ago.

I should like to thank you again very, very much for all you have done for me: for the work you devoted to *The Memorandum*, for the interesting production, for your kindness in enabling me to visit New York, and for your friendly reception. I think New York is amazing, and am quite smitten with this city. I never cease to thank you with all my heart; without you, I would never had the chance to see it. It has been all so incredibly interesting for me, and I often think of those wonderful days. The fact that my play has been produced so far from the country where it was written — and with such understanding — fascinates me. I would be very grateful if you could occasionally write me a few lines about the production, how the audience responded to performances, what people thought of it, how long it has been playing. Remember me most warmly, please, to your actors as well as to all other friends and associates of your theater.

With the hope of welcoming you in Prague some day, or of meeting you in New York once again in the future, I remain . . . (July 28, 1968)[16]

After his visit to New York, Havel was honored with the prestigious Obie Award for Best Foreign Play (1967–1968). That year, he also received the Austrian State Prize for European Literature — confirming his international status as a playwright. Papp accepted the Obie Award on Havel's behalf and promised to deliver it personally.

Sixteen years passed before Papp was able to make good on that promise.

1968: SUMMER

Cultural thaws have been known to freeze overnight.[1]
— Kenneth Tynan, *The New Yorker*, April 1, 1967

Back in Prague, Havel threw himself headlong into the politics of the Prague Spring, as if he hadn't missed a step. In June, he and dozens of other cultural leaders signed a statement, calling for the revival of the Social Democratic Party.

Elated but also enervated by the visit abroad, Havel and Olga tried to spend as much time as they could in the countryside. For at last they had acquired a retreat, and an idyllic one, too. Back in 1967, when Andrej Krob invited Havel to work on *The Increased Difficulty of Concentration* in the castle at Březnice, Havel had been so taken by the tranquil country setting that he told Krob he needed a place of his own where he could write his plays. At the time, Krob owned a cottage in the northern

Bohemian mountains a few hours northeast of Prague, near the Polish border. The cottage was in a tiny hamlet called Hrádeček (meaning "little castle"), named for the abandoned ruin of an old castle perched high on a hill. Just below it, Krob's cottage stood nestled in the trees, and in a small clearing below that was a lovely little farmhouse made of stucco and wood. It was surrounded by an orchard, bearing apple, plum, and pear trees, with a copse of birches rising on one side and a narrow road on the other. Around it were wooded areas, rolling hills, and low mountains in the distance. The farmhouse was up for sale in 1967, and Krob suggested that Havel consider it.

Havel knew Hrádeček already — he had visited it several times. He and Olga now had an apartment in Dejvice, a section of Prague, but welcomed the idea of a country retreat. So he decided to buy it with some of the royalties from his foreign productions. He paid an amazing price of 24,000 crowns for it (roughly $8,000) and immediately set about renovating it. During the rest of 1967, the couple went to Hrádeček and lived, slept, and ate in one room while working on another. Havel supervised the renovations himself with the help of Libor Fára, the set designer at the Balustrade. To create a workplace, they constructed a wing on the first floor that would house Havel's study. It had a separate entrance and a large picture window facing a softly rising slope dotted with fruit trees. Beyond it rose a dense copse of elegant birches. Every season was lovely there, but the summer was glorious.

During July and August of 1968, Havel and Olga spent as much time as they could at Hrádeček, although there were frequent interruptions pulling him into the political arena. In early July, he was invited to a social event at the Hrzánský Palace in Prague, attended by the Communist Party leadership and selected young artists. Along with Havel, guests included the playwright Pavel Kohout and the cultural and political writer Ludvík Vaculík. They laughed and talked with Dubček into the night. Clearly, Havel had already been identified as a leader.

Then Havel returned to Hrádeček. He handed in his official resignation as dramaturg of the Balustrade. But that had no bearing on his commitment as a dramatist. He had simply outgrown the years of being a playwright in residence. Now he was a resident of a larger arena, one that was becoming his stage.

The summer of 1968 at Hrádeček was an unusually hot one. At the Havel cottage, there was a nonstop housewarming celebration, with guests gathering by the dozens. Havel himself had laid a pathway from the garden to the front door in expectation of the flock of friends that had been invited. Guests spent day and night lolling on the lawn, walking in the woods or up the hill around the castle ruins, bathing in neighboring ponds, dining outside or in the main room. Havel himself did the cooking.

As Pavel Kosatík, Olga's biographer describes that summer, it was "a forgotten picture of paradise."[2] Everything was happening under a bright blue sky to the soundtrack of the Bee Gee's "Massachusetts," a record Havel had bought in New York and one Olga played continuously on their record player. Jan Tříska, an actor and close friend, recalled the time in a letter to Havel years later.

> We were self-confident, rebellious, and foolishly happy. We knew that this fantastic summer of 1968 was full of political decisions of consequence. With every new day came some exciting news; it was never-ending. The house was overcrowded with guests; one group of people would arrive, while another followed close on its heels. As people entered, they were greeted by the Bee Gees' "Massachusetts." Then Václav would call out to Olga: "Stop them! Stop them for a second!" while he played it once again for the next entrance. The floor of the basement was covered with bottles of white wine, which helped us smile all through the night. During those blissful evenings at the home of this celebrated but ever-modest playwright, Olga would ask me to perform short improvisations, to show him how a world-famous playwright should behave. . . . That marvelous summer, everything seemed so easy and so simple, as if the whole world were sitting down with us to dine, and we were happy and satisfied. . . . Next morning, we'd sit on the chaises longues drinking tea and coffee, talking and laughing. Conversation with Václav is always smooth, inspiring` and sharp. But mainly, we laughed. Olga was always the last to wake up. She'd appear at the door, pass among us, and head straight for the orchard to pick up apples, plums and pears. Then she'd come back bearing fruit, saying: "Good morning, gentlemen."[3]

Still, Havel felt that they were living in a state of suspended animation. The same unease he had expressed in his short plays earlier that year (*Guardian Angel* and *A Butterfly on the Antenna*) may have been soothed by those halcyon summer days, but still it lay there. For the first time, he began to suspect that he might be under surveillance.

There were signs. Early that year, in April 1968, the Soviet Union's ministry of foreign affairs had sent an official diplomatic document to the governments of all Eastern European countries; it included names of people who according to the Russians were members of antistate organizations and whose purpose it was to break down Socialism in Czechoslovakia. Among the names listed were the writers Václav Havel, Pavel Kohout, Ludvík Vaculík, Milan Kundera, Jan Procházka, and Václav Černý. As early as April 1968, Moscow knew about Havel and considered him part of a Czech anti-Communist conspiracy.

Alarmed by the growing liberalization in Czechoslovakia, the Soviet Union issued repeated warnings to the Czech leaders, which essentially went unheeded. A conflict was brewing between Dubček and Breznev. In July 1968, the armies of the Warsaw Pact began maneuvers on Czechoslovak soil. On July 29, Leonid Brezhnev arrived at a Slovakian border town in a special armored train for talks with Czechoslovak leaders. In an atmosphere of tension and hostility — Russian armed troops surrounded the meetings — the Russians warned Dubček that he was losing control.

On August 21, in the small hours of the morning, came the invasion. Havel, who was visiting friends in Liberec in northern Bohemia, heard the sound of airplanes flying overhead. Calls began to pour in from friends, with reports that trucks, tanks, and armoured cars carrying soldiers were rolling into Czechoslovakia at the German border. From Prague came reports of invading Soviet tanks rumbling through the cobblestone streets onto Prague's Old Town Square, just blocks from the Balustrade. At 4:30 A.M., Radio Prague confirmed the invasion and asked citizens not to resist.

What happened to Czechoslovakia on the night of August 21? The Soviets had mobilized twenty-nine divisions, 7,500 tanks and 1,000 planes from five Communist countries to invade Czechoslovakia. Dubček and his colleagues were handcuffed and abducted to Moscow for "discussions."

What happened that night to the playwright Václav Havel? His friend Jan Tříska described the tranquility of the summer that was doomed to be shattered:

> August 20: Hrádeček. First signs of the end of summer came without warning. There was a morning fog and it started to get colder, so we had to make a fire in the fireplace inside. . . . Still, we preferred sitting outside, and in this nostalgic light of early autumn

morning, we saw two ladies walking across the meadow and heading toward us. "Guten morgen," they said. "Guten morgen," we
replied in unison, and we welcomed them into the house. . . . .
Greta and Anna (the two ladies) were born in this house, to the
family of a German farmer and beekeeper. It was their first visit
after 23 years. . . . They were overwhelmed by a tender melancholy,
looking at the line of those old trees beside the road which they used
to pass every day on the way to school. The road leads to Vlčice, a
small village with (in those days) one German doctor and one
Czech baker. Their eyes were full of tears. . . . Václav suggested to
them that they take whatever they want as a souvenir. . . . But they
replied: "Nein nein, vielen dank." . . . They were standing at a point
between the pump and the wall of the house in the courtyard,
watching the skyline. It was exactly the same place, they said, where
they parted with their mother when they left for school every day.
Now they waved at us "Aufwiedersehen." . . . By the evening, another group of wild and prominent writers arrived. This time they
were welcomed by "Massachusetts" in Slovakian. We had two versions: one recorded by a Czech band and one recorded by a Slovakian band . . . Another party started. We had a big dinner and two
litres of white wine. When we finished eating, Václav winked at me
and said: "Tell us something more about your theory of literature."
I said that in fact I had no theory and even if I had, it would be
more irony than theory because in fact I was the only one at the
table who wasn't a writer. But Václav didn't agree and encouraged
me to say it, anyway. So I gave my theory at the table. Every writer
should try to write something about music. To catch the spirit of
music in words is a high-level challenge which no writer should ignore. It can be the decisive test of his literary talent. . . . Václav
rocked back and forth in his chair and rubbed his stomach. The
smile on his face said that he liked my literary theory very much.
Olga opened the door, and suggested that we all go outside, as there
was a full moon, giving a bright and wonderful light. We all went
outside and looked at the landscape. Nobody spoke. Next morning,
when all the guests had gone, Olga and Václav and I were alone,
surrounded by a certain nostalgia. By the evening we went to
Liberec to have dinner at a local gallery with its director. Several
minutes after midnight, after we had finished our dinner, Russian
tanks rolled into the city.[4]

For a playwright who wrote about the theme of identity in his conflicted culture, the event was a definitive one. Hereafter, Havel's identity, as well as his life in the theater, was to change. After 1968, Havel would be rehearsing a new role. And from that night on, Havel's life in the theater and his life in politics would become one and the same.

1968–1969: THE AFTERMATH

You know, sometimes it all seems like a beautiful dream — all the exciting opening nights, private views, lectures, meetings — the endless discussions about literature and art! All the energy, the hopes, plans, activities, ideas — the wine-bars crowded with friends, the wild booze-ups, the madcap affrays in the small hours, the jolly girls dancing attendance on us! And the mountains of work we managed to get done, regardless! — That's all over now. It'll never come back![1]

— Havel, *Protest*

When asked, "What does the year 1968 mean to you" in an interview with *Mladý svět*, Havel replied:

The year 1968 means — not only to me but probably to most Czechs — a completely new experience. The experience is that of participation. Ever since my childhood I was an observer of the society, an observer of political activities, sometimes an ironical critic, but without any need to take part in it. I was out of that orbit. And this has totally changed now. It's as if I lost my virginity. I am not outside of it anymore. I feel like I have been drafted into it. . . . For me, it is simply much more personal than it was before the invasion.[2]

An outsider no more, Havel participated ever more intensely in the weeks that followed the invasion. In Liberec, where he had been staying with Olga at the home of Jan Tříska, the Czech actor, they joined in the local resistance. Havel wrote speeches and prepared public statements for politicians and committees. He became a resistance journalist, appearing on television and writing provocative radio commentaries, which were read on the air by Tříska, urging the Czechs to fight back. As such, Havel was part of an electronic-media warfare against the invaders that was waged throughout Czechoslovakia. Expressions of support poured in from the international writers' community — Kingsley Amis, Samuel Beckett, Günter Grass, John Osborne, and Havel's idols, Eugene Ionesco, Arthur Miller, and Jean-Paul Sartre. There was a euphoria in the communal outburst of protest. But that did not last. After a week, Havel himself began to feel the exhaustion.

Meanwhile in Moscow, on August 26 at midnight, Dubček and his cohorts were forced to sign a fifteen-point Moscow Protocol, a document of capitulation. On August 27, Dubček returned to Prague and was reinstated in his position, a broken man. There were reports of cruel and grueling interrogation, isolation from all communication, and attempts to break his will and shatter his views. All this had reduced his capacity to rule effectively. At noon, he spoke to a nation on the radio and wept, and millions who listened wept with him. Listening to his broken voice, Havel's friends began to lose heart. Dubček's false assurances of optimism could not hide what the dreaded Protocol really required, that the Dubček government and the country undergo a period of "normalization," during which the regime's liberal reforms would be declared invalid, a new Congress would be elected, the media would be overhauled, and all alleged threats to Socialism would be purged. Only then would the troops leave. Even with Dubček's return, hope quickly gave way to depression.

Later in that dramatic year, Czech radio announced a short contest in honor of the country's fiftieth anniversary (the state had been founded in October 1918). Accordingly, Havel composed a collage that included recorded excepts of famous speeches from Czech politicians such as Masaryk, Beneš, and Dubček, all pillars of the Czech ideal of democracy. These alternated with excerpts from Bedřich Smetana's opera, *Libuše*. There is also a third sound on the recording, that of a man wordlessly eating lunch. The sense is that of "the common man" eating and drinking, oblivious to the speeches and their meaning. As the tape is played, the musical excerpts get shorter and shorter; the last speech to be heard is Dubček's on the futility of defending his country against foreign armies. He is weeping. The title of the collage, "Čechy krásné, Čechy mé" (Bohemia the Beautiful, Bohemia Mine), is also the name of a nationalistic Czech song. Havel won the prize, but it would be more than two decades before the collage was broadcast.

In 1969, the political theater was one of exits, leaving an empty stage as bleak as a Beckett landscape. During the uncertain, ominous year following the invasion, Dubček quietly withdrew from public life in defeat.

There were occasional spasms of protest. In January 1969, a young student named Jan Palach burned himself to death to protest the Soviet invasion. "Jan Palach's act of self-immolation was immediately understood by the whole society,"[3] Havel wrote later in an essay entitled "Second Wind." But these were acts of desperation that could come to nothing.

Shuttling back and forth from Hrádeček and his new apartment in Prague's Dejvice district, Havel doggedly continued his political efforts, writing and speaking out, expressing his concern about what might come, and calling again for democracy. In February 1969, he published a reply to Milan Kundera's article "The Czech Destiny" in *Tvář*, which had been briefly revived for a final time. In it, Havel objected to Kundera's optimism about the future, calling it typical Czech patriotic passivity and myopia.[4] Then in March 1969, Havel discovered an eavesdropping device in his apartment planted by the StB (Státní bezpečnost), which functioned as the secret police. His worst fears were confirmed. He was being watched. His war with the secret police had begun.

On August 9, 1969, Havel boldly wrote a lengthy, private letter to President Dubček. "Dear Mr. Dubček," it began, "I don't know whether you remember me; we talked once a year ago at a small gathering of writers and politicians. Nor do I know if you know me as a writer, nor even whether you will take this letter as I intend it, as a sincere expression of sincerely held convictions."[5] In bold, clear, forceful, direct language that would mark the style of his voluminous political writings for the next two decades, he called upon Dubček to exert leadership, to display courage, and to move ahead toward democratization. He ended with a passionate plea:

> It is not my intention to be a self-appointed spokesman of the people. But if anything is certain today, it is this: that most Czechs and Slovaks today think as I do. It's hardly possible to think otherwise. The matter is essentially simple. You, however, are at the center of extremely complex pressures, forces and viewpoints. The point is to be able to find your way out of this dark and tangled wood into the light of what we might call "simple human reasoning." To think the way every ordinary, decent person thinks. . . . Dear Mr. Dubček, in the coming days and weeks, I, along with thousands of my fellow citizens, will be thinking of you. I will be anxious, but will also expect great things of you.
>
> Yours sincerely, Václav Havel[6]

Two weeks later, Havel and nine others signed a declaration entitled "Ten Points," condemning the policy of normalization. As a consequence, in the months ahead he and the other signers would be interrogated, then arrested and charged with subverting the republic. All ten signers were to be tried on October 15, 1970, but the trial was postponed indefinitely.

As for his dramatic writing, there were only isolated attempts: a screenplay written with Jan Němec entitled *Heart Beat* that was never produced, and an outline for a play called *The Wedding* (in the mood of *An Evening with the Family*), which was never written. In that year of waiting for the inevitable, with no Theatre on the Balustrade as an anchor, Havel's dramatic imagination was set adrift in a Pinteresque no-man's-land.

Finally, and prophetically, in that downward spiraling year of 1969, the curtain fell on the works of Václav Havel, playwright and political writer. A volume entitled *Similes 2* (Podoby 2) was published by Československý spisovatel (Czechslovak Writer), with contributions from eighteen authors and a foreword by Havel. As a consequence, within less than three years, all those writers would be banned in the normalization process. By 1971 to 1972, Havel's writings would vanish from schools and public libraries. The theater he called home would shut its doors to him indefinitely.

THE 1960s: CONCLUSION

My early beginnings as a playwright coincided with the 1960s, a remarkable and relatively favorable era in which my plays, despite being so different from what had been permitted until then, could actually reach the stage, something that would have been impossible both before and after that. I don't suppose I need emphasize how important this was for my writing. It was not just the formal fact that my plays were permitted; there was something deeper and more essential here: that society was capable of accepting them, that they resonated with the general state of mind, that the intellectual and social climate of the time, open to new self-knowledge and hungry for it, not only tolerated them, but — if I may say so — actually wanted them.[1]

— Havel, "Second Wind"

The 1960s are the little heart in Havel's signature.[2]

— Pavel Kosatík

Shortly after the invasion, Havel wrote a commemorative typogram. Entitled "The Generation of August 21" (Generace 21 srpna), it was a poignant attempt to capture that fresh, free spirit of the 1960s, to preserve on paper, somehow, the energy of the exuberant era that had evaporated on that fateful late-summer night in 1968.

```
                        humanita
          pravda                         ! svědomí
     demokracie      HIPPIE ?
                                              BOBEK
                      flower power
permanentní   VACULÍK      !!    Yip
     statečnost            JOHN       suverenita
                             ?!      sexy    LSD
BEATLES  LSD !   SVOBODA     PAUL
   MAO  ?     !!   zrada              not war
       BE IN        svoboda               socialismus
         !  národ   čest   !!          BE IN
ČERNOCH        TGM   BE IN    ?          nezávislost
make love              ?? Yip
         kolaborant                 bezpečnost
              KENNEDY
OV KSČ      LOVE  idite!       Yip       WALDEMAR
kontrarevoluce    ?        BE IN    !   RINGO      ?
      okupace                      ?        svoboda
     ?         CÍSAŘ   Yip          INDRA  DUBČEK
   svoboda    !                    spojenectví
   psychedelic     vměšování        spojenectví
             !!  BE IN                        CHE
       vměšování   ŠILHAN        Yip      tanky
SEDLÁČEK ??      svědomí             TGM
       LENNON                    BE IN
    SVITÁK                KOLDER          neutralita
      ?      suverenita³
```

Václav Havel's life in the theater was born in that exuberant era of 1960s, the spring of his country's hope. It was a golden decade for the playwright, for the theater, and for the whole culture. As he described it:

> Back then the streets were full. People knew how entertain themselves spontaneously. They didn't just sit at home watching television, they went out. In the little bars and wine rooms you could find actors, painters, writers; wherever you went there was someone you knew. Life was somehow more relaxed, freer; it was as though there was more humor, ingenuousness, hope. People could get involved in something, go after something, take trouble with things . . . in other words — paradoxically — it made sense to deal with the absurdity of being, because things still mattered. And, in their own way, the small theaters reflected all that, gave expression to it, helped to create it. They were one of the important manifestations and mediators of this intellectual and spiritual process in which the society became aware of itself, and liberated itself, and which inevitably led to the familiar political changes in 1968.[4]

Invigorated by the spirit of the 1960s, by the gusts of fresh new ideas blowing in from the West, Havel felt a sense of freedom and an empowerment to write.

> In my writing . . . there was something like that first "heroic" period when — self-confident, uninhibited, without a lot of overblown ambition — I was simply mapping out my initial experience of the world.[5]

Above all, he had a place to write his plays, a home.

> At the Balustrade, there was something happening, and throughout the 60s this created extraordinarily favorable conditions for my writing: I knew why I was writing, and whom I was writing for.[6]

In the 1960s, Havel's life in the theater was distinguished by courage, cunning, cleverness, and timing, as well as by enormous productivity. He had the courage to write about things no other young Czech playwright had yet written about, namely, the tyranny of totalitarianism and the existential dilemma of modern man. He had the cunning to obscure his themes from the authorities; instead of writing about the crushing impact of Communism on the human soul, he wrote about bureaucracy. He had the cleverness to find a "code" in which to couch his dramatic writing, that of humor and absurd satire. He had a sense of timing; he knew he could write about what his audience was thinking but afraid to give voice to. As for productivity, during the decade he wrote both one-act and full-length plays, along with revues, essays, articles, and letters. It was an enormously prolific time.

By the time the tanks rolled into Prague, Havel was an internationally known dramatist — the best-known Czech playwright since Karel Čapek in the 1920s. Thanks to Havel's dedicated agent, Klaus Juncker, *The Garden Party* had already received over twenty productions in theaters in West Germany, as well as in Austria, Switzerland, France, Italy, Belgium, and Yugoslavia. *The Memorandum* had been performed throughout Europe, and at Joseph Papp's inaugural season at the Public Theater in New York.

Looking back on that decade, Havel could not have imagined a more fortuitous set of assets and circumstances or a life in the theater.

> Equipped with my view "from below" (i.e., as a bourgeois in a communist state) and the experience of Kafka and the French theater of the absurd and somewhat obsessed with the tendency to elaborate on things rationally to the point of absurdity, I found in those remarkable social conditions (hitherto unknown and therefore undescribed) a wonderful horizon for my writing. I am not claiming that in my first plays there was nothing more going on, or that my only concern was describing the dialectical mechanisms behind those pseudoreforms and the irresistible decay of the system that was trying to bring them about, but I can scarcely imagine having written them without the inspiration provided by that particular background.[7]

All that would change.

Within months, it had all slipped away. Havel lost both his theatrical home and his recognition as a playwright. For the next twenty years, he would to dwell in a no-man's land, searching for a life in the theater in a void.

above Landovský and Havel, appearing in Juráček's film *Every Young Man*, 1965 (Prague Theatre Institute archive)

below Havel (right) with his publisher/agent, Klaus Juncker, Prague

The Seventies

The Playwright at a Crossroads

John Lennon once said that the 1970s weren't worth a damn. And indeed, when we look back on them today . . . they seem, compared with the rich and productive 1960s, to be lacking in significance, style, atmosphere, with no vivid spiritual and cultural movements. The seventies were bland, boring, and bleak.[1]

— Havel, *Disturbing the Peace*

1970: A DARK DECADE BEGINS

Out of the rubble of the old world a sinister new world grew, one that was intrinsically different, merciless, gloomily serious, Asiatic, hard. The fun was definitely over and things began to get tough.[1]

— Havel, "Second Wind"

The decade of the 1970s began slowly and sluggishly. For Havel, playwright and political writer, it was filled with a sense of anxiety, of foreboding:

August 1968 did not mean just the routine replacement of a more liberal regime with a more conservative one; it was not just the usual freeze after a thaw. It was something more; it was the end of an era; the disintegration of a spiritual and social climate, a profound mental dislocation. . . . It was not just that the carnival-like elation of 1968 had come to an end; the whole world crumbled, a world in which we had all learned to live well and move with some ease.[2]

A sense of gloom set in, a resignation in the face of what was to come. It was called "normalization," and it cast its long shadow over the Czech terrain. It happened slowly, from 1970 to 1972. Three-quarters of the

Writing in isolation, 1975 (Oldřich Škácha)

higher echelon of government officials, including Dubček, were dismissed. The consequences of the punitive legislation passed in 1969 were becoming clear. There were purges. All those writers, including Havel, who refused to sign the petition welcoming "friendly armies" on Czech soil were punished. Their jobs were taken away from them; their children were denied schooling. Almost three-quarters of a million people lost their jobs. As for the creative and intellectual community, 475 of the 590 members of the Writers' Union were removed, and 130, including Havel, were officially blacklisted. Confidential and official lists were circulated with the names of authors whose writings were to be removed from all public libraries. There were widespread purges in the media. Slowly, the ranks of the "community of the defeated," as the novelist/playwright Klíma called it, grew among the intelligentsia and the artistic community.[3]

One by one, Havel's friends dispersed. Some, like Miloš Forman, emigrated. Others avoided Havel; after all, he had been attacked in the papers and called an enemy of the Socialist regime. When they saw him on the street, they crossed to the other side, fearing that contact with him would lead to trouble with the police. The doors of the Balustrade, his longtime artistic home and the theater that once hailed him as their leading playwright, were shut to him. Reluctant to cause discomfort to others, Havel went out less frequently. (To add to the encroaching gloom, his mother died in early 1970.)

Slowly, step by step, he became isolated. He retreated to Hrádeček, where he thought he might evade the watchful eye of the secret police. But Hrádeček, once teeming with the laugher and gaiety of Prague Spring fever, was quieter now. Regular visitors dwindled to only a few, the most notable being the actor Pavel Landovský. (Undeterred by his rejection at the Balustrade years earlier, Landovský continued performing and writing radio shows. In 1967 he had been invited to join the ensemble at the eminent Činoherní Klub, where he distinguished himself as a Chekhovian actor.) Another occasional visitor was Pavel Kohout, the playwright whose work, like Havel's, was banned. Zdeněk Urbánek, a close friend of Havel and Olga, was granted his own room at the top of the stairs. He wrote all day, Havel wrote all night, and the two met for dinner. In the afternoon, Urbánek hiked in the mountains, but Havel stayed close to the house doing odd jobs, wearing a Princeton T-shirt and bellbottoms from New York. His hair grew longer and more unruly. During that lonely year of 1970, Havel was searching. What was he to write about? How? And above all, for whom?

> Sooner or later, however, a writer (or at least a writer of my type) finds himself at a crossroads: he has exhausted his initial experience of the world and the ways of expressing it and he must decide how to proceed from there. He can, of course, seek ever more brilliant ways of saying the things he has already said; that is, he can essentially repeat himself. Or he can rest in the position he achieved in his first burst of creativity, subordinate everything he learned to the interests of consolidating that position and thus assure himself a place on Parnassus.[4]

But how could he repeat himself, or consolidate his themes of the 1960s? The times had changed, significantly.

> Once again, people's spines were bent, and lying, cheating and betrayal became common; once again, the theme of human identity and existential schizophrenia was everywhere — but now, it all seemed to take place on a completely different level: the time of oral juggling was over and it became increasingly obvious that human existence itself was at stake. Suddenly, instead of laughing, one felt like shouting. It is only natural that in this situation I felt twice as strongly that I must write differently than I had previously. But how to write — that, of course, I did not know.[5]

1970–1971: *THE CONSPIRATORS*

> You cannot judge the situation according to how many people celebrate the victory; the only thing that matters is how many people are able to fight for it.[1]
>
> — Havel, *The Conspirators*

For the first time in his life, Havel was without a theater, without an audience, without an idea. He was at a crossroads and, as he put it, paralyzed by this fact. So he entered a period of exploration and experimentation, a search for themes and forms.

In the ominous, threatening atmosphere caused by the occupation of foreign troops, his dramatic imagination turned to a plot of political intrigue. As he wrote in the accompanying commentary, this new play was provoked by the political and social changes in his country. These were serious times, and they called for a serious subject.

The Conspirators (Spiklenci), as he called it, is a political parable in fifteen scenes about government, power, and human nature. For the setting, Havel chose a nameless republic of which is nothing is known save that it was once ruled by a colonial regime. A cruel dictator named Olah has been recently overthrown by a brave and vigorous revolutionary movement and is now living in exile. A democracy has been instated, led by a benign and compassionate Prime Minister. Meanwhile, some of the top leaders representing the pillars of government — military, judiciary, security, and media — are concerned about protecting the stability of the new democracy they have fought so valiantly to create. Indeed, rumors are circulating that Olah, who now lives abroad, is still alive, and they fear that this news might cause unrest. In their discussions, an idea grows among them — that of creating a special agency that would preserve the order of the new state and its freedoms. They wish to create it legally and openly, to involve the public. When they hear, however, of another rumor that there is a conspiracy in the land that wishes to take control of the country, they decide to make their agency secret. Their efforts become increasingly illegal, and their alliance divisive. The plot thickens (with more twists and turns) when this "conspiracy" is further believed to be sympathetic to the deposed Olah. At the end of the play, the government leaders themselves decide that it is in the best interest of the land to recall Olah to ensure national security.

What the leaders never realize is that the "conspiracy" they've been warned of, which threatens their democracy, is in fact *they themselves* and their *own* initiative.

At the heart of the play is Havel's theme of identity — that "we have met the enemy and they are us." Do we understand the responsibility that lies in governing a democracy? Do we value freedom enough that we can sacrifice personal power for the sake of the nation's greater good? These are the questions Havel posed as he struggled to write the play in those gloomy years of 1970 to 1971.

Looking back on it decades later, the play — with its dark vision of a democracy in peril — is powerful and disturbing in its prescience and prophesy. At the time, however, Havel had no confidence in his efforts. He became increasingly frustrated, fearing that his plot was too convoluted and his dialogue too theoretical. Once more, he sought to clarify his intentions in an accompanying commentary, expressing his alarm at what was happening to his country, with Dubček's demise and Gustáv's Husák's rise to power under the program of normalization. But the writing of the commentary only compounded his frustration, bringing him no closer to solving the play's problems as he perceived them. Ultimately, writing *The Conspirators* was not a pleasurable or satisfying experience. It was Havel's first playwrighting attempt after the invasion — alone, without a theater and its collegiality and feedback for any of the dramaturgical frustrations he was experiencing. Furthermore, he was intensely preoccupied, brooding on the radical changes that had occurred and mourning the 1960s. As frenetically active as he had been in the 1960s, in the early 1970s it was as if the world had stopped turning.

> I tortured myself writing *The Conspirators*, the first play I wrote as a banned writer; after the excitement and stimulation of the years before, no play took me longer or was harder to write, and it's clearly the weakest of my plays. I once compared it to a chicken that has been in the oven for too long and completely dried out. Of course, no one was waiting for the play or pressing me to finish it, so it really was written in a kind of vacuum. As I worked on it, I spent too much time wondering how to come to terms with the completely new situation both in society and for myself personally, and inevitably, almost all the life was squeezed out of it.[2]

Looking back on *The Conspirators* today, Havel says: "I never liked this play very much, and to this day I don't really think it's a good one. Still, the principle idea of conspirators who conspire against themselves in defense of democracy is a good one. But I don't think it is very well executed."[3]

The Conspirators is meant to be a political parable of what was happening in that time from 1968 to 1971. As Havel said in the commentary, he had wanted to write a play about the anatomy of power, about politics, and about politicians and their modus operandi. He wanted to dramatize political behavior, to show how people change their minds, how people who were fighting against one thing suddenly shifted sides, just as the Czechs who fought for "socialism with a human face" (under Dubček's humanism) were suddenly fighting for normalization (under Husák's repression). He wanted to write about the psychology of politics, about the ambition and paranoia of leaders and their absolute and corrupting need for power. His message: A politician will do anything to stay in power, even if it is self-defeating. His ending: In the name of saving democracy, dictatorship is restored. *The Conspirators* is about contradiction and paradox in politics, and about why self-preservation is ultimately more important than the idea one works for. Once one becomes a politician, the idea doesn't matter.

In the end, he felt *The Conspirators* had failed to express this. In the afterword to *Hry 1970–1976* (Plays 1970–1976), published in Toronto by a dedicated Czech émigré group, Havel wrote harshly and unforgivingly about the play.

> It was the result of a spasmodic desire to take another step, whatever it was, in developing the theme of the crisis of human identity. The play is overdrawn, lifeless, bloodless, humorless, lacking in subtlety. I overwrote it. I forced it too much. I expected too much of it. And I put too many themes into it, so it had to fail. It's no accident that I have written fifty pages of commentary on *The Conspirators*, in which I try to analyze and explain all the complicated dimensions of this play.[4]

The Conspirators, Havel's least favorite play, became, ironically, the first Czech drama of the 1970s to be classified as a forbidden play. It was also the first Havel play to be premiered in a foreign land, in a foreign tongue, to an audience of strangers. It received its first production in 1974 at the Theater der Stadt in Baden-Baden, Germany, thanks to the efforts of Klaus Juncker. Havel, of course, was not permitted to attend the opening.

Not until 1992, twenty-one years after it was written, was *The Conspirators* presented in the land where it was written.

1970–1976: *MOUNTAIN HOTEL*

> I write abstractly, in a sense — for history, or for a foreign audience I don't know. And this hasn't been good for me. When you know it doesn't matter whether you finish a play today or a year from now, and when you don't know whom you're writing for anyway, it's not easy to write.[1]
>
> — Havel, *Open Letters: Selected Writings, 1956–1990*

I like it when a work can be interpreted in different ways, when it is something on an enigma . . . Art in general is a little like playing with fire; the artist deals with something without knowing precisely what it is; he creates something without knowing precisely what it will "mean." The work, it seems to me, should always be somehow "clearer" than its author and he should ultimately be able to stand before it filled with the same sense of awe and with the same questions in his mind as someone seeing or reading it for the first time.[2]

—Havel, *Letters to Olga*

After finishing *The Conspirators* in 1971, Havel continued with what he called his "theatrical research." He was searching not only for a home, but also for a form, an idea. He began another play, with the intent of experimenting with structure, just as he had done with his poetry and typograms. In this case, his idea was to gather all his favorite tricks — destroying the story line, doing away with chronology, exchanging lines of dialogue, using repetition — to allow the play ride on nothing but experimentation. What if all these techniques had autonomy? he asked himself. He felt a need to free himself from his obsessions with these experimental techniques, to explore the limits of their effectiveness. How far could he go? he wondered. So he started writing a play called *Mountain Hotel* (Horský hotel), not caring, he said, whether people would like it or not.[3]

The landscape of *Mountain Hotel*, the countryside, is Chekhovian. So is its ensemble, a collection of Chekhovian country types reminiscent of those in *The Seagull*, who have gathered on the terrace of a resort where they are spending their holiday. The coterie includes Orlov, a sentimental Russian count; Kubík, a blocked writer; Dlask, a plump provincial German type who plays cards; Titz, a sports addict; Milena, a pretty young waitress; Rachel, a mopey Masha-type who longs to get married; Pechar, a split personality; Pecharova, his dutiful wife; and Lisa, an ingénue. There is no plot to speak of, just a sequence of random and repeated actions. The Russian Count Orlov romances the lovely young Lisa, who is supposedly from Paris, although she says she has never been there. Dlask loves to play cards; he's friendly, but everyone ignores him. Pechar, who thinks he is two people, lathers sun cream all over his face, and openly cavorts with the hotel waitress, Milena, in front of his wife who meanwhile advises him about how to win her over. The next day, he tells Milena: "I don't like that fellow you were with yesterday."

As for the world of the play, one might imagine the characters of *Uncle Vanya* in *Alice in Wonderland*. For example, there's the scene wherein Drašar, the hotel director, welcomes his guests in a speech reminiscent of Falk from *The Garden Party*:

> Drašar: We are pleased that you are in the garden. *(Looks at his notes.)* Everyone must follow hotel rules. *(Looks at his notes.)* We provide more tea for the morning. *(Looks at his notes.)* As you make your bed, so you lie in it. *(Looks at his notes.)* There is no discrimination here. *(Looks at his notes.)* The light in the lavatory is working again. *(Looks at his notes.)* Everyone of us matters. *(Looks at his notes from both sides, realizes that there's nothing else. Puts it in his pocket. Moment of embarrassed silence. Short applause. Drašar motions with his hands that he'll continue, without his notes. Thinks for a moment.)* As it was, so it will be. And that's not so bad. *(The audience nods in acknowledgment. Drašar thinks again.)* Readiness is all. *(Everyone nods in acknowledgment. Drašar thinks again.)* Life goes on. *(Everyone nods in acknowledgment. Drašar thinks again, but nothing comes to mind. He starts to shake hands with those in audience.)*
> Titz: Good job, Pepik.
> *(Drašar doesn't react. He doesn't shake Titz's hand. But he stops to shake Kubík's hand.)*
> Drašar: Are you a writer?
> Kubík: Yes, I am, Mr. Director.
> *(Drašar shakes his hand seriously.)*
> Drašar: Literature is important.[4]

As with Chekhov, it's a play about several things — in this case, love, identity, and nature. Each character has a special desire. One character loves the woods and reading his own letters. A second plays cards. A third loves to walk. A fourth loves two women. All these characters are human, with human desires, and the audience is able to relate to them. But even those aspects disintegrate into nonsense. There are five scenes, during which the characters change love partners, engage in elliptical dialogue that goes nowhere, repeat each other's phrases and their own meaningless actions. "Do you remember Paris?" becomes a question asked throughout, while the play becomes a crescendo of jumbled scenes. By the end, all the characters are onstage, dancing, shouting one other's lines in a chorus-like fashion, exchanging identities, and losing their own. "Life goes on," echoes Drašar, as the play swirls round, dissolving into itself. It is Chekhov as interpreted by Fellini, an absurd cyclical dance of characters, words, and motions.

Some years later, Havel explained that his intention was to write "a nostalgic and vaguely unsettling poem about a world with no firm center, no fixed identity, no past and no future, with no coherence or order."[5]

That world with no firm center, to which he referred, was the gray, amorphous one of the early 1970s, in which he found himself adrift. And the central, Chekhovian image of the hotel? More than ten years later, when he had time to reflect on its meaning and the nature of his metaphor, he wrote:

> The hotel is in fact the human world. We have all come into it not knowing why, we can't move to another hotel, yet we enjoy relative freedom on its premises, and if that freedom is limited in any way, then only to the extent that we, as inhabitants of the "hotel," limit each other. And all of us sooner or later leave it. At the same time, most of us cannot find, either inside or outside this "hotel," any firm point to which we can unambiguously, enduringly and unproblematically relate, a point which in our eyes would lend to everything — and above all to our sojourn, our existence, in the "hotel" — a kind of central meaning from which would radiate, in a comprehensible way, all its other coherences and meanings . . . Things contradict each other, they lack order, continuity, logic, meaning and purpose; life in this hotel has a distressing restlessness to it. Again and again, we latch on to illusory values as substitutes for that missing firm point; we know all this, more or less, yet we cannot come to terms with it; on the contrary, we sink deeper and deeper into it.[6]

Mountain Hotel was an experiment that Havel would pick up and put down over a five-year period, like a bemused scientist laboring over a dubious experiment, before finally finishing it in 1976. Tiring of its novelty, he found it didn't hold his attention. The effort to find meaning in senseless repetition of words and action was unsatisfying. In a time in which nothing made sense to him or to anyone around him, a play without meaning offered no consolation. He remained at the crossroads.

At the same time, *Mountain Hotel* belonged to a period of theatrical experimentation that helped to free him up from his obsessions, as he called them.

I tried to conclude a whole period of theatrical research. As such, *Mountain Hotel* should be considered as a strange poem about nothing, a nonplay, containing none of the features which makes a play a play (story, time, continuity, characters, conflicts, etc.). Therefore, any concrete message about the world is absent. The only theme of the play is the play itself. It is rather a scenario of stage movement and speeches. . . . The play hasn't been produced yet, and I doubt that it will ever be, but I don't suffer much because of this. Because I wrote it in a certain way more for myself than for the audience. I know that it was the only way to free myself from all these obsessions, and no matter whether the plays will live on stage or not, it helped me to write it.[7]

The first half of the 1970s was, for Havel, a search for what he calls "a second wind," as he described it in an essay by that name. He had lost the opportunity not only to work as a playwright in residence at the Balustrade, but also to work in any position in any Czech theater at all. As a writer, he was, in his words, "one of the ones most completely prohibited."[8] The authorities couldn't prevent his plays from being produced abroad, but, at the time, that gave him little comfort.

I had learned to understand a play as something that could fly into the world only from a specific home that alone could breathe specific meaning into the play; it was not something you tossed experimentally into the air in the hopes that it would land somewhere, catch on, and only then gain some kind of meaning. . . . So for a long time, the search for that "second wind" meant trying to overcome a feeling of emptiness and futility.[9]

Ultimately, *The Conspirators* and *Mountain Hotel* taught him valuable lessons. To survive, he realized, he had to write plays that could be produced for an audience he knew, in a theater he could see, even if it were in his mind. He also realized:

(a) that I'd better write my plays thinking that they could really be produced here and now, because only real and concrete connections to reality can breathe life into my plays; (b) even the most highly developed idea for a play doesn't prevent it from resulting in the depths of banality. *The Conspirators* was written in one of those moments when a playwright knows that he stands at the crossroads, and he is sort of paralyzed by this fact.[10]

So now Havel faced the task of somehow constructing for himself a life in the theater, without a theater and without an audience. But in the gloom of 1971, that task seemed futile indeed.

1971–1974: WRITERS IN SEARCH OF A HOME

Všechno zlé je k něčemu dobré. (Everything bad must bring something good.)
— Czech saying

The years 1971 to 1994 were gray years for writers. Where would they find their inspiration? What would they write about? As Havel described it:

An era of apathy and widespread demoralization began, an era of gray, everyday totalitarian consumerism. Society was atomized, small islands of resistance were destroyed, and a disappointed and exhausted public pretended not to notice. Independent thinking and creation retreated to the trenches of deep privacy.[1]

During this long period of moribund silence, as he called it, Havel may have been isolated, but he was not alone in this predicament. Writers lived in a private ghetto, he explained. The public knew who they were, and sympathized with them, but at the same time were careful to avoid them, fearful of their own safety.

Each of us was stewing in his own juices. Having been marked in a particular fashion, with no hope for any kind of wider support, we had no way of actively expressing ourselves, so for the most part we passively accepted our situation and simply wrote.[2]

The early 1970s was a time of retreat. As the new leadership gathered strength, the islands of visible resistance or opposition in society grew smaller and smaller. People retreated to their apartments, and on weekends fled to their dachas in the countryside. It was lonely, but at least it offered privacy. As Olga described it:

After 1969, we became villagers, in fact. Most of our time was spent at Hrádeček. I took care of the garden and the orchard. Vašek missed the collaborative atmosphere of the theater terribly; he always saw the theater as team work and himself as part of the team. Writing is much more difficult for him now because there's no ensemble, no director, no dramaturg to press him to write. The publisher in Hamburg [Klaus Juncker] helps Vašek's plays abroad, but he is too far away from Hrádeček.[3]

Klaus Juncker, Havel's agent/publisher, contacted Dilia, the Czech state agency for writers,[4] hoping to renew the contracts between Havel and his publishing house. But Havel's name was no longer on their list. "When I asked about Havel," Juncker said, "everyone answered, 'We don't know any Havel.' It was so paradoxical because the former contracts were signed by the same people who suddenly couldn't remember Havel."[5] Desperate to get Havel's new plays out of the country, Juncker asked the cultural attaché of Reinbek, who was going to Prague, to bring back any work Havel had to give him. The attaché met Havel in a restaurant, where, in the men's room, Havel handed over a copy of a new play. It was *The Conspirators*.

Then, something began to happen. Gradually, writers who had lost their voices, who had been banned, silenced, barred from publication, removed from libraries, dismissed from their positions as writers, editors, and teachers, began to gather together.

Among the key figures in this group was the dynamic playwright Pavel Kohout, eight years Havel's senior. In many ways, Kohout was Havel's antithesis. As a teenager, Kohout wrote poetry praising the Communist Party, and the regime identified him as a great asset to Socialism. But in the 1960s, he bonded with Havel and his group (Ivan Klíma, Ludvík Vaculík, and Milan Kundera) at the Writers' Union congress in 1965. By the 1970s, Kohout was blacklisted along with his friends. His plays had been performed in Western Europe throughout the 1960s, and he had directed his own plays in Germany. A tall, stylish man who loved wearing Western clothes, Kohout had a strong voice, a broad smile, and a contagious wit. He exuded confidence. With his charm and charisma, he soon became a major organizer of these gatherings, reminding his fellow writers that if they couldn't publish, at least they could get together and read their work.

There was also the shy, soft-spoken Ivan Klíma, who had survived Thereizenstadt as a child and become an acclaimed novelist and short-story writer in the 1960s. Klíma was a friend of Havel's — they had met at Writers' Union congress in 1965. "At the time Havel and I met," Klíma recalls, "*The Garden Party* and *The Memorandum* were playing. They were something marvelous, the best we could see; actors loved performing in them."[6] Klíma was a retiring man and preferred to sit home writing his novels. But times had changed, and so he joined in the effort with Havel and Kohout to bring everyone together.

The gatherings began in Klíma's apartment in Prague. While primarily a novelist and short story writer, Klíma also wrote plays. He had just written a one-act based on the Soviet invasion called *A Bridegroom for Marcela* and wanted to hear it read. So in early 1970, Klíma invited some fellow writers to his apartment for a reading. "We invited people who were still working in the theater. Dissidents, nondissidents, anyone." he explained. So began a monthly ritual, wherein writers would come to his apartment to read their unpublished, unproduced dramatic words. Klíma served them spicy meatballs made from his own special recipe and known as "Klímakugeln." Both the readings and the cuisine became so popular that the monthly meetings filled his small living room. Havel attended and read *The Conspirators*. "Then," Klíma continued, "someone informed the police, and they filmed one of the readings with a hidden camera. A friend told me not to do any more readings because it would be dangerous. The last reading was in December 1971. And that started *samizdat*."

Samizdat (meaning the unofficial reproduction of unpublished manuscripts) was an idea that Klíma developed along with Ludvík Vaculík, the prose writer and journalist. As Klíma recounts its origins, Vaculík's girlfriend was a typist and had access to a Remington. She would type six carbon copies (the maximum possible at one time) of manuscripts written by Klíma, Vaculík, and their friends, including Havel, Kohout, and other "forbidden authors." Klíma would edit them, and Vaculík would circulate them. They called their endeavor Edice Petlice (Padlock Press). So began an effort that would save the work of so many writers and keep it alive. By 1980, the press had published two hundred volumes; by the end of the 1980s, more than 360.[7]

Another kind of writers' gatherings began in the early 1970s. In the summer, writers like Havel whose work had been banned by the regime gathered at Hrádeček for a small writers' congress. After all, in May 1972,

Havel and the other banned writers had been publicly attacked at the founding congress of the new "normalized" Writers' Union, the same event at which, seven years earlier, Havel had given the keynote speech. Why not start a congress of their own? At Hrádeček, they basked in the summer sun, inhaled the glorious Bohemian mountain air, wandered through the woods, bathed in the ponds, dined, laughed, argued, drank wine, and read their works aloud.

There were, in fact, two writers' camps, the one Havel referred to in the 1960s as the "antidogmatics" or reformed Communists, which included Kohout, Vaculík, Klíma, and Jan Trefulka, and a group of non-Communists, which included Zdeněk Urbánek, Milan Uhde, and Josef Topol. At Hrádeček, these two groups gradually blended together. The differences that once separated them no longer seemed to matter, now that they were all in a similar predicament. Some were surviving on royalties from abroad; others held manual labor jobs that left them little time to write. In the late 1970s and into the 1980s, these clandestine meetings were held four times a year, sometimes at Hrádeček, sometimes at Kohout's home in Sázava, sometimes in Moravia and Slovakia, but always at secret locations. The gatherings were called *Kvartál*, meaning quarterly, and they coincided with the beginning of each season.

As Kohout remembers it, all his colleagues suffered from a kind of writers' block during this period. He encouraged them to write, no matter what. Once, just for fun, he suggested that Havel write a play about a man with a minor speech impediment who can't pronounce the letter *R*. (Havel had this problem himself.) Havel wrote the play as a conversation between the man and his psychiatrist, and called it *Rrrrr* . . . He read it with Kohout at one of the writers' gatherings in the early 1970s.[8] Although copies of the work seem to have been lost, the actress Vlasta Chramostová, who was present, remembers the evening as hilarious. These readings were precious events. In that casual and inviting atmosphere, writers felt free. "Somewhere here, the character of Vaněk took roots," says Chramostová, referring to the character of a banned playwright Havel created later in the 1970s in a series of one-acts that would change the course of his writing.[9]

The 1970s also gave birth to a phenomenon called *bytové divadlo*, meaning "living-room theater." Vlasta Chramostová, who attended the Kvartál meetings, was one of many theater artists who found themselves "silenced" in the 1970s. Because she would not join the Communist Party, there was suddenly no work for her in theater, film, radio, or television. She could perform in the remote provincial theaters, but soon that privilege was taken away from her, too. She resorted to making lamp shades, but not for long. In 1976, on the occasion of the seventy-fifth birthday of Jaroslav Seifert, the greatest living Czech poet, Chramostová arranged a private reading of his memoirs at her apartment near the Prague National Museum. There were thirty-three people in Chramostová's living room, Kohout remembers, and it was aglow with the intensity of the acting and the enthusiasm of the audience. It was there that living-room theater was born. The following year, in December 1977, Chramostová hosted another evening of *bytové divadlo*, which she called "Appelplatz II," a collage of readings with the leitmotif of Cyrano de Bergerac. In July 1978, again at her apartment, Kohout's new play called *Play Macbeth* was read by Pavel Landovský, Kohout, Chramostová, and others. (The critic Sergej Machonin, who was present, described the author as "a playboy with shiny hair, shiny shoes and shiny plays."[10])

Kohout's biographer said of living-room theater: "This is theater that is shouting for the truth, theater as a protection against the devaluing of all values."[11] The royalty Kohout received for this performance, his biographer notes, was "one big pot of goulash and several litres of wine."

Play Macbeth became a cult piece; it was performed eighteen times in apartments throughout Prague. Then the secret police stepped in. As Karel Kyncl, a writer and journalist who was there, observed (in his book about the 1970s, *After the Spring Came Winter*): "The State Security tolerated only seventeen performances before coming to the irrevocable conclusion that William Shakespeare (1564–1616) was an enemy of real socialism and had to be silenced."[12]

One evening, during a performance of *Play Macbeth,* fifteen uniformed policemen appeared at Chramostová's apartment, saying that they had received reports of an orgy. It was just at the point when Macduff (played by Kohout) was to kill Macbeth (played by Landovský) in front of an audience of twenty. As Karel Kyncl described it, "Ivan Kyncl leaned out of a window to take a documentary picture of some distinctly non-Shakespearean police cars down below in a dark Prague street."[13] The audience did not applaud, fearing that the police might interpret that as an orgiastic activity. Instead, spectators and actors alike took out their identification cards and prepared for inspection.

Even with all this harassment, *bytové divadlo* continued in people's apartments. The police began to block access to buildings in which they suspected *Play Macbeth* would be performed. Meanwhile, Chramostová's husband, a cameraman, managed to film a performance and have it smuggled into Austria, where it was broadcast on Austrian television. The esteemed British playwright Tom Stoppard later wrote his own version called *Cahoot's Macbeth*, a minitravesty of Kohout's *Play Macbeth*. In Stoppard's play, a private performance of Kohout's abbreviated version of *Macbeth* is interrupted when a knock at the door is heard, only this time, instead of the murderers, it's the Czech secret police. The police accuse the actors of antistate activity and warn them that the apartment is under surveillance. Still, the play continues. As Klára Hůrková points out in *Mirror Images*, her study of the plays of Václav Havel and Tom Stoppard, *Cahoot's Macbeth* "is a comic satire of totalitarianism, pointing out the absurd aspects of the regime's attempt to control culture and people's private lives."[14]

The Czech saying *"Všechno zlé je k něčemu dobré"* (everything bad must bring something good) described the 1970s. These were dark times, politically and socially. But paradoxically, new friendships and alliances were formed, many of them unexpected and improbable; new resources were discovered, like the living room of a friend's apartment that could be turned into a stage. And so a new kind theater was created, with an audience eager for new work and writers eager to produce it.

Barred from theaters, the Czech writers found freedom within their own homes and their own souls. The gatherings, the readings, the friendships, the bondings — those were the unexpected fruits of this dark decade. Out of great adversity, a gradual change was occurring. A new intelligentsia was forming, and at its heart were forbidden writers, brought together and solidified by their common plight, any differences of the past having faded away. Slowly, the foundation of a new culture was being laid; a new literature was growing and a new leadership being established.

The question then became: How to get this new literature to the people? The solution evolved in a quiet and subtle way. During the early and mid-1970s, slowly and carefully, a system was developed by a group of dedicated and determined dissidents whose mission it was to preserve contemporary banned Czech literature by smuggling it out of the country. A key link in this chain was a young professor of sociology named Jiřina Šiklová. Dismissed from the philosophical faculty of Charles University in the early 1970s because she was not a Communist, Šiklová began working as a cleaning woman in the same building where she taught. "I didn't mind," she explained. "My students often visited me, and it was a good job because I could visit the reading room and do research."[15] She cleaned the halls of the State University and the Klementinum Palace in the center of the Old Town, too. Eventually she obtained a job as a statistician in a geriatric hospital. (As Šiklová explained it, she couldn't work in a hospital for mentally retarded children, because the authorities thought that dissidents might have a bad influence on the young.)

When Šiklová started working at the hospital, she was contacted by some fellow dissidents who were trying to find a way to get new work by Czech dissident writers out of the country to ensure its safekeeping. Once abroad, the work could be published by emigré presses — in London, the *Index on Censorship*, edited by George Theiner and Karl Kyncl; in Paris, *Svědetví* (Testimony), edited by Pavel Tigrid; and in Rome, *Listy* (Letters), edited by Jiří Pelikán. So it came to pass that Šiklová's Prague apartment, on a quiet side street near the Náměsti republic, became the secret depository for new manuscripts, a key stop in a highly organized underground chain. As she explains it, once the manuscripts were dropped off at the hospital or her apartment, she arranged for them to be hidden in various garages in the city. Then, six times a year, a white van was driven from Paris to Prague, each time by a different person. The van arrived at Šiklová's apartment, where the manuscripts were loaded into it; then it returned to Paris, where the works were distributed to emigré publishing houses throughout Europe. They, in turn, produced small printings to facilitate secret distribution back in Czechoslovakia. "In West Germany, for example," explains Šiklová, "you could make thousands of copies, whereas in Czechoslovakia it was so difficult to make those copies by typewriter with carbon paper." Once published, the works were collected again, loaded onto the white van, and brought back to Czechoslovakia, where Šiklová had a five-page list of the hundreds of names to whom the publications would be distributed. But the list had to be coded, to protect those whose names were on it. So she and Pavel Tigrid devised a system whereby they shared a novel, and its words, characters, and pages became codes for the names on the list.

No one knew who was part of this chain. The only word passed around was that if you wanted to get a manuscript outside Czechoslovakia, just get it to Jiřina Šiklová and she would take care of it. "I was just a part of a chain," she explained. "My mission was to take care of things here, to collect the manuscripts and get them into the van. As for the rest, I was kept in the dark. It was organic, how it developed." Above all, the system was designed to protect every link in the chain. Only Šiklová's name was known. "I wasn't in the dissident ghetto," she explained. "I belonged to the structure." Thus, Šiklová was not invited to attend the writers' meetings. To protect the system, she had to remain on the outside. "It wasn't possible to do both things together," she said. "You can't have your cake and eat it, too."[16]

As one of the unsung heroines of the dissident movement, Jiřina Šiklová would continue in her quiet but determined way to build up a system to ensure the preservation of Czech dissident literature, among which was the work of Václav Havel.

But in the early 1970s, that story was still unfolding.

1972–1975: *THE BEGGAR'S OPERA*

Let's put on my neighbor's play![1]

— Andrej Krob

The year 1972 found Havel in a state of gloom.

> For me, the first half of the decade is a single, shapeless fog; I can't say any longer how 1972, for instance, differed from 1973, or what I did in either of those years. Like most of my colleagues, I was driven out of every position I'd once held, I was publicly branded an enemy, and I was even indicted for subversion (there was no trial or prison sentence). Ultimately, I too had no choice but to withdraw into a kind of internal exile.[2]

Havel was "in exile," as he put it, at Hrádeček, avoiding any public notice, uncertain of what was happening, living in a kind of existential void. The only time he caused a public stir was on December 4, when he and thirty-four other Czech writers signed a petition asking the president to grant amnesty to all Czech political prisoners. Otherwise, the writer who worked twenty-four hours a day in the 1960s had time on his hands. So once again, Havel turned to writing a play.

Back in the late 1960s, Jaroslav Vostrý, the artistic director of the Činoherní Klub, thought it might be a good idea to invite Havel to write a play for its ensemble of actors. He had suggested an adaptation of John Gay's *The Beggar's Opera*, and Havel had accepted. Having nothing to do during those long shapeless days of 1972, Havel finally turned to the task. After *The Conspirators*, this was like "relaxation after suffering," as he put it. "It was easy for me. I didn't speculate about it, and I didn't feel the same pressure."[3] He completed the work during that quiet year at Hrádeček.

By the early 1970s, all the theaters were feeling the pressure of normalization, and Vostrý and Jan Kačer, the Činoherní Klub's leading director, began to worry. Havel, of course, was prominently blacklisted, and they feared for the theater. Kačer came up with an idea. Why not produce Havel's adaptation in a German translation in Switzerland, where Kačer had been invited to direct a play, and then bring it back to Prague as a German play and have it retranslated again into Czech? But that seemed somewhat convoluted, not to mention risky. So, in embarrassment, the theater retracted its invitation to Havel.[4] The play was, in effect, homeless.

Then one day in 1973 at Hrádeček, Havel nonchalantly handed Andrej Krob a copy of the new manuscript he had recently finished, his version of *The Beggar's Opera* (Žebrácká opera), subtitled "a play in 14 scenes based on the theme of John Gay." Neither remembers the exact date, nor do they recall whether Havel walked the script up the little hill to Krob's cottage, or whether Krob passed Havel while sitting in the garden. "Papers went back and forth between our houses often in those years — journals, articles, books," Krob explained. "He was always trying to 'educate' me."[5] Krob, like Havel, had lost his job at the Balustrade. He read the new play and asked Havel about his plans for it. Upon learning that the playwright had none, Krob announced: "I'd like to direct it." "But you're not a director!" Havel exclaimed. "And anyway, where and how would you do it?" At the time, Krob knew of several other stagehands, prop masters, set builders, and lighting-board operators who were also unemployed as a result of normalization and had time on their hands. He proceeded to spread the word around certain pubs in Prague that he was working on a new play by Havel and found a handful of willing participants — friends, friends of friends, even Krob's nephew. Although they were experienced workers in the theater, they had no acting experience. They eagerly agreed, despite the fact that Havel was a forbidden playwright.

So they started rehearsing, a process that lasted roughly eighteen months, during which time the cast members would go from apartment to apartment, house to house, so as not to be discovered by the secret police. Rehearsals weren't regular; they were scheduled based on who had time, who was available, and where they might rehearse safely. "All the actors were my friends, they had all worked in the theater, but none were professionals," Krob said. "We didn't have a heroic goal, or a terroristic goal, either." Krob thought of a name for his little band of amateurs: *Divadlo na Tahu*, or Theatre on the Road.[6]

In April 1975, the ensemble presented its work to Havel in the form of a staged reading at Krob's house in Hrádeček. They crowded into the small, low-ceilinged space that served as living room, dining room, and kitchen. To the left of the entrance stood an old-fashioned stove, to the right was an armoire, on top of which were perched props and costumes that Krob was assembling for the production. Havel was delighted, but Krob, who had never directed a play before, was highly anxious, unsure of himself and of the actors.

Havel left the little house elated, his spirits buoyed by the run-through. Once more, he was in a "theater," even though it was in his neighbor's house. On the night of April 24, he sat down and quickly wrote a twelve-page letter to Krob.

Dear Andrej:
At last I can keep my promise and write something about my impressions from your rehearsals [of *The Beggar's Opera*]. I shall simply write whatever comes to me directly into the typewriter, so excuse my imprecise formulations, the absence of system in my notes, and any errors of expression.

First of all, I want to say that no matter what play you rehearse, no matter whether you finish it or not and what the outcome might be, I consider it all to be wonderful. It is wonderful that you all stick together, that you search for something, and that you have time and energy for an activity which will not bring you any profit. In today's material world, this seems to me very precious, very meaningful, and I admire that very much. I think that the group of people you have put together is a very fine bunch, and I was fascinated by the atmosphere of your rehearsals; the collaborative spirit made me nostalgic because it reminds me so much of our beginnings at the Balustrade. I think that this is the only way to do theater which makes sense. More exactly, this is the only theater which attracts me and which I enjoy. Of course, my admiration is even greater because you've chosen a play which is not easy at all and which might cause some challenges for you. As an author, it excites me . . . As you know, I have been used to "team work" [he uses the English word] in the theater (as Grossman used to say), and I feel as if something that I missed for such a long time has returned.[7]

At first, Havel praised the actors for their amateurism.

Nobody does it like amateurs do. Which means that they don't imitate theatrical mannerisms. Everyone is simply himself/herself, without desperate attempts at making theater with a capital T.[8]

He was captivated by their guilelessness, touched by their earnestness, and delighted that they captured the complexity of his dialogue without any formal training.

As you know, it was my aim to write a play in which characters speak in a pretentious language. In fact, the whole play rises and falls on this tension. That is to say that thieves and tarts speak like psychologists and sociologists. Thanks to the actors, this works. And let me be honest — this was the thing I was afraid of most: how the actors would handle this literary language. It's remarkable, because the actors are untrained, but who knows? That could be the very thing which makes it easier for them. (They don't have to be burdened by the conventions of psychological acting.) And perhaps more experienced actors would have more problems. Whatever the reason is, I find the result to be perfection. It seems to me that all the characters are well cast and that most of the actors, especially those in the main roles, display what I would call a true actor's talent. Perhaps it is that natural, spontaneous, uneducated talent which a lot of people have and don't even know they have it, but in any event it's a fortunate coincidence.[9]

After reading the first few pages, Krob was elated. "The first part of the letter was all compliments. The more I read it, the more my self-confidence grew," he recalls. "And then, I read the second half of the letter." For the next ten pages, Havel gave Krob paragraph after paragraph of specific, detailed notes about the acting, the direction, the blocking, the scene work — notes so specific and detailed that Krob, for whom this would be his directorial debut, was thrown in a panic. Regarding the actors, Havel wrote:

> As for Mr. Černoušek, he doesn't show any special actor's talent, but if I may say so, he's so sweet that you want to kiss him! For me, a man like that on the stage is a hundred times better than all those handsome professional actors. By the way, don't let Mr. Černoušek "play" anything, and especially, don't let him play Mr. Černoušek. Don't let success go to his head, and don't let him overact. Let him simply be himself, and let him speak in his own manner of speaking. . . . Also, Arnošt as Lockit could be brilliant, if only he would learn his lines. . . . If Diana would play the whole play as well as she did in the first act, then she will fit the part perfectly. . . . Those small roles: Jim, Jack, Harold, etc. — you should rehearse with the actors who are playing them. At this point it seems like they're ad-libbing. . . . At this phase of rehearsals, everyone should learn the text perfectly. Without that, you're not going to progress, you'll just go around in circles. And it's not only about those who didn't memorize the text so far — it's also that those who already have learned the text should learn it exactly.[10]

Regarding the direction, Havel had this to say about Krob's fondness for a complicated directorial concept he had developed using chairs:

> As I already told you, your concept as a general principle is fine, and you definitely shouldn't give it up. It gives the whole performance a shape. . . . But you shouldn't fixate on the idea that at every moment every chair must be in its place. . . . In general, I would say that I don't like the fact that everyone who comes on and off the stage takes his chair with him. I know why you want it that way; I understand that you can explain it in theory. But no one else will understand it. I know that you will eventually do it in your own way and in fact that's the right approach: the director shouldn't listen to other people, and above all, he shouldn't listen to the playwright. Nevertheless, if you want my impressions, here they are: use your chairs only in the scenes in which it helps the play. Elsewhere . . . you should forget them. That is my advice. It will help the entire production, and it will also help your directorial concept.[11]

That summer, they rehearsed at Hrádeček, a raggle-taggle lot of blue-jeaned, T-shirted theater techies. The men were bearded, the women wore tank tops. Havel's curly blond hair was now below his ears. He wandered among his cast, smiling, wearing his Princeton T-shirt, a cigarette dangling from his fingertips. The lawn in front of the Havel house was strewn with lawn chairs, makeshift tables covered with beer bottles and ashtrays, and clusters of happy amateur actors, thrilled to have Havel their playwright amongst them, elated to have a purpose. They had a performance to put on.

1975: Horní Počernice

> If this play is performed one day, for me it will be a bigger success than all the premieres of my plays from Montreal to Paris.[12]
> — Havel, letter to Andrej Krob, April 24, 1975

The year was 1975. The time had come to perform what the fledging group, Theatre on the Road, had been rehearsing for a year and a half. The actors knew their lines; the blocking had been set. But the premiere of a new play by a banned author in a totalitarian state, as well as the debut of a new and unique theater company whose existence was as yet unknown — these objectives presented a challenge. Where could there be a performance of a play by Havel that would escape the scrutiny of the authorities? They needed to find a place where their friends might come that would also avoid the attention of the secret police.

A member of the cast came to Krob's rescue. The actor playing Macheath, Viktor Spousta, had produced several amateur productions in a Prague suburb called Horní Počernice, a remote, modest district to the north, with narrow lanes and small stucco red-roofed houses. They had performed in the large hall of hotel/pub called U Čelikovských, where dancing parties were often held on Saturday nights.[13] Spousta, who knew the local authorities, told them that a new amateur group wished to perform Brecht's version of John Gay's *The Beggar's Opera*, adapted into a nonmusical. The authorities didn't ask who had adapted it, and Spousta didn't tell them. According to Spousta, the ban on Havel was so successful that the local authorities had no clue who he was, anyway. Their only stipulations were that the performance could not be advertised, and no admission fee could be charged. Krob could not have been more relieved. The date was set for Saturday night, November 1.[14]

Elated, Krob and the company set out to invite their friends, and soon the list of audience members had grown to three hundred. Krob had three days in the theater to rehearse. He scurried around, making final arrangements, rehearsing, even personally repairing the one-hundred-year-old curtain in the hall of the hotel/pub. Jan Grossman was invited to attend a rehearsal. One official from the local authorities planned to attend the performance on November 1, but according to Krob he had no idea what was going on.

The first public performance of *The Beggar's Opera* is one of the most moving stories in twentieth-century theater. On the evening of November 1, for the first time since 1968 and for one night only, a new play by Václav Havel, the country's foremost living (and banned) playwright, would be performed on Czech soil.

The account of what happened on that night is rich in detail, and like all legends, it has some variations. By Krob's account, an hour before the curtain hardly anyone had arrived, and he was terrified. By the account of the actor Jan Hraběta, who was playing Peachum, no one had arrived even ten minutes before the curtain. Edá Kriseová, Havel's biographer, who was also there, helped stack mattresses against the side doors of the hall to muffle the roaring of drunks in the adjacent pub. Nervous and watchful, Havel had slipped through the gate to the hotel courtyard, wearing a white shirt, a tie, and a jacket over his bell-bottom jeans. The brisk November night air sent an additional chill through him. He had just turned thirty-nine a month before, and he had not seen a play of his performed for seven years.

Then suddenly, the auditorium began to fill. People had been driving through the dark, unfamiliar streets of Horní Počernice, afraid to ask for directions lest the secret police discover their destination. Some three hundred excited people — friends, relatives, artists, writers, theater folk, even Havel's father — took their seat in thrilled disbelief. As Kriseová describes it:

> In the audience were sitting three hundred wonderful, splendid, talented people whom the Communists had demoted to the nation's boiler rooms. They sat on creaky chairs. On stage, people who installed insulation in windows, stage hands, workers, repairmen, and drivers performed the play, and suddenly the action shifted from the stage to the audience. It was an enormous "happening" with *The Beggar's Opera* as the theme.[15]

The evening began dramatically with a hush, then an audible gasp. The lights dimmed, and a face peered from behind the drawn curtain. A tall, thin frame slipped out onto the stage. "There was a great tension and alertness in the audience," recalls the actor Jan Tříska, who was there. Wordlessly, the man took out a cigarette, lit it, and blew puffs of smoke while he coldly surveyed the audience row by row, as if taking account of who was there. The spectators became uneasy, sensing this was not part of the play itself. They were right. The tall man was Krob, and the moment, which was his invention, had been orchestrated with Havel's approval. Who are you out there in that audience? his silent, menacing presence seemed to ask. We know who you are, we're watching you, the moment said. "It was an unbelievable moment," said Tříska, "because everyone in the auditorium knew there was going to be big trouble for everyone who came."[16] Grossman was in the audience; so were Klíma, Urbánek, Vaculík, and many other writers and theater artists. As both Krob and Havel knew, those who were there would be marked forever.

The performance itself is precious in Havel's memory:

> The performance was marvelous; the laughter and delight of the audience seemed endless, and for a moment I was back again in the atmosphere of the Theatre on the Balustrade in the 1960s. Thanks to the circumstances, it was, understandably, even more exciting. The matter-of-factness with which these young people acted in my play gave their performance a special theatrical charm. It was a human act that somehow, miraculously, had been transformed into a highly suggestive theatrical act.[17]

The audience laughed and applauded for the next two hours. "Beautiful!" "The atmosphere was so special!" "What a feeling of freedom!" So went the chorus of praise from the actors, thinking back on that evening years later. "It was so strange," said one cast member. "We were so happy and at the same time we were so scared."[18] "It was like a miracle," Ivan Klíma recalls. "We applauded for fifteen minutes. We had such a feeling of greatness."[19]

At the curtain call, the beaming actors took their bow before their elated public. Havel remembers a special moment. "It was very touching. I was very moved. . . . At the end, Andrej Krob did something very courageous. After the curtain call, he came out and descended into the audience and gave me a flower."[20]

After the performance, many in the audience went to the cast party for the Theatre on the Road at the pub called At the Sign of the Bears (U medvídků) on Bartholomew Street, located right around the corner from the police station. Seated around long tables decked out with rows of bottles of red wine, there were toasts, laughter, and merriment into the night. Havel told the cast, "I had more joy from this premiere than from all my foreign premieres, from New York to Tokyo."[21]

The production at Horní Počernice was a triumphant experience for those who attended. There were different artistic communities in the Prague theater world; some artists had been banned, some had lost their jobs. But on that night, they all met at one place, united. "Because," as Vlasta Chramostová, who was there, said, "there are some moments when people stop to think, and others when there is only 'yes' or 'no' and you stop thinking and stop doubting."[22] They came, and they were glad they did.

The playwright, of course, was thrilled. As Havel wrote, in the afterword to *Hry 1970–1976*, which includes *The Beggar's Opera*:

> It's interesting that this play, although far more appealing that *The Conspirators*, hasn't been produced frequently. So far it has only been produced by two professional theaters: Teatro Stabile in Trieste [Italy] and the Schlosstheater in Celle [West Germany]. This minimal foreign interest in the play disappoints me, but the production in Horní Počernice makes up for it one hundred fold. The inner freedom and moral responsibility of a group of young people who were brave enough to perform in *The Beggar's Opera* gave the production an unexpected theatrical thrill which was so intense, that after many years once again I experienced the feeling of theater in the deepest and best meaning. It was an electrifying place of joy, truth, freedom, and collective understanding. I appreciate this premiere night more than any that I have ever attended.[23]

The Beggar's Opera: The Aftermath

> No good deed goes unpunished.[24]
>
> — Havel, from the documentary
> "Once Again, *The Beggar's Opera*"

By most accounts, nothing happened for a few days. Krob and his cast sat back and waited. "I was afraid, of course, because I had a child and I was worried about her future," he said.[25]

The following Tuesday, one of the actors, Viktor Spousta, who had returned to his job at a local slaughterhouse, heard from a fellow worker that news of a production of a new Havel play had been broadcast over Radio Free Europe. "Trouble," Spousta thought to himself. On Wednesday, a report of the event appeared in the West German newspaper *Der Spiegel* by a journalist who had attended the performance; unbeknownst to Krob, the audience had included two West German journalists.[26] The authorities were outraged. How had a performance by a banned author escaped their scrutiny? What was to be done? The Helsinki Agreement, an international human rights proclamation, had been signed just three months earlier by Czechoslovakia along with other nations, so to punish the artists or the audience would be violating the agreement. On the other hand, the government could not ignore what had taken place.

So one by one, they began rounding up actors and audience members to interrogate them. Although Bohdan Holomíček, a photographer and friend of Krob and Havel, had hidden the photos he had taken at the performance, the authorities were nonetheless able to identify dozens of people who were involved with the production or in the audience. Many were punished. Krob himself was called in for questioning on November 17, and a team of secret police interrogated him for for eleven hours. (He used the idea of rotating interrogators in directing Havel's next play, *Audience*). As a result, Krob lost his job as technical director at the Balustrade and was no longer permitted on the theater's premises. But he refused to leave, and since his contract prohibited him from being fired on such grounds, Vladimír Vodička, the theater's managing director, allowed him to stay but demoted him to stagehand. Then in June 1976, his job was eliminated, allegedly because of staff restructuring, and he spent the next thirteen years installing insulation in windows. Others involved lost their drivers' licenses, still others lost their jobs. The persecution went even beyond those present; an actress lost her job, only because her father was present in the audience at Horní Počernice.[27]

Jan Grossman, whom the authorities assumed had directed the production, had his passport revoked simply for being in the audience. He could no longer leave Czechoslovakia to direct elsewhere in Europe. He went to work in a theater in the remote provincial town of Cheb, in Western Bohemia, far from Prague. But he refused to let his situation break his spirit. "Here in Cheb, we must work as if we were working in the Burgtheater in Vienna or the Comedie Française," he said.[28] He was to remain in the provinces for fourteen years. Jan Tříska, the actor with whom Havel had spent his last "free" night in August 1968 before the invasion, was fired from the National Theater because he was in the audience. He ultimately emigrated to the United States in 1977.

For Havel, the most shocking and painful thing was the reaction of the theater world. The authorities immediately put out the word that there would be a tightening of policies toward theaters and that Havel should be blamed for these reprisals.

> There were interrogations and sanctions; enraged bureaucrats spread the word through the official Prague theaters that because of me (!) the cultural policy of the government would be that much more stringent, and the whole theater community would suffer. Many a shallow-minded actor fell for it and got very upset at me and my amateur actors for frustrating their artistic ambition, by which, of course, they meant their well-paid sprints from job to job — in dubbing, theater, television, and film — that is, from one center for befuddling the public to another.[29]

The authorities cancelled a number of productions at official theaters, spreading rumors that these cancellations were the result of the production at Horní Počernice. As a result, other professional actors, playwrights, and directors became angry with Havel and Krob. Havel despaired.

> I was really angry about the artists' official response, especially because one could see how easy it was to manipulate people's minds, opinions and behavior. Artists should be the last people who can be manipulated. They should be the most independent. It made me angry, sad, depressed.[30]

After all, Havel pointed out, the union actors were gainfully employed, and they were angry at the young amateurs who did this all for free. Pavel Landovský and Vlasta Chramostová were among the only actors who supported the Theatre on the Road.

Havel, of course, was called in for interrogation by the police, and even tighter controls and restrictions were placed on him. Now more than ever, he was a marked man.

Almost two months after the performance, Havel wrote a letter to the Minister of Culture entitled "Facts about the production of *The Beggar's Opera*." In the letter, published in 1976 in *Listy*, a monthly Czech émigré journal in Paris, Havel was responding to the aggressive crackdown by the secret police and the media. The Communists were calling the production of *The Beggar's Opera* "a kind of illegal political congress, the action of an organized opposition group working according to some conspiratorial plan."[31] The media was depicting the performance as a political meeting held by dissidents. By then, Havel said, the secret police had interrogated almost everyone in the ensemble and the audience, trying to find evidence that the performance was a political provocation. As a result, many other performances and cultural events had been banned, even ones having nothing to do with Havel or the "dissidents." And Havel, of course, was being blamed for all this.

So Havel wanted to to set the record straight, to present the facts about what really happened.

1. The production of *The Beggar's Opera* was officially approved by local authorities in Horní Počernice. It wasn't public. There were only invited guests present. It was a clearly a theatrical event, and during the performance, nothing political happened.
2. In the script of my play, you cannot find anything that could be directed against our state, its regime, or public policy.
3. I know that professional theaters in Czechoslovakia do not produce my plays, but I don't know about the existence of any official law or public notice which would ban anything I wrote. So nobody can be accused of breaking the law.
4. The audience was invited by the director, actors, or me; they were our friends and colleagues, people of different occupations and opinions, but all of them are law-abiding, working Czech citizens who have the right to go to the theater. They came to Počernice just to see the performance, and nothing else. No other intention. Some of them knew that I wrote the play, others didn't.[32]

The letter went on to speak about Krob's ensemble.

They were young people, workers, students, who decided to rehearse and perform the play on their own. It was their own decision, they weren't searching for any publicity or celebrity, not abroad, not in Czechoslovakia. They just wanted to do the play.[33]

Just as *The Beggar's Opera* was a story of betrayal, collaboration, and informing, so did the same story embrace the lives of those involved in its production at Horní Počernice in 1975. The playwright, the director, and the actors were a cast in a much broader drama. And there were no signs of a happy ending.

The Significance of The Beggar's Opera

> They serve best who know not that they serve.[34]
>
> — Havel, *The Beggar's Opera*

As in *The Garden Party* and *The Memorandum*, what Havel put on the stage in *The Beggar's Opera* was a reflection of what was happening in the lives of his audience.

In John Gay's underworld of crime in seventeenth-century London, with its themes of betrayal, informing, collaborating, double-agenting, and signing one's name, Havel found an uncanny match for the Czech reality in the 1970s. He adapted the story astutely for his own audience. If everyone from the greengrocer to the politician must hang the sign of compliance outside his window, if everyone is forced to conform, how can one know the true identity of another? The questions: Who are you? Who are you working for? Whose side are you on? These were the questions of John Gay's world, and of Havel's, too.

Havel pared down *The Beggar's Opera* to its basic story, divesting it of music, singing, and a happy ending. Keeping the same names as Gay's characters and the same locales, Havel presented a political allegory to a Czech audience who readily understood it. He also preserved Gay's well-known plot of convolutions and entanglements. There are three protagonists who form a triangular balance of power: Macheath, a "boss of a criminal organization," as Havel calls him, and a flamboyant ladies' man; Peachum, a rival boss of another crime network who collaborates with the police and whose pretty daughter Polly is Macheath's wife; and Bill Lockit, chief of police, whose equally pretty daughter Lucy is also

Macheath's wife. Others inhabit this world of crime, among them Mrs. Peachum, who conspires with her husband to the detriment of their own daughter; Filch, the honest thief, who moves among the three protagonists; and Diana, the proprietor of the "ladies' salon," where Jenny, a former lover of Macheath, also lives. To achieve their ends of power and control, the three protagonists flagrantly use daughters, wives, lovers, friends, and the "little man" on the street; they, in turn, readily use the protagonists. By the end, everyone uses everyone else, everyone betrays everyone else, everyone gets what he or she wants.

When Peachum discovers that his daughter Polly is in love with his rival, the ne'er-do-well rake Macheath, he is not outraged, he is intrigued. Here is an opportunity to use his daughter to spy on his enemy. When he discovers, furthermore, that she has betrayed her father and has already married Macheath, he sees it as a felicitous opportunity and enlists Polly as his double agent to infiltrate the Macheath organization with the aim of destroying it and sending Macheath to the gallows. Polly in turn betrays her father and warns her husband of her father's plot. At the same time, Macheath is seduced by Jenny, who entraps him in Madame Diana's brothel. Amid cries of "rape," Macheath is arrested by prisoners dressed as policemen, hired in return for favors, and sent to prison.

As the cunning, corrupt police chief ostensibly fighting crime but using it to his own advantage, Lockit is shrewd: if he kills Macheath, he reasons, his organization will fall apart and he will have no source of information. So Lockit betrays Peachum, his collaborator, and instead of doing away with Macheath, tries to recruit him into Lockit's organization. Meanwhile, Lucy, who (unbeknownst to her father) is also married to Macheath, helps her husband escape. Polly takes refuge in her father's home, having been told by Macheath to renounce him and say that she would cooperate with her father. Instead, she confesses to her father that she is a double agent and that now she sees Macheath does not love her, but only wants to use her. Peachum promises to forgive her if she will betray Macheath and help entrap him. Once again in hiding at Madame Diana's, Macheath is confronted by both his wives and is arrested once more.

The merry-go-round of betrayal, collaboration, and double, triple, and quadruple agenting spins on and on. Meanwhile, in this satire on power and human behavior, Filch, the honest thief and the character who represents the condition to which the ordinary Czech has been reduced, has the only moment of human dignity. Peachum states the case for collaboration, as he tries to convince Filch, an independent "freelance" thief, to work for him.

> Peachum: The real heroes of the underworld today are a different breed of man altogether. They may not constantly flaunt their fidelity to the pure code of honor among thieves, but they do modest, inconspicuous and risky work in that no-man's-land between the underworld and the police. And they make a real contribution to our objective interests. By not hesitating to dirty their hands from — as you put it — trafficking with the enemy, they expand the range of our business opportunities inch by inch, strengthen our security, keep us informed, and slowly, inconspicuously, with no claim to glory, serve the cause of progress. The era of romantic highway man of the Middle Ages is long past, sir. The world has changed, other standards have prevailed for some time now, and anyone who fails to understand that has understood nothing . . . let me give you this piece of advice: get rid of your illusions while there's still time. Come down to earth from your ethereal heights, look at the world around you, try to understand it, free yourself from the thralldom to abstract principles! It's in your own interests.[35]

Filch refuses, saying that he would prefer honest labor to stealing under police protection. He refuses to rat on Peachum, his former boss, even though Filch despises his corrupt practices. "I am a man of principle," he says. "And one of my principles is: never rat on a colleague, no matter what reservations I may have about him."[36]

Finally, Filch asks to be sent to the gallows.

> Filch: I don't want to go on living anyway. I'm not suited to this world.
> Lockit: On the contrary. I think this world needs more people like you. A pity, but what else can I do.[37]

In a corrupt world in which collaboration means survival and the slogan *někdo tu práci dělat musí* (someone has to do the job) is a frequent alibi, Filch the thief is the only one who refuses.[38] So he perishes. The (ironic) moral of the story? Do your job. Collaborate. Work within the system, without caring who you work for. That's the way, and the only way, to survive. As Peachum says: "Why do you think I cooperate with the police? Because I love the king? I'm just doing what everyone else is doing — in one way or another: working for my own ends and covering my back at the same time."[39]

In the end, Peachum proposes to Lockit the formation of a new crime syndicate, with Lockit controlling the whole of London's underworld. If Macheath signs on, he will be spared execution, says Lockit. This is the offer Macheath ultimately cannot refuse:

> Macheath: If I were to turn that offer down, those around me would understand it as an ostentatious expression of my own superiority and conceit . . . everyone will ask: where does he get the right to be so different from the rest of us, to step out of line, to thumb his nose at the opinions of the majority and to spit on that minimum of discipline without which no society can function properly? I would be seen as a pompous and arrogant exhibitionist, someone who wanted to play the conscience of the world. I'd be giving my life for something no one but me believes in. My death would therefore remain uncomprehended; it would reinforce no values, it would help no one, and merely cause pain to those closest to me . . . And I can understand that: to utterly reject the rules of the game this world offers may well be the easier way, but it usually leads nowhere. It is far more difficult, and at the same time far more meaningful, to accept those rules, thus enabling one to communicate with those around one, and then to put that ability to work in the gradual struggle for better rules.[40]

At the same time, Lockit negotiates a deal whereby Macheath will serve as a double agent for him and inform on Peachum. Thus, at the curtain, a perfect balance of power is maintained. The epilogue sums it up:

> Mrs. Lockit: It's still bizarre though, Bill. No one knows about our organization, yet everyone works for it.
> Lockit: They serve best who know not that they serve. Bon appetit.[41]

As such, the Havel version of *The Beggar's Opera* is a political parable. In John Gay's world of thieves, crooks, and swindlers, Havel intuitively saw the same systems of entrapment, manipulation, and collaboration in the world of Communist Czechoslovakia around him. He also saw the existential dilemma of man in that system. After the Russian invasion of 1968, the lives of Czech citizens changed dramatically. Under the new Czech Communist leaders, who were collaborators with the Russians, it was a question of whose side you were on. Whoever refused to sign the Declaration on the Entrance of Friendly Armies in 1969 (condoning, in effect, the invasion) lost their job, their passport, and educational opportunities for their children. They were forced to work as manual laborers. On the other hand, once you signed the agreement, you were signing a contract with the regime. You were its hostage. We don't care what you think, said the new regime, we just want you to be "loyal." We will let you earn money, buy your dacha and your car. Just keep a low profile, do your job, and hang a Russian flag in your window on holidays. The need to make such accommodations profoundly affected the everyday life of the citizens of Prague in the gray 1970s. They quietly did their job during the week, then retreated from the cultural graveyard of Prague to their *chatas* (dachas) in the countryside, away from the scrutiny of the invisible secret police.

Without having intended it, Havel accomplished in *The Beggar's Opera* what he set out to do in *The Conspirators*, to write a play about power and its effects on human identity. Where *The Conspirators* was theoretical and didactic, *The Beggar's Opera* was entertaining and provocative.

But Havel clearly loved to "exercise" his ideas in a variety of genres. Just as he wrote commentaries for his plays, so he also wrote essays that expressed, in another form, what his plays were dramatizing. "The Power of the Powerless," written a few years later in 1978, illuminated many of themes dramatized in *The Beggar's Opera*. In the 1970s in Czechoslovakia, normalization was the official policy of the day. As Havel said in his essay, it meant playing by the rules of the game, which in turn meant survival at any cost, especially at the cost of what Havel called "living in truth." The result, as he said, was "a deep moral crisis in society." Havel cites the example of the greengrocer who, to survive, puts the sign "Workers of the World, Unite!" in his shop window. As Havel put it, in a posttotalitarian system, where conformity, uniformity, and discipline are demanded, everyone is affected. And whoever plays the game becomes part of the game.

> Individuals need not believe all these mystifications, but they must behave as though they did, or they must at least tolerate them in silence, or get along well with those who work with them. For this reason, however, they must live within a lie. They need not accept the lie. It is enough for them to have accepted their life with it and

in it. For by this very fact, individuals confirm the system, fulfill the system, make the system, *are* the system.[42]

For these reasons, the dark terrain of the 1970s was far more dangerous, rough, and corrupt than in the 1960s. Moral dignity was lost through collaboration with the new regime. Souls were sold, except those who held out, like Havel. For holdouts, there would be consequences, and Havel was beginning to feel their approach.

These consequences would be meted out by the StB, the secret police, who were slowly casting their shadow over Havel's life in the early 1970s while he was writing *The Beggar's Opera*. In the 1960s, Havel was an established author who had hardly any contact with the police. Now, in the 1970s, they were beginning to watch him. The story of *The Beggar's Opera* gave Havel a chance to think about the police — about how they work, how they talk, and what manipulative tactics they use to ensure the loyalty of those who were with the regime and to watch those, like Havel, who were not. Once again, Havel the playwright was able to see ahead and to catch a glimpse of how dire the consequences might really be.

In the 1960s, Havel wrote from "below," as he put it, from the perspective of an outsider looking in at the system. Now in the 1970s, it was too dangerous to be on the outside. Those who refused to sign the Declaration on the Entrance of Friendly Armies felt that the only choice was to emigrate. Those like Havel who stayed, who refused to sign, who could not collaborate, were in a new and uniquely dangerous position, one they did not yet understand. In *The Beggar's Opera*, Havel began to explore that dangerous terrain and the whole phenomenon of collaboration, where it begins morally, where it ends. What is excusable, what is not. Thus, the paradox of the thief Filch, as the only man who could be trusted, because he was the only one who was not a collaborator.

What Havel discovered, in exploring the notion of collaborating, was its insidious impact on identity, his favorite theme of the 1960s. "In a world of double and triple agents," Havel himself said years later, "they don't know who their master is, and the individual loses his identity in the end."[42] Jenny, the "prostitute with a heart of gold," who herself collaborated with the police to give up Macheath, in return for a pardon for her father who has been sentenced to die, gives the warning:

> Jenny: Look, Mack — you can't exist as two different people — one
> who does the will of others, and the other who looks on in disgust.

We all need — to a certain extent, anyway — to belong to ourselves, because not belonging to ourselves means not having a identity, and therefore, de facto, not to be at all. As you know, my profession compels me to belong to myself less than other women. The thing they often consider their most valuable asset, doesn't, in my case, belong to me at all, but to the marketplace. Yet I want to belong to myself because I want to be myself. Is it any wonder that I am all the more protective of the little of me that is still under my control, and thanks to which I still *am* at all?[43]

In the end, save for the courageous Filch, all the characters are equally caught up in the system. Play the game, so you can communicate with others, so you can join in the struggle for change. Is that the moral of Havel's *The Beggar's Opera*?

At one point, Peachum cries out in momentary agony at the consequences of collaboration:

Peachum: Do you have the slightest inkling of what that means? Wearing two faces for so long? The ceaseless vigilance, day and night, the deception, keeping secrets, pretending to be someone else? Constantly trying to fit into a world you condemn, and to renounce the world to which you really belong?[44]

It is an anguish that everyone in the audience on November 1, 1975, could understand. That is why they were there, because they chose to wear one face only.

Looking back on that unique event, Havel's biographer Edá Kriseová was overwhelmed by its significance. A theatrical event had transcended the theater.

Something happened up there that I've never been able to understand. For me it was a mess of fuck-ups — curtains opened poorly, slips of the tongue, sweating faces. But with the passage of time, I realize it wasn't a matter of a theatrical performance at all, but of something that managed to happen under absolutely incredible circumstances.[45]

Indeed, nothing could alter the spirit of the event. Something had happened that night. People had gathered, people had risked their safety, their livelihoods, their reputations, all for a performance in the theater. It would bond them together. It would become the basis for a new society.

From that day on, the answer to: "Were you at Horní Počernice?" would become one of identity. It would define who you were on November 1, 1975, and in the years to come. That is why Krob's appearance in front of the curtain as the play began had a double meaning. "Were you at Horní Počernice?" was not only a question that was being asked by the authorities; it was also a question being asked by the courageous few who chose to live in truth by putting on a play.

Twenty years later in 1995, Krob would assemble his actors from the cast at Horní Počernice to perform once again *The Beggar's Opera*, this time at the Theatre on the Balustrade. "Putting on Havel's play was important for me," he said on that twentieth anniversary. "I replaced the word 'theater' with 'life.' And if you live like that, it won't be easy; you'll have a lot of conflicts, problems, doubts, but at least you won't sign something that you would be ashamed of later."[46]

Meanwhile, the performance of *The Beggar's Opera* on November 1, 1975 proved that attending a play could be an act of protest, that performing in a play could be an act of courage, that a theatrical event could be an expression of freedom — the highest expression, in fact, in that culture at the time.

For Havel, in that hopeless chapter of his life in the theater, a public performance of his play had taken place and a new ensemble had been created.

> For me the most important thing was that, for the first time in seven years (and the only time in the next [fifteen] to follow), I had seen a play of mine on the stage, and I could see with my own eyes that I was still capable of writing something that could be performed. All these events made me feel I had something left in me, and gave me energy for further enterprises.[47]

1974–1975: "SECOND WIND"

> A writer . . . can abandon everything proven; step beyond his initial experience of the world, with which he is by now all too familiar; liberate himself from what binds him to his own tradition, to public expectation and to his own established position; and try for a new and more mature self-definition, one that corresponds to his present and authentic experience of the world. In short, he can find his "second wind."[1]
>
> — Havel, "Second Wind"

Because Havel had lost a life in the theater, he was forced to rediscover himself as a playwright. But in the mid-seventies, he was still searching for that "second wind," as he called it.

In 1974, Havel drove his Mercedes, bought with royalties from his productions in Europe and America, and parked in the parking lot of the Trutnov Brewery, ten miles from Hrádeček. It was his first day of work at the brewery, a job that was to last for ten months.[2]

Finances were not the only reason that he took the job. Nor was it Czechoslovakia's "antiparasite" law, which said that if you did not work, you could be jailed. (In fact, you had to have a stamp on your identification papers saying you were employed.) Rather, it was, primarily, the pain of isolation. He needed a change. The long stretch of inactivity was becoming unbearable. He wanted to get out of his hiding place, to be among people. There was another reason, too, for his gloominess at that time. During this period of détente, many of his western friends and collaborators avoided the banned writers in Czechoslovakia, so as not to provoke the authorities and sabotage attempts at rapprochement. After that exhilarating taste of freedom abroad in the spring of 1968, this withdrawal only intensified his sense of isolation.

During that time, Havel was not the only writer who was frustrated, isolated, bored, and in need of money. Countless writers and intellectuals had lost their jobs either because the institutions or journals where they worked were liquidated under normalization, or because they were fired from television or movie studios because they had not supported the Soviet invasion. They were taking all kinds of manual jobs, the only ones available to them — water surveyors, geological researchers, garbage collectors, window cleaners, ambulance drivers, coal stokers, castlekeepers, night watchmen. "Reading plays by Ionesco was boring in comparison," says Tomáš Vrba, a professor of cultural history, who worked as a metal construction worker and a bricklayer.[3] The novelist/playwright Ivan Klíma held numerous jobs, including messenger, surveyor's assistant, and smuggler of books and manuscripts. "I even drove a train without derailing it," he wrote.[4] Klíma described these experiences in his book of short stories entitled *My Golden Trades*. In his afterword, he said of the value of these experiences to writers:

> Life sometimes put them in situations writers in a free country almost never experience. . . . I believe . . . that most of what I have

written does not rely on the existence of any particular regime; it is linked to our human existence, to our civilization and its problems.[5]

At the brewery, Havel was assigned the task of rolling barrels in the basement, which he did along with a number of gypsies who were also employed there. He was surprised at his coworkers' reaction:

I must say they accepted me wonderfully well. You know, I've done many things in my life, and I've even worked manually for a number of years, but I have always suffered, and still suffer, from something that might be called awkwardness or shyness . . . perhaps it's a holdover from my ancient experience as a "son of the manor," that is, the child of a bourgeois family who had certain privileges which he saw not as an advantage, but as a handicap. When I started working at the brewery, I understandably took those feelings of awkwardness and fear with me, and I was all the more delighted to discover that the other workers liked me and accepted me without the slightest reluctance.[6]

Andrej Krob recalls Havel's fascination with his new occupation:

He had been in the brewery only a few weeks and he was sold on it . . . it was like a trip into another universe for him. For a few months he rolled barrels in the basement, but he soon wanted to learn how the barrels were manufactured, who made the iron hoops, what was put into the barrels, and suddenly he was giving us long lectures on the world of beer brewing. He was a world-class expert. He has an ability to understand things quickly, to perfectly analyze a situation he finds himself in out of the blue, something he has minimal information on. . . . With him, not a single thing remains unfinished; not a single word is said in vain. Every second, every hour has purpose, he knows what for.[7]

Somehow, Havel's experience at the brewery provided a respite from the monotony and gloom. After almost four years of isolation, he was again in an active mode.

For me personally, the first noticeable break in the long and boring sentence of the 1970s was 1975. . . . [I]t was time to stop being merely a passive object of those "victories written by history," as Václav Bělohradský calls them, and to try to become their subject for a moment. In other words, it was time to stop waiting to see what "they" would do, and do something myself, compel them for a change to deal with something they hadn't counted on.[8]

Then, in 1975, three events broke this long sentence of silence and inactivity. One, of course, was the performance of *The Beggar's Opera* at Horní Počernice. Another was in the form of a letter, and the third was the writing of two new one-act plays.

In the spring, Havel decided it was time to stop taking a passive stance and to do something instead. So he sat down and wrote a long "open" letter to Dr. Gustáv Husák, General Secretary of the Czechoslovak Communist Party. Dated April 8, the letter was a bold articulation of what Havel later summarized as "the sad situation in our country . . . the profound spiritual, moral and social crisis hidden behind the apparent tranquility of social life."[9] He urged Husák to take responsibility for the general state of misery in which his fellow countrymen lived, a state of fear and apathy produced by the policies of normalization and the surveillance of the secret police. The spiritual and moral void in which the country found itself was in fact very much like a living death, he said. He expressed his deep fear for the consequences to national consciousness and history itself.[10]

According to Havel's friends, the writing of this letter was an act of political suicide. Since 1969, Husák had been carrying out the policies of normalization with low-key and deliberate efficiency, stifling any possibilities of protest. Until now, no one had challenged him publicly. After Havel sent his letter on April 8, Pavel Landovský secretly photocopied and distributed it to theaters in Slovakia. Copies also made their way through underground channels to sources abroad, where it was published and broadcast in Prague on Western radio stations. Husák did not respond, at least not publicly, but that was not the point. With this first open expression of protest, a new era in Czech history began. For the first time, the country's leading and banned playwright had given clear, cogent voice to the oppression by the regime that was suffocating its people. A bold and courageous act of dissidence had been performed.

> The letter, on a primary level, was a kind of autotherapy: I had no idea what would happen next, but it was worth the risk. I regained my balance and my self-confidence. I felt I could stand up straight

again, and that no one could accuse me any longer of not doing anything, of just looking on in silence at the miserable state of affairs. I could breathe more easily because I had not tried to stifle the truth inside me. I had stopped waiting for the world to improve and exercised my right to intervene in that world, or at least to express my opinion about it. At the same time, it had a wider significance; it was one of the first coherent — and generally comprehensible — critical voices to be heard here, and a general response was not long in coming. Obviously I had hit a moment when all this endless waiting around had begun to get on a lot of people's nerves, people who were tired of their own exhaustion.[11]

Once again, Havel was displaying an uncanny instinct for the times and his place in it, as well as the courage to define his identity in those times. It was this act of courage and self-liberation that freed Havel and helped him find his "second wind" in the theater.

1975: *AUDIENCE* AND *VERNISSAGE*

The important thing is that we're all in the same damn boat here, so let's act like it —[1]

— Havel, *Audience*

After he wrote the letter to Husák, Havel awaited a response, but none was forthcoming. Meanwhile, summer was approaching and, with it, the annual gathering of writers for a weekend at Hrádeček. He was looking forward to the camaraderie. As he described it in an essay called "Light on a Landscape": "After 1969, they all had found themselves in a situation similar to mine; that is to say, they were banned in their native country and publicly disgraced for their beliefs concerning society."[2]

Feeling freer and more invigorated than he had in years, Havel sat down, and, in the spirit of the moment, dashed off a one-act play to amuse the friends who would be gathering at Hrádeček. Unlike his earlier plays, this one was written in a matter of hours, and he made no changes. After all, it was all in fun, and all in the family. He dedicated it to the memory of Alfred Radok, his mentor at the ABC Theater.

Called *Audience*, this two-character play was inspired by his experiences at the brewery and featured characters brand new to the Havel canon: a burly foreman named Sládek and a reticent dissident named

Vaněk, who is also a banned playwright. The time is the present, and their brief conversation takes place in Sládek 's office at the brewery. His desk is covered with glasses and empty beer bottles. A case of beer lies on the floor beside the desk. There are piles of junk along the walls, and in the corners are broken valves, an old radio, piles of yellow newspaper, and other odds and ends. On the wall is a painting of the good soldier Schweik with an innkeeper. A decorative sign beneath it reads: "Living Is Easy Where Brewers Keep Busy." Sládek is seated at this desk, wearing a worker's smock, his head in his hands. He is snoring loudly.

Vaněk enters, wearing a heavy work coat and boots. He sits down timidly and politely declines the beer that his boss presses upon him, explaining that he is not a beer drinker. But Sládek prevails:

> Sládek: Well, don't worry, we gonna break you in over here. Oh yeah, you gonna get used to drinking beer, no problem. We all drink it here, everybody — it's kind of like a tradition or something we got in this brewery . . .[3]

While Vaněk pretends to sip the beer, Sládek inquires about his work — rolling barrels of beer along with his fellow workers who are mostly gypsies (notably, the inebriated Sherkezy). How's it going? How does he like it here? Is he getting along with everyone? "Not too bad" or "Fine, thank you," Vaněk replies alternately. Good, says Sládek, just do your job and stay out of trouble, "especially in your case."[4]

The "case" to which Sládek refers is, of course, Vaněk's status, that of a forbidden playwright. Sládek inquires about Vaněk's writing — "Theater plays, huh?" — and even suggests he write a play about a brewery some day. And by the way, since he is a celebrity, does Vaněk happen to know his favorite star, the popular stage and television actress Jiřina Bohdalová, whose poster is on his wall? And what about the singer Karel Gott? (Both were actual performers, known to Havel personally. Indeed, throughout the play, Havel makes no attempt to hide the similarity between Vaněk's circumstances and his own, while at the same time not insisting that they are in fact the same.)

As multiple bottles of beer are consumed by Sládek, who keeps pouring it into both their glasses, and multiple trips to the lavatory are taken (during which Vaněk pours his beer into Sládek's glass), Sládek reminds Vaněk that if anyone else were sitting at his desk, Vaněk wouldn't be working there ("And quit thanking me all the time, will ya! . . . Lemme tell ya, these days everybody's afraid of gettin' their tits caught in the ringer . . . the important thing is that we're all in the same damn boat . . .")[5] All he asks for, in return, is that Vaněk bring Jiřina Bohdalová to the brewery to meet Sládek. That's not too much to ask, is it?

More beer is consumed (by Sládek), and then finally he comes to the point of their conversation: "They" have come around to the brewery to inquire about him, "they" being the StB, as represented by a man named Mašek, who is actually a friend of Sládek — new on the job and anxious to succeed. It becomes clear that Sládek envies Vaněk for all the attention he is getting. For the first time, Havel is giving the perspective of the silent majority in a society condemned to silence that only the dissidents had broken:

> Brewmaster: You don't know shit! You've got it made! You write your damn plays — you roll your barrels — and they can all go to hell for all you care! What more do you want? The fact is, they're even afraid of you, man!
> Vaněk: That I would doubt —
> Brewmaster: They sure are! But what about me? Nobody gives a damn about me! Nobody's sendin' no reports about me nowhere! They can squeeze me every time they feel like! They got me by the balls! They can squash me like a bug — whenever they decide! Like a goddamn bug! You — you got it made![6]

For promoting Vaněk to a job in the warehouse, Sládek wants something from him in return. His friend Mašek needs "information" on Vaněk to pass on to the authorities each week, and frankly he has run out of ideas about what to tell them. After all, he explains, he hardly knows Vaněk.

> Brewmaster: You're what they call an intellectual, right? You keep up with politics, don't you? You're writing stuff, ain't you? Who the hell should know whatever the fuck it is they wanna know if not you?
> Vaněk: I'm sorry, but this would —
> Brewmaster: Look, in the warehouse, you'd have tons of time — so what's wrong with jottin' somethin' down on paper for me once a week? You could do that much for me, couldn't you? Look, I'm

gonna take care of you! You'd be happier there than a pig in shit! You can even take beer back there — as much as you want, too! It would be child's play for you! You're a writer, damn it, right? This Tonda Mašek really is a decent guy and he really does need it, so we can't just leave him hangin'! Damn it, didn't we just finish sayin' that we're all in this together? That we gotta give each other a hand? That we're gonna be a team here? Didn't we just toast to that now? You tell me — did we or did we not just toast to that?[7]

Vaněk refuses on moral grounds, saying he will never inform on anyone, including himself.

Vaněk: . . . I can't be snitching on myself.

Brewmaster: What do you mean snitch? Who's talkin' about snitchin' here?

Vaněk: It isn't because of me — it couldn't hurt me any more — but it really is a matter of principle! I just cannot, as a matter of principle, become a part of —

Brewmaster: A part of what? Go ahead and spell it out! You can't be a part of what?

Vaněk: A part of a way of doing things that I don't agree with — (A short, tense pause.)

Brewmaster: Well. So you can't. You can't then. That's great! Now you're showin' your true colors! Now you've really said it all! (Brewmaster gets up and begins pacing nervously around them room.) And what about me? You're just gonna let me sink, right? You're just gonna say, fuck you! It's okay if I end up being an asshole! Me, I can wallow in this shit, because I don't count. I ain't nothin' but a regular brewery hick — but the VIP here can't have any part of this! It's okay if I get smeared with shit, so long as the VIP here stays clean! The VIP is worried about the principle! But he don't bother about other people! Just as long as he comes out smellin' like a rose! The principle is dearer to him than another human being! That's typical of all of you!

Vaněk: Who?

Brewmaster: You, damn it! You intellectuals. VIPs! All that stuff's just smooth bullshit, except that you can afford it, because nothin' can ever happen to you, there's always somebody interested in how you doin', you always know how to fix that, you're still up there, even when you're down and out, whereas a regular guy like me is bustin' his ass and ain't got shit to show for it and nobody will stick up for him and everybody just fucks him and everybody blows him off and everybody feels free to yell at him and he ain't got no life at all, and, in the end, the VIP's will say, hell, he ain't got no principles! A soft job in the warehouse, you'd take that from me — but to take a piece of that shit I gotta walk knee-deep in every damn day along with it, that you don't wanna! No way! You're all too goddamn smart, you got everything worked out ahead of time, you know exactly how to look out for yourselves! Principles! Principles! Damn right you gonna fight for your damn principles — they're worth a fortune to you, you know just how to sell them principles, you're makin' a killin' on them, you're livin' off them — but what about me? I only get my ass busted for havin' principles! You always got a chance, but what kind of a chance have I got? Nobody's gonna take care of me, nobody's afraid of me, nobody's gonna write anything about me, nobody's gonna gimme a hand, nobody's interested in me, all I'm good for is to be the manure that your damn principles gonna grow out of so you can play heroes! And lookin' like a damn fool gonna be all I'm gonna have to show for it! You're gonna go back to all your actresses one day — you gonna floor 'em with how you rolled barrels — you gonna be a hero — but what about me? What can I go back to? Who's ever gonna pay any attention to me? Who's ever gonna appreciate anything I did? What the hell do I ever get out of life? What's in store for me? What?[8]

Sobbing, the crushed and bereft brewmaster finally begs Vaněk for one night with Jiřina Bohdalová, as the only consolation to his meaningless, anonymous existence.

For the first time, Havel is depicting real people in a real situation speaking real language. The play is full of references to contemporary figures like Jiřina Bohdalová, Karel Gott, and even the playwright Pavel Kohout. The absurdity arises not from an exaggeration of the language or the plot. Instead, Havel has found it in the truth of the scene, and he lets the story tell itself. The absurdity is part of the reality.

As in *The Beggar's Opera*, Havel is writing about man in the system, where values, morals and ethics are forsaken and in its stead a balance of power is created. Everyone is part of it, everyone is is involved, everyone profits together or goes down together. Never mind that everyone is corrupted in return, that everyone lives a lie rather than the truth. As Sládek says: "You'll scratch my back, I'll scratch his, he'll scratch mine and I'll scratch yours — so nobody's gonna get shortchanged in the deal. Let's not make life hell for each other!"[9] But Vaněk simply cannot be in the system. He can only "be."

Although language is not the main character of the play, as it is in *The Garden Party* and *The Memorandum*, Havel uses repetitions here to make his point. "Everything's all fucked up" is a phrase that Sládek keeps repeating. "We're all in the same boat" is another. "You married? Any kids?" is a question Sládek asks Vaněk four times during this half-hour play, although Vaněk answers on each occasion. Even with all this information, can we ever really know anyone, under the system as it is? At the end, Vaněk exits, leaving the sobbing Sládek with his head down on his desk. Then he hesitates, turns, enters again, sits down at the desk, and this time it is Vaněk who says: "Everything's all fucked up."

And so the story begins, all over again, just as it did in *The Garden Party* and *The Memorandum*, just as it does in Ionesco. Life is absurd, but in this deeply humanistic play, as Sládek says, at least "we're all in the same boat."

As such, *Audience* is a morality play, too, and a complex, richly layered one. As funny and entertaining as it is, it also has a dark side. We all may be in the same boat, but it is a sinking one. What, then, is the value of friendship and trust if it means betraying yourself? On the other hand, in a world where one can live in truth only in isolation from one's fellow man and ultimately at his expense, what is the value of truth?

On June 28, 1975, sitting in his living room at Hrádeček, Havel read the play aloud to fellow writers and friends. Kohout was there, and so was Ivan Klíma. "To my surprise, there was a wonderful response to that play," Havel said.[10] His fellow writers loved it, and they were unanimous in their enthusiasm for Vaněk.

Surprised and delighted that a work produced so effortlessly could provoke such a response, Havel dashed off another one-act that same year featuring the same character. Entitled *Vernissage*[11] (translated as *Unveiling* or *Private View*), it tells of Vaněk's visit to the new apartment of his friends, Věra and Michal, an upwardly mobile young couple, who proudly show off their new furniture and possessions, and try to seduce Vaněk to their lifestyle. The apartment, which the actor Pavel Landovský says was modeled after one occupied by a close mutual friend (though he won't say who), is described in detail. By normalization standards, it is lavishly decorated, chock-full of antiques and an eclectic assortment of objets d'art that the couple has obsessively collected, including a Chinese vase, a limestone Baroque angel, a Gothic Madonna, a folkloristic painting on glass, a Russian icon, a rococo musical clock, a bear hide with a stuffed head, and, inexplicably, a huge wooden confessional. The apartment also boasts high-tech appointments such as a stereo and a fully stocked bar cart with a bowl of stuffed oysters. It's a far cry from the simple apartment of *An Evening with the Family* of 1959, with the broken television and the dead canary in its cage.

As the curtain rises, Vaněk stands in the doorway, holding a bouquet of flowers behind his back for his hosts. He is the first guest in their newly decorated apartment, and once he crosses the threshold, he is in the land of the Lotus Eaters.

Vaněk has barely tasted his whisky (with ice, of course) before the hosts pounce upon him and begin their interrogation. Does he like their Turkish scimitar, and isn't that the ideal place for it over the fireplace? Did he know how much they paid for the confessional? The Gothic Madonna is Michal's favorite, it looks just right in that niche, doesn't it? Meanwhile, Vaněk had better get started on his place; after all, he can't live out of boxes forever. And meanwhile, what about Eva? When are they going to finally . . . ? There's an awkward moment. They put their records from Switzerland on the stereo; they pass around the bowl of sautéed groomblies ("Groomblies?" replies Vaněk, startled. "Never heard of them."). Season them with woodpeak, Věra suggests, and he should also taste her latest culinary adventure, liver with walnuts. By the way, how's it going in the brewery — pretty tough, hmmm?

On and on Michal and Věra up the ante, their aggression punctuated only by the chiming of the musical clock on the mantelpiece (an homage to Ionesco's *The Bald Soprano*), which periodically breaks into a classical tune. There's their son, Petr. You should see him! What a child! Only yesterday, he asked them: "Daddy, can a frog drown?" Outstanding, isn't he? Having a child is, well, everything. Why don't you and Eva . . . ? Never mind. Věra's such an ideal wife; Michal can't say enough about her. She works, she's a good homemaker, a good mother. And as for their sex life:

Věra: Why do you think Michal isn't drawn to other women? Because he knows that he doesn't have some mop-swinging wifey at home, but a real woman who knows how to take as well as give —

Michal: Of course. Věra is still just as attractive as always — I'd even say that now, after Pete, she has ripened even more — she has an astonishingly fresh and youthful body now — well judge for yourself! *(Michal undoes Věra's clothes, uncovering her breasts.)* Not bad, right?

Vaněk: Great —

Michal: Do you know what I will do, for example?

Vaněk: No —

Michal: I'll kiss her, switching from her ear to her neck and back — which really turns her on and I like it too — like this, look! *(Michal starts to kiss Věra, alternating between her ear and her neck; Věra groans excitedly.)*

Věra: Don't, darling no — please — wait — a little later, okay — come on — *(Michal stops kissing Věra.)*

Michal: We'll talk a little more first, then we'll show you more — to give you an idea of the range of our technique —[12]

The clock chimes again. The demonstration over, they encourage Vaněk to try married life with Eva. Who knows, it might solve all his problems; he'll stop making the rounds, chasing waitresses. After all, they're only saying it for his own good; they really care. Vaněk is their best friend.

Back to the interrogation, first Michal, then Věra. Why not try a sauna? Why the brewery? Get away to Switzerland, why don't you? Is it really necessary to mingle with Kohout and his crowd? (the Communists, you know). Can't you find a better job? As they assault him, Vaněk gets up quietly and backs toward the door. They press themselves on him.

Věra: You know that we're only trying to help you —

Michal: That we like you a lot —

Věra: That you are our best friend —

Michal: You cannot be this ungrateful!

Věra: We don't deserve this — not while we're trying to do so much for you!

Michal: Who do you think Věra has spent the whole afternoon baking the groombles for?

Věra: Who do you think Michal has bought that whiskey for?

Michal: Who do you think we wanted to play these records for? Why do you think I wasted all that hard currency on them, and dragged them half way across Europe?

Věra: Why do you think I dressed up like this, put the makeup and the perfume on, got my hair done?

Michal: Why do you think we fixed this place up like this anyway? Who do you think we're doing all this for? For ourselves? *(Vaněk is by the door now.)*

Vaněk: I'm sorry, but I'll be off now —

Věra: *(Agitated.)* Ferdinand! You can't just leave us here! You're not going to do that to us! You just can't pick up and go now: there's so much we still wanted to tell you! What are we going to do here without you? Don't you understand that? Stay, I beg you, will you stay here with us!

Michal: You haven't even seen our electric almond peeler yet!

Věra: See you later! And that you for the groombles —
(Vaněk is leaving, but before he closes the door behind him, Věra breaks into hysterical sobs. Vaněk stops and looks at her, not knowing what to do.)

Věra: *(Crying.)* You're selfish! A disgusting, unfeeling, inhuman egotist! An ungrateful, ignorant traitor! I hate you — I hate you so much — go away! Go away! *(Věra runs to the bouquet that she got from Vaněk, tears it out of the vase, and throws it at Vaněk.)*

Michal: *(To Vaněk.)* See what you're doing? Aren't you ashamed?[13]

As with *Audience*, the play ends in a standoff, without resolution. Vaněk remains, and they listen to the record playing the same song over and over again, "until the last spectator has left the theater," the stage directions say.

As with Sládek's need for Vaněk, Michal and Věra's need for him presents an irreconcilable paradox. They are dedicated to converting Vaněk to their way of life, and yet his opposition gives their life a purpose, a justification. Their efforts escalate until they break down, saying they need his approbation to justify their own morally bankrupt existence. But neither side can change. The play ends in a standoff, a frozen dialectic. Any change by one would jeopardize the identity of all. Once again, the system defines them in polarity. As for Vaněk, in neither play does he have what others think he has. Vaněk is not about "having." He is about "being."

Like *Audience*, its companion piece, *Vernissage* is grounded in reality, more than any of Havel's previous plays. But it takes a leap into an exaggerated hyper-reality bordering on the absurd, with the incongruous décor of the couple's apartment, their bizarre cuisine and their exhibitionist behavior.

Audience was subsequently typed out and printed by the *samizdat* press Edice Petlice (number 47, 1975) and reprinted at the end of the year in the new *samizdat* press Edice Expedice, or Expedition Express, (number 3, 1975), which Havel and his wife Olga founded together.

In contrast to the serious-minded preparation and deliberate dramaturgy of his previous full-length works, *Audience* and *Vernissage* were written spontaneously and effortlessly by a playwright who hardly took them seriously. Imagine, then, his surprise at their impact. By popular demand, they were staged the next summer at a festival (also called a garden party) at Hrádeček on the first weekend in August, 1976. Up the hill from Havel's house, the barn next to Andrej Krob's house was readied by the eager members of the Theatre on the Road, energized after their performance of *The Beggar's Opera* the previous November. Under Krob's direction, Havel found himself reluctantly playing Vaněk. Krob had a further surprise for his author/actor. Drawing from his own traumatic experience following *The Beggar's Opera* only months before, when he had been questioned for eleven hours at the police station by a rotating team of interrogators, Krob cast three actors in the role of Sládek (Jan Hraběta, Jan Kašpar, and Krob himself). One actor would exit during the course of the play and another would replace him.

The audience response was more than enthusiastic. Still, there was a larger question. What would happen to *Audience* and *Vernissage*? Where would they be performed? Havel's plays were banned throughout his country. Would they have a life?

Klaus Juncker had been working on this problem for several years. Increasingly alarmed about what was happening in Czechoslovakia, Juncker visited his playwright twice, once in 1974 and once in 1975. Šiklová's network was still getting underway, and of course Juncker was eager to obtain Havel's new work. But the surveillance of Havel was tight, and Juncker, as his foreign agent, was under suspicion too, as Havel fully realized. On one visit, the first thing Havel asked when they got into the car at the airport was whether Juncker had something with him that was typically Western. Juncker replied that he had brought Havel two bottles of his favorite whiskey. "No," Havel replied, "that can be bought in the foreign shops here." Then Juncker said that he had brought along a book by Rolf Hochhuth, with a picture of the Statue of Liberty on the cover. Havel instructed Juncker to put it visibly on the seat of the car, so it could be seen clearly. "Why?" asked Juncker. Havel replied: "Today there is a nice StB agent assigned to watch me, with nothing to report to his boss; now he will be able to report something. He's a good guy; we exchange sport results when we hear the football [soccer] scores." Then Havel added that the fellow who was assigned to watch Juncker could report it to his boss, too. Juncker was not amused. "It's easy to joke about those things today, but it was an extremely difficult situation," said Juncker.[14]

On his second visit in 1975, Juncker managed to smuggle copies of Havel's *Audience* and *Vernissage* out of the country.

> I was really scared; 30 years later, I can remember shaking and sweating as if I were going to be executed, every time I crossed the border. I had invented a kind of trick of how to get those manuscripts across the border: I asked Dilia [the Czech state writers' agency] to give me piles of prospective scripts and programs, and then I put Havel's short one act plays into those piles. The customs officials were of course too bored to check all these Dilia prospects, so they never found Václav Havel's manuscripts in the pile.[15]

After that visit, Juncker was denied a visa to return. The authorities had identified him as an agent who helped the dissidents, and he was not allowed in Czechoslovakia for the next thirteen years.

But Juncker had accomplished his mission. He had Havel's newest plays in hand, and immediately set to work placing them in European theaters. Thanks to Juncker, the popularity of *Audience* spread at a remarkable speed. Within months of the second reading at Hrádeček, Juncker had found the play a home for its foreign premiere, the Burgtheater in Vienna. Its artistic director, Achim Benning, admired Havel greatly and was sympathetic to his circumstances. Benning produced *Audience* and *Vernissage* on the Akademietheater stage, the Burgtheater's five-hundred-seat house. Thus began a long-distance artistic relationship that would sustain Havel over two dark decades. During that period, Benning willingly provided a "home away from home" for every new Havel play, so that Havel would know his work would see the light of day, and that somehow he was not writing in a void.

By the end of 1976, there were performances of *Audience* and *Vernissage* throughout Germany, at Trier, Gottingen, Munich, and Ingolstadt. In 1977, there were more than a dozen more in West Germany and Austria; in 1978, productions spread to Sweden, Switzerland, Finland, Belgium, and Holland. That year, the plays were performed at the Royal National Theatre of London and on BBC television. Meanwhile, on Czech soil, the circulation of *Audience* by *samizdat* (both as a written text, and later on a tape that was recorded in Sweden and smuggled back into Czechoslovakia) made it something of a cult work. As Havel describes it:

> Things began to happen to me. For example, I once picked up a hitchhiker and, without knowing who I was, he began to quote passages from that play [*Audience*]. Or I'd be sitting in a pub and I'd hear young people shouting lines from the play to each other across the room. That too was very encouraging, not only because it was a flattering reminder of happier days, when my plays were being performed, when it was almost a cultural duty to know them, but above all because it suggested to me that even a playwright who is cut off from his theater can still have an impact on his own domestic milieu. He is still an integral part of it.[16]

In September 1976, the Austrian Minister of Education invited Havel to the premiere of *Audience* and *Vernissage* at the Burgtheater. But Havel was not allowed to attend. As the Czechoslovak Foreign Ministry put it, he was "not a representative of Czech culture."[17] That year, he received the prestigious Austrian State Prize for European Literature.

In fact, Havel had no idea that what he thought of as an effortlessly written trifle (*Audience*), written just for the fun to it, would become a popular culture favorite and inspire a remarkable cycle of plays. Moreover, he had no clue that the character of Vaněk would resonate far beyond the borders of his land, and that these two plays — *Audience* and *Vernissage* — would be performed more than any of his other works. Above all, he never would have imagined that these plays would generate that "second wind" he had longed for as a writer.

> *Audience* and *Vernissage* are plays whose life is the most paradoxical. I wrote them quickly and spontaneously, just to amuse my friends.

I had no idea that these plays might entertain somebody else, somebody abroad. But now it seems that I was wrong. These two one act plays are the most frequently produced plays I've ever written [outside Czechoslovakia]. . . . It makes me feel slightly embarrassed, because somehow I cannot believe that my second wind is in these two miniatures and that all those long months and years of searching [*The Conspirators* and *Mountain Hotel*] were for nothing. The truth is that I really must write for a concrete audience (I wrote these two one act plays for my friends, for concrete persons, for concrete occasions, e.g., Kvartál). It means that I have to depend on what I know, on my concrete life experience and background and only through this authenticity can I give a more general testimony about the times we live in. It means that somehow I have to forget all those rational calculations and speculations, and open myself up to something which I call the existential dimension of the world.[18]

The character Vaněk appeared once again three years later, in a Havel one-act play called *Protest*. By 1978, Havel's situation had changed drastically, and he needed Vaněk to help dramatize these changes. It was as if Vaněk had come back of his own accord. And, remarkably enough, *Protest* was not the only play in which Vaněk reappeared in 1978. Tumultuous events would prompt his return.

1976: A NEW THEATRICAL HOME

I experience a lot of small, everyday pleasures. I feel happy when the weather is fine, when our roses aren't frostbitten, when my letter to Dr. Husák speaks to someone's soul, when I get a beautiful letter from Alfred Radok, when my friends come to see me and we have a good party, when I cook a meal that everyone likes, when we burn less fuel that we thought we would, when the carpenter makes us a nice piece of furniture and charges us less than I expected, and so on. But I get the greatest pleasure — and unfortunately this is becoming rarer and rarer — when I finish writing something and feel it's finished and that I accomplished what I set out to do.[1]

—Havel, "It Always Makes Sense to Tell the Truth"

In 1975, when asked in by an interviewer: "Have you experienced something you might call happiness in the last few years?" Havel responded with the above. The answer was to be found at Hrádeček.

Indeed, it was becoming clear that Hrádeček would provide him with more than a safe haven. The Balustrade in Prague had been Havel's theatrical home in the 1960s. Now, after eight years of exile, Hrádeček and the Theatre on the Road had become Havel's theatrical home in the 1970s.

By 1976, Hrádeček was identified as a haven for writers, artists, actors, musicians — a safe place to retreat, far from the pressures of Prague. There was a warm and welcoming atmosphere, and Havel and Olga's hospitality became famous. During the summer, friends gathered on the weekends and sat on the lawn, picnicking, laughing, talking, walking in the woods, picking mushrooms. Adjacent to the main farmhouse there was a side building that used to be a hayloft. The Havels used as a studio, where rock concerts were held and equipment for visiting bands was stored. The studio bore a street sign saying "Na zbořenci,"[2] which had been torn down along with others in 1968 — a common sport enjoyed by the intellectuals to make it difficult for Russian soldiers to find their way through Prague. Olga kept her scythe there, and Havel stored his tools; he had numerous projects, including the construction of a white picket fence, of which he was extremely proud. The set designer Libor Fára built furniture there, and his sculpture made from farm implements was placed in the garden. On the other side of the house was Olga's vegetable garden. And that was Hrádeček, the center of cultural life in the 1970s.

The special time at Hrádeček was an extended weekend in early July around Olga's birthday, July 11. As Olga's biographer, Pavel Kosatík, describes it, people began coming on Thursday and would leave as late as Wednesday. These events were rich, with many things happening at the same time. There were exhibitions of photos and paintings. There were rock concerts in which several bands would perform. There were costume parties and contests for children organized by Olga. Sometimes, there were open rehearsals of Theatre on the Road organized by Krob. Almost everyone, it seemed, had a guitar. People played in the meadow or by the fire. Dozens of people slept in the house, with the overflow relegated to the forest or to Krob's house. (One of the reasons that Havel had renovated his house, says Krob, was to create more bedrooms for guests.) Every room was open, no place was forbidden. Olga did not particularly enjoy cooking, though she was fond of reading recipes. Usually, Havel did most of the cooking, though according to his friends, he seasoned food with too much pepper. "Cooking is his passion," Olga recalls. "He cares more about his reputation as a cook than as a playwright. He loves to

experiment in the kitchen. . . . He doesn't cook for himself; only for others."[3] For this long weekend, the Havels devised a special solution: people could also bring food and prepare it themselves. Havel kept the freezer
stocked. He and Olga both hated disorder, and yet, paradoxically, they
had created a casual and open system of hospitality. After these long
weekends, they spent two to three days cleaning up the house, but during the visits they were permissive and free.

Play readings, Kvartál meetings, theater performances, garden parties,
rock concerts, festivals. A rich and lively cultural life blossomed at
Hrádeček around that first production of *Audience* in the barn. It would
last, in varying capacities, through traumas and triumphs, for twenty years.

1976–1979: *LIVING IN TRUTH*

> When I speak of living within the truth, I naturally do not have in
> mind only products of conceptual thought, such as a protest or a let-
> ter written by a group of intellectuals. It can be any means by which
> a person or a group revolts against manipulation: anything from a
> letter by intellectuals to a workers' strike, from a rock concert to a
> student demonstration, from refusing to vote in the farcical elec-
> tions, to making an open speech at some official congress, or even a
> hunger strike . . .[1]
>
> —Havel, "The Power of the Powerless"

All those events of 1975 — the letter to Dr. Husák, the production of
The Beggar's Opera at Horní Počernice, the writing of the first two Vaněk
plays — imbued Havel with a new energy and a sense of possibility that
something indeed could happen. And something did.

Earlier in 1975, Havel and Jan Lopatka, critic and editor, had met in
a favorite wine cellar on Panská Street to dream about founding a new underground *samizdat* press that would complement the existing Edice
Petlice. This underground press essentially published work by well-known
authors who had been banned, whereas Edice Expedice (Expedition Press),
as they called the new one, would also provide opportunities for younger,
underground writers. With the newly founded Edice Expedice, Havel introduced a courageous new policy, that of taking responsibility for the publication itself. That is to say, the author did not sign the publication, but
rather, the publisher did. For example, the volumes were signed: "In 1976,
Václav Havel made copies for himself and his friends." That way, he took

all the risk. The new press also provided the invaluable service of reproducing work that had been published elsewhere in the world but was forbidden in Czechoslovakia, as well as the work of banned translators. In its early stages, Edice Expedice published a number of authors, including Havel, Bohumil Hrabal, Jiří Dienstbier, Pavel Kohout, Edá Kriseová, Pavel Landovský, Osip Mandelstam, George Orwell, Jan Patočka, Jaroslav Seifert, Egon Bondy, and a newcomer named Ivan Martin Jirous.

Jirous, or Magor, as they called him, was the manager of a raggle-taggle rock group called the Plastic People of the Universe. The group was named after a song by Frank Zappa, the American singer of the 1960s who was worshipped by the Czech underground culture. It started in 1967 as a neighborhood band from Břevnov, a residential quarter of Prague — a scruffy bunch of teenagers in love with the Rolling Stones, the Velvet Underground, and the Doors, whose music they had learned from records. By the early 1970s, they had begun to develop their own style, setting their music to poems by Egon Bondy and other original compositions. Known for their long hair, rough lyrics, and provocative antiestablishment style, the Plastic People became a favorite target of the police. Under normalization, rock music was in effect suppressed, and groups had to conform to the rules (no long hair, no English lyrics) or disband. So the Plastic People's license was revoked, and they were forbidden to play in public, in Prague or anywhere. Instead, they went underground, playing at private parties and in remote countryside villages. The police hunted them down, broke up their concerts, beat the musicians, and carted them away in patrol wagons. At one concert in 1974, hundreds of spectators were arrested, and students who attended were expelled from school.

Havel knew of Jirous because he published some of his poetry through Edice Expedice. Jirous represented the underground musical culture, a segment of society that fascinated Havel. He was eager to learn more about it. A mutual friend suggested that the two men meet and get to know each other better. They spent an evening together and listened to music all night long. Havel sensed that Jirous' circle of underground musicians, with its protest lyrics and passionate youthful following, was an ally.

[T]he music was a profoundly authentic repression of the sense of
life among these people, battered as they were by the misery of this
world. There was disturbing magic in the music, and a kind of inner

warning. Here was something serious and genuine, an internally free articulation of an existential experience that everyone who had not become completely obtuse must understand. . . . Suddenly I realized that, regardless of how many vulgar words these people used or how long their hair was, truth was on their side . . . in their music was an experience of metaphysical sorrow and a longing for salvation.[2]

Jirous invited Havel to attend a concert, but it never happened. A few weeks later, in March 1976, nineteen people were arrested by the police, including the Plastics and some of their followers. Jirous' wife sought out Havel's help, albeit with some trepidation, fearing that an association with Havel might further anger the police. But a trial date had been set for September 16, and she was desperate.

Havel was at Hrádeček when he learned of the arrest. He was outraged by what he saw as an "attack by the totalitarian system on life itself, on the very essence of human freedom and integrity . . . on the spiritual and intellectual freedom of man, camouflaged as an attack on criminality, and therefore designed to gain support form a disinformed public."[3] He immediately set out for Prague to do something about it. Anger was mounting in various segments of society, and people who ordinarily would not have banded together were united in protest. Seeing this as a precious opportunity to mobilize various factions behind the common cause of freedom, Havel began his campaign, aided by the philosopher Jiří Němec, a colleague from the 1960s.

With the same passion for plotting the structure of his plays, he plotted the strategy to protest the arrest. Havel arranged interviews with the musicians through Radio Free Europe, and the fate of the band became an immediate focus of international attention. He sent messages of protest to all the embassies. Along with Němec and other Czech writers and philosophers, Havel wrote an open letter to the German novelist Heinrich Böll, appealing to writers and artists from other countries to join them in support; that letter resulted in a petition signed by over seventy people. They organized protests, they circulated petitions. Above all, their campaign mobilized different factions, hitherto isolated and adversarial, who united for a common cause. Once the cause attracted international media attention, the campaign took on a life of its own.

The trial was held in September 1976; in a subsequent article entitled "The Trial," Havel likened the event to a performance of absurdist theater. In the hall outside the courtroom, Czechs of many different factions, from long-haired youths to former Communist Party functionaries, waited together. As Havel, who was in the group, describes it, there was a sense of "equality, solidarity, conviviality, togetherness and willingness to help each other, an atmosphere evoked by a common cause and a common threat."[4]

That gathering, that sense of solidarity, laid the groundwork for a new initiative. As Havel told the playwright Tom Stoppard: "The government thought they could hurt them without anyone caring. But to their surprise, the worst thing happened — the fate of the musicians made a unity among different kinds of people."[5]

And so the cast was assembled and the stage set for a new drama. It was to be called Charter 77.

CHARTER 77

No society, no matter how good its technological foundation, can function without a moral foundation.[1]

— Jan Patočka

As the months passed after the trial, they all agreed with Havel — the playwright Pavel Kohout; the journalist Petr Uhl; the politician and diplomat Jiří Hájek; Zdeněk Mlynář, the former general secretary of the Communist Party (under Dubček); and Ludvík Vaculík, the founder of Edice Petlice . Something had happened around that trial, something, as Havel said

that should not be allowed simply to evaporate and disappear but which ought to be transformed into some kind of action that would have a more permanent impact, one that would bring this something out of the air onto solid ground.[2]

Furthermore, it should be put in writing, the group decided, not a one-time manifesto but a document that would represent something more permanent and would unite two hitherto disparate elements: the dissidents (forbidden writers, intellectuals, artists, philosophers) and the hippie movement that called itself the underground (inspired by the West and the image of John Lennon). The dissident movement was tiny, just a handful of people, whereas there were thousands in the underground. Havel and his fellow writers represented the former, the Plastic People the latter.

And so it came to pass that on December 10, 1976, and in meetings that followed, a statement was prepared, a declaration on human rights called, at Kohout's suggestion, Charter 77. It was brief — just 1,800 words — and to the point. Its primary thesis was that the government of the Czechoslovak Socialist State was in violation of the Helsinki agreement on human rights.

This agreement, developed at the 1975 Helsinki Conference on Security and Cooperation in Europe, had been in effect since March 1976. It was binding on the countries that signed it, including Czechoslovakia. And yet, the human rights and freedoms set forth in its covenants were, according to Charter 77, nonexistent in Czechoslovakia. The Charter maintained that Czech citizens were currently denied the freedom of public expression, the freedom to live without fear, the right to an education, the right to form trade unions, the right of free religious expression, the freedom to criticize the society through the media, the freedom to leave and reenter the country, and the right to privacy. Czech citizens, the Charter maintained, were subject to police threats, surveillance, and harassment. Their homes were searched, their mail was open, their phones were bugged, they were followed.

The group kept silent as to the Charter's actual authorship. Havel maintained that it was not important; the point, he said, was that the statement was a "an expression of a collective will."[3] During these meetings, the group refined the declaration, and it was decided that Havel, Jiří Hájek, and Jan Patočka, the eminent Czech philosopher, would be the spokespersons. Hájek, age sixty-four at the time, had been Dubček's Foreign Minister, and prior to that ambassador to the United States and the UN. Patočka, age seventy, was a revered Czech professor of philosophy, forbidden to teach in 1948 by the Communists. Havel, age forty, was the youngest of the group (and the only one who had a car, a considerable asset under the circumstances). Hájek represented the Communists; Patočka, the anti-Communists; and Havel, the dissidents and the underground. It was an eminent group that offered wisdom, experience, and perspective. And it was an alliance with representation across the spectrum, from Marxists to anti-Marxists, from Catholics to agnostics, from intellectuals to artists.

With the declaration now prepared, the next task was getting signatures. Fortuitously, it was Christmastime, so the ten appointed gatherers could collect signatures in the normal course of holiday visits and hopefully avoid scrutiny by the police. Each was given assignments: Mlynář would recruit signatures from the ex-Communist circles, Havel from the writers' circles, and so on. The plan was that these signatures would be brought to Havel's apartment in Dejvice and arranged in alphabetical order, to be readied for delivery to the Federal Assembly. Typed copies of the petition would be sent to each signer. The deadline for collecting signatures was targeted for January l, 1977; they would be delivered to the officials one week later.

As the group gathered in Havel's apartment during those last days of December — former university professors, ministers, Communist Party secretaries, writers — the air was tense with anticipation. Above all, there was a feeling of solidarity. As Havel described it:

> Something had taken shape here that was historically quite new: the embryo of a genuine social tolerance . . . a phenomenon which — no matter how the Charter turned out — would be impossible to wipe out in the national memory. . . . It was a stepping out toward life, toward a genuine state of thinking about common matters, a transcendence of their own shadow.[4]

By January 5, 1977, the first round of collecting signatures was completed, with some 243 names, according to Havel. Signers included Marxists and anti-Marxists, Catholics and Trotskyists, professors and factory workers, the broadest representation the group could recruit. The next step was to deliver Charter 77 to various seats of government, along with the signatures.

As if the dramatic buildup weren't enough, there was another player who made an explosive entrance in the already combustible scene. Pavel Landovský had been recently fired from the Činoherní klub for his political sympathies, along with several other actors. He had been writing episodes for a radio series under a nom de plume. In 1976, as with Havel, his life in the theater and in politics began to intertwine.

On the morning of January 7, Landovský found himself cast in a leading role of an absurdist political thriller: the delivery of Charter 77. The plan was a two-step one: to mail 243 individual copies of the Charter to each of the signers, and then to deliver the master copy to the government, along with the 243 original signatures. Havel would drive the lead car; Landovský would follow in his Saab.

What actually transpired was a scene that couldn't have been more dramatic if Havel had written the screenplay and cast himself and Landovský in it. Havel had been up almost all night before, punchy with laughter and nervousness, addressing envelopes at Zdeněk Urbánek's apartment to be mailed to the signers. Returning to his apartment for a few hours sleep, he found that someone (the police, sensing that something was about to happen) had slashed the brakes of his Mercedes. He called Landovský, who immediately recruited a friend (a car mechanic) to go to Havel's apartment and repair them. That served as a decoy for the police, who were watching Havel's car, while Havel walked back to Urbánek's apartment to get the envelopes. Landovský drove to Urbánek's, where Havel and Vaculík were stamping envelopes, their giddy laughter now tinged with nervous anticipation. The task now completed, the three men loaded the sacks of envelopes into Landovský's car and started out on their journey.

Within blocks, the scene became wild. Landovský had noticed with suspicion several Škoda MB cars parked outside. As it happened, the police had purposely picked the beat-up Škodas for the occasion. Landovský relived what follows with relish:

> As soon as we left Urbánek's apartment, I could see in my rear-view mirror that they were chasing us. So I stepped on the accelerator and I turned on a curve to the right, but it was January, the roads were icy, and the car was spinning. But because I'm a good driver, I kept going. The police, however, weren't quite as good as I was — they crashed, six cars in all. I said to Havel: There's a mailbox over there. Put all those envelopes in. Vašek got out of the car and started stuffing envelopes into the mailbox. I could see that other police cars were approaching, so he only had time to put 40 envelopes into the mailbox. He got back into the car, and the chase continued. I was driving down Lenin Street, and there was a red light at the intersection. Vaculík shouted: it's a red light! I said: I see. But I wanted to test the guy following us. So I went through the intersection and so did my pursuer. So it was clear that it was a policeman in an unmarked car. Then, I made an error. I went down a one-way street, and there were 4 police cars in front of us, and two behind us. So it was all over. I stopped and locked all the car doors. The cops got out of their cars, surrounded the Saab, and put their ID cards against the

windows — about 6 to 8 of them. They were beating the windows and yelling: "Open the car in the name of the Republic!" Havel said: "Well, this is a fine start for the fight for human rights. But Pavel, I suppose these gentlemen are really police officers. We should open the door." So I opened the door, the cops dragged Vašek out of the car and then Vaculík, but I was fighting with them and yelling. Within seconds, there were two circles surrounding us — the first, consisting of cops. But there was another circle of ordinary pedestrians who stopped to see what was happening. Someone said: "Come here, look! Landovský is shooting a movie again." The cops realized that this was going wrong now (they didn't want an audience) so one of the cops sat down in my car, took out his gun, and said: "Follow the car in front of you." So I drove myself to prison. On the way to prison, the cop sitting beside me was saying things like: "Jesus, you're going to be in a lot of trouble. They're so mad at you. I wouldn't be surprised if they shoot you."[5]

In Edá Kriseová's account, Landovský also threatened the policeman who was taking him in, saying that unless the policeman promised to bring him toothpaste and cigarettes in jail, Landovský would drive the car straight into a wall.

Havel, Vaculík, and Landovský were detained and interrogated, and their houses were searched. The period following the arrest, which included an all-night interrogation and his (temporary) release, was, according to Havel, "the wildest weeks of my life." Havel and Olga's apartment in Dejvice looked, as Havel described it, "like the New York Stock Exchange must have looked after the crash of '29, or like some center of revolution."[6] Friends and signers of Charter 77 were interrogated all day long at Ruzyně Prison; at night they returned to the Havels' to compare notes, draft statements, meet with the press and make telephone calls. Finally, on January 24, Havel was taken in for interrogation at Ruzyně and locked in a seven-by-twelve-foot cell together with a burglar of grocery stores, where he remained until May 20. He was charged with subversion of the republic for his letter to Dr. Husák and for being the chief organizer of Charter 77. The authorities also concocted a convoluted charge related to the smuggling of texts from Prague to Paris. He was sentenced to a term of fourteen months in jail.

During this imprisonment, which would last almost five months, a number of traumatic events occurred.

First, and particularly painful, was the anti-Charter campaign promoted by the regime, which succeeded in mobilizing members of the artistic community against the Chartists. On January 28, actors, television personalities, journalists, musicians, and visual artists gathered in the National Theater to hear speeches against the Charter delivered by leading performers, and then lined up to sign an anti-Charter declaration. The event was broadcast live on Czech national television. Especially devastating was the condemnation of the Charter by the actors at the Theatre on the Balustrade. Meanwhile, the authorities mounted an aggressive anti-Havel smear campaign. He was denounced in the newspaper *Rudé právo* and accused of being a CIA agent; his past was dug up and scrutinized, and a television program was produced to discredit his character.

Then Professor Patočka and Jiří Hájek, the Charter cospokesmen, were dragged into police headquarters and subjected to intense interrogations. Traumatized, Patočka suffered a heart attack on March 4 and died nine days later. As over a thousand sympathizers gathered for his funeral, the sound of the police helicopters overhead and the revving of the police motorcycles drowned out the priest's eulogy. The police also photographed the mourners, many of whom found themselves fired from their jobs or expelled from school.

In an essay entitled "Last Conversation," written from Ruzyně prison on May 1, 1977, Havel spoke of Patočka and his influence. Havel had first heard him speak when he was sixteen, at a lecture on phenomenology, existentialism and philosophy (Patočka was a student of Heidegger). Havel was struck by the "inconspicuous moral greatness of this man,"[7] and how, thanks to Patočka's influence, Havel came to understand himself better and became more confident in his thinking. He also remembers their last conversation during a break between interrogations in the prison waiting room for interrogees. They talked about death, of all topics, and Havel was so looking forward to their next conversation, feeling that he had so much to learn from Patočka and so much to say to him.

> And then came the news that my last discussion with Patočka will truly remain the last. I will not describe here how I bore the news, what I felt . . . for me the news also had the peculiar and paradoxical context . . . we had been talking about death! I have always been struck by a strange thing: that people who spent their whole lives thinking about death, who understood it and its meaning so well, die too. [D]eath should at least have some respect for them, or be

ashamed in the presence of those whose spirit lived with him so long, so intimately. And again and again I am shocked by the realization that this is not the case and that the exact opposite seems to hold: that it is precisely those who are most aware of him he cares most about, perhaps out of fear that eventually they would be able to discover his secret; so for them he often comes sooner than for others. But has he really outwitted them? . . . [I]t seems that those like Professor Patočka, with all they were, thought out, did, somehow keep being — here — there — somewhere — more *urgently* than the many of whom death has nothing to fear, and thus no reason to rush.[8]

Finally, and most traumatic, were the circumstances under which Havel was released from prison. Procedure required that a prisoner write a request for release, which Havel did. The authorities used this as an opportunity to attempt to damage him permanently. They added a clause to the text of his request, saying that he had resigned as spokesperson of Charter 77, and publicized this falsification in the press. Nothing could have humiliated Havel more.

The public disgrace was worse than I'd expected: they said, for instance, that I'd given up the position of spokesman in prison, which wasn't true. . . . The first days after my return, my state of mind was such that every madhouse in the world would have considered me a suitable case for treatment. In addition to all the familiar, banal symptoms of post-prison psychosis, I felt boundless despair mingled with a sort of madcap euphoria.[9]

This event, or as he called it, this "public disgrace," would become his greatest trauma of the 1970s, one that would shape his future life in politics and in the theater for years to come.

Meanwhile, despite all their efforts to the contrary, the authorities made a major strategic error: By making their campaign against Havel so public, they stimulated the interest of the foreign press, who flocked to Havel's apartment in early January to interview the Chartists directly. They also provided extensive publicity for the Chartists' cause. During Havel's five months in prison, the Chartists continued to recruit signers, and the number increased form the original 243 to 750, despite that fact that the government had been taking out a systematic revenge on the original signers ranging from arrest, interrogation, and imprisonment to revocation of drivers' licenses, cutting of telephone wires, confiscation of typewriters, and general public embarrassment. So, upon his release on May 20, despite what he perceived as a public humiliation, Havel discovered, in fact, that the Charter movement had not been destroyed; on the contrary, it had flourished. And thanks to it, he later wrote, "History had taken a greater step forward than during the preceding eight years."[10]

But at the time, that was small consolation for Havel. A turbulent two-year period would follow, one devoted to staving off the inevitable. It was only a matter of time. His life as a prisoner was about to begin. In that period, Havel found himself on a mad, emotional seesaw.

> In time, of course, I recovered from the psychotic state of those first few days and weeks after my return from prison, but something of the inner contradictions and despair of that time remained within me and marked the two years between my release in May 1977 and my "definitive" imprisonment in May 1979.[11]

On the one hand, there was a full burst of dissident effort. Havel threw himself into a frenzy of activity, his pen as his weapon, his signature of protest as his identity. In December 1977, along with a group of Czech writers, he signed an open letter to colleagues abroad, appealing for support in the publication of prohibited works under to the Helsinki Agreement. In January 1978, he and Landovský were arrested again on the trumped-up charge of disturbing the peace and sent to Ruzyně Prison. In March, out of prison again, he and 298 other citizens signed a petition, calling for the abolition of the death penalty. In April, he and twenty-three other Charter 77 signers signed a statement called "A Hundred Years of Czech Socialism" for the Czech Social Democratic Party's Congress. Also in April, he cofounded VONS, the Committee for the Defense of the Unjustly Prosecuted. In August, he began to attend clandestine meetings with Polish dissidents, hiking through the forest to the top of a mountain at the Czech/Polish border. Andrej Krob remembers one of those arduous journeys:

> Years ago, when I accompanied Václav Havel to a spot in the mountains where we were to meet the Polish dissidents, I led him on a very rough road through the forest, because I thought that the path would be shorter. And at some point where the traversing was ex-

tremely difficulty, Havel turned to me and said: "About people who do these foolish things and survive, you can say that they are men of adventure. When a man does something spontaneously and it works, nobody believes that it happened just like that. One has to ascribe better and more credible reasons for his actions."[12]

All the while, Havel participated in a continuing debate within the dissident community about Charter 77. His pace was unstoppable.

I may have gone somewhat overboard; I was too uptight, if not hysterical, driven by the longing to 'rehabilitate myself' from my own public humiliation.[13]

In October, Havel expressed his feelings in an essay, "The Power of the Powerless," dedicated to Patočka, which was published by Edice Petlice (number 149). In the essay, Havel put forth the notion of "living in truth" that became his credo. The next month brought the essay "Reports on My House Arrest," about the police harassment campaign against him. Police were now watching Havel continuously, keeping surveillance over his apartment in Dejvice as well as Hrádeček. He was shadowed, interrogated, threatened, insulted. His apartment and his house were broken into; his car was vandalized. The authorities even constructed a look-out house on stilts at the turn of the road opposite his house at Hrádeček, which Havel dubbed "Lunochod" (after the Soviet remote-controlled moon module). It was from there that StB agents watched him day and night. Olga remembers, one frigid morning, when Havel brewed a potion of hot tea with rum and brought it out to two agents who were sitting in a car in front of the Lunochod. They refused it. Havel left the glasses on the hood of the car. When he returned later, the glasses were empty.

In the midst of all this frantic political activity, Havel's character, Vaněk, kept reappearing. In the summer of 1978, at the annual summer writers' conference at Hrádeček, *Audience* was performed again, with Havel playing Vaněk, Landovský playing Sládek, and Krob directing. At the time, Vaněk and his activities seemed all the more relevant. "*Audience* was our reality. Those absurdities really happened. It was our normal life, our daily truth," says Landovský, recalling that year.[14]

Then in the fall of 1978, the idea was proposed that a tape recording be made of Havel and Landovský reading *Audience*. It would then be smuggled across the border to Upsala, Sweden, where it would be made into a record and released by a company called Šafran, founded by a Czech émigré named Jiří Pallas. The recording was made at the home of Vladimír Merta, a Dylanesque Czech folk singer who had some recording equipment in his small apartment on a side street in a quiet section of Prague. The group spent several days rehearsing it, under the direction of Luboš Pistorius. It was a tense and unpredictable effort; Havel was watched constantly by the police, so he couldn't attend rehearsals regularly. It took three days to record the play, and one to edit. They recorded it in the kitchen, Landovský recalls, because they needed the sound of running water for the segments in which Sládek goes to the lavatory.

After the recording session, they made plans to take a photo for the cover of the record. As Landovský tells the story, he and Havel met at Pavel Kohout's house outside Prague, away from police scrutiny, on a freezing January day in 1979. After the photo was taken, Landovský drove Havel and Olga to the train station in Těšnov. It was bitterly cold outside. Havel and Olga boarded the train, which had a heater, as the train pulled out, Havel took off his sweater and handed it out the train window to Landovský. That was the last time they would see each other for over a decade. Three days later, Landovský left the country and went to work at the Burgtheater in Vienna; he would not return for eleven years. Meanwhile, the record was smuggled into Sweden, where it was made into a record and smuggled once again back into Czechoslovakia. People made their own copies, and for the next eleven years, until the Velvet Revolution, it became the most popular underground recording in the country.

With all this activity, Havel had a sense, almost a wish, that there would be an end to it. Then the inevitable happened. In the spring of 1979, the security police began a massive campaign against the VONS Committee, searching homes and arresting fifteen of its members. On May 29, ten members, including Havel, were charged with criminal subversion of the republic. Havel was detained behind the grim red walls of Ruzyně Prison until October, when he was tried along with six others (Petr Uhl, Jiří Dienstbier, Otta Bednářová, Václav Benda, and Dana Němcová). On October 23, they all were convicted. Havel's sentence was four and a half years in prison.

> When they finally did lock me up during their campaign against VONS, all my former uneasiness suddenly vanished. I was calm and

reconciled to what would follow, and I was certain within myself. None of us know in advance how we will behave in an extreme and unfamiliar situation (I don't know, for example, what I would do if I were physically tortured), but if we are certain at least about how we will respond to situations that are more or less familiar, or at least roughly imaginable, our life is wonderfully simplified. The almost four years in prison that followed my arrest in May 1979 constitute a new and separate stage of my life.[15]

While in Ruzyně prison over the summer months before his trial, two things happened. On July 22, Havel's father died, and the authorities permitted him to attend his funeral. Then in August, Miloš Forman, who was already living in New York and working as a film director, heard of Havel's imprisonment and impending trial. He talked to the playwright Michael Weller, who in turn talked to Joe Papp about what could be done to help Havel. Papp contacted the U.S. State Department, who made inquiries with the Czech authorities. They said that if Papp would write a formal letter offering Havel a position at the Public Theater in New York as dramaturg for one year, he would be released from prison and allowed to go.

Papp wrote the letter, and the authorities presented it to Havel in prison. Havel was shocked: one day he was taken from his cell and walked to the prison office; there they uncuffed him and even offered him coffee. The Deputy Minister of the Interior himself came in and said that Havel would be allowed to go to New York to be a writer-in-residence at the Public Theater. Havel said he would think about. He talked it over with Olga. First of all, he sensed it was a trap, a one-way ticket to compulsory emigration. More important, he didn't want to abandon his fellow VONS members who were also being brought to trial. So he flatly rejected the offer, saying, years later: "I have never regretted refusing the chance to travel to the USA . . . and my choice to remain in prison instead."[16]

According to Forman, Havel later explained his reason in a letter, saying that he hadn't wanted to abandon his fellow dissidents and the dissident community in Czechoslovakia. He wanted to set an example, so they would not lose hope. "Havel realized he was the model of moral courage to his fellow dissidents," Forman explains.[17] Furthermore, he apologized to Forman, saying he didn't want him to think he wasn't grateful. In fact, later on, Havel thanked him, saying that Forman had helped him more than if he had been allowed to go free. As Havel would later explain:

When I was in custody facing trial, it was at Joe Papp's initiative that I received an offer to go to the United States to study. That offer — although I did not take advantage of it and chose trial and prison instead — was of immense political significance: our state was thus compelled to offer me the trip to the United States in exchange for not disgracing itself by bringing me to trial. That, in turn, gave me the opportunity to humiliate the totalitarian power by declining the offer.[18]

As for Olga's response to the invitation, here is an excerpt from an interview between Eva Kantůrková and Olga in the following year:

Question: Your husband was offered in prison to go to New York. . . . He refused, he didn't leave prison; he remained there with his friends [Dienstbier and Benda]. Did you participate in this decision on this part?

Answer: They called me to Ruzyně. Vašek told me very briefly what he thought about this offer. And I said that it's OK with me. I was happy that he decided as he did.

Question: Didn't you give him any advice about it?

Answer: I wouldn't advise anybody in a situation like this. I couldn't, because I don't know how I myself would react.[19]

Looking back on these two frantic years between his first arrest in January 1977 and his impending trial in October 1979, it seemed almost as if Havel were driving himself back to prison. "Havel realized he was the model of moral courage to his fellow dissidents," Forman said. "We always expected this," Olga said.[20] Was Havel seeking punishment, to atone for the mistake he felt he made in writing the letter of release in 1977 that the authorities had altered and then publicized? Did Havel seek reimprisonment to set the record straight, to restore his good name as a dissident and moral leader, to reestablish his credibility as a spokesman for Charter 77? Was Havel getting even with the authorities, who had humiliated him by falsifying that identity?

Friends felt helpless to stop him. His close friend Zdeněk Urbánek commented on Havel's determination to serve this spiritual sentence:

He could not do anything but provoke the police to arrest him again. Naturally, they soon found something to charge him with.

It's frightening, of course, when you hear such a person — someone you've known for a long time — declare that he's going to get himself caught. You could see from the expression on his face how badly he was taking it. No other solution presented itself; there was nothing else that would have been as risky but would not have led straight to prison. His way is to give an answer, without posing the question directly. He's a person who needs to discuss a difficult decision openly, but he alone bears the unconditional responsibility for his actions.[21]

Later on in prison, Havel ruminated over and over on that fateful letter of release he wrote in 1977. In one of his letters to his wife, Olga, he wrote:

I came out of prison [in May 1977] discredited, to confront a world that seemed to me one enormous, supremely justified rebuke. No one knows what I went through in that darkest period of my life (you may be the only one who has an inkling): there were weeks, months, years, in fact, of silent desperation, self-castigation, shame, inner humiliation, reproach and uncomprehending questioning. For a while I escaped from a world I felt too embarrassed to face into gloomy isolation, taking masochistic delight in endless orgies of self-blame. . . . I felt best of all, relatively speaking, in prison.[22]

That purgation through suffering, that atonement for what he thought to be his sin, became a deeply spiritual experience for Havel:

I have my failure to thank for the fact that for the first time in my life I stood — if I may be allowed to make such a comparison — directly in the study of the Lord God himself; never before had I looked into his face or heard his reproachful voice from such proximity, never had I stood before him in such profound embarrassment, so humiliated and confused, never before had I been so deeply ashamed or felt so powerfully how unseemly anything I could say in my own defense would be.[23]

During that four-and-a-half-year sentence, Havel endured spiritual suffering such as he never had before. It would provide the groundwork for his major plays of the 1980s.

1978: *PROTEST*

You think the nation can ever recover from all this?[1]

— Havel, *Protest*

Somehow, in that turbulent, traumatic time of protest, between imprisonments, waiting for the inevitable, Havel managed to keep his life in the theater alive, through his character Vaněk. Vaněk had become a kind of ironic hero of the times, a dissident with a life of his own, an island of continuity in a sea of confusion and uncertainty. Just the act of writing a play with Vaněk in it provided an identity for a playwright who felt helplessly swept along in the tides of political turmoil.

In addition to the performance of *Audience* at Hrádeček and the recording of *Audience* with Landovský in 1978, Havel found time to write a new one-act play, entitled *Protest*. Once more he summoned Vaněk, this time to tell the story of Charter 77 and its aftermath, those painful, traumatic times when actor turned against actor, writer against writer, friend against friend.

In *Protest*, Vaněk, the blacklisted playwright, has been invited to the home of his friend Staněk, an established, official writer. Like Michal and Věra in *Vernissage*, Staněk is successful, connected, and well-to-do, far more so than his impoverished, shabbily dressed guest, Vaněk, to whom Staněk offers a comfortable seat in his well-appointed study. While Vaněk remains, characteristically, a man of few words, Staněk talks on and on, boasting about his superb garden. Does Vaněk have such flowers at his dacha? Would he like to see Staněk's apricot trees? How about a cigarette? What about some brandy? Would he like some comfortable slippers? Staněk continues, luring him with liquor and plying him with questions. Was he followed to Staněk's apartment? (He offers helpful tips on how to shake police tails.) How was it in prison? Was he beaten? Do they leave him alone now? Staněk reminisces nostalgically about the 1960s, and criticizes the current regime. But in light of his affluence, his rants seem hypocritical, as they are born of his official association with the regime he is criticizing. Clearly, he and Vaněk were in the same milieu in the 1960s; now they are worlds apart, Staněk in the protective, insulated comfort of the establishment, Vaněk out in the cold with the other dissidents. Staněk flatters Vaněk with acknowledgments of his fight for human rights, but his words seem patronizing and laced with pitying innuendo that Vaněk is on a fool's errand.

As in *Audience* and *Vernissage*, they talk about real events and people, about Landovský, about Kohout, about Vaněk's "one-act play about the brewery." During a lull in the one-sided conversation, Staněk grandiosely offers to send Vaněk's wife some gladiolus bulbs. "I've got thirty-two shades, whereas at a common or garden nursery you'll be lucky to find six," he boasts.[2]

The "light talk" dispensed with, Staněk comes to the point of his invitation. (First he turns up the background music, the inference being that he is trying to avoid any bugging of the conversation.) He has invited Vaněk to his home to ask for a favor. Staněk wants to help a popular singer named Javůrek, who has been arrested during one of his performances. Staněk has been trying to use his connections and influence to right this injustice, but hasn't gotten anywhere. So he is turning to Vaněk. Will Vaněk write a petition of protest on Javůrek's behalf? After all, Vaněk is so experienced in these matters. And who knows, it might be published abroad, create public pressure. By the way, he adds, Staněk's daughter is pregnant by this musician, but Staněk assures Vaněk that he would be trying to intervene in any case. Of course, he would.

Vaněk replies by pulling from his briefcase a petition that he has already written. Perhaps this is the kind of protest Staněk had in mind? Startled, Staněk seizes the document and reads it through. Yes, just what he'd had in mind. And so professional, so well written, too, although, Staněk suggests gently, it could stand a few changes, some rewording here and there. Still, how much he admires Vaněk! And how glad he is that Vaněk is around as the person to whom one can turn to and rely on in such a situation! Although, of course, he says, Vaněk has had to pay a price — ostracism, betrayal by all those around him including his fellow theater friends. Vaněk shouldn't tolerate that, he remarks (knowing, as he says it, that Vaněk couldn't have stopped it if he tried.)

Staněk asks Vaněk if he has sent off the petition yet, to which Vaněk replies that signatures are still being collected. Then Staněk's avoidance dance begins. How many signatures has Vaněk collected? Fifty? Too bad, Staněk says, that it's too late for him to sign. Vaněk replies: "But it's still open — I mean —" Staněk doesn't let Vaněk finish his sentence with its inevitable request for Staněk's signature. He sidesteps with further questioning. Do the police know? Who else has signed it? Staněk then changes the subject and out of pity offers Vaněk some money. Vaněk accepts it, saying that he can pass it on to some of his needy friends. Staněk tries to distract Vaněk further, by offering to show him the garden.

But clearly, Staněk feels cornered. He has run out of diversion tactics, and he can't avoid the list of signatures Vaněk is holding before him, waiting for Staněk to add his name. In a deft countermaneuver, Staněk changes his strategy and goes on the offense, trying to put Vaněk on the spot and force Vaněk to back off. First, Staněk points out the unfairness of the system, noting that it actually puts Vaněk at the advantage, while Staněk is helpless.

> Staněk: Just think: even I, though I know it's rubbish, even I've got used to the idea that the signing of protests is the business of local specialists, professionals in solidarity, dissidents! While the rest of us — when we want to do something for the sake of ordinary human decency — automatically turn to you, as though you were a sort of service establishment for moral matters. In other words, we're here simply to keep our mouths shut and to be rewarded by relative peace and quiet, whereas you're here to speak up for us and to be rewarded by blows on earth and glory in the heavens! Perverse, isn't it?
>
> Vaněk: Mmm —
>
> Staněk: Of course it is! And they've managed to bring things to such a point that even a fairly intelligent and decent fellow — which, with your permission, I still think I am — is more or less ready to take this situation for granted! As though it was quite normal, perfectly natural! Sickening, isn't it? Sickening the depths we've reached! What do you say? Makes one want to puke, eh?
>
> Vaněk: Well —
>
> Staněk: You think the nation can ever recover from all this?
>
> Vaněk: Hard to say —
>
> Staněk: What can one do? What can one do? Well, seems clear, doesn't it? In theory, that is. Everybody should start with himself. What? However! Is this country inhabited only by Vaněks? It really doesn't seem that everybody can become a fighter for human rights.[3]

As Vaněk, embarrassed, offers his apologies, Staněk escalates his attack, accusing Vaněk of enjoying his position in this system and humiliating Staněk. His speech echoes the brewmaster Sládek's cry of "What about me?" But Staněk's maneuver is self-serving. His aim is to avoid the responsibility of signing the petition at any cost and to make that avoidance Vaněk's fault:

> Staněk: Let me tell you something, Ferdinand. (*Drinks. Short pause.*) Look here, if I've — willy-nilly — got used to the perverse idea that common decency and morality are the exclusive domain of the dissidents — then you've — willy-nilly — got used to that idea as well! That's why it never crossed your mind that certain values might be more important to me than my present position. But suppose even I wanted to be finally a free man, suppose even I wished to renew my inner integrity and shake off the yoke of humiliation and shame? It never entered your head that I might've been actually waiting for this very moment for years, what? You simply placed me once and for all among those hopeless cases, among those whom it would be pointless to count on in any way. Right? And now that you found I'm not entirely indifferent to the fate of others — you made that slip about my signature! But you saw at once what happened, and so you began to apologize to me. Good God! Don't you realize how you humiliate me? What if all this time I'd been hoping for an opportunity to act, to do something that would again make a man of me, help me to be once more at peace with myself, help me to find again the free play of my imagination and my lost sense of humour, rid me of the need to escape my traumas by minding the apricots and the blooming magnolias! Suppose even I prefer to live in truth![4]

In a two-step dance of convoluted logic, Staněk delivers a dazzling, five-minute speech during which he presents both sides of the argument: to sign or not to sign. If he signs, of course, he regains his self-respect and that of others; he loses a job that he hates anyway. Of course he wants to sign. On the other hand, Staněk argues that if he signs, he will bring more discredit to the dissidents, who are in enough trouble already. In a smoothly Machiavellian move, Staněk presents the argument that his signing would hurt the dissidents even more than it would hurt Staněk.

> Staněk: . . . these people (the establishment) secretly hate the dissidents. They've become their bad conscience, their living reproach! That's how they see the dissidents. And at the same time, they envy them their honour and their inner freedom, values

which they themselves were denied by fate. This is why they never miss an opportunity to smear the dissidents. And precisely this opportunity is going to be offered to them by my signature.[5]

In conclusion, reasons Staněk, the dissidents will be accused of dragging Staněk down, and that will hurt them, and those they want to help, like Javůrek the singer, even more. Therefore, Staněk says in a stunning summary, should he think of himself and sign, or should he think about the dissidents and not sign?

> Staněk: In other words, if I'm to act indeed ethically — and I hope
>   by now you've no doubt I want to do just that — which course
>   should I take? Should I be guided by ruthless objective consider-
>   ations, or by subjective inner feelings?
> Vaněk: Seems perfectly clear to me —
> Staněk: And to me —
> Vaněk: So that you're going to —
> Staněk: Unfortunately —
> Vaněk: Unfortunately?
> Staněk: You thought I was —
> Vaněk: Forgive me, perhaps I didn't quite understand —
> Staněk: I'm sorry if I've —
> Vaněk: Never mind —
> Staněk: But I really believe –
> Vaněk: I know — [6]

Staněk has played his hand so brilliantly, that his tacit refusal to sign never needed to be uttered. He never took the responsibility; he didn't have to. Vaněk spares him, saying "I respect your reasoning."

Staněk returns the protest letter and signature sheet to Vaněk, who puts them in his briefcase. But Staněk's maneuver isn't complete. He goes on the offensive. Didn't Vaněk know how much he wanted to sign the petition? Why doesn't Vaněk level with him? Why has Vaněk been a hypocrite? Staněk plays his final card with perverse pleasure:

> Staněk: I'm not an idiot, Vaněk!
> Vaněk: Of course not —
> Staněk: I know precisely what's behind your "respect"!
> Vaněk: What is?

Staněk: A feeling of moral superiority!

Vaněk: You're wrong —

Staněk: Only, I'm not quite sure if you — you of all people — have any right to feel so superior!

Vaněk: What do you mean?

Staněk: You know very well what I mean!

Vaněk: I don't —

Staněk: Shall I tell you?

Vaněk: Please do —

Staněk: Well! As far as I know, in prison you talked more than you should have!

(Vaněk jumps up, wildly staring at Staněk, who smiles triumphantly.)[7]

A tense pause. The threat of violence hangs in the air. Then comes yet another plot twist. Before Vaněk can respond, the phone rings. It's Staněk's daughter. Javůrek has been released. Staněk's behind-the-scenes moves have succeeded. Nothing more needs to be done.

Once again, a Havel play ends as it begins, with Staněk, his mask of friendship now restored, offering Vaněk cuttings from the garden (as well as compassionate advice to throw the protest petition into the furnace):

Staněk: My dear fellow, you mustn't fret! There's always the risk that you can do more harm than good by your activities! Right? Heavens, if you should worry about this sort of thing, you'd never be able to do anything at all! Come, let me get you those saplings—[8]

What was Staněk referring to in that final accusation that made Vaněk jump up so wildly? What had Vaněk actually said? Havel seems to be exposing himself in a dangerous, potentially self-destructive fashion. What was he hinting at? What else had happened during Havel's first imprisonment that upset him to the point of psychosis, that made him want to be imprisoned once more? What had he told the authorities?

Written in 1978, *Protest* seems laden with Havel's shame and guilt — guilt for the "public disgrace" caused by the authorities' distortion of his letter of release of 1977, as well as self-doubt as to the merit of his identity as a dissident. He paints a bleak portrait of the dissident, one who is hated by the establishment, misunderstood by the general populous, and betrayed by his friends. Ostracized from society, he is isolated, blamed, ridiculed. In a void.

Furthermore, he is ineffectual. In the end, Vaněk not only fails to get Staněk's signature, he also fails with the protest itself. It is rendered useless. If the musician is saved by the Staněks of the world who work from within, what is the value of the dissident? What is his purpose? Need he exist at all?

And what about the ethical considerations — decency, loyalty, friendship — that are part of his commitment to "live in truth"? Yes, as Staněk, Michal, and Věra say, they are friends, dear friends, longtime friends, but what is the value of that friendship? "Come, let me get you those saplings," are Staněk's parting words, as he sends Vaněk on his way, with only the illusion of collegiality. Behind the mask of friendship is Vaněk's existential anguish. Vaněk is alone, just as Havel is alone.

Protest is a morality play. However, in a system where the concepts of right and wrong have been so twisted and warped, there can be no clarity, no resolution. In the end, the dissident lives as much in a void as he does in truth. All that is left for Vaněk, and for Havel, is simply to "be," to live in a state of suspended animation. And to wait for the inevitable.

Nowhere else in dramatic literature, perhaps, is the role of the dissident more poignantly portrayed than by the all-but-silent Vaněk. In the whirl of paradoxes, ironies and absurdities around him, Vaněk remains fixed at the center, opaque in his reticence, yet clear in his steadfastness to "being," to living in truth, however murky, contradictory, absurd, and misunderstood that truth is.

THE VANĚK PLAYS: A "LIGHT ON A LANDSCAPE"

What pleased me most is that something apparently happened which, I think, does or should occur with all art, namely that the work of art somehow exceeds its author, or is, so to speak, "cleverer than he is," and that through the mediation of the writer — no matter what purpose he was consciously pursuing — some deeper truth about his time reveals itself and works its way to the surface.[1]
— Havel, "Light on a Landscape"

One of the great ironies of Václav Havel's life in the theater is that while he sat in prison, his character Vaněk was alive and free.

Havel may have doubted the value of his existence as a dissident, but there could be no doubt as to Vaněk's value. They could take Havel's plays off the stage, but they could not remove the character of Vaněk from the dramatic imagination of others. They could imprison Havel, but not his creation.

And gradually, a remarkable thing happened. Vaněk stepped outside of Havel's plays and took on a life independent of his creator. He became a separate being, who inhabited the works of three other writers whose lives were closely intertwined with Havel's. Through Vaněk, these writers continued to tell their mutual story. While Vaněk remained Havel's "spiritual property," he journeyed through their work.

How Vaněk came to life, independent of his creator, is a phenomenon that is "truly an uncommon, if not a unique, occurrence in modern literature," according to the scholar Marketa Goetz-Stankiewicz.[2]

This is how it happened: Back in the summer of 1975, at the very first reading of *Audience* at Hrádeček, the playwright Pavel Kohout and the actor Pavel Landovský, both of whom were present, were deeply affected by both the play and the character of Vaněk. Here was something new — real people in real situations to which everyone present could relate. Vaněk was alive to them.

Kohout remembers how captivated he was by the character of Vaněk:

> I was sitting in Václav Havel's hillside cottage that summer day when, for the "entertainment of friends," as he remarked with characteristic modesty, he read his one-act play *Audience* . . . With characteristic immodesty, it was I who, after the reading, drew his attention to the fact that he had discovered a vehicle for translating concrete information about concrete people and problems in a concrete period into a dramatic form capable of sustaining life on stage.[3]

Kohout was so excited, in fact, that he called Klaus Juncker and translated *Audience* into German over the phone:

> Suddenly I realized that I had an empathy for Vaněk as if I'd written the play myself. . . . This is a new genre of theater. And it's not only to amuse friends, this is something more.[4]

Then, after *Vernissage* was written, Kohout asked Havel for permission to use Vaněk to record his own experiences. Havel agreed enthusiastically. Furthermore, out of their conversation came an idea for a jointly composed evening of one-act plays, both with the character of Vaněk.

The results were Havel's *Protest* and Kohout's *Permit*, both written in 1978. The hope was that they could be staged together — somewhere.

Kohout's *Permit* takes place in a government office, where Ferdinand Vaněk, the playwright, is applying for a breeding license for his dog. (A poster saying "Love Your Country, Love Your Dog" graces the wall). The dog, a pedigree and passive like his master, Vaněk, is denied breeding papers because his owner does not have the proper papers. One of the other dog owners points out the absurdity of this notion, but to no avail.

> Čech: Are we breeding Mr. Vaněk or his dog?
> Supervisor: That's not the way the application for the breeding permit reads.
> Čech: So how does it read? We aren't breeding Mr. Vaněk, and his dog hasn't signed the Charter![5]

None of the employees in the office will help Vaněk obtain breeding papers, because they all are too afraid of the consequences, such as the loss of jobs or passports. Vaněk's only option is to sell his dog. Finally, one employee gets her father, a Communist Party member, to agree to take him. At that point in this hilarious play, there's a final, chilling reversal. As they try to lead off Vaněk's passive dog, he suddenly turns into a raging beast and attacks them all.

Consistent with the precedent Havel set in his Vaněk plays where real people and events are mentioned, the names of Havel, his play *Audience*, and Charter 77 are all mentioned in *Permit*. Kohout puts this device to particularly effective use with numerous references to himself, including the lurid story of how Kohout's own dog was poisoned and the inference that the secret police were involved.

Just after *Protest* and *Permit* were written, Havel was imprisoned once more, and Kohout, who was working at the Burgtheater in Vienna, was barred from returning to Czechoslovakia. So, on November 17, 1979, Achim Benning produced *Protest* and *Permit* on the Akademietheater stage (of the Burgtheater) in an evening called "Tests."

By 1981, Havel was still in prison. As an homage to him, Kohout, indefinitely exiled in Vienna, wrote another play with Vaněk as a character. Entitled *Morass*, the play takes place in the administrative offices of the secret police at Ruzyně Prison, where both Havel and Kohout had been incarcerated after Charter 77. On the title page, Kohout has written:

Dedicated to the convicted
Václav Havel,
writer
recipient of the Austrian State Prize for European Literature
currently inmate of Correctional Institution Heřmanice
PS 2 Ostrava 13 71302[6]

In *Morass*, Vaněk's door is beaten down and he is dragged in for interrogation at Ruzyně prison. He is questioned by a team of crafty, determined interrogators, who pressure him to reveal the authorship of Charter 77. "Wasn't it Havel, by any chance? It was Havel, wasn't it?"[7] they taunt Vaněk. The first interrogator is a joke-cracking comedian who pretends to work for the department of vehicle licenses and quotes lines from Vaněk's poems (which are, in reality, Kohout's). The second, a former miner, is a brutal, intimidating bully. The third, a poet and "almost" a dissident ("my first poem was returned because it had ten misspellings. That was capitalism, Mister Vaněk") tries to convince Vaněk to renounce the Charter and collaborate with the regime[8]. This third interrogator even proposes to release information to the newspaper, saying Havel didn't really sign the charter, but that his name was added by — the interrogator reaches for a name — "your Beckett."[9]

While all this is taking place, an attractive administrator named Mary offers Vaněk cigarettes, while talking on the telephone (arranging school transportation for her child) and fending off advances of the first interrogator. Meanwhile, the latter tries to frame Vaněk with photographs of Vaněk together with Olga Havlová. Finally, a fourth interrogator enters. He asks if Vaněk has a driver license — he hasn't, since it was confiscated by the authorities. He then proceeds to give Vaněk a driver's license exam.

There are wisecracks alluding to Kohout's former Communist leanings (a sore point for Kohout); there are references to other Chartists under interrogation (including Patočka and Landovský); there is even an allusion to "men like Staněk (the character in Havel's *Protest*), decent authors, who didn't do anything underhanded; they just couldn't say no."[10] Like the Vaněk plays of Havel, *Morass* is an absurd world where the boundaries of reality and fiction are blurred, and the truth inhabits neither, a world in which, as Kohout's Vaněk says, "My biggest fear is — of fear."[11]

Another author who borrowed Vaněk for his own work was Pavel

Landovský, who was captivated by the character at the very first reading of *Audience*. Indeed, Landovský claims it was he who first had the idea of borrowing Vaněk to appear in one of his own plays. He says he did so in 1976, in a full-length dark comedy entitled *Sanitation Night* (Sanitární Noc). (It was first performed in Bonn in 1976, directed by a friend of Havel's named Hans Paul Fieber, whom Landovský had met in Hrádeček. As Landovský describes it, the premiere was a fiasco. The title of the play had been translated into German as *Wegen disinfection geschlossen* (Closed for Disinfection), so when the theater put up the name of the play on the marquis on opening night, passersby took it literally and no one came.[12])

Vaněk became part of Landovský's life. After he performed in Havel's *Audience* at Hrádeček and recorded it in 1978, Landovský found himself, like Kohout, exiled from Czechoslovakia and working at the Burgtheater in Vienna, where the two writers kept the memory of Vaněk very much alive. In 1981, Kohout suggested that Landovský write a one-act play in which Vaněk, "the hero whom we three have come to pass back and forth among us like a challenge cup,"[13] is a major character. Landovský readily agreed, and the result was *Arrest* (1981), a gritty, bitter situation comedy set in Pankrác Prison. In it, Vaněk has been incarcerated in a cell along with some gypsies. Like Havel's Vaněk, Landovský's Vaněk is polite and humane; he has taught his cellmates how to read, write, and count and has even instructed them in French. He also supplies them with cigarettes. (In return they wanted to teach him the neck jab, but he politely declines.) They share novels by Dostoyevsky and other books. They discuss philosophy and the meaning of justice, a topic of special interest, since it pertains to them all. One of the gypsy prisoners, a deaf mute named Matte, has been unjustly condemned, because during the trial the deaf-mute interpreter didn't know that Matte was in fact Hungarian and misinterpreted his responses as a confession. Suddenly, the sound of machine-gun fire is heard, and a voice in Russian shouting, "We have freed you!" Terrified, the prisoners barricade themselves in the cell. Finally, a guard enters, only to inform them that Vávra, the movie director, is shooting "The Liberation of Prague" trilogy in the next section of the prison.

Knowing that Landovský's limited German would restrict his castability at the Burgtheater, Kohout had suggested that he write a play with a mute character, one that Landovský could therefore perform. Thus, with *Arrest*, Landovský accomplished two goals at once: he wrote a Vaněk play to honor his friend Havel, and he created in it the colorful and mute gypsy Matte for himself.[14]

Again, Achim Benning showed his abiding commitment to Havel, his fellow writers, and to the character Vaněk, and produced Landovský's *Arrest* on the Akademietheater stage (of the Burgtheater) on February 24, 1982.

A third writer to create a Vaněk play was Jiří Dienstbier, a journalist, foreign correspondent, essayist, and playwright. Banned in Czechoslovakia since 1969, Dienstbier had become a founding member of VONS and a spokesperson for Charter 77. He was sentenced with Havel and spent three years in prison with him from 1979 to 1982.

Dienstbier's play *Reception*, written at the end of 1983, is inspired by the two men's shared experience in prison. In his essay "On Reception," Dienstbier recalls how he bid Havel farewell in the prison courtyard at Plzeň-Bory in 1982:

> "I'll write you a new *Audience*," I jokingly said . . . And when we said good-bye to each other in the Bory prison-yard, I repeated my joke. If I ever took it seriously, then it was only to the extent that I planned a parodic sketch to welcome him back to civilian life.[15]

In his dedication on the title page of the play, Dienstbier writes:

> This play, inspired by *Audience* and by my stay, together with its author, in a place where life takes off the social mask, is dedicated to Václav Havel on the occasion of his first New Year's Day out of jail — 1984.[16]

Reception takes place in a prison office, and both Vaněk and the Brewmaster from *Audience* are characters in it. In fact, the play is clearly written as a sequel. The Brewmaster is now a prisoner (convicted of theft) working in the prison's administrative office; Vaněk is also a prisoner (convicted of subversive activities). They refer to Sherkezy, the offstage gypsy character in *Audience* who rolled barrels with Vaněk, and about how Vaněk never did bring Bohdalová to meet the Brewmaster. Once again, the Brewmaster has been asked to report on Vaněk. Once again, a favor is asked: If Vaněk would write a play for the Brewmaster on Liberation Day to show his "positive attitude to reeducation," then the Brewmaster would get a chance for early parole.[17] In return, the Brewmaster will try to get Vaněk a job in the prison laundry, where he would have the time and opportunity to do his writing. Vaněk agrees to dictate reports against himself to the Brewmaster, which the latter will in turn give to the prison authorities. In the end, Vaněk is heard dictating what is in effect an accurate report to the Brewmaster; since it is true, it contains no incriminating evidence. Dienstbier's variation on Havel's theme of living in truth is, therefore, that if Vaněk were to have informed on himself in *Audience*, he would have told the truth, which is not incriminating and therefore would not have helped the Brewmaster anyway.

In fact, *Reception* commemorates the most painful of circumstances. While in Plzeň-Bory prison, the writers of reports, themselves prisoners, approached Havel and Dienstbier, saying that if the two men were to dictate reports about themselves, this would help the report writers get parole. In his essay "On Reception," Dienstbier looked back on his original intent to write a light-hearted Vaněk play to welcome Havel back from prison:

> Months passed, and I realized that there would be no fun and no "welcome-parody." More and more it became clear to me that, in fact, this whole thing wasn't about prison — and even less about a concrete one — and that neither is this anecdote. Actually, the world of prison hardly differs from the world surrounding it . . . When hair and civilian clothes are shed, the masks fall along with them. Of course, nearly everybody immediately tries to put on another one, but the new mask is dreadfully transparent. The least awkward thing is confronting the discomfort with one's own face.[18]

The last play in which Vaněk appears was written by Pavel Kohout in 1986. As he explains it:

> Five years later still when, for the first time, I felt the need to reflect in dramatic form the experience of my involuntary stay in the West — a consequence of a trip to Vienna — I added to the hitherto formed sequence my third work, *Safari*.[19]

The title page reads:

Safari
the last (?) one-act play about the life of the writer
Ferdinand Vaněk[20]

Set in a television studio in Vienna, *Safari* is a hilarious and bitingly satirical view of the dubious celebrity status foisted upon Vaněk, the dissident. In overtly absurdist tones, it dramatizes an interview with Vaněk, who had been discovered in the Danuvian marshes (a territory along the Danube near the Czechoslovak border, occupied at the time by protesters against the building of a hydroelectric power plant). Vaněk is described as "corpulent, sporting badly wrinkled overalls and incessantly munching peanuts," and it is assumed that he has allegedly defected, "probably in a diplomatic courier-case."[21] The interview is in the form of a discussion among a panel of notables, including an actress (Ms. Greiner), a critic (Mr. Grumpo), a playwright (Mr. Rednek), a poet (Mr. Forniker), a journalist (Mr. Blumann), and a very attractive moderator. Vaněk is alternately interrupted, misunderstood, ignored, and shouted down by the self-serving panelists, who are far more interested in gaining attention, voicing their own views, and attacking each other than in learning about Vaněk, whose name none of them bothers to pronounce correctly ("Vanick," "Vejnek," and "Vanye" are frequent alternatives). As the backstabbing, attention-grabbing behavior crescendos, it is interrupted by viewers who call in with questions on topics ranging from sex to recipes to who is the best tailor in Prague. The scene ends in a mêlée of shouted answers; meanwhile, Vaněk has escaped. The play closes with a news flash, reporting that an unidentified naked man crossed the Danube heading for Czechoslovakia; it is none other than "Ferdinand Funyet," who had left a few days earlier mysteriously and has returned just as mysteriously. "In accordance with the three-year prison term imposed on him for his defection, he was immediately committed to a medium-security prison as a recidivist."[22]

As is the custom, the names of authors associated with the Vaněk plays — "Vaklaf Havell," "Pavel Cohoot," and "Pavel Landowski" — are mentioned — as the vaudevillian travesty of an interview becomes an absurd jumble of mangled political references and outrageous celebrity behavior. And so the cycle of Vaněk plays, which extend from 1975 until 1986, ends on an almost defiant note: that of absurdist farce.

How can this phenomenon — one character, four authors — be explained?

Kohout tries, in his essay "The Chaste Centaur (Havel's Vaněk and Vaněk's Havel)." It happened out of a necessity of the times. Taking over the character of Vaněk, he says, was his attempt at closeness, to reclaim a friend who had been taken away by cruel circumstances. He was also fascinated by the purity of Vaněk, which makes him somehow impervious to his surroundings. Vaněk is a survivor, something that gives Kohout hope in the desperate times in which he and his friend live. So Kohout "borrowed" Vaněk from Havel, as he put it, out of his need to be close to Havel and his need to survive. The two men talk about Vaněk as if he has taken on a life of his own, independent of his creator. As Kohout explained it:

> My last piece, *Safari* [1986], summons him [Vaněk] on a first investigation of Western society. At the end of the play I, honest debtor that I am, return him to the country of his original owner. He cannot cross over to me a second time; I can only rejoin him. This I hope for; but I also believe that he will not wait, that he will, shyly yet without hesitation, enter into further plays which, in turn, will chart the features of our time on the blank map of contemporary Czech theater.[23]

All Havel's seminal Vaněk plays — *Audience*, *Vernissage*, and *Protest* — are about the issues of identity, friendship, and betrayal. In *Audience*, Sládek the brewery foreman feels that Vaněk has betrayed him by not informing on himself. In *Vernissage*, Michal and Věra feel that Vaněk has betrayed them by not becoming like them. In *Protest*, Staněk turns the tables and makes Vaněk feel that he has betrayed Staněk by not understanding why he will not and cannot sign the petition. The asylum offered to Vaněk, by letting him live in the plays of Landovský, Kohout, and Dienstbier, is the strongest gesture of friendship these three could offer to their suffering friend and fellow playwright.

Through Vaněk, four writers — Havel and Dienstbier imprisoned in Czechoslovakia, Landovský and Kohout exiled in Vienna — shared one identity. They expressed their commonality through one character, Vaněk, who their shared identity — a man who stood alone, isolated, abandoned, betrayed, misunderstood, ostracized, ridiculed. Through Vaněk, they lived together "in truth," as Havel called it. Vaněk was their point of connection, their mutual reality, their mode of survival. Vaněk endured the dark days of the 1970s for them; Vaněk faced the uncertainty of the 1980s for them. As Kohout says in his essay about the Vaněk plays:

No matter how different the life and style of the authors who have appropriated Vaněk so far, each of their Ferdinands preserves symptomatic traits of his spiritual father. Invariably, each and every one of them is in essence Havel portrayed by different painters, including himself.[24]

They could imprison these writers, they could separate them, isolate them, exile them; but they couldn't imprison Vaněk. As Landovský writes in his essay "Ferdinand Havel and Václav Vaněk," Vaněk roams free.

When Václav Havel was in jail, Ferdinand Vaněk visited me a few times in Vienna, but it has been a long time since he last appeared. In my opinion, he has probably moved from Prague to Havel's Hrádeček near Vlčice, and there he and Václav chat about what was, what no longer is, and what may some day be again. But who knows?[25]

How did Havel feel about his character walking through the dramatic worlds of his friends? In his essay on the Vaněk plays, entitled "Light on a Landscape," he uses that phrase to describe his character's purpose:

For me, personally, all that remains is to be pleased that, having discovered — more unconsciously than on purpose — the "Vaněk principle," I have inspired other Czech writers who, as it happens, are also my friends, and have provided something of a key for them to use in their own way and at their own responsibility. And if the present collection of Vaněk plays says — as a whole — something about the world in which it was given us to live our lives, then the credit should be given collectively and in equal measure to all the authors involved.[26]

Václav Havel's life in the theater during the dark, dreary decade of the 1970s began in one kind of void and ended in another. Of the three full-length plays (*The Conspirators, The Beggar's Opera, Mountain Hotel*) and three one-act plays (*Audience, Vernissage, Protest*) he wrote during that decade, he was to see only one, *The Beggar's Opera*, on a stage in front of an audience in a public performance, for one night only, one exhilarating night of consequence. Beyond that, he had to make a life in the theater elsewhere — in the living room at Hrádeček where he read *Audience*, in Andrej Krob's barn where he performed *Audience* and *Vernissage*, in the kitchen of his friend Merta's apartment where he recorded *Audience* with the window shades drawn.

By the end of the decade, separated from his audience, family, friends, and fellow writers, Havel was in prison. His life in the theater would be suspended. But those thrilling, isolated moments in the 1970s were, by his own admission, more gratifying than any performances of his plays in theaters around the world.

Havel and Olga, 1970s (Oldřich Škácha)

The playwright without a theater is like a bird without a nest.[1]
— Havel, "Far from the Theatre"

MAY 29, 1979–JANUARY 23, 1983:
SERVING THE SENTENCE

I always bite my tongue before I speak, and remind myself of what Patočka once told me: the real test of a man is not how well he plays the role he has invented for himself, but how well he plays the role that destiny assigned to him.[1]

Across from Havel's house in Hrádeček, at the bend in the road, there was a watchtower built by the secret police. Havel and Krob called it "Lunochod," named after the Soviet spaceship. "When they took it down at the end of the seventies," said his neighbor, Andrej Krob, "we knew he'd be away for a long time."

On October 22 and 23, 1979, Havel and six other signers of Charter 77 were tried and found guilty of the crime of subversion of the republic "by assembling, copying and distributing, both on the territory of the Czechoslovak Socialist Republic and abroad, written material which the senate considered indictable."[2] They were sentenced as follows: Otta Bednářová, three years in prison; Václav Benda, four years in prison; Jiří Dienstbier, three years in prison; Dana Němcová, two years in prison; Petr Uhl, five years in prison; Václav Havel, four and a half years in prison.

Olga Havlová found the trial surreal, grotesque. "Very bad theater of the absurd," she described it. "Humiliating, inane . . . to be overcome —

After prison, writing again (Jaroslav Kořan)

not by some magnificent power from above — but simply crushed by an ordinary, foolish, undignified old judge."[3]

Havel's time in prison was divided among three locations. The first seven and a half months were spent behind the dark red walls of Ruzyně Prison outside Prague, where he was kept from his arrest on May 29, 1979, through the trial in October, until his sentence began. Then on January 7, 1980, he was transferred to the grim prison of Heřmanice outside Ostrava, "the city of smokestacks," a remote, rough town in an industrial and coal-mining area of northern Moravia. There he began to serve his sentence. By some miracle, Benda and Dienstbier, his colleagues from VONS (the Committee for the Defense of the Unjustly Prosecuted), were transferred to Heřmanice with him. Then eighteen months later, in July 1981, after a week at the prison hospital in Prague, Havel was again transferred to the prison at Plzeň-Bory, where he served the rest of his sentence. (Jiří Dienstbier was transferred there, too.)

During his imprisonment, Havel was required to work in a variety of capacities. At Heřmanice, he made heavy steel mesh with a spot welder. Working conditions were brutal, and productivity quotas were double what they would be in civilian life. Failure to meet them meant extra hours of labor, less food and pocket money, and the loss of other privileges. Havel struggled to meet these quotas, but just as he began to fulfill them, he was shifted because of his deteriorating health to the less demanding job of working with a welding torch, together with Jiří Dienstbier. At Plzeň-Bory, he worked in the laundry and then at a scrap-metal plant where he stripped insulation off wires and cables.

For Havel, the years in prison were a deeply complex experience. On the one hand, he saw it as his destiny; at the same time, it was a voyage he felt compelled to make. He began it with stoicism, purpose, determination, resourcefulness, and even a degree of curiosity. In an early letter to Olga, written on January 27, 1980, just after he arrived at Heřmanice, he described it as an opportunity:

> I certainly can't complain about a lack of interesting experiences and I'm almost surprised at how soon, and how precisely in the spirit of my own expectations, I have been thrown into the kind of experience that, as I wrote you from Ruzyně, might serve as an instrument of my inner, psychic reconstitution and the renewal of my primordial relationship with the world.[4]

Determined to make prison a spiritual journey, he read a striking variety of material: Camus' *The Stranger*, Brod's biography of Kafka, Maupassant's "The Darling," *The Pickwick Papers*, Hemingway's *To Have and Have Not*, Robert Louis Stevenson's *Treasure Island*, Stendhal's *Lucien Leuwen*, Saul Bellow's *Herzog*, Heidegger's *Sein und Zeit*, works by Kafka and Georges Sand, biographies of Muhammad, Toulouse-Lautrec, and Karl Hermann Frank. He read anything he could find in the prison library or that could be sent to him by his brother Ivan, who collected reading material and copied poems and essays by himself and others. He read works in English and German, trying to learn these languages.

But soon his determination became muted by the indignities of daily prison life: being shaved bald; living in tiny spaces with strange, sometimes violent men; struggling to make sense of time; haunted by dreams, memories, fantasies; longing for favorite foods, cigarettes, liquor, friends, family, nature, the open air, Hrádeček; enduring physical pain caused by colds, flu, fevers, chills, toothaches, hemorrhoids, even a bowel operation; enduring spiritual pain caused by depression, anger, doubt, despair. The reasons for anguish seemed endless.

As the months and years passed, Havel, traumatized, anxiety-ridden, and exhausted, succumbed to the cumulative effect of endless spiritual and physical pain. He sank into a kind of mental, spiritual, and physical torpor. Still, being Havel, he found himself involved with the people who surrounded him. He served as priest, judge, counselor, mentor, tutor, and psychologist to his fellow prisoners. He wrote love letters for one, advised another on whether he should divorce; he settled disputes, consoled the homesick, talked some out of committing suicide, befriended younger prisoners and gave them reading material.

Meanwhile, a helpless world looked on. No amount of foreign pressure could sway the Czech government in its determination to punish Havel and his VONS colleagues. And there certainly were attempts. There were the valiant efforts on the part of Miloš Forman and Joseph Papp to invite Havel to New York. It was an invitation that Havel had rejected, but it preyed on his mind. Concerned that Papp might not know of his gratitude, Havel wrote to Olga on his first New Year's eve in prison:

> When you speak with the lawyer, ask him if he's been able to determine whether my letter to Mr. Papp has been forwarded by the

court. If not, write him yourself, thank him for his offer and explain
to him why I could not accept it.[5]

Havel maintained that he never regretted refusing the invitation. At
the same time, he was to dream often of Forman and of the freedom he
might have enjoyed:

> I dreamed again I was in the USA filming something with Miloš
> Forman. Miloš has been haunting me in my dreams. (Do you sup-
> pose I subconsciously envy him his luck and his success?) I know of
> no other way to explain it, even though my conscious ego harbors
> no such feelings.[6]

Two and a half years later, still in prison, the dreams continued to
haunt him.

> An interesting thing: the person I still dream about most often is
> Miloš Forman. Ever since I've been in prison, he's never let me
> alone. What does that mean? Is it perhaps an incarnation of my an-
> cient dream to become a film director? Or does he — the most suc-
> cessful of my buddies from my youth — wish to remind me
> constantly of what I have not achieved in life? God knows![7]

There were other attempts to help Havel. On June 18, 1981, the European Parliament drafted a resolution calling for the release of Havel and
others imprisoned on political charges. It went unheeded, and later in
December the Plzeň District Court rejected Havel's petition for condi-
tional release after serving half his sentence. The world continued to
watch and to give him recognition. On February 17, 1982, the International Committee for the Defense of Charter 77 awarded Havel the Jan
Palach Prize for his literature and his efforts on behalf of human rights.
In June 1982, Toronto's York University awarded him an honorary doctorate in absentia. So did Toulouse University in August 1982.

Paradoxically, during this three-year, nine-month imprisonment,
Havel did have a life in the theater of sorts, even though from afar. There
were passionate expressions of support from the theater community outside Czechoslovakia. In December 1979, the Cartoucherie Theater in
Paris presented a dramatic recreation of the trial of Havel and the other
five condemned members of VONS. This performance was repeated in

Munich on February 9, 1980, and at the Greenwich Theatre in New York on November 12, 1982. The German performance was subsequently televised in Austria and Switzerland.

In July 1982, the 36th International Theater Festival at Avignon presented a memorable "A Night for Václav Havel," consisting of a six-hour evening of theater. Playwrights from around the world were invited to write scenes for Vaněk, making it possible for the character to live in freedom, even though his creator could not. Ten scenes were chosen and performed with intervals of songs and music by Czech emigrés. Included in the evening were two new plays dedicated to Havel — Samuel Beckett's *Catastrophe* and Arthur Miller's *I think about you a great deal . . .* In the scene written by Jean-Pierre Faye, called "A Seat," Vaněk was offered opportunities for betrayal and surrender, with the chance to sit in a chair as his reward. The evening was sold out, but the organizers finally let in everyone who wanted to see the performance, so there were hundreds of young people sitting on the grass and the surrounding ramparts. During the course of the evening, a letter of support for Havel from the French minister of culture was read aloud.[8]

While Havel sat in prison, Vaněk roamed freely around Europe. On November 17, 1979, the world premiere of *Protest* took place together with Kohout's *Permit*, under the title of "Tests," at the Akademietheater (of the Burgtheater) in Vienna. In March 1981, the Paris Theater des Mathurins presented Havel's *Protest* on the same bill with Sartre's *No Exit*, in aid of the imprisoned members of VONS. In November 1981, Havel's trilogy of Vaněk plays, *Audience*, *Vernissage*, and *Protest*, were presented at Warsaw's Malá Scéna Teatru, where they played for three weeks, until martial law was declared. Also in 1981 at the Akademietheater in Vienna, Vaněk appeared once again in Landovský's *Arrest*. The ever-popular *Audience* received productions in Germany, Norway, Belgium, Sweden, Austria, Italy, France, Yugoslavia, and Poland, all in expression of support. His brother Ivan translated the reviews and sent them to him in prison.

The highlight of Havel's "life in the theater" during those three years and nine months in prison came with the world premiere of *Mountain Hotel* at the Akademietheater on May 23, 1981, directed by Peter Palitsch. When word came to Havel in prison that the opening would take place, he actually developed a case of "opening night nerves,"[9] as he called it. The afternoon of the opening, he worked his regular shift, and in the evening, assuming the performance was over, he celebrated with hot pow-dered milk and an American cigarette.

Foreign opinion could not bring enough pressure on the Czechoslo-vak government to release Havel and his colleagues. But clandestine at-tempts were made to have Havel leave the country. In 1981, the secret police offered Olga and Havel passports to emigrate to Germany. Again, Havel refused, as he had in 1979 when he had the chance to go to New York. By 1982, there were signs that his government was beginning to see him as a political liability, and that fall, the authorities made a strange ges-ture. They sent him a message in prison, saying that if he were to write them a single sentence asking for pardon, he would be released in a week. According to Havel, the reason was that Dr. Husák was planning to go on a state visit to Austria and wanted to announce Havel's release as a ges-ture to the Austrian president, who had once been the Austrian ambassa-dor in Prague and had recently awarded Havel the Austrian State Prize for European literature. Havel set what he called a "curious condition," the right to meet with three of his fellow prisoners and consult them each in-dividually on the issue. The consensus was against his asking for pardon, so he remained in prison.[10]

In fact, Havel would have served his entire four-and-a-half-year term, had he not developed pneumonia. On January 23, 1983, he suddenly spiked a high fever, and violent chills wracked his body. He feared he was dying. By morning, although his temperature had gone down to 104 de-grees, he reported for sick call, fearing that he would be punished other-wise. He languished for several days in the prison clinic with nothing but aspirin. Finally, he was transferred, handcuffed, to the Pankrác Prison hospital in Prague. From prison, he had written of his plight to Olga, who immediately came to the hospital and demanded to see him. Permission denied, she returned home and called Pavel Kohout in Vienna, who in turn started calling heads of state throughout Western Europe. Interven-tion began, and the Czech government, fearful of international pressure, used Havel's illness as an excuse to release him. This news was announced to him in the prison hospital by a group of guards, accompanied by a doc-tor and an official. It was, as Havel remembers, an extraordinary moment:

> I was flabbergasted and asked them if I could spend one more night
> in prison. They said it was out of the question because I was now a
> civilian. I asked them what I was supposed to do now, in my paja-

mas. An ambulance was waiting to take me to a civilian hospital, they said. It was a shock to hear the doctor suddenly calling me "Mr. Havel" instead of just "Havel." I hadn't heard myself addressed that way in years.[11]

1979–1983: LETTERS TO OLGA FROM "THE CONVICTED VÁCLAV HAVEL"

Writing those letters helped to save my life and give it a meaning, but what can they mean to others, outside the prison world?[1]
— Havel, *Disturbing the Peace*

During the three years and nine months Havel spent in prison, his life in the theater took place only in his imagination.

In the early days, at Ruzyně, he was able to make notes on an idea he had for a new play. However, that lasted only a few months. After he was sentenced and transferred to Heřmanice, writing of any kind was strictly forbidden, except in the one form permitted to a prisoner by law. That was a weekly letter to his wife.

As the translator Paul Wilson observes, for Havel, those weekly letters to Olga were all that gave his time in prison meaning.[2] They gave him a purpose, a reason for living. They became living testimony to the endurance of the human spirit and, for Havel, the absolute necessity — indeed the right — to write. And somehow, through these letters, he managed to maintain a life in the theater, too.

The rules were severe to the extreme. As Havel describes it in *Disturbing the Peace*, the weekly letter was limited to four sheets of standard writing paper. It had to be legible, with nothing corrected or crossed out, and there were strict rules about margins and graphic and stylistic devices. Quotation marks, underlined words, and foreign expressions were strictly forbidden. If Havel made rough drafts of these letters, he was punished. No copy of the letter could be retained. No one but the immediate family could be written to. There could be no mention of prison conditions or political issues. The subject matter was strictly limited to family matters; even humor was forbidden. If prisoners wanted their letters to pass the prison censorship and be mailed, they had to follow the guidelines. Any infraction was punished.[3]

These rigid rules were set by "an absolutist and much-feared, half-demented warden"[4] who took sadistic pleasure in enforcing them. This particular warden, as Havel describes him, looked upon the VONS prisoners as a kind of prize in his career. In his early days, he had been in command of a Stalinist prison camp in the 1950s. Thereafter, he had ruled for years over prisoners of the lowest rank, like petty thieves and rapists. Now, with the arrival of Havel and his colleagues, it was for him "like a return to the good old days,"[5] as translator Paul Wilson points out. Once again, he had political prisoners and was delighted by the opportunity to terrorize them. The letters home became his favorite focus, and a battle ensued between the warden's cruelty and the cleverness of his prisoners Havel, Dienstbier, and Benda to outwit him. The warden's behavior, by Havel's description, was both unpredictable and dangerous, and he soon focused his enforcement of these rules on Havel, interpreting his polite manners as a sign of weakness.

For Havel, the letters became the focal point of prison life. He became so wrapped up in them that almost nothing else mattered. All week long he would develop his letters in his head, while working, exercising, or preparing for bed. The day he was permitted to write them, he did so amid constant interruption and, as he put it, "in a kind of wild trance":[6]

> Writing them is always the most important event of the week for me and it's a small ceremony: I usually write you on Saturday, sometimes on Sunday. First I discharge all my weekend duties, such as washing my socks, etc. so my writing won't be interrupted by thoughts of what remains to be done or seen to, then I wait for the moment that is relatively the quietest. I try, if possible, to attain a state of inner harmony (as a matter or principle I never write when I am sad, nervous or angry about something) . . . and then I seek out the quietest corner where I set up my writing camp and once there I leave only in cases of direst need.[7]

Writing these letters became a passion, an obsession, a ritual, a raison d'être. It was also something of a challenge, a kind of test. Could he keep his thoughts together throughout the week, without making notes, and that way triumph over his tormenter, the sadistic warden? Could he pour out all these thoughts, pent up throughout the week, into one cogent expression that would fit exactly onto four pages?

On Sundays, enervated, he would fall into a depression. After the "performance" of writing home, as he called it, he felt empty. And because he was not allowed to keep copies, he would lose track of what he had written. Eventually, he developed a system whereby he would categorize the themes of the letters in his mind. He numbered the letters, so that he and Olga could keep track of them. He also found clandestine ways to write rough drafts, which were forbidden and had to be hidden. In Plzeň-Bory, for example, he hid them in mountains of dirty sheets in the laundry room, where he revised them during lunch break, all the while trying to dodge any informers.

Then there was the question of content and tone. Since discussion of political issues was forbidden, Havel learned to couch political statements in obscure language, to elude his censors, ever eager for the opportunity to harass and punish: "Slowly, I learned to write in a complex, encoded fashion which was far more convoluted than I wanted and certainly more complicated than the way I normally write."[8]

There was also the issue of intimacy. When Havel realized that his letters to his wife would circulate amongst their friends, he learned to accept the fact that the deepest expressions of his heart and soul could never be private.

Only two people were allowed to write to Havel: Ivan and Olga. Their letters to Havel were confiscated by the authorities and have never been published. Ivan kept copies, but has never published them. Ivan's letters were always four typewritten pages long. According to Olga's biographer, Pavel Kosatík, Ivan's correspondence provided Havel with a cultural and intellectual lifeline during those years. For example, Ivan would chose a book, a performance, or an exhibition and devoted several pages to discussing and analyzing it. In this way, he gave his brother Václav what he craved, a cultural context. Ivan also wrote about philosophical matters. In fact, says Kosatík, the long philosophical passages in Havel's letters to Olga are responses to Ivan's letters. Ivan then assembled a group of philosophers who sat down and discussed Havel's letter, and once more Ivan wrote back, continuing the dialogue.

The letters served a variety of purposes. Fundamentally, they represented Havel's legal right as a prisoner to communicate to his family about his well-being. But of course they were so much more. They became, essentially, his only form of self-expression, an emotional and intellectual lifeline. As he put it: "The letters gave me a chance to develop a new way of looking at myself and examining my attitudes to the fundamental things in life."[9] Accordingly, they became the vehicle through which Havel tried to work out a basic philosophy about a number of vital topics. As such, the writing of them became a source of great personal fulfillment, as well as an order and a purpose to his existence. "In short," he said, "they gave meaning to my life in prison, and helped me to endure."[10]

During his imprisonment, Havel wrote 144 letters to Olga. As the translator Paul Wilson explains in his preface to the *Letters to Olga*, all but nineteen were included in the published collection; of these nineteen, four were never delivered and fifteen were dropped from the original Czech edition because of redundancy. What is striking about the letters is the progression and flow of their major themes over the 189 weeks of imprisonment. These subjects are philosophy, the theater, and Havel's relationship with his wife.

In the 144 letters to Olga, there are so many rich passages about the theater that, excerpted, they could make a separate book. The letters illuminate how much theater meant to Havel, how crucial to his life it was, and how important playwriting was to him. They provide and *explication du texte* on a number of his own plays, as well as those of others. They articulate his philosophy of the theater. They include a "running commentary" on many aspects of the theater, and what it meant to him during his incarceration. Furthermore, the letters contain material for his future plays.

At first, he had a sense of stepping out of himself, of being a character in a play or a novel, and watching it all happen. "This is a little like the hopes with which Dostoevsky's heroes go off to prison," he wrote in an early letter in 1979. "In my case, however, the hopes are neither as dramatic nor as absurd, nor as religiously motivated."[11] There is even a strange appreciation of the experience at its outset. Ten days after his sentencing, he wrote:

> Sometimes I have the strangest feeling that I don't really want to leave this place. At least not now. Here you enter a state somewhat akin to hibernation, allow yourself to be swept along by the stereotypical routine of prison life, sink into a kind of sweet mental lethargy and the prospect of going back into the evil world, with its constant demands that you be decisive, becomes somewhat terrifying . . . p.s. there is far more truth in this world than in the world outside. Things and people manifest themselves as they really are."[12]

In the early months of his imprisonment, Havel's love of theater and his need to stay connected to it kept his spirits high. The process of playwriting provided a welcome diversion for his agitated mind while awaiting trial. Thinking about a topic and turning it over in his mind warded off fear and anxiety about what was to come. In his second letter, written on June 5, after only a week in prison, Havel reported to Olga with excitement that he had a new play almost half written in his head, based on the Faust theme. In August 1979, he reported that ideas for the play were chasing around in his head, but as the trial approached, he felt too inhibited and distracted to put them in writing. In September, bedridden by painful hemorrhoids, he found it a welcome opportunity to mull over the play some more.

After the trial and sentencing, thinking about the play became a welcome distraction. And when the initial shock and numbness subsided, he actually began to work on it. His excitement was palpable, as he wrote about it to Olga in November:

> I've started writing a play! That is, I've gone directly from just thinking about it and making notes to writing the text. I consider this a great achievement because I didn't believe I could do it in these circumstances. I've never written like this before; I have very little room, I can't write at night, I mustn't waste paper, I have nothing to stimulate me while I write etc. The fact is I haven't written much yet — about ten pages. (I had to stop because of the pain [from hemorrhoids]). The main thing is I know I can do it. Theoretically, there should be nothing to prevent me from actually writing a new play here sooner or later. (Of course I don't know what conditions will be like when I'm finally sentenced — I'll certainly have less time then). I'm delighted by this turnaround because, as you know, for me writing a play is like giving birth (I don't write easily, like most of my colleagues). Of course I don't know how it will turn out — but then I never do.[13]

On New Year's Eve, Havel celebrated by writing an enthusiastic letter about the play's progress.

> I've abandoned the original Faustian conception and left only the basic theme, which I have shifted to a different milieu — prison. Yet it is not going to be a play about prison but — in a manner of speaking — about life in general; the prison milieu should serve only as a metaphor of the general human condition (the state of

"thrownness" into the world; the existential significance of the past, or recollection, and of the future, the spinning of hopes; the theme of isolation and pseudo-hope, the discovery of "naked values" etc.). It will be a Beckettian comedy about life; all that remains of Faust is that theme of temptation (the swapping of one's own identity for the "world of entities"). There will only be three people onstage, chatting about trivialities — in other words, everything will be in the subtext. . . . I'm struggling against a number of odd psychological inhibitions; it's not that I have any doubts about the subject itself and the way I've worked it out, it's more that, technically, I'm having trouble writing about prison in prison. It's hard to explain. If I can't overcome this block, I'll set the play aside till later and work on something else, a one-act comedy, perhaps. In short, it's hard to write here. . . . Ideally, I'd like to get some extraordinarily fortuitous and sustaining idea for a one-act play (like the one that gave rise — in a single week — to *Audience*), one that would carry me along with it: then, in all likelihood, I could overcome those obstacles and inhibitions and write something funny, spontaneously. If I could manage that, the rest would follow more easily. So far, however, no such idea has occurred to me.[14]

On January 7, 1980, he was moved to Heřmanice Prison and his official sentence began. He braced himself for the infinite stretch of days to come, having no idea that playwriting would become an impossibility there.

Still, thoughts about the theater kept him alive during that first year. They gave him a sense that things were somehow normal, that he still was who he was, a playwright whose identity would not be eradicated by his current circumstances. His letters were laced with eager inquiries and requests to Olga about the theater. How was the record of *Audience* progressing? A pity that *The Conspirators* was included in the publication of his collected plays in 1977; that was unauthorized. There should be an addendum instructing readers not to read it. Please write Klaus Juncker and ask him to push *The Beggar's Opera* for production. But first, it must be translated. It just needs to be discovered, that's all. Meanwhile, it's such good news that there will in fact be a production of it in France, but they might rewrite it; the French theater is known for that tendency. Perhaps they need some notes from the author for the director and translator. What about the response to *Protest?* Did Joseph Papp get his letter? The court was supposed to pass it on to him. Yes, that's wonderful that the Vaněk plays will be produced in France. On and on he wrote, keeping his life in the theater alive.

Desperately needing an escape, he focused his energies on worrying about his unproduced play, *Mountain Hotel*. Who would produce it? Couldn't Klaus Juncker find a home for it somewhere in Europe? And if he did, wouldn't they need an explanation of the play? After all, it was an experiment, one that needed an *explication du texte* from the playwright. Over thirteen months (from April 1980 until the play opened in Vienna in May 1981), Havel wrote a series of letters flooded with commentary on the *Mountain Hotel*, similar to the kind he'd written about *The Increased Difficulty of Concentration* and *The Conspirators*. All week long he composed commentary in his head, and on Saturday it poured out in letter after letter. Letter 31, dated April 27, 1980, for example, was devoted entirely to a discussion of *Mountain Hotel*, seeking to define it in a variety of ways: as "an anthology of dramatic principles," "a so-called abstract play," "a nostalgic and vaguely unsettling poem," "an endless merry-go-round."[15]

Because he was not able to make copies of letters or notes on what he had written, and because he often ran out of space in his weekly letter, unfinished thoughts about the play remained on his mind. In Letter 37, written several weeks later on June 22, he found himself picking up where he had left off, cascades of commentary still pouring out, focusing on human identity, the theme, which he explains, is common to all his plays.

Later, in August 1980, he expressed delight over news from Olga that Achim Benning had indicated interest in producing *Mountain Hotel* on the Akademietheater stage (of the Burgtheater) in Vienna the following spring. But he suffered from the thought that a new play would be premiered without his input. Over the following months, he wrote Olga lengthy explanations of his unproduced play, which he urged her to convey, with apologies, to the artists at the Burgtheater:

> I still worry that those who are putting it on won't have the proper notion of how to go about it. When thinking of how best to convey my own idea of the play, I realize that it is, in fact, a fugue. If they think about the staging while listening to *The Art of the Fugue* or the *Brandenburg Concertos*, they will certainly see what I have in mind. . . . It might be of some help to pass on these notes of mine

to the friends who have something to do with the upcoming production. On the other hand, perhaps I'm just carrying wood in to the forest, in which case so much the better.[16]

Months later, Havel was still worrying. As the production of approached, he continued to defend the plays' experimental qualities. After a long discourse about the techniques he was using (in Letter 71, March 13, 1981), Havel added a revealing coda. Evidently, he had tried to describe *Mountain Hotel* to a fellow prisoner:

He listened to me with great interest and astonishment, and when at last I asked him what he would think if he hadn't known me and for some reason had to see the play, he replied quite candidly that he'd think I was a fake who was trying to make a fool out of him and he would be royally offended.[17]

The opening night of *Mountain Hotel* at the Akademietheater in Vienna arrived on May 23, 1981. It is poignant to think of Havel in his cell, celebrating the occasion with a cup of hot powdered milk, an American cigarette, and as much good cheer as he could muster. Maintaining a stoical attitude was not easy, especially with the news of other playwrights who were emigrating and savoring their artistic freedom:

On of the more frequent themes of my meditations and daydreams are the friends that have left the country. Initially, I feel a slight nostalgia and even some envy (of their artistic achievements) and a slight anxiety (they are doing what they enjoy at last, they are involved in their work, free from endless complications, no doubt viewing our toiling and moiling as pointless now, while I on the other hand am deprived of all that, without the slightest chance of working in a theater and reveling in the ideas that theater has always inspired in me). That is how such meditations begin, and they always end with a peculiar sensation of inner joy that I am where I should be, that I have not turned away from myself, that I have not bolted for the emergency exit and that for all the privations, I am rid of the worst privation of all (one that I have known myself too): the feeling that I could not measure up to my task, though I may not have set it myself — at least not in this form and to this degree — but merely accepted it from the hand of fate, accident and history.[18]

With all hopes of finishing his new play abandoned, he nonetheless continued to crave discussion about the theater; indeed, any mention of it by Olga would inspire a letter from him on that subject. For example, he dedicated almost three of the precious four pages of Letter 58 (December 6, 1980) to a discussion of Tom Stoppard's *Rosencrantz and Guildenstern Are Dead*, analyzing the closeness of Stoppard's sensibility to both his own and the Balustrade's.

As time passed, Havel's letters became more and more philosophical, showing an awareness of how he had been using the theater to express his ideas. Increasingly, his letters on the theater became springboards to ever deeper philosophical meditations. The day after New Year's, 1981, for example, he wrote of the connection between his ideas and his plays:

> It's customary at New Year's for people to give some thought to what they went through during the preceding year; I do so now, giving some thought as well to things I thought about over the past year. . . . The problem of human identity remains at the center of my thinking about human affairs. If I use the word "identity," it is not because I believe it explains anything about the secret of human existence; I began using it when I was developing my plays, or thinking about them later, because it helped me clarify the ramifications of the theme that most attracted me: "the crisis of human identity." All my plays in fact are variations on this theme, the disintegration of man's oneness with himself and the loss of everything that gives human existence a meaningful order, continuity and its unique outline.[19]

During 1981, he also became increasingly aware of a strange encroaching melancholy, tinged with "a general existential anxiety."[20] He even starting making lists and charts of his various moods. He began to daydream, to sink into reveries. Standing by the welding machine, he found himself dreaming about being backstage at the Balustrade, aroused by the smell of the machine, which evoked the aroma of old theater textiles mixed with pancake makeup.

In July, when he was transferred to Pankrác Prison hospital, they discovered that he had a bowel tumor. The interlude relieved him greatly. He relished the peace and quiet of the hospital, where his daydreams continued. He imagined himself in Prague, looking out at the rooftops from the window of his den in the family apartment, where he had written his first play.

Poetics

> And so, in fact — though at a distance — I remain with the the-
> ater.[21]
>
> — Havel, *Letters to Olga*

In August 1981, Havel was transferred to Plzeň-Bory Prison. He was approaching the halfway mark of his sentence with increasing anxiety. What lay beyond? What was there to look forward to? From the time of his transfer onward, he slid into a downward spiral of depression. Increasingly, his letters marked a retreat from reality into abstract, theoretical philosophizing.

The reveries continued. He imagined himself in a sauna, swimming, sunbathing, then dressing and going out with Olga to a restaurant. Or the most stimulating of daydreams, starting to write a play:

> If I imagine that rare and wonderful moment when I get an idea for a play, an idea so fine and so gratifying that it practically knocks me off my chair, and if, in a kind of joyful trance, I imagine actually turning the idea into a play I'm happy with, then having it neatly typed out, reading it to some friends who like it, and even finding theaters that express an interest in putting it on — imagining all that, I must also necessarily imagine the moment when it's all over and the awful question comes up again: "Well?" "Is that all?" "What next?"[22]

What longing is expressed in this passage, longing for the joy and the anxiety of the theater, of writing for the theater. His depression increased. He complained of feelings of "vacancy and barrenness; there no longer seems to be anything to look forward to, cling to, to hope for and therefore, in fact, to live for."[23] He reported "spleen, melancholy, anxiety, a sense of futility."[24]

Then one night, while watching a variety show put on by prisoners for other prisoners, he was overcome by the feeling of how much he loved being in the theater. He had had the same feeling in Heřmanice, attending a performance put on by inmates there. How he missed it! There was something about being in a theater that made him feel like nothing else. And somehow, in the prison environment, the theatrical experience became even more remarkable. Feelings from the 1960s, feelings of exhilaration, excitement, nervousness, and the rollercoaster emotions of a young playwright, feelings he had not permitted himself for so long, flooded back. He could not wait to report them in the next letter to Olga:

> It's hard to explain why, but these things moved me a lot back in Heřmanice too; its entire human context makes it something strange and unrepeatable, something scarcely to be found on any stage "outside." I don't suppose many playwrights have had this experience; it's difficult to know what to make of it. I've long since put out of my mind any thought of what I'll write once I'm free.[25]

Inspired by the experience, Havel found a renewed focus in his letters. For a seven-month period starting in September 1981, Havel set out to write an overview of his life in the theater, past and present. In one letter after another, following perfunctory greetings, messages to friends and personal details, he spun out paragraph after paragraph of beautifully shaped meditative discourse about the nature of the theater, or about a play that had deeply affected him, or about his own plays, or about his place in the theater as a playwright. Given the conditions under which the letters were written — in a tiny cell, deprived of freedom for two years — they are more than a reflection on his life in the theater. They are a reaffirmation of it. And they are remarkable in their development and progression, given that he was forbidden either to take notes or to make copies.

First came letters trying to define his place in the theater. In the 1960s, when he began as a playwright, he wrote for a specific audience. That was his reason for being in the theater. Now, after a decade of being both a banned playwright and an imprisoned one, what was his reason for being in the theater?

> I am definitely not what we call a "divadelník" — a professional theater person, someone for whom theater is the only imaginable vocation. When I was involved in theater it was always with a specific theater, and when I write for theater, I do so in a way specific to myself — and if no one were interested in my way, I'd prefer to write only for myself or stop writing plays altogether, rather than try to do it differently just because someone asked me to, as playwright.[26]

This sense of personal freedom was essential to Havel. And it was precisely this sense that kept him wanting to write for the theater, or simply to be in the theater. As he says of the Balustrade, in retrospect:

Had it not been for that lucky combination of circumstances [that led to the Balustrade] I don't know what I would have done, or whether I'd have had anything to do with theater at all. I might have begun writing plays sooner or later anyway; then again I might not have. But all that is long past . . . that time is over. But writing plays, in a sense, has remained with me to this day. . . . I don't think I've written myself out as a playwright. I have a lot of vague but therefore all the more exciting ideas about what I could and would still like to do on that territory, so I can still torment myself with that. As you know, I'm a man of obsessions, and I hate giving something up before I've exhausted all (my) possibilities. And so, in fact though at a distance — I remain with the theater. At the same time, I feel entirely free.[27]

Other letters were filled with philosophical discourse about the theater, or what Havel calls "the poetics" of his plays.[28] Havel would pick a theory — the social nature of theater, for example — and plunge into it with relish. Pointing out that he was a social person and that theater is a social phenomenon, he wrote that what attracted him to the theater was the mutual participation, the shared experience that transforms a group of people into a community.

It is that special moment when their mutual presence becomes mutual participation; when their encounter in a single space and time becomes an existential encounter; when their common existence in this world is suddenly enveloped by a very specific and unrepeatable atmosphere; when a shared experience, mutually understood, evokes the wonderful elation that makes all the sacrifices worthwhile.[29]

On and on he wrote about the theater with a heated intensity, oblivious of his surroundings, as if the act of writing about it would keep the theater alive in him and in that tiny cell. Theater as a new experience, as a new sense of community. The social aspect of each individual performance that creates a special, instant bond in the audience, united once and forever. Theater as an institution, a focal point of social life and thought, an expression of national spirit, "a small organism bound by thousands of threads to the great organism of society."[30] Theater as a spiritual home, a social club. The culture of theater — the foyer, the exhibition, the programs, the posters. The code among habitual theatergoers. Theater's impact on the self-esteem of society as a whole. Theater that can "attract, provoke and shock." Theater as an "adventurous path." Theater as a "collective spirit." Theater as an "eddy in the river."[31]

Ideas about the theater continued to flow. "The artifice of the world of plays." The playwright's bondage in the world he has created, limiting him far more than he would be limited in a film, a poem, or a painting. The playwright as "'victim' of his own creation."[32] The "pitfalls inherent in drama's artificiality."[33] The lament over the state of modern drama, "infected . . . with didacticism or ideology."[34] The celebration of Aristotle because he insisted on the importance of structure. The composition and development of motifs, the way they are arranged, what makes a play a play.[35]

A list of what theater has given him: an opportunity to become part of a community that creates; an inner stability; a heightened sense of order.[36]

A statement about the theme of every play, as well as his own: that of identity. The "Who's there?" question in *Hamlet*. The theme of recognition (disguises, doubles, mistaken identities). Jocasta recognizing that Oedipus is Oedipus. Lear recognizing who his daughters are. In one way or another, "every play involves the gradual disclosure of someone's true identity." That's the "logic of the world of plays."[37] In fact, he continued, all modern art and modern drama is about this crisis of human identity. It is the central issue that humanity now faces.

Still other letters were filled with references to plays written by others, plays he loved, plays he revered, plays about which he had thought for years and now had the time to reflect, to draw from their richness as he formulated his philosophy of the theater. A nod to Aristotle. A reference to Beckett. A mention of Edward Albee. An entire letter devoted to the character of the Orator in Ionesco's *The Chairs*, a play that had impressed Havel deeply over twenty-five years ago when he read it, sitting in the Café Slavia. In this letter, he wrote about the celebrated moment at the end of the play, when the Orator is to deliver a speech on the meaning of life, and of course it is in gibberish. Havel uses this moment as a springboard for a discussion on his own attempts to develop a system of philosophy.

I don't know any other way of dealing with the question of "the meaning of life." . . . In one way or another, I've been trying to do this in my letters from the start and I intend to continue, in the hope that whatever I manage to squeeze out of myself in these difficult circumstances will be taken neither literally nor too seriously, but understood as a stream of improvised attempts to articulate my unarticulated "inner life." The point is, I would not want to sound like Ionesco's *Orator*.[38]

It was a remarkable feat: a philosophy of the theater, developed and articulated in letters over a period of seven months, with no notes, no rough drafts, while suffering the cumulative trauma — physical, psychological, and spiritual — of imprisonment. And all graced with a sense of humility, self-awareness, and humor. Consider, for example, the letter in which he described a terrible toothache, in the midst of a discussion on the poetics of theater:

I've been through a hellish week: the combination of an aching tooth and being in prison (one multiplies the impact of the other) belongs to the trials of Job. For the first time since May 1977, when you brought me home from prison, I wept (!) Don't worry, no one saw me. I'm not counting, of course, my response to *Libuše*, *The Bartered Bride*, etc.[39] It happened at the height of my agony when I was denied permission to lie down after work. . . . A short time ago, I lanced my gums with a needle, a quart of pus ran out and the pain stopped. I sterilized the needle in a flame and I am taking penicillin, so I trust I won't get sepsis and die before morning and that I may be around awhile longer to burden the world with my identity.[40]

A Word About the "Heroine"

"Olga and I have not professed love for each other for at least two hundred years, but we both feel that we are probably inseparable. It's true that you won't find many heartfelt, personal passages specifically addressed to my wife in my prison letters. Even so, I think that Olga is their main hero, though admittedly hidden. That was why I put her name in the title of the book. Doesn't that endless search for a firm point, for certainty, for an absolutely horizon that fills those letters say something in itself, to confirm that?"[41]

— Havel, introduction to *Letters to Olga*

When Havel consented to the publication of this collection, he chose the title: *Letters to Olga*. It is a revealing title, one that suggests the importance of this hidden heroine, as he calls her, and of their relationship.

We only have one side of the correspondence, as Olga's letters to Havel were confiscated by the authorities. (Tragically, we don't have Olga to ask about them; she died in 1996.) Yet, even without her responses, we sense her presence and her strength, as if the letters were a theater monologue delivered to an unseen but vivid offstage character.

From one perspective, the collected *Letters to Olga* provides a portrait of a marriage defined by extraordinary times and circumstances. Contrary to what the title suggests, the nature of this communication from husband to wife is neither romantic nor intimately revealing, but rather extremely practical and real. The letters are filled with the details of everyday life: shopping lists of items to bring him on her next visit (she and Ivan were allowed to visit four times a year), requests for foods (powdered juice, lemons, cheese, cigars), requests for cigarettes and dictionaries, instructions on how the fuse box works, worry over the cost of heating oil. Has she renewed the drivers' licences? Has the contractor come? Has she painted the apartment? Did she have the car repaired? (And yes, it's all right to buy another Russian automobile.)

Havel's letters also reveals his sharply fluctuating moods. In the early letters, he remonstrates her for not writing long enough or often enough, for not answering his questions. He critiques her letters, corrects them, complains about illegibility; he reprimands her, scolds her, chides her about various issues. On the other hand, there are expressions of tenderness. Once she broke prison rules and wrote about matters beyond the family; they withheld her letter, and he expressed his compassion for her plight. On one occasion he apologizes for his own "wretched appearance."[42] He always sends her love and kisses, and reassures her, saying that "a large bucket of bitterness probably awaits me. Of course I'll have to drink it alone, but I'll manage somehow. Don't let it depress or bother or upset you."[43] And he shows appreciation for her slightest efforts — like scenting her letters with jasmine, or sending funny family photographs.

Readers and critics have commented on the lack of professions of love and romantic content. One reader complained specifically about this. Olga had been sharing the letters from Havel with Kamila Bendová, wife of Václav Benda, Havel's fellow VONS member and inmate. In a letter Kamila wrote to her husband, she remarked about the absence of declarations of love in Havel's letters. Benda in turn shared this remark with Havel in prison. In response, Havel wrote the following "love letter" to Olga (Letter 42, which was, in fact, not published in the collected *Letters to Olga*). He begins: "I was provoked to write this letter, in fact, by Kamila, because in her last letter to her husband she mentions that you don't receive any love letters from me, whereas Kamila receives them from her husband."[44]

It is true, he continued, that he writes about himself, about everyday problems concerning Hrádeček, and not about personal issues. He goes on to say:

> It seems to me that it is your pride and my shyness which do not allow us to talk or write of love. . . . I don't know if I would be who I am if I didn't have you by my side, if I didn't have your presence as a kind of self-control and censorship and permanent grounding. You are a kind of mirror which helps me validate myself . . . If I were to say what you mean to me, I would have to say that you're a part of me. You're my inner certainty; you give me meaning. You're the bulwark — the pillar of strength — of my life. In light of these facts, it seems to me that to simply say that we love each other is not enough. Naturally we both have our own lives, our so-called separate interests, relationships, loves, connections. But these elements cannot divide our symbiotic existence. . . . Therefore: "I love you." (Kamila: it's not as romantic as Vašek's [your husband's] letters, but there it is. It has been said.) It is love-dependence, love-addiction, love-destiny. It's a lifelong matter, at least from my side. Amen.[45]

Not much is known about Olga's life during those years in prison. Her letters to Havel in prison were confiscated by the authorities, and it is not publicly known whether she, like Ivan, kept copies. In any case, they were not published before her death in 1996 and have not yet been. According to her biographer, Olga spent most of the time at Hrádeček and in Prague, surrounded by friends. The summer weekend at Hrádeček around her birthday continued, although in a modified form. She sent photos of these gatherings to Havel, to cheer him up. She visited him regularly and brought whatever he asked. But her suffering remained private.

Miloš Forman recalls the one time he saw Olga during those years of Havel's imprisonment. Forman had emigrated to America in 1969 and had become an American citizen in 1977. He had wanted a visa to return to Prague, but had been denied one until 1980, when he was finally allowed by the authorities to return to shoot his movie *Amadeus*, on the condition that he not seek out dissident friends. He agreed, provided they in turn agree that if a dissident were to seek him out, neither the dissident nor his film would be harmed. While in Prague, he ran into Olga on the street. As it happened, she was on an infrequent visit to Prague and was not being followed. They sat in a café, undisturbed, and talked, savoring a few moments of renewed friendship under such extraordinary circumstances. "She was a rare and courageous woman, full of energy," he said.[46]

In a few rare instances, however, we have a record of her private thoughts. In 1981, Eva Kantůrková interviewed a number of women whose dissident husbands had been imprisoned. The answers to some of the questions posed to Olga give a glimpse of her life while Havel was in prison. In the directness, simplicity, and honesty of her answers we sense the "pillar of strength," as Havel put it, that she provided for him.

> Question: Do you support your husband and his opinions or do you argue with him?
>
> Answer: Vašek makes his decisions always very quickly. I am more careful; I always try to see things from every angle. But with the imprisonment, it was something that we expected from the very beginning. Every time we spoke about these things (political matters, etc.), I was the one to remind him that he can expect the worse.
>
> Question: How do you cope when your husband is in prison?
>
> Answer: As I said, we aways expected this. Perhaps I would see it differently if we had children.
>
> Question: How do people there [neighbors in Hrádeček] relate to you?
>
> Answer: In a normal, human way.
>
> Question: Meaning in a brave, supportive way?
>
> Answer: I wouldn't call their behavior brave; simply human. In the 1960s they didn't care about us. We were only another couple of Praguers to them. Later, when the police started to visit us there, the neighbors began to greet us. I'll give you an example: we couldn't drive our own car. [Havel had lost his license around 1971 to 1972; it was confiscated by the police.] One of the neighbors had seen me on the road walking into the village, and

picked me up and drove me into town. After that, he lost his driver's license. But he still greets me today.

Question: Do you feel isolated from the world of so-called normal
people?

Answer: I don't like this distinction. I just do what I think I should
be doing. One should do whatever one can do. To me, abnormal
people are those who behave as if nothing happened here, as if
they couldn't hear, couldn't see, couldn't speak. In my eyes, the
abnormal people are those cops who guard us at Hrádeček.[47]

Biographers have probed their marriage and alluded to infidelities on
both sides. But these probings miss the main point. The love between
Havel and Olga transcends such observations and judgments; indeed the
bond goes far deeper than people in more normal circumstances could
ever understand.

And this period in prison only served to strengthen that bond. Olga
became his lifeline, a source of strength and continuity. She became his
anchor, his focus, his only expression of reality. The endurance of each
helped the other to endure. As he wrote to her: "I am happiest of all to
see that you are living and acting — if I may put it this way — 'in my
spirit' and that you are effectively standing in for me. (Now if you could
only write a new play for me as well)."[48]

As Havel said, his letters to Olga saved his life. They were his only
mode of communication to the outside world for almost four years. They
were his only form of creative expression, which, for a writer who wrote
as prodigiously as Havel did until the time of his imprisonment, meant
survival. They were the only thing that made him feel he was doing something worthwhile. They gave his existence order, purpose, and meaning.
They provided him an opportunity to reflect on his life in the theater and
the theater in his life. They enabled him to keep his identity as a playwright alive.

As those who urged their publication have shown, the collected letters stand as one creative effort. Their value does not lie in their philosophical content alone; many of the philosophical passages are repetitive
and obscure, largely because Havel could not keep copies of the letters
and because his writing had to be coded. Nor does their value lie in the
long passages about the theater alone or in the commentary on one play
or another. Rather, it lies in the profoundly powerful and moving self-

portrait of an extraordinary man and writer struggling to survive under extraordinary circumstances. They clarified to Havel, and to the world, that for him, writing was his essential form of being, of expression, indeed, his identity. If ever anyone could say: "I write, therefore I am," it would be Václav Havel.

Ultimately, the letters are a reaffirmation of his life and work as a writer, thinker, playwright, humanist — and playwright. And the writing of them — finding the will, the discipline, the determination, to do so in those darkest of hours, under impossibly cruel conditions — was in itself an act of supreme courage.

1983: *MISTAKE*

> I sometimes have the feeling that I'm acting the part of myself instead of being myself.[1]
>
> — Havel, *Largo Desolato*

It would take Havel years to recover from the trauma of prison. But the experience had set him on a new path, whose destination was yet unknown. It also gave him material for two new full-length plays.

The month that Havel spent in the hospital in February 1983, was strangely euphoric. On February 7, he received the City Court's decision to suspend his sentence for health reasons, and was transferred from a prison hospital to a public hospital. There he entertained friends and colleagues, relishing their delivery of piles of new *samizdat* publications. As he said, during that month in limbo he felt like royalty.

> Released from the burden of prison but not yet encumbered by the burden of freedom, I lived like a king. . . . The world — beginning with loved ones and friends and ending with the doctors, nurses and fellow patients — showed me its kindest face. I had no responsibilities, only rights. I was no longer in prison, and at the same time, I did not yet know the post-prison depression suffered by a returnee who is suddenly cast loose in the absurd terrain of freedom. But the beautiful dream had to end. The day came when I had to step back into the world as it really was . . . and I've been moving along its uncertain surface ever since.[2]

On March 4, Havel was released from the hospital. He and Olga returned to the family apartment, although his sentence wasn't formally waived until September 1985. In the meantime, he resumed work, compiling documents related to Charter 77, editing his letters, writing essays, giving interviews. But for the next six months, he lived in a state of suspended animation and high anxiety, afraid that at any time there might be a knock on the door from the secret police, who would drag him off to prison once again.

While he was not yet a free man living in a free society, Havel noticed that there were some changes. In his first interview after he had been released (to a French journalist, published in *Le Monde* in April 1983), he observed that the lines between the "official" and the "other" culture, so rigidly drawn throughout the 1970s, were starting to blur. Meanwhile, the Charter 77 movement had maintained a base of public support. As an opposition movement, it continued to force the regime to engage in dialogue. At the same time, VONS continued to inform the Western press about the fate of those who had been accused and imprisoned. All this attention was gradually helping to discredit the Czechoslovak regime abroad more and more.

But above all, Havel wanted to return to the theater.

> Returning from prison is no joke — some in fact say that it is more difficult than going in. I first have to get my bearings, try and fit in, try to understand the world in which I have arrived. And that means meeting a great many people, reading a large number of important texts, going to various performances and concerts, in short, again learning to breathe the air of my times. Without that, you cannot write. And then I'd like at last to start writing another play — it's about six years since I last wrote one.[3]

At the same time, he urgently felt the need to justify himself, his existence, his choices. Out of touch with society for nearly four years, he was in a state of high anxiety. How had people perceived his imprisonment? What had been its value to them, let alone to him? Perhaps he was too stunned, too unprepared to contemplate the latter question, but he wanted to address the former. He wrote to Miloš Forman, who had tried to arrange for his release from prison in 1979 with Joseph Papp. A letter of apology became a letter of explanation as well:

I returned from prison, and immediately discovered all you had done on my behalf, to try to get me out. And I suddenly had a terrible pang of conscience. That is to say, I had a feeling that I hadn't been fair with you, and I felt the need to apologize to you as soon as possible. . . .

Perhaps you were offended that I hadn't accepted the offer to go to America. After all, it must have been so difficult for you; you accomplished close to the impossible: a jailbird in sweat clothes and handcuffs, awaiting trial and a sentence of about seven years, is suddenly sitting in an office. They remove his handcuffs, offer him coffee, shake his hand (!), even call him "Mr. Havel" (!!!), and propose a stay in New York instead of a Czechoslovakian slammer! My cellmate (the gypsy Čonka who got 13 years for illegal manufacturing) called me a fool and nagged me for days and nights to take the offer. It's hard to explain, but I simply couldn't accept it! You play *maryáš*,[4] so you know that when one is dealt a bad hand, one doesn't just say: "Screw it, so long, I'm leaving." I was in a situation in which I felt that I couldn't simply give up my cause and back down whenever they tried to frighten me. The stakes were too high, there was far too much invested in the game. To give up at that point would have been catastrophic for too many people and especially for me; I would have suffered over it it for the rest of my life!

At the time, no one had lost his citizenship yet,[5] but I wasn't that stupid not to understand what they were after. I could see what a rush they were in; Kohout's return from Vienna was imminent, so they had to get me out of the country first before refusing to let him back in. They knew that after that, I wouldn't have agreed to their offer at all. They tried to assure me, they gave me guarantees, etc. A week later, I read in my cell in *Rudé právo* that Kohout wasn't allowed to come back. Then later, as you know, after I was released from prison, people assured me that my refusal had been a turning point in our situation, and stressed how meaningful it was, etc. etc. — all of which, naturally, I had no idea in prison.

It wasn't an easy decision because it wasn't entirely clear what game they were playing. That they were playing a game, however, was clear, and there were a number of possibilities as to what that game might be. Theoretically, it might have been possible that after my departure they might have released everyone, and the trial would not have taken place at all. So the implications were serious; I didn't know whether I was deciding for myself alone, or for the lives of my fellow prisoners and friends as well. But as it turned out, I made the right decision. None of my "accomplices" would have agreed to a release on those terms — we had already discussed that many times. But please bear in mind that my refusal to accept their offer doesn't mean that I don't appreciate your efforts on my behalf. On the contrary! That's what I explained to Joe [Papp], who understood perfectly. If it hadn't been for your efforts which resulted in their offer, there would have been no chance for me to have refused anything, and for me thereby to manifest that my truth is a matter of my own choice! Only thanks to the fact that I had this choice, could I take this moral stand. The long term effect of your efforts is much greater than it would have been, had I accepted it!

So your efforts were not in vain, as you may have thought they were. On the contrary, because of your efforts, my refusal accomplished its purpose. You provoked the situation, perhaps in a different way than you might have imagined. If it hadn't turned out as did (we were the last "monster trial"[6]), who knew how many friends might still be in prison today! Perhaps from America it seemed like a proud or crazy gesture, but I know that through it — no matter what you may think — I helped to improve the situation. Slowly, they realized that the Chartists were serious in their intentions, so they had to start getting used to it. Today, we're a hundred times more active than we were before our imprisonment, and no one thinks about putting us in jail.

Of course, I'm not saying that I'm the only one who should be taking the credit. I'm only saying that in taking that "cross" upon ourselves without having to, we contributed to the improvement of the situation. I may be expressing myself poorly here, but what I mean is that we redeemed ourselves in a way, and perhaps others too, as well. And if this is the case, then the true value of what you were doing for me from abroad is that you actually gave us a chance to prove our credibility. Anyway, I'm not going to analyze this further. I've never written about such things before, and now, all of a sudden, I feel rather foolish.[7]

Havel had other debts of gratitude to pay, too. An opportunity presented itself in November 1983, when the Stockholm Stadsteater presented an "Evening of Solidarity" for Havel and Charter 77. For that occasion, Havel wrote a play that he dedicated to Samuel Beckett. It was a gesture of thanks and indebtedness for *Catastrophe*, the play Beckett had written in 1982 for the Avignon Festival and dedicated to Havel while he was in prison.

Havel's one-act play was called *Mistake* (Chyba). Like *Catastrophe*, it was five pages long and set in a prison cell. *Mistake* dramatizes the orientation ritual of a new inmate to prison life. Four prisoners, one named King and the others called First, Second, and Third Prisoners (all with shaven heads and tattooed arms and torsos), indoctrinate a newcomer named Xiboj to prison regimen and customs. King explains the rules, while Xiboj huddles silently on a top bunk. First, the rule about no smoking before breakfast is articulated. Second, the regulation about bed-making is presented. Finally, the procedure of how to scrub the wash-basins and the floor is explained. When King demands that Xiboj come down from the top bunk, he simply smiles in embarrassment and does not respond. Interpreting it as provocative behavior, the Second Prisoner drags Xiboj down to the floor and kicks him. Xiboj rises slowly, not comprehending their attacks. There is a pause. Then it dawns on the other prisoners:

> Third Prisoner: *(Softly.)* Know what? He's some kind of bloody Hungarian . . . *(Everyone, surprised, looks at King.)*
> King: *(After a pause, softly.)* Well, that's his mistake . . . [8]

The five-minute play ends with the circle of inmates closing in menacingly on Xiboj, with a promise of more violence to come.

In the end, *Mistake* is a curious fragment about a seemingly simple misunderstanding. At first, we are led to believe that Xiboj is a Vaněk-type, shy, introverted, polite. But the truth is that he is a foreigner who cannot speak or understand a word of Czech. Who is responsible for this misunderstanding, the play asks? On the surface, it is no one's fault. There is a language barrier, and the assumption is that Czechs do not understand Hungarians, and Hungarians do not understand Czechs. But this play is about more than a simple misunderstanding. It is about prison life, where the notion of human responsibility is different. In prison, it's every man for himself. Everyone is responsible only for his own survival. In this new world to which Havel has been exposed, man is fated never to comprehend the language of another, nor the cruelty.

"It's an experience which I myself have had twenty times," Havel says in a videotaped interview about the play.[9] Since Havel was continuously moved from one prison to another, and from one cell to another, he fell victim to this ritual frequently. What Havel sought to dramatize was the deterioration of human behavior under totalitarian systems. This time, the example was prison, a place where people become worse than even the system requires them to be, where a fellow prisoner becomes crueler than a guard. As for the experience of prison itself, the play tries to present a fragment of that strange, traumatic reality. As Havel describes it in that same interview: "For every prisoner, to move from one cell to another is a tragedy. To us, it's the same, but to him it's a completely different world. The slightest change of the view from the window, the different flakes on the wall."[10]

But there is the deeper meaning to the play's title, *Mistake*. In the videotaped interview, Havel talks about the mistake he made when he was in prison in 1977, the mistake that had tortured him for years. He is referring to the letter he wrote requesting a release, which the authorities distorted by adding a sentence, to make it sound as if Havel was relinquishing his position as a spokesperson for Charter 77. As he had written to Olga from Ruzyně just after his sentencing: "I can't help thinking that in fact it's punishment for everything I've done in recent years."[11]

The word *mistake* can also be interpreted in other ways. Did Havel compound what he considered his first mistake (writing the letter of release in 1977) by making another one in 1979, one of dire consequences to his soul? In other words, was it an even a greater mistake that he had sought imprisonment to be punished for this "crime"? What had it really brought him? What had it accomplished? Were those years in prison, after all, a "mistake"? After he was released, he realized that he could never write about prison. And the shock of this realization has rendered him silent, like his character Xiboj in the play.

All this may explain why *Mistake*, which was to be his only play set in prison, seems like a fragment of an unfinished play, the beginning of a larger one dealing with the guilt that he could not yet express. For after he was released from prison, he realized that he would never be able to write about the experience.[12] The reasons that he gave, years later, in *Disturbing the Peace*, were threefold. First, he said, he was not a narrative author, nor was he a storyteller. Second, his nature was such that he became involved with life in the present, leaving him no time to return to that remote time out of time. Third: "the most important thing about it is uncommunicable. No, I mean it: it was a deeply existential and deeply personal experience, and as such I'm simply unable to pass it on."[13]

But the effect of that profound, otherworldly experience in prison was to remain with him indefinitely. He would simply have to find another way of writing about it.

1984: *LARGO DESOLATO*

> If I understand you correctly, you want me to declare that I am no longer me — [1]
> — Havel, *Largo Desolato*

> I have a feeling sometimes that all I am doing is listening helplessly to the passing of the time.[2]
> — Havel, *Largo Desolato*

In the early 1980s, Andrej Krob looked out the window of his cottage at Hrádeček. A group of prisoners were building a small house on the other side of the road, the headquarters where the secret police could watch the house of Václav Havel. A good sign, thought Krob. His neighbor would return home soon.[3]

And so he did, on March 4, 1983. Then the postprison depression set in. He had anticipated it, and it came.

Friends saw signs of it almost immediately. His biographer Edá Kriseová remembers a train ride she and Havel took together three days after his release from the hospital. They were on their way to Moravia along with eight other writers, to one of those quarterly writers' meeting called Kvartál. In the 1970s, Havel had hosted them at Hrádeček, and Kohout, before he was exiled, had hosted them at his lovely modern villa in Sázava, twenty miles southeast of Prague. Havel was talking about how much he wanted to write a play, but no idea had come to him. "He had dreamed that an owl sat on his shoulder and hooted into his ear that it was a singer," Kriseová recalls, "and then its head changed into a woman's head."[4]

On that train ride, they were sitting in a compartment, where no smoking was allowed. As Kriseová remembers it, some of the writers were smoking. Havel was afraid, because there was a stern conductor aboard, notorious for being an ogre. Goaded by his fellow writers, Havel lit a cigarette, and had smoked half of it when one of the writers spotted the conductor coming down the corridor. They put out their cigarettes in haste. The conductor stuck his head through the door and, suspicious, accused one of them of smoking. A silence reigned over that compartment while the conductor cast his eye over all its occupants. His eye settled on Havel, who was blushing furiously.

> The ogre savored his victory, and I knew then that Vašek is like Schopenhauer's saint, who is punished for peccadillos the way other people are punished for great sins. As soon as he does anything, he gets slapped. There was nothing he could do. The conductor, moved by Vašek's inability to lie, bent over and said: "I don't want [to give you] a fine. Just promise me you'll never do it again."[5]

As soon as the conductor left, one of the writers lit a cigarette and smoked happily the rest of the journey. Havel did not. That incident stuck in Kriseová's mind, as she reminisced about Havel's state after his release from prison. "At the time," she said, "it seemed that Václav would never again be able to be happy."[6] In *Disturbing the Peace*, written in 1986, Havel confirms this assessment. He had a bad case of nerves. He was depressed. Everything was a chore.

Meanwhile, his plays continued to be performed abroad with respect and recognition. On November 20, 1983, the day after *Mistake* premiered at the Stadsteater in Stockholm, Havel's Vaněk plays — *Audience*, *Vernissage*, and *Protest* — opened at the Public Theater, produced by his friend Joseph Papp and directed by Lee Grant, under the title of *Private View* (an alternate translation of *Vernissage*). Critic Mel Gussow in the *New York Times* called the production "an event of artistic and political urgency:

> The dehumanizing effects of totalitarianism are demonstrated with wounding honesty and irony in Václav Havel's *Private View* [the production] reminds us of the importance of the artist as provocateur. Despite his victimization, Havel has retained his comic equilibrium and his sense of injustice. Confronted by public and private absurdities, the artist clings to first principles: self-respect and an unquenchable morality. . . . Watching Mr. [Stephen] Keep [who played Vaněk in all three works] move from menial labor to strained

sociability with his superfluous friends to a reunion — and a memory of a time of freedom — one necessarily thinks of Havel, an artist who has lost his liberty but not his creativity.[7]

But the news of these productions did not help lift Havel's bleak mood. To ward off his depression, he threw himself into political activity. In that first year after his release, he wrote a number of powerful political essays, including "Responsibility as Destiny," "Politics and Conscience," and "Six Asides About Culture." But nothing could give him pleasure. Wracked with guilt, he worried constantly about his friends who were still imprisoned, like Petr Uhl who was in solitary confinement at Mírov, and Ivan Jirous who was at Valdice, one of the most punitive prisons. Havel was finding it difficult to adapt to being "outside," fearing that since he had not finished his sentence, they might come at any moment. He drank heavily and slept poorly. To compound his despair, according to biographer John Keane, his marriage was suffering understandable strain in the aftermath of his imprisonment.[8]

Then one summer night in July 1984, holed up in his apartment overlooking the Vltava River, drinking brandy, listening to his favorite tapes, he plunged into the writing of a new full-length play. As he himself describes it, he wrote it "with increasing impatience, in feverish haste, in a bit of a trance,"[9] as if possessed by a demon flogging him on to finish it in a hectic rush. It took him four days and nights, a record for Havel, who had struggled over multiple drafts with all his previous full-length plays, which took anywhere from a year to five years to complete. It was as if the play sprang from him, whole and complete. A twelve-character play in seven scenes,[10] he called it *Largo Desolato*, a title derived from one of the movements of a composition by Alban Berg. It was written by a playwright in his most vulnerable state.

Largo Desolato tells the story of Leopold Kopřiva, a philosophy professor who struggles to keep his sanity in a frightening world. He has a problem. He is under the intense scrutiny of the authorities, who are mistrustful of the books he has written on phenomenology, ontology, and other suspicious subjects. Therefore, he is subject to frequent and unpredictable visits by sinister looking men in trench coats, who keep appearing at his door. They interrogate him, wanting to know what he is writing, referring to his "essay" that is causing so much trouble. They ask him to sign a statement that he is not who he is. Otherwise, he will be sent "there," on the charge of intellectual hooliganism. Then there are the two workers from a paper factory who keep delivering reams of paper. Both named Láďa, they are cut from the same cloth as Sládek in *Audience*, representing the Czech "little man" or everyman. They leave him with blank paper to write the plays he cannot seem to write, as well as mountains of "official" factory documents they thought he might find of interest. His apartment gradually fills with papers and books and uninvited guests who keep reappearing. In short, he is a nervous wreck.

Disheveled and unkempt, Leopold hides out in his apartment in his dressing gown, suffering from agoraphobia, paranoia, writer's block, and loss of sexual drive and subsisting on pills, rum, and a diet of salted almonds and onions. He lives in a state of acute anxiety, constantly lamenting to his wife, Zuzana, that if only he were not the man who signed that "thing," he would be safe. Meanwhile, Zuzana, who has long since given up on him, resorts to a relationship with his best friend, Olda, with whom she goes to the theater and the cinema, leaving Leopold with his eyes fixed on the peephole, his ear glued to the door, nervous, paranoid, waiting for the next threatening visit that will ultimately send him "there." She is sick of all the dissident literature that his friend Olbram keeps bringing him; all she wants is to go to the movies, to dinner, to the opera. Also, she is worried that if Leopold recants, he will not go to prison and she will be stuck with him.

Like Eduard Huml's apartment in *The Increased Difficulty of Concentration*, Leopold's is a thoroughfare through which a succession of women come and go. Zuzana brings food and supplies; Lucy, his mistress, recites choruses of "I love you/I need you"; Markéta, a philosophy student, listens adoringly. Zuzana turns a deaf ear and blind eye to it all and, in the end, goes dancing with Olda.

In the final scene of seduction and confession, while Leopold plies Markéta with rum, he confides in her of his need for punishment, to be sent "there," to yield to a higher will.

> Leopold: I have a feeling that my only way out is to accept a term
> there — somewhere far away from my nearest and dearest — and
> put my humble trust in a higher will, to give me the chance to
> atone for my guilt — to lose my apathy and regain my price —
> and as a nameless cog in a giant machine to purify myself —
> thus and only thus — if I manage to drain the bitter cup with

dignity — I can get back — perhaps — something of my lost human integrity — renew the hope inside me — reconstitute myself emotionally — open the door to a new life —[11]

Horrified, Markéta tries to bolster his self-esteem, entreating him to resist this self-destructive path. She offers herself to him as salvation. At that point, the scary men in trench coats arrive; anticipating their demands, Leopold finally takes his stand. He will not sign the statement. "I'd rather die than give up my own human identity — it's the only thing I've got."[12] But the trench-coated men have news. His case has been "adjourned indefinitely for the time being." And Leopold does not have to sign, because he is now no longer himself.

> Leopold: Are you trying to say that I am no longer me?
> Second Chap: You said it, not me.
> *(Short pause. Leopold gazes at the first and second chap and then shouts.)*
> Leopold: I don't want an adjournment! I want to go there! *(Leopold suddenly falls to his knees in front of the chaps and starts to sob.)* I'm begging you — I beseech you — I can't go on living like this —
> First chap: It seems you'll have to —
> Markéta: *(Calling to him.)* Leopold, get up! You're not going to beg them, are you!
> Leopold: *(Shouting at Markéta.)* Leave me alone! All of you leave me alone! *(Leopold collapses on the floor, banging his fists on it.)*[13]

As the stage directions indicate, the play ends as it began; Leopold is in his apartment, sitting on the sofa, starring in terror at the front door. After a pause he rises, crosses, peers through the peephole, and glues his ear to the crack in the door. Again, Havel uses familiar techniques of revolving-door entrances, repetition of action, ending at the beginning — and we're on the terrain of the absurd once more. But in this case, it's a far more personal one, and therefore all the more perilous.

When reflecting on how he could have written a play so soon after he left prison, Havel said that perhaps it was "an act of self-preservation, an escape from despair, or a safety valve through which I sought relief from myself"[14] In any event, springing as it did from him whole and complete, it came directly from that profound and powerful experience of prison, the consequences of which had only begun.

Largo Desolato offers an interesting perspective. It is a play about a man who is about to enter prison by a man who has just left prison and is writing the play in a state of deep aftershock. As such, it is a full study of the paradoxical existence of the dissident. It dramatizes his isolation, paranoia, and low self-esteem. It exposes his tortured lifestyle with its infidelities and betrayals. It depicts his identity crisis in trying to be all things to all people. On the one hand, he is pressured by the unrealistic expectations of the "common man," represented by the Ládas who admire him for his leadership. (Note the vague reference below to Charter 77 — "that thing you wrote" — and its perception by the ordinary citizen.) They need him as a dissident to change society; they goad him on, saying he could do even more. Their visits are punctuated by pleas in an overlapping, almost Ionescan, dialogue:

> First Láďa: That thing you wrote — even if we don't fully understand it —
> Second Láďa: We're ordinary people —
> First Láďa: — and the fact that you're right behind it —
> Second Láďa: — regardless of the consequences —
> First Láďa: — straight away leads one to hope that you will take the final step . . . to put it simply that you'll come up with the pay-off to all your philosophizing —
> Leopold: The trouble is that opinions differ about quite what the pay-off is —
> Second Láďa: You'll find it —
> First Láďa: Who else but you is there to get things going again?
> Second Láďa: I'd say that's just what people are waiting for —
> Leopold: What people?
> First Láďa: Everybody —
> Leopold: Isn't that a bit of an exaggeration?
> Second Láďa: Forgive me but you probably don't realize —
> Leopold: What?
> First Láďa: Your responsibility —
> Leopold: For what?
> Second Láďa: For everything — [15]

On the other hand, he is pressured by Olbram, his friend and fellow dissident. Speaking as an emissary from the dissident community, Oldram expresses their shared concern that Leopold is possessed by "great demons" who are driving him to turn inward. They are concerned that his personal life is in shambles, that he has lost his perspective, determination, humor, sense of irony, in short, his identity. It is implied that he will crack under pressure, and, once sent to prison, who knows? Other dissidents might be in jeopardy. Olbram preaches to Leopold about the importance of the dissident's identity, urging Leopold to play the part with conviction and not just go through the motions. In cheering him on, Olbram sounds very much like the Ládas: "Don't weaken! Keep at it! Get a grip on yourself! Pull yourself together! Straighten up!"[16]

Leopold is Eduard Huml (from *The Increased Difficulty of Concentration*) with a real, contextual problem. Huml is an intellectual; he feels pressure from within. Leopold is an intellectual, too, but he is also a dissident. And that label imposes an identity on him that is not of his choosing, one that becomes more than he can handle. Leopold's is the dissident's lament, the articulation of suffering over all these irreconcilable expectations, the pressure, the feeling of being responsible for everything and everyone, the limelight that is too bright. He longs for ordinariness, for anonymity:

> Leopold: I'd rather be there than here like this. Why can't I get my life clear! It was wonderful when nobody was interested in me — when nobody expected anything from me, nobody urging me to do anything — I just browsed around the secondhand bookshops — studying the modern philosophers at my leisure — spending the nights making notes from their words — taking notes in the parks and meditating — why can't I change my name . . . and forget everything and start a completely new life?[17]

At one point, all the characters in the play surround Leopold in a choric, almost surreal fashion (just as they surrounded Huml at the end of *The Increased Difficulty of Concentration*), and chant their simultaneous and conflicting demands on him. In that moment, Havel is dramatizing the overwhelming feeling of confusion and pressure that he feels as a dissident, and the fundamental doubt of the value of this identity, as well as his own.

Following the four frenzied days of writing his first full-length play since imprisonment, a sense of danger overcame Havel. As he described it:

There is one [neurosis] that probably every dissident knows: fear for his manuscript. As long as the text into which you've put your best effort, or which you consider very important, is not safely hidden away somewhere, or reproduced and distributed in a sufficient number of copies, you live in constant suspense and uncertainty. And this does not improve with time: you never get used to the notion that your manuscript is constantly in danger. On the contrary, your fear becomes a genuinely pathological obsession.[18]

It was an accumulation of experiences: house searches, body searches, passing a manuscript on to a neighbor (usually Andrej Krob) in the small hours of the morning before searches usually begin, that led to this "obsessive neurosis," as Havel called it. And as he drew to the end of the play, how "you begin to fear that someone will trip you just before the finish line."[19]

This fear may well have accounted for the unprecedented speed at which Havel was able to write *Largo Desolato*. Consumed by anxiety as to its safekeeping and well-being, Havel took two steps to preserve his new manuscript. First, he hid it. In fact, as he told Juncker on the telephone one night at midnight: "To avoid confiscations of my manuscripts, I had to take everything I wrote out of my house — immediately."[20] They might search his house at any time of the day or night, he told Juncker. So he would steal out in the middle of the night to give a new manuscript to a neighbor.

When the play is done and safely tucked away somewhere, I don't care what anyone does to me. I'm happy; I feel I've triumphed over the world once more. As long as it's lying out there on my table as a practically illegible manuscript, I tremble — not just for the play but for myself — which is to say for that part of my identity that would be irrevocably torn away from me if the manuscript were confiscated.[21]

But it was not paranoia that provoked Havel to hide his manuscript. His fears were justified. In August, the police broke into his house at Hrádeček and ransacked it without a warrant, seizing books, letters, papers, documents, magazines, even family photographs and tapes. In addition, his phone was tapped. Once, while on the telephone with Havel, Juncker recalls a conversation during which they heard the sound of clicking. Havel said suddenly, in English: "Wait a minute, Klaus: we have to stop. Our friends have to change the tapes."[22] (Juncker adds an ironic footnote to the story of these constant, harassing house searches. In the late 1990s, at an auction in Berlin, a copy of a novel by Günther Grass was sold at an auction. In it was an inscription from Grass to Havel, to whom he had given the book as a gift in the 1960s. The book was sold for 2,800 marks. When Havel heard about this, he was horrified with embarrassment. He begged Juncker to explain to Grass that he would never sell the book — on the contrary, it had undoubtedly been confiscated in one of these searches by the authorities, and found its way back to Germany. When Günther Grass heard this story, he laughed, and said: "Auctions like these should be more frequent; they enhance my prestige." And he immediately sent another book to Havel with a new inscription.[23])

Meantime, his new play was safely hidden away. In addition, Havel initiated the postprison practice of reading his plays into a tape-recorder and hiding the cassettes.

There was yet another precautionary step Havel took, to help preserve his manuscript. For fifteen years, Havel had not been permitted to see a play of his performed on a stage in his own country. While the news of the numerous productions throughout Europe pleased him, he felt uneasy. At the Balustrade, he had been used to close, intimate collaboration with the director and actors. But since 1968, everything he had written for the stage had been delivered into the hands of strangers. Would they alter the text? How would they interpret the meaning of the play? These concerns plagued him.

So, once again, Havel found himself writing a commentary. In it, he called attention to his continuing theme in *Largo Desolato*, that of identity and how hard it is for a man to maintain an identity in the face of an anonymous power who wants to destroy it. He wrote about the strange contradiction between man's potential and man's destiny, the one his society has imposed on him. He wrote about how easy it is to know how to live in theory, but how hard it is in reality.

At the heart of *Largo Desolato*, he wrote, is paradox and ambivalence. Leopold is an example of paradox, in that he is both a hero and a coward. He is sincere, and at the same time he cheats. He desperately defends his identity, and at the same time he loses it. He is both the victim of his environment and at the same time he is its creator. Consequently, says Havel, we feel both compassion and disgust for Leopold. The Ládas have good intentions; at the same time, they are indiscreet, they bother Leopold, they waste his time. Olbram is a fair, reasonable man, he cares about Leopold, but he is also judgmental and his visits upset Leopold. In summary, Havel writes in his commentary, there are no good or bad characters in the play, only paradoxical ones, living in a paradoxical world in which everyone has good intentions, everyone is a little right, but nevertheless, everyone makes things worse and worse. In a poignant plea, Havel expresses his fear of losing control over the interpretation to unseen, unknown artists: "So I beg the future director to let the characters live their lives their own way."[24]

Years later, Jan Grossman said of *Largo Desolato*: "It is a very brave play. One day, when someone writes a biography of Václav Havel, they should pay attention to this play, because there is something very self-critical about it. You might even say that it is a caricature of a dissident."[25]

Havel himself had been quick to acknowledge, in *Disturbing the Peace*, the autobiographical content of *Largo Desolato*. However, he has said he would never think of rejecting a theme inspired by his own life experiences. On the contrary, he feels that as a dramatist, he would have no right to censor his own dramatic impulses, which are, as he put it, at the very heart of the creative process. He also offers acknowledgment that, in the process of drawing the play from his life experiences, he may have hurt others. He regrets this, and offers an apology: "In *Largo Desolato*, all those I may once have hurt can see an instrument of divine justice taking revenge on me for them. The damage I inflict in this play is on myself, for a change."[26]

But in the end, Havel maintains that to experience the play as autobiography is to miss its larger implications.

> The play was inspired by my own experiences, certainly more directly than any other play I've written, and this is true not only of the individual motifs, but also about its most basic theme. I really did put a bit of my own instability into Kopřiva's instability, and in a certain sense it is a real caricature, containing elements of me and of my postprison despair. At the same time, it is not an autobiographical play; it is not about me, or only about me as such. The play has ambitions to be a human parable, and in that sense it's about man in general. The extent to which the play was inspired by my own experiences is not important. The only important thing is whether it tells people something about their own human possibilities.[27]

In speaking of *Largo Desolato* as a caricature of the life of a dissident, Grossman is referring to the play's satirical elements, which highlight the absurdities of Leopold's situation. There is the persona of Leopold himself — his disheveled state, his paranoia, his ear glued to the keyhole, his eye glued to the peephole. There is the merry-go-round of Leopold's personal life. There is the absurdity of the demands placed on him by the outside world. The Ládas bring Leopold useless bureaucratic papers from their plant because they are stamped "confidential," thinking Leopold can decipher or decode them. Well, of course, he's a dissident; he can do that sort of thing, or anything, for that matter. The Ládas want Leopold to write a declaration. What kind? "Quite simply a kind of general declaration covering all the basics," replies the second Láda.[28] Here, Havel is questioning the value of Charter 77 itself. If the ordinary citizen doesn't understand what it means, if it hasn't brought change, then what is its value, if people's lives (including his) have been sacrificed for it?

Then there are the expectations of others, which are repeated over and over by everyone in his life: "We know everything." "We're your fans." "We're of the opinion that you could be doing more than you are in your place." "We believe in you and we need you." "The main thing is you mustn't weaken." "There's lots of people looking to you." "The more they count on you the harder it would be for them if you failed to hold out in some way." The crescendoing chorus must have echoed in Havel's mind during all those years since his arrest, as he suffered in prison in solitude and silence, unable to express the burden of failure and guilt publicly until now.

Underlying it all is the fundamental absurdity of Leopold's situation. He did not have to go to prison at all, whereas Havel did go, whether he had to or not. That is what Havel may have been wondering, dazed, depressed, demoralized, alone in his apartment in that hot summer of 1984. Why had he gone to prison, after all? What had it proven, and to whom? If it was about preserving his identity of a dissident, then what exactly is the value of that identity?

As a play about a man on the threshold of going to prison, *Largo Desolato* is ultimately the prison play Havel said he was not capable of writing. For it is not about the prison and its four walls, it's about the four walls of the soul, the need for punishment, the need for atonement he felt so keenly, that it was, as he said, "incommunicable." As Leopold explains:

I have a feeling that my only way out is to accept a term there —
somewhere far away from my nearest and dearest — and put my
humble trust in a higher will, to give me the chance to atone for my
guilt — to lose my apathy and regain my pride — and as a nameless cog in a giant machine to purify myself — thus and only
thus — if I manage to drain the bitter cup with dignity — I can get
back — perhaps — something of my lost human integrity — renew
the hope inside me — reconstitute myself emotionally — open the
door to a new life — [29]

For Havel, in the summer of 1984, only eighteen months out of
prison, it was too early to tell.

Largo Desolato was first published by Edice Expedice (number 185,
1984), Havel and Olga's *samizdat* press. It had its premiere at the Burgtheater in Vienna on April 13, 1985, in a strange land, in a strange tongue.
It was Havel's most personal play to date, and he was not present on
opening night.

In September 1984, just after Havel had finished writing *Largo Desolato*, he received a long-promised visit from Joe and Gail Papp. Papp had
been invited to Moscow to discuss an upcoming production of *A Chorus
Line*, and he and Gail decided to stop in Prague on the way. When Havel
learned of this, he invited the Papps to visit him and Olga at Hrádeček.
Havel dispatched his brother to the airport to greet them. "How will I
recognize you at the airport?" Papp asked Ivan Havel. "I'll be the only one
carrying a book," replied Ivan.[30]

The Papps arrived at Hrádeček in glorious, September weather. They
presented Havel with a framed copy of the Obie Award for *The Memorandum* that he had won sixteen years earlier in New York, which they
had hidden in the bottom of their suitcase. "In those days, cultural trips
were highly suspicious. It was better to say you were going skiing," Gail
Papp remembers. Although they had been stopped at the airport, the authorities had not found it, she said. As she recalls:

> Havel was under house arrest. Olga was there, took, looking stately,
> beautiful, and sad. Ivan spent the whole weekend working on a photo
> album. Joe and Václav were marvelous together. There was a great,
> warm feeling between them. They showed us the ruins at the top of
> the hill, and the police stake out near the old castle ruin. There was a
> big stucco fireplace in the living room. It was a lovely country home,

very warm. We slept in a guest room with psychedelic posters on the wall from New York City and a picture of the Pope.[31]

During that visit, Gail Papp recalls, Havel spoke of how he was plagued by the secret police, who would periodically enter his home and search it without notice or provocation. To illustrate the absurdity of these searches, Havel brought out a typewritten list prepared by the police, itemizing the objects they had confiscated from Havel's home after a recent search. Havel showed it to the Papps, pointing out that one of the items the police had confiscated was a copy of *Hamlet*. "It was so crazy," Gail Papp remembers. "No wonder he wrote the kinds of plays he did."

Havel told Papp that he had just written a new play, *Largo Desolato*, and promised to get a copy to them. "He didn't give us the manuscript of *Largo* then and there, because he was afraid we might be stopped and searched at the airport," Gail Papp said. "He had other ways, then, of getting his scripts out of the country."

The "other ways" were the network established in the 1970s to smuggle dissident manuscripts out of the country, for publication by the Czech emigré press. Much had happened since the network was founded to test and traumatize it. In 1981, the chain was broken. An informer had contacted the police, who were ready and waiting at the border to detain the white van the next time it traveled from Paris on the way to the drop-off at Jiřina Šiklová's Prague apartment. They arrested the drivers, a young French couple, who knew nothing about the piles of books, manuscripts, and magazines they were carrying in the back of the van, only the name of the person to whom they were to deliver it. Among the materials, the authorities found the list of three hundred to four hundred names in code, a priceless document that represented the infrastructure of the Czech dissident movement. They made an offer to Šiklová: either decode the list, or go to prison for ten years. Šiklová chose the latter. While in prison, she recalls sitting in her cell and overhearing Olga being interrogated in the next room. When asked by her interrogator: "Who is Jiřina Šiklová?" Olga was overheard to answer, truthfully: "I don't know." Until then, the network was so tightly designed, everyone had been protected. "When I got out of prison [fourteen months later]," Šiklová recounts, "Ivan Havel was waiting for me with flowers and an identification card, to prove that he was not an agent and that he really was who he said he was. That was the first time Ivan and I met face to face."[32]

Once Šiklová was released from prison, the network reconfigured. Now that Havel had also been released and was writing again, getting his new plays safely out of the country was a top priority and a dangerous one. "We used embassy people — namely, Wolfgang Scheuer," Šiklová said. Scheuer was the West German cultural attaché in Prague from 1981 to 1986. The new configuration was a triangle, according to Vilém Prečan, former executive director of the Scheinfeld Center.[33] Located at Castle Schwartzenberg near Hanover, the center's purpose was to distribute independent literature and information that had been banned or confiscated in Czechoslovakia. Šiklová passed the manuscripts on to Scheuer, who made sure they got out of the country to Bonn via diplomatic courier. Once in Bonn, the manuscripts were sent to the Scheinfeld Center, where Prečan made copies and sent them to Klaus Juncker in Reinbek and to other Czech emigré publishing centers. The network operated swiftly. Both *Mistake* and *Largo Desolato* arrived within weeks after they were completed. This illustrates both how eager Havel was to get his manuscripts out of his hands, and how efficiently the network functioned.

"It was hard to work with Havel," Šiklová says, "because (a) he was always followed and (b) he didn't have a good sense of conspiracy. 'Don't tell me anything,' he would say.'" So Olga, Ivan, and Ivan's wife Dáša became the intermediaries between Havel and Šiklová. Like his character Leopold Kopřiva, Havel was always in an intense state of anxiety about his manuscripts. Šiklová recalls a notable example of this. Havel was working on an essay at a hotel in Český Krumlov (a medieval village several hours from Prague), when he noticed some secret police around the hotel. Desperate that the essay be sent abroad, he took a piece of carbon paper, typed the essay in carbon, put one copy in an envelope and mailed it from his hotel to Jiřina Šiklová at her address in Prague. Once he left Český Krumlov and was driving on the road to Prague, he was stopped by the police and searched. They found the original copy of the essay and confiscated it. "He arrived in Prague and was a nervous wreck with apprehension that the only copy of that essay would get to me," Šiklová recalls. "When I received it, I knew it had to be smuggled out immediately. But I couldn't meet Havel to tell him, so we had to wait till after it was out of the country. Days passed before he would learn it arrived safely in the West and would soon be published."

Through the 1980s, Šiklová maintained as low a profile as possible. "By the 1980s, the system was well reorganized, but I had to be prepared to be arrested at any moment," she says. "It was important, if you were a contact person, never to do anything that would attract unusual attention." Ruefully, she recalls all the tickets to the Plastic People of the Universe concerts she had received in the 1970s. "I gave the tickets to my children's friends, but I couldn't give them to my own children," she says.

When asked today why she did all this, Šiklová replied: "We did it for ourselves. We did it because it was important to do."

1985: *TEMPTATION*

> You simply cannot serve all masters, and at the same time deceive them all. You can't just take and give nothing in return. Every one of us has to decide where he stands.[1]
>
> — Havel, *Temptation*

> The devil is present in everyone of us, if we do not live in truth.[2]
>
> — Ivan Jirous

The torrent of playwriting, unleashed after release from prison, had not yet subsided. Havel still had to deal with the Devil.

Ever since Havel was first imprisoned in 1977, he had been haunted by the Faust theme. As he described it in *Disturbing the Peace*, it was in the air while he was in prison, where he was plagued by "strange and somewhat psychotic states and feelings"[3] and sharp pangs of guilt. After all, he was one of the authors of Charter 77 and had brought harm to so many people. He felt he should shoulder that responsibility for their misery and shoulder it alone.

The Faust theme hadn't yet taken name or shape. Then came the "trap" that he said was laid for him in May 1977, when the authorities suggested that he write the usual formal request for release, and he did so, without knowing that the authorities would take that request, falsify it, and discredit him in the eyes of his country. Yet, looking back at that very dark time, he remembers that strange things began to happen — things beyond his control. A copy of Goethe's *Faust* was delivered to his cell, unrequested, and thereafter, Thomas Mann's *Doctor Faustus*. Was someone setting him up, he wondered, trying to warn him and at the same time tempt him with the idea of "temptation" itself? Strange dreams and ideas haunted him.

I felt as though I were being, in a very physical way, tempted by the devil. I felt that I was in his clutches. I understood that I had somehow become involved with him. The experience of having something misappropriated in this way — something I had actually thought and written — something that was true — clarified for me with fresh urgency that the truth is not simply what you think it is; it is also the circumstances in which it is said, and to whom, why, and how it is said.[4]

Then, of course, he was released, and found out about the falsification of his letter. The work of the devil had begun. And the unconscious wish to be punished for the crime he had committed against himself and consequently against others pursued him until, at last, he was sentenced to prison again. That period between "crime" and "punishment" he called the darkest one of his life.

The theme of Faust haunted him through his second, long imprisonment, too. There was no way he could exorcise this demon, although he tried. During the presentencing months at Ruzyně, he took vigorous notes of drafts for a new play on the Faust theme. First it was going to be a "Beckettian comedy about life,"[5] as he described it; then it was reduced to three characters. But he discarded these notes. After he was transferred to Heřmanice and then to Plzeň-Bory, he was forbidden to take any notes at all, let alone write a play. But the feelings of humiliation and devastation at having been "tempted by the devil" still tormented him. He wrote of them in a letter to Olga, and in a way, the expression of these feelings were a continuation of the notes on the play he wanted to write, to exorcise this demon.

> I came out of prison [in 1977] discredited, to confront a world that seemed to me one enormous, supremely justified rebuke. No one knows what I went through in that darkest period of my life (you may be the only one who has an inkling): there were weeks, months, years, in fact, of silent desperation, self-castigation, shame, inner humiliation, reproach and uncomprehending questioning. For a while I escaped from a world I felt too embarrassed to face into gloomy isolation, taking masochistic delight in endless orgies of self-blame. And then for a while I fled this inner hell into frantic activity through which I tried to drown out my anguish and at the same time, to "rehabilitate" myself somehow. Naturally, I felt how

tense and unnatural my behavior was, but I still couldn't shake that sensation. I felt best of all, relatively speaking, in prison.[6]

After leaving prison, he continued to make notes, but it wasn't until over a year after the completion of *Largo Desolato* that he began work on the Faust play in earnest. Perhaps it was provoked by his revisits to prison in January 1985, where he was held in police custody for forty-eight hours in connection with the nomination of the new Charter 77 spokesman. He was detained twice again in August, for forty-eight-hour periods each, in connection with the drafting of a Charter 77 statement on the anniversary of the 1968 Soviet invasion. Yet these incidents did not distract him from his formulation of a new play; indeed, they seemed to stimulate it.

Meanwhile, earlier that year, Havel had been reading some books on black magic that he had borrowed from his friend Zdeněk Urbánek. In the fall of 1985, an idea for a new play came to him. He was alone at Hrádeček; the leaves on the birches outside his study window had turned, the days were chilled and gloomy, and visitors were rare. He began to sketch the play out in his usual fashion, with graphs and charts, entrances and scenes and acts.

Then one October evening (Havel had the habit of writing late into the night), he sat down in his study and began to write. The room was on the ground floor on the side of the house and had a large picture window. Facing away from the courtyard and from the Krob's house, it looked out over a lawn and a copse of birch trees, into a dense, dark forest. There he wrote the play in ten days straight, at breakneck speed, a scene a day, as if in a trance, scarcely gazing out the window at the overcast fall skies as he plumbed the darker depths of the past ten years. He emerged from his study, exhausted, with a fifteen-character play in ten scenes. Its title was *Temptation* (Pokoušeni), and it was dedicated to his friend Zdeněk Urbánek. As he described the experience later in a letter to Pavel Landovský:

> The speed of this process — which is unusual for me because it usually takes me two to three years to write a play — had a bad effect on me. I collapsed, physically and psychologically. Thereafter, I spent several terrifying weeks at Hrádeček — the devil must have taken revenge on me for writing about him. But part of that collapse was that I was more unsure about that play than about

anything I'd written in my life. And never before was I so dependent on the opinions of others. I was even ready to finish my senseless life, if someone were to have said that the play was bad. But there was one thing for certain: I cannot touch the play any more. I can't change a thing. It's simple — I have a choice: either I let the play live its own life, or throw it away, or hang myself.[7]

One day during that period, Andrej Krob, his neighbor, found an envelope at his door. With it was a note:

Andulko and Andrej: This is my new play, which a short time ago burst forth from me. It only took 10 days to write. I'd appreciate it if you'd read it. Your friends can read it as well. And then please let me know what you think. So far it's the only copy, so please read it quickly and return it to Olga. Thank you.[8]

The plot of *Temptation* is drawn from the medieval legend of Faust, about a man who sold his soul to the devil. It is one of Havel's most ambitious and complex plays, the story of two worlds, the official and the "other world," the scientific and the occult, and a soul who is tempted to cross the border from one to the other. As in *The Garden Party* and *The Memorandum*, the "official" world in *Temptation*, a scientific institute, is a structured one, with its own rules and regulations. At the same time, Havel introduces its opposite: the unknown.

The soul that gets sold belongs to Dr. Jindřich Foustka, a respected young scientist who works in a institute where scientific research of an unspecified nature is being conducted. Foustka secretly opposes the institute's scientific purposes, doubts its methods, and hates its dull, white-coated routine and structured, sterile environment. In scene one, we are introduced to that world, its employees and its bureaucratic double-talk and speechifying. It is a far cry from Foustka's dim, smoke-filled lair, filled with books, papers, a globe, and a map of the heavens. There we find him in scene two, kneeling in the middle of his room, clad in his dressing gown, with four burning candles on the floor around him, a fifth candle in one hand, and a piece of chalk in the other. He draws a circle around himself and the candles, while consulting an old tome on the occult, which lies open on the floor. He is experimenting, trying to break through to the "other side." Enter his aging housekeeper, Houbová, to announce the arrival of a visitor. As the stranger takes the first step over the threshold, the ceremony of temptation has begun.

As devils go, Fistula looks more like a character out of Beckett's *Endgame* than out of Faust. He cuts a rather nondemonic figure; a small, slender man "of dubious appearance" with a limp, he enters carrying a paper bag containing slippers. According to Houbová, he smells rather like cheese. In fact, he is quite pleasant and nonthreatening, this agent of darkness. Foustka fears Fistula, thinking that he is a representative from another world that he has conjured up (his fears are increased by Fistula's icy handshake). But Fistula reassures him, saying: You're afraid of me, I know, I don't blame you, you think I'm an agent provocateur, you don't know if I'm a devil or only pretending to be. Duality in life and truth — they are always up to us to decide. I can't give you any clear proof of what I am and what I'm not. I might be, and then again I might not be. I'm not able to convince you. I have no arguments. Here I am: you must decide what I am.

Fistula tempts Foustka by suggesting that Foustka keep an open mind about who he really is, and meanwhile that they work together, so that Foustka can take advantage of Fistula's knowledge and special powers. After all, says Fistula, who knows? It may be Foustka who is the agent provocateur, not he. Thus, preying on Foustka's fear as well as his curiosity, tantalizing him with his offer of special powers, the "pact with the devil" is made. As proof of his capabilities, Fistula offers to make Markéta, the office secretary, fall in love with Foustka at the institute's garden party that evening.

At the party, Foustka, possessed by a sense of freedom and empowerment, waxes philosophical to Markéta. Boldly and recklessly, he speaks out on antiscientific issues:

> Foutstka: When man drives God out of his heart, he makes way for the Devil. What else is this contemporary world of ours, with its blind, power-crazed rulers and its blind, powerless subjects, what else is the catastrophe that is being prepared under the banner of science . . . other than the work of the Devil? It is well known that the Devil is a master of disguise. Can you imagine a more ingenious disguise than that offered him by our modern lack of faith? No doubt he finds he can work best where people have stopped believing in him.[9]

Seduced by his philosophical outpourings, Markéta falls madly in love with Foustka. Fistula has triumphed. And Foustka, intoxicated by his own transformation, is not yet aware of its consequences.

> Foustka: . . . Something is going on inside me — I feel I'd be capable of doing things that were always alien to me. As if something that had lain hidden deep inside me was suddenly floating to the surface.[10]

Meanwhile, the director of the institute has sensed Foustka's subversion. He announces to the staff that something serious has happened: the institute, that "lighthouse of true knowledge" and scientific progress, has been infected by a virus of dissent. Someone in the institute has been engaging in hermetic practices, astrology, alchemy, and magic for the purpose of prescientific investigations. Someone has made "contact" with the world of occult practices. He accuses Foustka by name, announcing that he is "on trial" and must respond to the accusation. When Markéta protests, she is fired.

Foustka returns home, to find Fistula already installed at his desk. Enraged, Foustka lashes out at Fistula for what has happened. But why, says Fistula? Isn't it just that something has been liberated in you that was already there, dormant until now? "If the devil exists," says the agent of the devil, "then he is within all of us."[11] I am just a catalyst, says Fistula. I just "stimulate" things that are already there. Through my efforts, they find the courage to lead a more exciting life. Fistula didn't tempt Foustka, he insists; Foustka exercised his free will to choose temptation.

> Fistula: You know why you called me a devil? To rid yourself of responsibility — and to ease your conscience . . . you must understand that I — an insignificant invalid — could not budge you by so much as an inch if you did not want to be budged, if indeed you had not dreamed about being budged long ago. Our little experiment was merely designed to bring these trivialities home to you.[12]

Ultimately, says Fistula, Foustka is suffering from self-deception. Disguised as an innocent seeker of truth, he not only fooled others, but also himself. Anyway, continues Fistula, truth is a tricky thing. It is not only a question of what we think the truth is, but it is also to whom and under what conditions we articulate it. Fistula has simply revealed to Foustka his darker side.

Foustka is done for, basically. He is "tried" by the institute's director and deputy director, and he confesses to the study of hermetic literature, a fascination for mysticism and the supernatural, and the practice of magic. The director is dismayed: How could Foustka, as a scientist, deal with magicians? Foustka's answer: If mysticism, the occult, and superstition pose a threat to science, then why not study it and learn more about it? Foustka goes a step farther, saying that to study the other side, he in fact took "an oath of silence," to string along their emissaries so as to infiltrate them and observe them better. In short, Foustka has become a double agent. Yes, now, as a scientist, he sees it was a mistake to undertake this new line of research.

With this argument, Foustka has convinced the Director, who promises to exonerate Foustka and even let him continue his research of the "other side," if he supplies the Director with information on his research. In other words, the Director wants Foustka to act officially as a double agent. And in fact, this research will be a feather in the institute's cap. Delighted, the Director announces that the theme for the next evening's garden party will be a Witches' Sabbath.

Along the way, there is Havel's familiar subplot of multiple love interests, replete with intrigues, seductions, betrayals, and the like. However, they are of little consequence to the main story. Meanwhile, the most interesting female character in *Temptation*, and an unusual one in the Havel canon, is Houbová, Foustka's landlady. She is not involved in any love intrigue; moreover, she takes a stand, expressing her doubts about Fistula in the play's penultimate scene, when he appears at the door again. But Foustka does not heed her. Instead, Foustka declares that he wants to keep working with Fistula, who in turn congratulates him for it, saying that not only has Foustka kept his job at the institute, but in fact has been promoted. Then the tables turn. Fistula (the agent of the devil) begins to fear Foustka (the man of science) — is Foustka trying to deceive him? After all, they have begun to trust each other. Not at all, Foustka replies. He is now in a position to inform on both sides. He can give information on the other world to the institute; he can give information on the institute to Fistula. At the end of the scenes, they embrace each other in agreement — and this time, Fistula jumps away. Foustka now is colder than he!

In the final scene, the Witches' Sabbath garden party, the tables are turned once again. The Director announces to the unsuspecting Foustka that the game is up, and Fistula appears from behind the bushes. The Director reveals that Fistula has been working for the institute all along, that he is an old and trusted collaborator and friend, that he has never lied to them. Fistula had been sent to tempt Foustka, to test him, to see how he would conduct himself. All the characters form a semicircle around Foustka, dancing an ever-quickening tango as the music rises.

> Foustka: *(To Fistula.)* So I fell into your trap, after all, didn't I? . . .
> Fistula: Well, I'm sorry, Jindřich, but here you go again — simplifying everything. Did I not let you now all along that you had a range of choices and that you alone could decide your fate? You didn't not fall into any trap of mine, you (are undone), thanks to your own pride, which led you to believe that you could play both ends against the middle and get away with it. Have you forgotten the pains I took to explain to you that man has to respect someone in authority — whoever that someone may be — unless he wants to come to a bad end? . . . So my conscience is clear . . . I did what I could. I'm afraid it's your funeral if you failed to understand . . .[13]

The moral? "You simply cannot serve all masters, and at the same time deceive them all," the Director says. "You can't just take and give nothing in return. Every one of us has to decide where he stands."[14]

Foustka confesses his folly: to think he could use the devil without having to render his soul unto him! "As if the devil could be deceived," he admits.[15] The Director praises Foustka for seeing the error of his ways. To acknowledge this moment, the ensemble surrounds him, and as the music crescendos, they start clapping in a rhythmic fashion, swaying side to side, until they are all dancing in a swirling motion. According to Havel's stage directions, the dancing escalates into an orgiastic carnival, a frenzied *Walpurgisnacht* echoing with dark, derisive, laughter. Foustka does not participate, but stumbles among them, disoriented, entangled in the mêlée. Suddenly, a character who has been carrying a bowl containing a burning flame accidentally sets fire to Foustka's coat. Foustka runs up and down the stage in panic. Thick, sulphurous fumes come pouring out from the bowl, which has been set at the edge of the garden. The music is deafening, and the stage is engulfed in smoke. Havel's directions indicate that it should even invade the audience. In the most flamboyantly theatrical ending that Havel has yet written, his play goes up in a puff of smoke.

Then the music subsides, the curtain falls, the house lights rise. A lone figure takes a bow; it is a fireman in uniform, with a helmet on his head, holding a fire extinguisher.

The parable is evident: Foustka is a scientist, who wants to understand the "other side," the world of the occult, the unknown. Havel is a dissident, who tries to deal with the "other world," the world of the official regime. How could Havel even think of communicating with the other side? he seems to be asking himself. Even the act of writing the letter that released him from prison constitutes "dealing with the devil." How could Havel have possibly been tempted by their promise of a rational response to his letter? Did Havel actually believe that he could make contact with the other side without getting tainted? Was that belief an act of naïveté or of hubris, a belief in his own imperviousness? And by that act, did Havel in fact not become a double agent for the authorities? Worse, could Havel have been used as an example to others in his society?

These are the questions that tormented Havel since 1977. Fascination, fear, curiosity, seduction, self-deception, self-delusion, quest for knowledge, control, power over his situation — all the demons that possessed Foustka — are the demons that Havel sought to exorcise in the writing of this play. The burden of all this self-torture, self-reproach, and self-doubt was finally articulated. No wonder he collapsed when he finished writing it.

If Havel's traumatic experiences led him to ponder the existence of the devil, it was logical that they would also lead him to ponder the existence of God. And that is what happens in *Temptation*. Says Foustka to Markéta:

> Foustka: Have you ever thought that we would be quite unable to understand even the most simple moral action which is not motivated by self-interest, that in fact it would appear to be quite absurd, if we did not admit to ourselves that somewhere within it there is concealed the prerequisite of something higher, some absolute, omniscient and infinitely just moral authority, through which and in which all our actions gain a mysterious worth and through which each and every one of us constantly touches eternity?[16]

Havel's *Temptation* does not answer that question. But it does acknowledge a higher power that transcends good and evil. That power, the theme that unites all his postprison essays, is truth.

Imagine the frustration Havel must have felt, having poured out his heart into *Largo Desolato* and *Temptation*, and then not having the opportunity to see them performed or to participate in a theatrical production of their premiere.

> It's very trying, worse than when a poet or a novelist can't publish in his own country. A play is bound, to a far greater extent, to the "here" and a "now." It is always born out of a particular social and spiritual climate, and it is directed at that climate. That is its home, it needs that home, and it only truly becomes itself when it can be seen in that home as theater. As a text it's incomplete. For the past seventeen years I've been deprived of these basic conditions, and, understandably, it doesn't make writing any easier. I come to terms with it by simply not admitting that this is the situation, by writing as though my plays could still be performed at the Theatre on the Balustrade and as though my contemporaries could still see them here today.[17]

So bound was he to the concept of a home, that Havel realized that he had written *Largo Desolato* and *Temptation* with both the original company of the Balustrade in mind and the actual physical dimensions of the Balustrade stage itself.

But he couldn't have his plays performed at the Balustrade, or anywhere in his country, for that matter. Once again, he relied on the Šiklová-Scheuer-Prečan network. Within weeks of the play's completion, a copy of *Temptation* was sent out of Prague by Scheuer via diplomatic courier, and arrived at the Scheinfeld Center in Hanover on November.[8] Again, Prečan made copies immediately and sent them to Klaus Juncker and others. (Meanwhile, Havel made a tape of his own reading of the play, which he circulated among his friends.) Once again, thanks to Juncker and Achim Benning, *Temptation* received its world premiere, in German, on the Akademietheater stage at the Burgtheater.

As rehearsals progressed, Havel's anxiety for his new play increased. A true offstage drama was brewing in Vienna; no one understood the play, not even his friend Pavel Landovský, who was performing in it. Havel received calls daily from the theater, asking him to explain the meaning of its different themes, and even requesting line readings. Despairing that he was so far away, frustrated that he couldn't be in the rehearsal room, he found that these calls made him more nervous than ever. Why didn't they stop discussing the play and just learn the lines, he told his fellow playwright, Josef Topol, and the critics Sergej Machonin and František Pavlíček, in a round-table discussion for the *samizdat* journal *Lidové noviny* (People's News)? As he complained to them:

> The European theater is full of Brecht's assistants. Everyone who ever made coffee for him is now saying he is Brecht's disciple, and behaves like an authority. They want the play to be explained in sociological and psychological terms . . . They don't understand that every play has its secret and it should be played as it is written . . . But they're not interested in this at all and they waste rehearsal time searching and analyzing and trying to make metaphysical sense of it all.[18]

His anxiety increased to the point of alarm after receiving a call from Landovský, who said the director and the dramaturg had some strange ideas about *Temptation* and were having problems with the play. In fact, Landovský was having problems with the play too, so the production team had asked him to help them make some cuts and changes. Panicked, Havel wrote Landovský a desperate letter:

> What should I do in this situation? Should I beg you to like my play and to go on supervising it? Should I defend my play against your objections? Should I ask the theater not to produce my play? I really don't know. And I feel helpless . . . I cannot influence the production from a distance. . . . Meanwhile, I'm pleased to tell you that 95% of the reaction to the play here has been positive so far. About six people already have written essays or commentaries on the play. If you are interested, the translator has them and will be glad to send you the copies. Many people are shocked by it (in the best sense): one psychiatrist even said that after he read this play, it changed his life (I don't know how). Philosophers like it, too; my fellow playwrights like it — Josef [Topol], Karel [Steigerwald], Daniela [Fischerová]; others say it's my best play. All this, of course, encourages me. There were also some critical voices: three by experienced dramaturg, but you know dramaturgs, they always want to make changes, that's what dramaturgs do. Some Christians said that the play should have more hope. I don't care about that at all,

because I know that the question of hope and hopelessness in the theater is much different than in the church.[19]

He begged Landovský to reconsider. Perhaps, because the play was being done in a foreign theater, the director and actors may be missing something. Perhaps Landovský's own judgment was being influenced by the foreign environment. Havel ended with a final plea to Landovský to put aside whatever reservations he had about the play and convey Havel's intentions to the director.

Landovský delivered the message; the director stepped down from the production, and opening night took place on May 23, 1986. That night, while the actors performed *Temptation* in Vienna, Olga gave a simultaneous opening-night party at the family apartment at Rašínovo nábřeží. There, Havel read the play aloud to a group of his closest, most enthusiastic friends. Anna Freimanová, Krob's wife, recalls the exuberant atmosphere of that evening, which included dining, laughing, and an animated discussion about the play, while they eagerly awaited the phone call from Vienna. Finally, after the curtain came down in Vienna, a call came from Pavel Landovský and from Pavel Kohout, who was in the audience. "How long did the applause last?!" was the first question from Havel to his friends.[20]

The contemporaries of Havel who understood his postprison plays best were those who also had experienced despair, temptation — and imprisonment. Of all his friends, Havel felt that Ivan Jirous, director of the Plastic People of the Universe, had the greatest insight into what he was trying to write. Jirous recognized that the play was inspired by Havel's traumatic experience in prison in 1977 when he wrote the letter to the authorities that brought his release. Jirous knew it because he too had had such an experience; so many of their friends had. As far as he was concerned, Havel had redeemed himself through all his brave civic deeds. But, as Jirous wrote in an essay on the play:

> Nevertheless, now we see that this old story was deeper in him than we would have expected. The topic of temptation had to be transformed into a play which we now have. For Havel, it was the only way to purge himself of this obsession, to kill it by transforming it into art. In my opinion it is the most thrilling play Havel ever wrote.[21]

Calling *Temptation* a return to the absurdist world of *The Garden Party* ("like a snake biting his own tail," as Havel puts it), Jirous praises the play for its humor and at the same time notes that the ending is not at all funny:

> We are confronted with the fact that the real devil has nothing to do with theosophy and Agrippa's magic. We see that the existence of the devil is in reality; that the devil is present in every one of us, if we do not live in truth. And the one who thinks that he's able to deceive life, falls into the devil's embrace . . . When I finished reading Havel's play, I felt upset for a long time. It is deeper than his plays of the 1960s. But Havel himself hasn't changed that much; he is only wiser now. He has known about the existence of the devil since the beginning of his career, although that's not what he was called then. Since that time he has met the devil face to face; hence Havel is a playwright who has the right to adapt the seductive Faustian theme. Some Christian friends of mine say there's no hope in this play. I don't think the purpose of drama should be to give us hope. Nevertheless, there is hope in *Temptation*. The hope is: to refuse to collaborate with the devil.[22]

Jiřina Šiklová, key organizer of the network that smuggled dissident literature out of the country, also understood the meaning of *Temptation* and of *Largo Desolato* from personal experience:

> I know what the problem of temptation is. It's about playing both sides. And it's about the devil. The devil is like the StB. The temptation is to play the game and to try to outwit them. But if you play this game with the devil, you can never win. I remember when I was interrogated, I was tempted to play along with them. I thought it would work. But it didn't. I knew it from the moment I thought: "I'll give you the information you want — maybe it won't be quite accurate, but I'll give it to you anyway." I thought I could play the game. So that's why these are my favorite plays of Havel [*Largo Desolato* and *Temptation*] — because I know about all this from my personal experience.[23]

1986: "FAR FROM THE THEATER"

> In this desperate situation, there is one advantage. I don't have to
> care about the critics any more.[1]
>
> — Havel, "Far from the Theater"

Although the opening night of *Temptation* in Vienna had come off well,
and Havel was ever grateful to the Burgtheater for another premiere, he
still longed for a theatrical home where he could participate in the production of his plays. He poured out his heart in an essay called "Far from
the Theater" (Daleko od divaldla), first published in *O divadle* (About
Theater):

> The playwright without a theater is like a bird without a nest. My
> situation is even worse because since my theatrical beginnings, up
> until 1968, I was not only writing for the theater but also I was
> working there. I took part in rehearsals and I cocreated the face of
> the entire theater. . . . People sometimes ask me: "How can you still
> write"? I must confess that I'm not able to answer these questions.
> In fact, I just try to behave as if it weren't true.[2]

But there were consolations. The Akademietheater (of the Burgtheater) was one of numerous theaters in Europe ready to provide a home
away from home for Havel. Theaters in Europe and America were only
too pleased to raise their curtains on his new plays.

Within months of the *Largo Desolato* premiere at the Akademietheater in Vienna, there were productions in Norway, Yugoslavia, Germany,
and Paris. The loyal Joseph Papp produced the play at the Public Theater
in New York, directed by Richard Foreman. The play opened on March
25, 1986, in a translation by Marie Winn. Josef Sommer played Leopold
Kopřiva, and the cast included Sally Kirkland, Larry Block, Diane
Venora, and Richard Russell Ramos. Papp also produced *Temptation,*
opening on April 9, 1989, in a translation by Marie Winn), directed by
Jiří Žižka, with David Straithairn as Foustka and Bille Brown as Fistula.
(The *New York Times* critic Frank Rich had issues with the direction in
both productions, and thereby abstained from judging the strength of the
plays themselves.) As was the case with productions in Europe during his
imprisonment, if Klaus Juncker could arrange it, he would make sure that

since Havel could not be present on opening night, there would be a huge picture of him at the theater, either on the stage after the performance or in the lobby.

Largo Desolato received its next English-speaking production at the Theatre Royal in Bristol in a version by Tom Stoppard, directed by Claude Whatham. Irving Wardle of the *Times* (London) called attention to the universality of the play as well as its humor, describing it as a

> wonderfully comic and unself-pitying piece . . . that . . . extends beyond its own country to the civil rights public at large. To me, sitting comfortably in a Bristol hotel, cheering Havel on to take his next prison sentence on the chin, it takes a comic writer of genius to make something funny out of that.[3]

Jon Peter of the Sunday *Times* called the play "an essay on responsibility" and saw the play in darker terms. Catching Havel's profound desperation under the comic absurdity of a dissident's situation, Peter wrote: "Under regimes like this you are so conditioned to deviousness and resistance that, once they stop accusing you, there's nothing left to live for."[4]

As for *Temptation*, the Royal Shakespeare Company (RSC) was pleased to give it a second production, as well as its English premiere, in the following year (1987) in the Other Place Theatre in Stratford. The play had been submitted to the RSC by Peggy Ramsey, a leading British agent (who in turn had received it from Klaus Juncker). Roger Michell was named director and journeyed to Prague in 1986 to meet Havel and prepare for the production. (Michell had lived there in 1965 to 1969 while his father was in the diplomatic corps.) "I didn't want to frighten him by telling him it would be directed in the round," Michell said. The director was struck by Havel's dissident persona; he found the playwright "not a glorious romantic or a freedom fighter, but culpable, real, humorous." Meeting Havel gave Michell a deeper insight into the play:

> Foustka is trying to find a more human way of looking at the world. On one level, it's about an intellectual rebelling against a corrupt system — on another level, it's about the self-doubt of the dissident. Am I being ridiculous, vain, selfish, unreasonable? he asks. Because many of the dissidents at heart are foolish, and that's what humanizes the plays.[5]

Michell's insight into *Temptation* and the heart of the dissident proved fruitful. Given a translation by George Theiner (of the *Index on Censorship*), *Temptation* received its British premiere on April 22, to glowing reviews, with John Shrapnel as Foustka and David Bradley as Fistula. By many accounts, the production was sharp, searing and sparkling, thanks to Michell's understanding of the text and his skillful, tour de force rendering of its comedic and sinister tones. Irving Wardle of *The Times* said that "this new piece gloriously demonstrates that he (Havel) has lost none of his early powers." At the same time, Wardle noted that "an immense weight of pain lies behind these events, which emerge from years of subjection to an environment of enforced lies in which the victim has come to doubt his own good faith. But the play represents a comic triumph over lacerating experience."[6]

Jon Peter of the Sunday *Times* called *Temptation*

the writer's most substantial play so far. . . . Havel's point is that, in a totalitarian society, the only protection of personal freedom and integrity is the lie. A private moral act has to be safeguarded by an immoral public gesture. The very act of breaking free will involve you even more deeply in complicity. You become an intellectual double agent. The price of survival is corruption.[7]

He praised Michell and the cast for capturing the work's dark comedic tone and for delivering "an exhilarating performance." In April 1988, the play moved to London, where it was performed in the Pit Theatre of the RSC at the Barbican. Jane Edwardes of *Time Out* called *Temptation* "a bewitching, Faustian comedy with nightmarish implications."[8] Milton Shulman of the *Evening Standard* praised Roger Michell's direction, calling it a mise-en-scène of "balletic brilliance."[9]

After the production, Michell returned to Prague and personally delivered a copy of a videotaped production into Havel's hands. One evening shortly thereafter, Havel held a party at his apartment to screen the videotape. At that party, he read the play aloud, and invited comments from friends who were in attendance. Sergej Machonin, the critic, was present and gave Havel criticism. Not only did Havel take it well, he also made some changes right then and there.

Thanks to all this attention abroad, Havel was not as "far from the theater" as he thought. But that was a small consolation. Ever since his release from prison, he struggled not only with postprison depression, but also with persecution by the secret police. He was shadowed, hounded, and harassed. From the small lookout tower the police had built on the winding mountain road opposite his dacha in Hrádeček, he was watched constantly. Havel himself stripped the walls of his apartment at Rašínovo nábřeží, looking for concealed microphones. His telephones were tapped. According to the biographer Keane, his dog was shot on the doorstep by the secret police.[10] In the Kafkaesque world in which he lived, paranoia was justified. Someone was indeed watching.

Between the writing of *Largo Desolato* in August 1984 and *Temptation* in October, 1985, Havel was arrested three times and held in custody. The first time, on January 3, 1985, was in connection with the nomination of new Charter 77 spokesmen; Havel was held for forty-eight hours. In August 1985, Havel set out in a Volkswagen Golf on a journey across Czechoslovakia to visit friends, during which he was detained twice in connection with the draft of a Charter 77 declaration that was being prepared for the anniversary of the Soviet invasion. First he was picked up at a friend's house, charged with intention to commit hooliganism, and dragged in and interrogated about what he knew about the forthcoming declaration. The police also ransacked his friend's house, looking for documents. Released after forty-eight hours, Havel continued on his journey, followed by a procession of police tails. When he arrived at the house of another friend in Bratislava, the doorbell rang, and police again entered, arrested Havel, and ransacked the house. This time he was arrested on the charge of incitement. While in the Bratislava Prison, Havel protested by holding a hunger strike. Released again after forty-eight hours, a police escort followed to the border of Slovakia, where his escorts changed.

After this episode, Havel wrote to the attorney general, protesting these arrests and pointing out that his trip across Czechoslovakia had involved three hundred members of the police force, costing the Czech government almost one hundred times more than the trip had cost Havel.[11]

In a visit to Havel during that period, British journalist Timothy Garten Ash describes the strain of the constant surveillance and harassment:

> He talks about the nervous strain of writing under these conditions, when at any moment the police might walk in and confiscate a year's work. How he has crept out into the woods at night and

buried parts of his typescript in the hole of a tree. How as a manuscript piles up he writes faster and faster: the fear of a house search concentrates the mind wonderfully. Far more effective than any publisher's deadline. Just yesterday he was writing about this nervous tension. Then his wife came in and said "The police are outside again. I'm afraid they aren't our usual ones." And so he got nervous about writing about the nervous strain of writing when . . . [12]

Still, there were times when Havel was able to deal with the constant surveillance with humor, even compassion. Once, when his police tail got stuck in a ditch, Havel stopped his car and helped get the vehicle out. Another time, when police were ransacking his home and came upon his cassette collection, they began to investigate its contents. Putting one cassette into the recorder, they ended up listening for an hour and a half to a lecture by Havel on "how everything can change, how it is never too late for anyone."[13] Yet another time, Havel and some friends were traveling in a car and stopped by the bank of a lake to go swimming. Minutes after they dove in, they were joined by his police tails, who jumped in after them. One of them almost drowned. They all spent the afternoon laughing together in the water.

Havel found another way to keep his life in the theater alive in those postprison years — by writing about it. Early in 1985, Karel Hvížďala, a Czech journalist living in West Germany, proposed to Havel the idea of a book-length interview. Havel accepted the invitation, appreciating the opportunity to reflect on his life as he approached fifty. During that year, the two communicated by underground mail, with Havel responding to a series of questions that Hvížďala posed. But, feeling that the answers were too essay-like, they devised another way. Hvížďala sent Havel about fifty questions; and over the Christmas holidays, Havel sequestered himself in a friend's apartment in Prague and emerged seven days later with eleven hours worth of tape-recorded answers. Back and forth they worked together, transcribing, editing, refining. By June, 1986, Havel completed the final version.

The book was first published by Edice Expedice, under the title of *Dálkový Výslech*, meaning, literally, "Long Distance Interrogation." It was subsequently translated by Paul Wilson, a Canadian teacher and translator who had lived in Czechoslovakia in the 1960s and had also played with the Plastic People of the Universe. With Havel's approval, Hvížďala retitled the work *Disturbing the Peace*. While it reads like an autobiography in a stream-of-conscious format, it also contains the richest, most concentrated personal commentary that Havel had written about his life in the theater to date. *Disturbing the Peace*, along with *Largo Desolato* and *Temptation*, represent an intense outpouring of autobiographical writings in the postprison period of 1984 to 1986. As such, they are an act of exorcism as well as expiation. The writing of them contributed to the calming and comforting of Havel's troubled soul. For an understanding of Havel's life in the theater, *Disturbing the Peace* is invaluable.

There were other consolations during that period. The year after writing *Temptation*, Havel turned fifty, and in honor of his birthday, his friends compiled a collection of essays about *Temptation*. They were published by Olga by Edice Expedice in 1986 under the collected title of *Fausting with Havel*. Among those essays, the one by Jirous, former leader of the Plastics People, especially pleased Havel because he felt that Jirous understood best the meaning of the play.

Those essays gave Olga the idea of founding a journal dedicated to the theater. A meeting was called in the Havels' apartment in Dejvice, attended by the playwrights Ivan Klíma and Josef Topol, the actress Vlasta Chramostová, the writer Zdeněk Urbánek, the critic Sergej Machonin, and others. Anna Freimanová was appointed the managing editor. The result was *O divadle* (About Theater), a *samizdat* theater review that appeared five times over the next two years. Each issue was 350 to 400 pages and devoted to a specific theme.

The significance of this journal was threefold. First, it united different segments of the theater community — young and old, dissidents and mainstreamers, Communists and anti-Communists. Second, it stimulated a rebirth of theater criticism, which had not had a platform or a focus for fifteen years. Third, it united the official theater community and the banned community, with writers from both contributing to it. By the fifth issue, writers even stopped using pseudonyms. (The production stopped when Havel was imprisoned again in the fall of 1988).

More international recognition came that year. On January 22, the Erasmus Prize Foundation in Amsterdam announced that Havel would receive its 1986 award. One of Europe's most prestigious awards, the Erasmus Prize is given "in order to honour persons or institutions that have made an exceptionally important contribution to European culture,

society or social science." Its winner, of course, was not permitted to attend the ceremony (held just after his fiftieth birthday in November) at
the Rotterdam Cathedral, which was attended by the Dutch royal family.
The authorities might have given him a passport, but he feared the same
fate that had befallen Pavel Kohout and Pavel Landovský, who were given
permission to go to Vienna and not allowed to return. The actor Jan
Tříska accepted the prize on his behalf and read Havel's prepared speech.

In honor of that occasion, another Czech friend in the emigré community, Jan Vladislav, compiled a book that included six texts written by
Havel and sixteen others written for Havel. The title of the collection is
Václav Havel or Living in Truth. "It is the search for truth in its purest
form that drives him," wrote the president of the Erasmus Foundation in
the foreword about Havel.[14] The centerpiece of the collection are Havel's
eloquent political essays, including new ones written after his release from
prison: his "Letter to Dr. Gustáv Husák" (April 8, 1975); "The Power of
the Powerless (October, 1978); "Six Asides About Culture" (August 14,
1984); "Politics and Conscience" (February 1984); "Thriller"; "An Anatomy of Reticence" (April 1985). The collection also includes a number of
significant theater works: Samuel Beckett's play *Catastrophe*, and Arthur
Miller's play *I think about you a great deal* (both written for the 1982 Avignon festival); Tom Stoppard's introduction to *The Memorandum*, and
Pavel Kohout's "The Chaste Centaur," an essay about the Vaněk plays.

One of the texts included in *Living in Truth* was a letter written
under rather extraordinary circumstances. Zdeněk Urbánek, Havel's and
Olga's close friend, had been particularly distressed by Havel's time in
prison. Olga had shared Havel's letters with his brother Ivan, Urbánek,
and a few others, and Urbánek was particularly struck by the remark in
one letter that Havel had found a life in the theater by a "series of coincidences."[15] Urbánek was determined to respond by saying that there are
no such things as coincidences. Since only Olga's letters could be delivered to Havel, she agreed to include his response in one of hers. The text
of Urbánek's letter, written in the spring of 1982, concerns the significance of Havel's life in the theater and contends that it was the hardly a
coincidence, but rather his destiny:

> All good plays, all good theater, repeatedly put our views and pre-
> cepts to the test. The play of Arthur Miller's which was here given
> the colourless title of *The Witches of Salem* was called *The Crucible*

in the original. But of course a literal Czech translation would have looked odd on the posters. On the other hand, I know of no more appropriate title for a play — perhaps all the better theaters should be called that. Alas, there exist tougher and more severe tests of human minds and characters, but among the more humane ones the theater comes top in the arts as a "crucible" sensitively revealing what kind of metal we are made of. Both on stage and in the auditorium.[16]

Whether near from it or far, Havel's life in the theater had revealed, and continued to reveal, what kind of metal he was made of.

1987: *REDEVELOPMENT*

> In other words, time marches on! Not only here, the world over! And if anyone here thinks otherwise — ![1]
>
> — Havel, *Redevelopment*

By 1987, change was in the air.
As Michael Simmons, author of *The Reluctant President*, wrote:

> There could be no doubt that the Husák leadership was seriously losing ground and authority. Though there was no statistical way of measuring it, the standing of the small band of people seeking to hold the country together was alarmingly low.[2]

The main event of the year was the visit of Mikhail Gorbachev, the first Russian leader to attempt to change the system from a position of power. Gorbachev came to Prague on April 10 to 11, 1987. For the first time in history, the Czech Communists were shown to be more conservative than the Russians. In contrast to Gorbachev and his vision of perestroika, Miloš Jakeš, the new general secretary of the Communist Party (Husák was now in his mid-eighties), made the Czech regime seem reactionary. Also at that time, the Russian embassy began to contact people from the underground, to test the water. Change was clearly in the air.

Havel was being drawn deeper and deeper into the political vortex, with increasingly less time for writing. When foreign ministers and political leaders from the West visited Prague, they met not only with the official representatives of the Czechoslovakian government, but also with representatives of the opposition, like Havel and other Charter 77 spokesmen. The police tried to prevent this by putting opposition members under house arrest or detaining them during these visits, but they were not always successful. Meanwhile, Havel was made a member of the editorial board of *Lidové noviny* (People's News), a *samizdat* monthly. The opposition now had its own newspaper.

In October, in the midst of all these meetings and the drafting of petitions, Havel managed to write a new play called *Redevelopment* (Asanace). In this fourteen-character play, Havel returns to the world of the organization to deliver an overtly political metaphor about perestroika (meaning reorganization, reformation, reconstruction, or rebuilding), the other meaning of the word *asanace*. Like *The Garden Party* and *Temptation*, the play takes place in an "institute," this time an architectural one, housed in a medieval castle somewhere in Czechoslovakia. The castle rises above the ancient town it once ruled. A team of architects has been installed there, to prepare a plan for the town's redevelopment. The implication of "architectural" changes is a provocative one, given that the Communists call themselves the architects of life, those who build new worlds.

As the curtain rises, the lights go up to reveal something unusual in a Havel play. A lone figure sits to the side of the stage, playing a violin. It is Kuzma Plekhanov, a young architect with an overtly Russian name. Wearing a dressing gown and slippers, his costume throughout the play, he is completely absorbed in playing the well-known Russian song "Dark Eyes." Like a chorus, he will comment on the action of the play with his music, which he reprises at the end of each of the play's five acts.

The play begins with the arrival of a two-member delegation; they bear a petition signed by 216 people, protesting the redevelopment of this old castle town. The people like their lives as they are. Bergman, the principal project director and a man of enlightenment and reason, tries to deal humanely with the petitioners. But he is interrupted by the Special Secretary of the institute, who explains that the redevelopment project will convert the old social order into a new humane one, that it will transform the medieval town, whose two thousand inhabitants are crammed into small dark quarters with inadequate facilities that breed poverty and disease.

Special Secretary: What a relic of the old social order, when the lords lived here in the castle and their subjects, their souls, down in the town. What a sad heritage. This project is not just for you, you know, it's for the good of us all.[3]

The delegates remains unconvinced, so the Special Secretary places them in the castle dungeon, until they name the petition's author. This action causes a schism within the institute. Bergman is deeply disturbed by these events. He fervently believes in his institute's mission, but does not want to force its vision on people. He is for "progress . . . with a human face."[4] Albert, an idealistic young architect, is equally disturbed. But their expressions of despair are interrupted by a newcomer, the First Inspector. Like a character out of Gogol's *Inspector General,* he is a jovial, open, and cheerful fellow and takes everyone completely off guard. He has come to say, in a friendly, informal fashion: Don't worry, relax, the redevelopment project was worthless, it would not have helped people at all, it wasn't responding to their needs. "What they don't dig up there is that people are individuals, they want to do their own thing, know what I mean?"[5] the First Inspector explains congenially. But "we" don't want you to stop, he continues. You're the experts. Go back to the drawing boards, keep working, develop some new ideas of your own, he encourages them. With a flourish of "Good luck!" he turns on his heels and makes a grand exit, leaving the research team dumbfounded.

Suddenly, a dialogue begins between the different factions in the institute, and in this new atmosphere of freedom, they drink champagne to toast a new era. "To urbanism with a human face!" Bergman offers, and they raise their glasses.

But everything is turned on its head once more. A Second Inspector arrives, only to read a prepared statement reversing the first one. And so, the Second Inspector restores "normality." The redevelopment project has been reinstalled. Using slogans similar to those in the *The Garden Party* — here, it's "Let's not throw out the baby with the bathwater" — he appeals to the workers to apply themselves with vigor, and off he goes, with a "Good luck!" too. Says the chorus:

Plekhanov: Well, it was nice while it lasted.
Luisa: Like a dream.
Plekhanov: Better than a dream.

Luisa: At least we had a little dance.
Plekhanov: I just hope they're not tuning up for the big one.
Luisa: How is it we're so easily fooled?
Plekhanov: Only a corpse is never fooled.[6]

Like Staněk in *Protest*, Bergman is a realist; he entreats his colleagues to endure, to make the best of everything. But Albert, the young idealist, explodes in frustration and expresses his rage against his colleagues' passivity and self-deception.

Albert: Do you remember yesterday? You were all trying to outdo each other! Never again would you betray your beliefs! Truth must destroy fear! Freedom must prevail over stupidity! And so on and so on, and then, suddenly, it's as if someone waved a magic wand and you've been wiped clean, there's nothing left but how not to wet your pants as you run for cover! Is this normal? Does it go on everywhere? Are people just jellyfish? Am I mad, or are you?[7]

At that point, the Special Secretary enters and drags Albert off to the dungeon. Luisa and Renata, both of whom love Albert, throw themselves at the Secretary's feet, but in vain.

In the final act, the play crescendos to a cacophony of confusion. The imprisoned petitioners' wives arrive, bearing provisions for their husbands who had been released but are once again locked up in the dungeon. The reason for this reversal? The Secretary explains that now he knows the real intention of the petition — to unleash mass hysteria. The Second Inspector reappears, reading a meaningless statement filled with absurd political doubletalk. Upon his exit, there is a lull in the action. A strange tranquility descends on the scene, as the characters lapse into conversation about simple, everyday life.

Plekhanov: Did you know we have a stork nesting on the tower?
Ulch: Is that good luck or bad luck?
Plekhanov: It depends how you look at it . . . *(A long, oppressive pause.)*
Bergman: While we're on the subject, there's a hole in the vegetable garden fence. The rabbits are eating the cabbages.

Ulch: I noticed that. I've been meaning to repair it but things
   come up . . .
Plekhanov: I'll fix it tomorrow . . . *(A long oppressive pause.)*
Ulch: The magnolias in the park are in bloom already.
Plekhanov: Except for two; a later variety.[8]

The calm is short-lived, however. Albert enters, released from the
dungeon, broken, wordless, dazed. (Idealism has been silenced.) This af-
fects Plekhanov deeply. He inquires about the fate of the other two in the
dungeon, but no one knows. Plekhanov rises silently and exits. In the
next moment, there is a terrible sound offstage. Word comes that
Plekhanov has committed suicide (the first in a Havel play). It is Albert's
struggle that has kept him alive and given him hope. When Albert is
silent, Plekhanov has no reason to to live.

   Bergman, the play's raisonneur, quickly steps into the breach of silence, with a speech that accepts responsibility for the one romantic character of the play.

   Bergman: . . . we are all responsible for the sad shape our world is
   in, which has hounded a sensitive man beyond the limits of endurance. We're callous, indolent, indifferent, deaf to the voices of
   those near and dear to us and blind to their pain . . . Let us therefore promise ourselves at this difficult time that we will never
   again allow human apathy to rule and destroy. Let us vow never
   again to connive in the "redevelopment" of the souls of ourselves
   and others. Our mission is not to dance to the frivolous beat of
   an incompetent conductor, but to hold fast to he truth we have
   found, and dedicate ourselves to the work we have begun.[9]

   As the play ends, the strains of "Dark Eyes" subside to be replaced by
the swelling sounds of Strauss's "Blue Danube" ("the swansong of the
emigres,"[10] as Kohout calls it in his Vaněk play, *Morass.*) What is Havel
saying, with the ebbing of the Russian music and the flowing of the German? Are they the Habsburg echoes? Is time marching backward? Who
knows? The songs represent the pulls from both cultures (the Russian and
the Germanic) that have influenced the Czechs throughout their history.
   Whatever its historical echoes may be, the play is clearly contemporary. A world where there are petitioners and imprisonments, where there

are slogans like "progress with a human face" or "urbanism with a human face" (variations on Dubček's "socialism with a human face"), where people get locked up in dungeons, where wives visit husbands in prison, where missions change every day — this is a world clearly drawn from Havel's own experience.

Redevelopment is a political parable, inviting several interpretations. On one level, it can be seen as a parable for the whole "project" of Socialism in Czechoslovakia. The petitioners in Act I might represent the ordinary citizens of the early 1960s, who were tired of the repressive Communist regime of the 1950s. Then in act 3, the (new) First Inspector can be construed as Dubček, the new General Secretary of the Communist Party, who ushered in the enlightened period of the Prague Spring. Like Havel's First Inspector, Dubček was warm and smiling, and his style, in contrast to that of his predecessors, was personable and human. Then, in 1969, came Husák (a.k.a. the Second Inspector) to restore order in the form of normalization (or "normality," as it is called here). In fact, when Husák became General Secretary of the Communist Party, he made a speech about Dubček that is very reminiscent of the Second Inspector's speech about the First Inspector.

> Second Inspector: My predecessor, whom you met here recently, was not a bad fellow. Unfortunately, as you no doubt surmised during your brief meeting, he fell short intellectually, temperamentally and professionally of the demands of the situation. A tragic figure, one could say: a native of this area, well intentioned and attuned to the mood of the people but inexperienced in management, weak in public relations and conceptually unsound. Thus it was that, failing to sense the moment when freedom turns to anarchy, unable in the hysterical atmosphere of unregulated discussion to distinguish between those with honest ideas and those without, he lost control of the situation.[11]

There is another possible interpretation. In *Redevelopment*, Havel also draws from the specific political circumstances of the times, namely Gorbachev's 1987 visit to Prague, bringing his policies of perestroika and decentralization. For the first time, a Russian leader was saying: "It's your business." Now, Havel is asking the Czech people: Is the Old Guard really capable of starting something new? Can Husák talk about perestroika? Can he talk about change when for twenty years he has been fighting against it? Once Czechoslovakia had "socialism with a human face" (hence the mockery in Bergman's toast). Can the Czech nation return to that golden decade of the 1960s? Can a nation deceived by the invasion, numbed by normalization, ever be young again, vulnerable to hope? Can a people factionalized for decades — young versus old, official versus underground, Communist versus non-Communist — unite with hope for change?

There is a further irony. Perestroika was, in a sense, a threat to Havel's struggle against the regime. As long as the situation was clear, as it was in the 1970s, with Husák and the totalitarian regime pitted against the dissidents, the struggle was defined. Now along comes perestroika, saying that Socialism wasn't all that bad, that it can be modified, rebuilt, reconstituted. In a sense, *Redevelopment* is an expression of disbelief in perestroika, and a warning to others not to believe in it either. After all, if it were to succeed, there would be yet another three decades of a Communist regime in Czechoslovakia. For Havel, perestroika was only a mask, a cosmetic face-lifting of totalitarianism. "Socialism with a human face" had been overcome by the dark forces of normalization. Why trust such a redevelopment once again? No wonder Plekhanov loses hope in the end.

Redevelopment may be one of Havel's lesser plays, reminiscent of *Temptation* in its institutional setting, repetitive of *The Garden Party's* empty phraseology, familiar in the multiple love intrigues (*The Increased Difficulty of Concentration*) that do not illuminate the central action. But, with its allusions to perestroika, it is a play that is specifically rooted in the changing times. It is a play that asks if people are up to the task of riding the crest of the waves of change. Are people's weaknesses, self-deceptions, cowardice, avoidance mechanisms so ingrained after years of living in a duplicitous, untruthful society that they cannot rise to the occasion when real change presents itself? With idealism (Albert) silenced, romanticism (Plekhanov) dead, and pragmatism (Bergman) droning on, deluding itself by the sound of its own voice, who is there to heed? Who are the heroes? One would have welcomed a silent Vaněk in this scenario.

As always, Havel immediately sought the network, to get the new manuscript out of the country and into the hands of Klaus Juncker. When Wolfgang Scheuer retired as cultural attaché in 1986, he arranged that his associate, Peter Metzger, would continue to be part of the network. *Redevelopment* was completed in October 1987, and through Metzger's efforts, a copy arrived at the Scheinfeld Center in Hanover before the month's end. Once again, Prečan made copies and distributed them to Klaus Juncker and elsewhere.[12]

As was his custom since imprisonment, Havel made a tape of a reading of the play that Anna Freimanová and others circulated among their friends. He also gave a copy of the script to the director, Karel Kříž, and the dramaturg, Vlasta Gallerová, who were working at the Realistické Theater in Prague. They were eager to produce *Redevelopment*, but to stage a Havel play was, of course, forbidden. In May 1989, an opportunity presented itself. "Open Dialogue," an underground event at which works by banned authors would be read, was to be held at a club on Pařížská Street, at the center of the Old Town. (The "Open Dialogue" events had started in Brno in the early 1980s, using small galleries and shops; far from the Prague police, they had successfully provided a forum for the works of banned authors.) At the time, Havel was in prison once again. Kříž and Gallerová had an idea. Using a copy of Havel's recording, they spliced the parts where he read the character of Bergman into the reading with live actors. But the event never took place; on the morning of the performance, the police, who had learned of the plan, closed the club.[13]

Redevelopment received its world premiere at the Schauspielhaus in Zurich on September 26, 1989. Within three months, Havel's plays would be no longer banned in his own country. But he did not know it at the time.

1988: *TOMORROW WE'LL START IT UP*

> I've never kept it secret from you that I'm putting my life at risk. But if the nation is at stake, then the life of one man doesn't matter. We stand before a great historic challenge, and we must be brave enough to face it — even though we have no guarantee that we will succeed without sacrifice.[1]
>
> — Havel, *Tomorrow We'll Start It Up*

Times were indeed changing.

In 1988, Havel was still hounded by the police. But change was accelerating rapidly. Everyone felt it. When French President François Mitterrand visited Prague, Havel was permitted to meet with him. On August 21, there were anti-Communist demonstrations on the streets of Prague, commemorating the twentieth anniversary of the Soviet occupation.

On September 3, Havel made his first public appearance in more than nineteen years, at a music festival in Lipnice. There he was greeted like a celebrity; he signed autographs and clasped hands. At the Lyre music festival in Bratislava, Joan Baez sang and uttered words of praise for Charter 77 and Havel, who happened to be in the audience. There was a standing ovation (although that was the end of the Lyre festival, at least for the time being).

For every two steps forward, there was one step back. In September, the quarterly writers' meeting was supposed to take place at Hrádeček. Edá Kriseová, who was among a group traveling there, remembers the day vividly. As a car full of writers pulled off the highway at the turnoff toward the dacha, they encountered a road block. When they tried another access road, the same thing happened. Eventually a procession of several cars parked in a nearby village, and the passengers set out through the countryside on foot, past fields of corn stubble and occasional mushroom pickers. They spotted policemen far ahead at a fork in the road, who were already questioning two of the writers who were serving as "advance men." Clearly, Hrádeček was surrounded. Edá Kriseová hid a *samizdat* manuscript she'd been carrying in a tree. They pressed on, not wanting to give up. Soon they encountered Olga and her dog. Olga suggested an alternate route to avoid the road blocks. So they traipsed through the forest that bright September day, stopping to picnic on the provisions they had intended for the meeting, figuring that in case they were arrested, it would be best to dine beforehand. Laughing and talking, they pried open a bottle of wine with someone's nail file, which they also used to cut the roast pork and plum cake, and proceeded with their impromptu picnic. When they finally got to the orchard beside Havel's house, they were surrounded by plainclothesmen and arrested. "And what am I supposed to do with all the goulash?" Havel cried, as he watched them lead his friends away. He was soon to accompany them. That evening, they were released, and as the car full of writers headed back to Prague, a police car followed them.[2] And so it still went, in 1988.

As the lines between official and unofficial culture continued to blur, the antiestablishment theater community grew bolder. A new generation was replacing the old guard, and they were experimenting in the smaller theaters, using all their wiles to test the parameters of possibilities, exploring hitherto forbidden themes.[3] And so, in 1988 a remarkable thing happened, something unprecedented for the past two decades. On October 21, a new play by Václav Havel was produced on a public stage in Czechoslovakia. His name was not attached to it. But it was presented, nonetheless.

The production was spearheaded by a spirited new personality emerging in the Czech theater. His name was Petr Oslzlý, a tall, rail-thin, bespectacled young director/dramaturg/actor from Brno (in Moravia), with tangled hair, an intense demeanor, and a gentle voice. A determined young idealist when he was a student in the 1970s, he made a list of the great European theater people he most admired — Havel, Otomar Krejča, Peter Brook, Jerzy Grotowski — and set out to meet them. Later in the 1980s, after Havel was released from prison, the two men resumed contact. Indeed, Oslzlý was the first person who invited Havel to the theater after he had been released from prison to see a performance by his company while it was touring in Prague.

During the 1970s, Oslzlý had founded a theater company in Brno called Theater on a String (Divadlo na provazku). Originally, the troupe had been called Divadlo husa na provazku, meaning "Theater of a Goose on a String," but one night, someone added the letter *k* to the word *husa* (meaning "goose") on a billboard, thereby spelling the name of the Dr. Husák who ran the Communist Party. This angered the authorities so much that the company was forced to drop *husa* from its name. Theater on a String was one of a new generation of small Czech theaters emerging in the early 1970s called "writers' theaters" (autorska divadla). Their purpose, in Oslzlý's words, was to sustain intellectual and spiritual contact with the audience as people began withdrawing into their homes to seek refuge from normalization.[4]

By the late 1970s, Theater on a String had become the most popular theater in Czechoslovakia. It opposed the regime, but because of its intense popularity, the authorities were reluctant to close it down. Since it was far from Prague, they let it continue. From 1973, when it was founded, until the 1990s, its 150 seats were sold out every night. When the company came to Prague on tour, all the performances were sold out, too.

In 1987, in an effort to start a theater review for new writing from the unofficial culture, Oslzlý began collecting new essays and articles. The subject for the first issue was to be "democracy." But the authorities forbade a journal of any kind to be published by his theater. So he and his collaborators came up with the unconventional and daring idea of having a group of actors get up on stage and simply read the essays aloud. They would call the event a "stage magazine," and it would commemorate the seventieth anniversary of the Czechoslovak republic, founded in 1918. It would be entitled "Rozrazil I/1988," taking its name from the Czech word for a small mountain flower, a tiny yet hardy plant that grows high in the mountains between the rocks. It is fragrant and extremely resilient.

Up until that point, Oslzlý had not asked Havel to contribute an essay. But now he faced the issue of how to keep an audience's attention during an evening of readings that would last up to four hours. So he asked Havel to write a short play about the founding of the democratic republic in 1918, which would be a part of the whole production. It had been an emotional era; after three hundred years of foreign rule under the Habsburg empire, the Czechoslovakian state had broken free and prepared itself for self-government. It was an era of turbulence and change, one that appealed to Havel because he sensed the potential for change in his own times. Here was an opportunity to put this sense of history on the stage, and he seized it. The result was a short new play, *Tomorrow We'll Start It Up* (Zítra to spustíme), subtitled "a historic meditation in five acts." The name came from the slogan of the Czech soldiers who defected to France rather than fight on the German-Austrian side in World War I. A Czech legion was formed under French command, and the phrase "tomorrow we'll start it up" referred to their hope that one day there would be a movement for independence for the Czech and Slovak peoples.

Havel's only historical drama, *Tomorrow We'll Start It Up*, is a retelling of the dramatic events during the night of October 27 to 28, 1918, as the coup d'état was taking place. Havel creates an ensemble of contemporary actors to narrate the story, while the characters of the period reenact it in five short scenes. (The cast is large, calling for seventeen actors.) Because Tomáš Masaryk, philosopher, statesman, and the champion of free rule, was living abroad at the time, the mantle of leadership fell on the shoulders of a politician named Alois Rašín. He soon became the driving force behind the independent Czechoslovakian state. Havel found him a compelling figure and chose him as the leading character in his play.

Alois Rašín was a deputy in the Austro-Hungarian parliament and an important figure of the day. In 1916, he was tried for treason as a member of the resistance movement and sentenced to death. In the meantime, the Emperor Franz Josef I died; and his successor, Karel II, commuted Rašín's sentence to life imprisonment. A year later, the emperor granted amnesty to all political prisoners, and Rašín was released. He became a member of the national committee that was seeking to establish a new independent Czechoslovak Republic. After its establishment, he was named Minister of Finance in the first Czechoslovakian government. His financial policies became famous throughout Europe. (On January 5, 1923, he was shot in the back by a young Communist; he died on February 18.)

At the curtain's rise, the ensemble is in place on the stage, ready to tell the story. Nine actors portray the main characters; the other eight serve as narrators and chorus, weaving in and out of the story in various roles, as well as members of the crowd. Music punctuates the many scenes. The play opens with a narrative introduction that states the playwright's intent to set the historical record straight and to distinguish between truth and illusion:

> Actor A: *(To the audience.)* As the more informed among you already know, we are trying to reconstruct what happened in the apartment of Dr. Alois Rašín on the night of the twenty-seventh to the twentieth-eighth of October 1918. The reconstruction will be a combination of historical truth and fiction, but you don't have to worry that we will confound you. At the right time, and as always, we'll give you a warning as to what is fabrication and what is reality . . . [5]

The Rašíns are at home that evening, elated by the news from Vienna that the war is lost and the Austrians are capitulating. The Czechs and Slovaks will have their nation at last.

> Actor B: *(To the audience.)* After the first explosion of joy, she will probably call her husband —
> Rašín: What?
> Rasinová (Mrs. Rašín): What are you actually going to do? Do you have a plan?
> Rašín: Karla, this is a revolution! Can you possibly plan a revolution?
> Rasinová: I know, but still . . . [6]

During the night of October 27 to 28, Rašín becomes the master-mind and implementer of an action plan from his home in Prague, communicating with colleagues as they strategize how to take over the Office of Supplies and the Vice Regent's Office. While he strategizes, he is also drafting the constitution and reading it to his wife. Meanwhile, in a moving cameo appearance, the greengrocer František Kopecký, a real historical figure, leads a parade of euphoric citizens through the streets of Prague from his home in Havelská Street though Wenceslas Square.[7] Like Sládek, the brewery foreman in *Audience*, the grocer is one of the few "ordinary citizens" in Havel's canon. The ensemble performs this parade to the cheers of "Long live Masaryk! Long live Wilson!"

As the night progresses and the story flashes forward and backward again, the actors continue their narration to the audience:

> Actress B: *(To the audience.)* The more memorable the day of October twenty-eighth became in the public consciousness, the more people claimed credit for their own contribution and downplayed the contribution of others. Year by year, as the anniversary drew near, new witnesses, new analysts, new protagonists appeared. We can close with the most likely version that, as it often is the case with history, the truth lies somewhere in between. The people would have been nothing without their leaders, and the leaders would have been nothing without their people. So the contribution came from both sides. The spontaneous demonstration of the people's will, in that moment, provided the main support for the political leadership. Similarly, the acts of the leaders were the only thing that could transform the will of the people into the political reality of an independent Czechoslovakia —
> Kopecký: *(Begins to sing the national anthem.)* Where is my home, where is my home — [8]

The Rasins speculate into the morning about the future of their newborn state, only hours old. At the same time, they ponder the enormous responsibility the nation is facing. Who will fill the vacuum in Europe? Will Germany be expansionist? Will Czechoslovakia have support from the allied powers? What about the economy?

Rašín dozes off, and according to Havel's directions, the actors circle around him, while the strains from Smetana's opera *Libuše* (with its closing prophesy of the shining future of Prague and the Czech nation) are heard. Then, in the style of a sound collage, superimposed on the strains of *Libuše*, are speeches by various Czech and Slovak statesmen made at the important historical moments from 1918 until today. The sound crescendos till *Libuše* ends. In deep silence, the actors stand motionless. The play ends in the small hours of the morning.

> Actor C: *(To the audience.)* We have no historical proof that Dr. Alois Rašín fell asleep in the early hours of October twenty-eighth, 1918. Moreover, we have less proof that he dreamed such a dream!
> Actress D: *(Exclaims.)* Then who is to dream it? *(Darkness.)* [9]

The play is rich in historical detail, and sparkles with idealistic themes: the idea of Czech independence as historic inevitability; the sovereignty of the Czech language (under Habsburg rule, the official language of Czechoslovakia was German); the responsibility of self-rule; the notion of pan-Slavism, wherein the Slovenian nations would function as one family in a pan-Slavic union. Many forces were fighting for the cause of independence at the time: Beneš and Masaryk in Washington, Tusar in Vienna. (Beneš and Tusar are characters in the play.) But the play also asks the question: Whose revolution is it? The leaders, or the "man in the street"? The answer: It doesn't matter as long as it takes place. [10]

The play ends with Rašín pondering the enormous responsibility that the nation is undertaking to gain self-rule and the reality of what that entails. (Rašín himself was assassinated by a political opponent on January 5, 1923.) He was a man of vision, who saw his country's past, present, and future, who rose to the occasion that history presented, who died in his country's service. Rašín, too, had been in prison and on trial; destiny intervened in both cases. Was Havel thinking, possibly, of his own place in his country's history? Was he thinking of himself and Olga when he told the story of how Rašín had written the Constitution and how his devoted wife stayed up all night to read it? Was this a prelude in his imagination of what might come, "the art of the impossible," as he calls it in one of his essays? Was his choice of Rašín as hero of his story (one who had a tragic end) a reflection of his own fears as to the price might one pay for changing the course of history?

In Act II of *Tomorrow, We'll Start It Up*, there is an interchange between husband and wife:

> Rašín: *(Speaks into the telephone.)* Austria has capitulated. You're the first to hear it. I must hurry. We're going over to the Vice Regent's Office —
>
> Rasinová: *(Into the telephone.)* This is the most important event in our country's history for the last three hundred years! I'm so happy you're a part of it![11]

One cannot help think of the year 1988 and the changes Havel himself must have been sensing. When asked today about the writing of *Tomorrow We'll Start It Up*, he said: "In *Tomorrow*, some of the things which I predicted in the play happened later, so in the end I am gratified by that."[12]

Tomorrow We'll Start It Up is both a play of history and of prophecy. It is about the making of a revolution, its strategies, its tactics, its negotiations, its dangers, and its challenges, such as how to take power without violence. It is a play about leadership, about rising to the occasion, about a carpe diem spirit. As for the play's protagonist, Rašín was a man who loved his country, who had a vision for it, who had been imprisoned and sentenced to die. But it was his destiny to survive and lead his country. He had a keen sense of historical timing and a strong, resilient partner in his wife; he had strength, courage, and humanity, as well as soundness of mind and the ability to express his fears. No wonder the playwright showed such an affinity for his protagonist.

Was Havel writing a rough draft for the Velvet Revolution?

1988–1989: PROLOGUE FOR A REVOLUTION

> Mrs. Rašín: I would never have believed you could found a state on half a sheet of paper!
>
> Rašín: In the time of revolution, anything is possible. Shall I read it to you?[1]
>
> — Havel, *Tomorrow We'll Start It Up*

The writing and producing of *Tomorrow We'll Start It Up* was yet another act of courage in the theater. It was also a prologue to the drama to come, a revolution in which Václav Havel would play the leading role.

The fourteen months between October 1988 and November 1989 were an intense period in which the theater community found itself at the vanguard of the movement for change. It was a traumatic time, marked by petitions, protests, demonstrations, police brutality, intrigue, and plots. For Havel, the symbol of resistance and the target of the authorities' wrath, there was a rapid, repetitive cycle of entering and exiting prison, just like a scene from one of his absurdist plays. During this period, the story of Havel's life in the theater and his life in politics became one.

October 1988: Theater on a String could not put Havel's name on its program, so Havel asked that Oslzlý's name be listed as the author of *Tomorrow We'll Start It Up*. Instead, Oslzlý decided that if Havel's name could not be listed, then none of the authors' names would be.

As Oslzlý tells the story,[2] normally he had to invite the censors to attend the rehearsal before the opening night. But in this case he tried to outwit them, telling them that the production was not ready, blaming logistical problems caused by the fact that it was a coproduction with the HaDivadlo Theater in Brno. And so the opening of "Rozrazil I/1988," which included *Tomorrow We'll Start It Up*, on Friday evening, October 21, 1988, was a great success. Oslzlý knew that the censors would be away for the weekend, so performances were also held on Saturday and Sunday.

On Monday, Oslzlý learned that in fact the censors had been present on Friday; but as he predicted, the secret police were away at their dachas for the weekend, so in fact they couldn't issue a "stop the performance" order till Monday. No, replied the theater — we can't stop the performances, we're already presold. The authorities had to come up with a reason for their order; they couldn't do it on the basis of the theme of democracy because, according to official party lines, democracy as a concept was acceptable. Instead, they said they were stopping the performance because the theater had used the Czech flag in the production, and that wasn't allowed. But Oslzlý refused to accept that reason, and in fact engaged a lawyer to argue on behalf of the theater that the flag that was being used onstage was in fact not the exact size as the official flag, and therefore not against the law. The authorities then found another cause for closing the production: One of the plays in "Rozrazil I" consisted of reportage on the street, with actors asking passers-by "What is democracy?" and using the answers in the performance. The authorities maintained that, without a license, the theater could not do this. Oslzlý replied that the Helsinki Agreement permits freedom of speech. Back and forth it went, for over a week, between the theater and the authorities. During all this conflict, the play went on tour to Prague and was performed there for one week. So, despite threats from the authorities, the play was actually performed ten times over a ten-day period. "We outwitted the secret police," said Oslzlý, triumphantly.

According to Oslzlý, Havel came to a performance in Prague, but the fact that he had written *Tomorrow We'll Start It Up* was not publicized till after the revolution. Actually, the audience and the authorities had suspected that another play on the program, *Hostina* (Banquet), was by Havel because it was about a group of philosophers — including Plato, Pericles, Locke, Hobbes, and St. Augustine — who sit in prison and talk about philosophy. (*Hostina*, however, was by Vladimír Chermá.)

While "Rozrazil I/1988" was being performed in Prague, there were large demonstrations on Wenceslas Square commemorating the founding of the Czechoslovakian democratic state on October 27 to 28, the very dates Havel had dramatized. As Havel remembers it: "There were various demonstrations and a slogan very similar to 'tomorrow we'll start it up' was being shouted in the squares. In the streets there were armored vehicles driving around, trying to impose order."[3] The police broke up the demonstrations with billy clubs and water cannons.

In another act linking the playwright to the date, Havel was arrested on October 27. This time, the arrest was in connection with a new initiative called the Movement for Civic Liberties, a consortium of groups over a wide political spectrum. Its founders sensed the growing tension between the general population and the authorities and wanted to connect that opposition with the dissident community. The movement drafted a petition that they wanted signed by the broader segment of the population, a statement that would be acceptable to the establishment and at the same time affect change.

The result was "Democracy for All," a document stronger than Charter 77, one that openly challenged the Communist Party's right to lead the government. It demanded democratic freedom for society and the release of various writers and artists held as political prisoners and had 260 signers. Sensing a demonstration would be held on October 27, the authorities rounded up the signers of "Democracy for All" on the day before and held them for forty-eight hours. On October 27, the secret police broke into Havel's apartment and searched it and his house at Hrádeček, as well, seizing books, papers, and his computer. Not finding him at home, they tracked him down that evening, arrested him, and once again held him at Ruzyně Prison, this time for four days. On October 31, the day of his release, five thousand people gathered in Wenceslas Square to demonstrate. The police ran rampant, attacking the crowds with riot control squads and water cannons, snatching cameras and smashing them on the cobblestone streets. People were beaten and wounded.[4]

Two days before Havel's arrest, a review of *Tomorrow We'll Start It Up* was printed in a local Brno paper. Like all the others in the audience, the reviewer was oblivious of its author's identity. He described it as a documentary-like reconstruction of one crucial night in Czech history that determines the future of the state. In it, the critic observes how the main character of the play falls asleep and dreams about the future of Czechoslovakia. This critic is concerned, given the political realities of the day. "We are not ready to speak about democracy yet," the critic wrote.[5]

November 1988: Havel was arrested again on November 10, this time for organizing Czechoslovakia 88, a symposium on the country and its history that had been approved by the Communist Party. He was arrested in front of the entire symposium as he conducted the opening ceremony and held for four days. The authorities were becoming increasingly desperate, intensifying their efforts to impose control on an increasingly agitated public. Upon his release, Havel wrote about this experience to the French President Mitterrand, who was about to visit Prague. A few weeks later, Havel breakfasted with President Mitterrand in Prague to discuss the ever-worsening situation.

December 1988: In a month of polarizing developments, Havel participated in the first authorized political demonstration in twenty years under normalization. It was held in Prague on Skroupovo Square. Havel and other dissidents spoke, and a petition was circulated, protesting the recent imprisonment of Ivan Jirous of the Plastic People.

The same month, the authorities closed down the production of "Rozrazil I/1988" at the Theater on a String in Brno, after twenty-seven performances. In response, Theater on a String and HaDivadlo Theater wrote an open letter in protest. The plot thickened. According to Petr Oslzlý, the Soviet embassy started to contact Oslzlý in secret, to ask about the situation in Czech culture and inquire how they could "help." One day, they even invited Oslzlý to a secret meeting at the So-viet embassy. "There, we had a friendly talk — they were all new guys, one had even been to the Sorbonne," Oslzlý said. The "new guys" were embassy staff sent over by Gorbachev, who were collecting information about the theaters in Czechoslovakia and were deeply interested in what Oslzlý had to say.

January 1989: Colleagues from other theaters — the Association of Alternative Theater People, the official stone theaters and, under pressure, the official Union of Theater Artists — rallied around Oslzlý and his Theater on a String. They met in Brno to declare open support of their protest letter, and call for a revival of "Rozrazil I/1988." While they met, Havel was being arrested once more, this time on January 16 in Wences-las Square, at a memorial commemoration of Jan Palach, the student who had burned himself to death in protest of the Soviet invasion in 1969. Demonstrations, which continued over a week, were met with violent po-lice reactions. People were clubbed, rounded up, and detained.

February 1989: Theater on a String and HaDivadlo Theater, sup-ported by colleagues and friends, won their fight. The authorities finally gave permission, and "Rozrazil I/1988" was restored to the repertoire of Theater on a String. Meanwhile, on February 21, Havel was tried and sentenced to nine months in prison for inciting participation in a demon-stration, despite the fact that he had only been an observer. Still, he was hopeful. The barriers between the dissident culture, the general popula-tion, and the official culture were blurring. Change seemed more possi-ble than ever.

March 1989: Incensed by Havel's sentence, a group of his closest friends, including Anna Freimanová, managing editor of *O divadle* (About Theater) and Sergej Machonin, the theater critic, decided that the publication should initiate a public protest and that a petition should be circulated demanding his release. They collected twelve important names, and the petition was read on Voice of America and Radio Free Europe. As a result, the petitioners were able to collect hundreds of additional signa-tures at exhibitions, theaters, and other gatherings. The names repre-sented a broad spectrum, including artists and workers from the theater community, writers, intellectuals, and names from the general population. Any actors who signed would be blacklisted from appearing on television or radio, Oslzlý reported. But they signed, anyway.

April 1989: At Kvartál, the quarterly writers' meeting in Slovakia, another petition demanding Havel's release was drafted, and the organizers recruited signers from amongst the leadership of official cultural groups. They collected 3,800 signatures.

May 1989: Exhausted, Havel was released conditionally from prison after four months. Olga gave a welcome-home party, with hundreds in attendance.

Meanwhile, the theater community was consolidating to take a political stand, and Oslzlý was at its vanguard. In his article "On Stage with the Velvet Revolution," he describes the rest of that dramatic year, month by month, as theaters became the vanguard of change in the society. (The Czechs actually referred to it as *něžná revoluce*, meaning "the gentle revolution." The word *sametová*, meaning "velvet," was introduced by the Western press.) During the second half of May, a meeting of Czech dramaturgs and directors from all theaters, official and unofficial, was held to address the issue of forbidden authors. In his keynote speech, Oslzlý spoke out against what he called the immorality of banning plays. "We must start a new season without any taboos to Czech drama,"[6] he said publicly, in front of the entire audience, which he knew included some secret police. An amazing thing happened: Nothing. The authorities did not react. And so theaters began to include productions of banned plays in their repertoires.[7]

June 1989: At an official conference of Czech theaters held in early June, a secret ballot was taken, and the opposition group emerged victorious. Under Oslzlý's leadership, a new group was formed called the Union of Dramatic Artists, which stood for protest against the totalitarian control of culture. Meanwhile, sensing that the time was right for an alliance between leaders of official cultural organizations and the dissidents, Havel and Jiří Křížan, a screenwriter who had organized the petition for Havel's release, drafted a seven-point petition demanding democratic reforms and religious freedoms. Entitled "Just a Few Sentences," it represented an alliance between the official and the dissident cultures, between Communists and non-Communists.

Following the previous pattern, the petitioners first sought signatures from prominent actors, writers, and artists. Then they tried to recruit signators from the broader theater world and from the general population. Havel challenged those circulating the petitions to see if they could find someone who hadn't signed a petition before. A fund was established to pay for government fines against signers. Havel masterminded the entire campaign, which eventually met with attacks against the petitioners in the official press. This publicity caused even more people to sign.[8]

July 1989: Prague welcomed a traveling theater festival of nine experimental European theaters for three days of performances. At the event, prompted by a letter from Charter 77 and other groups within Czechoslovakia, the Western troupes declared their solidarity with the persecuted artists. This public declaration was met with thunderous applause. "The secret police tried to prevent this," Oslzlý said, "but were helpless in the face of the solidarity of the actors and their public."[9]

August 1989: The cultural community experienced a backlash. Increasing numbers of artists were banned, although according to Oslzlý, these bans were ignored. On August 21, massive demonstrations were held in Prague to commemorate the anniversary of the Russian invasion. Havel stayed away, retreating to Hrádeček to avoid being arrested.

September 1989: By September, 40,000 signatures were collected for the petition "Just a Few Sentences," representing the entire spectrum of society. Also that month, *Redevelopment* premiered at the Schauspielhaus in Zurich. (Achim Benning had moved from the Burgtheater in Vienna to Zurich, taking his commitment to Havel's plays with him.)

October 1989: As more and more protests mounted against the totalitarian regime, tensions rose. Oslzlý and his colleagues began preparing a second "issue" of "Rozrazil," this time on environmental themes. "It was also on the ecology of the human soul," Oslzlý said.[10] The purpose was to bring his company to Prague on November 17 to perform this new piece, because he knew there would be student demonstrations in honor of Jan Opletal, the student who had been killed on that date fifty years ago by the Nazis. Many students would enjoy the performance, he thought.

And that was the night when the revolution started.

NOVEMBER–DECEMBER 1989:
WRITING AND STAGING A REVOLUTION

> We must not be afraid of dreaming the seemingly impossible if we want the seemingly impossible to become a reality.[1]
> — Havel, foreword to *The Art of the Impossible*

> [T]he Revolution, which was called, not by us but by Western journalists, "gentle" or "velvet," had, as a whole, some sort of theatrical dimensions. It had the structure of an ancient drama, at the same time of a fairy tale, and then again of a musical. It was very strange, and I believe that some day someone will write a study of it. [2]
> — Havel, "Not Only About Theatre"

The day the revolution started, no one had predicted it. It was as if suddenly there were an audience, a public, and an opening night without even a dress rehearsal. But the core dramatis personae found that, without knowing it, they had been preparing their roles for a long time. So they scrambled to cast the ensemble, improvise, and rehearse the revolution as they performed it.

What was the plot? A drama, written and staged by a playwright in collaboration with others. A play in forty-three scenes (days), guided by a skilled hand, one that knew structure, dialogue, and interaction with the audience.

Where was this revolution set? On the stages and in the lobbies and dressing rooms of the theaters of Prague. The ensemble? The theater community of Prague. The leading man? Václav Havel.

Friday, November 17: On the anniversary of Jan Opletal's death, Havel stayed at Hrádeček. He knew there would be demonstrations of some kind — everyone did — and he couldn't face another arrest and imprisonment. The multiple arrests over the past eleven months had exhausted him.

But Olga joined the march in Prague along with Havel's writer friends. It was a dark and dreary day, and by the afternoon a crowd of 15,000 students had gathered peacefully outside the Pathology Institute. The authorities had preapproved the gathering, as well as the route to the cemetery where commemorators would lay wreaths on Opletal's grave. The crowds cooperated up until the end. Then, buoyed by the spirit of the occasion, they turned and started for Wenceslas Square, the traditional gathering place for all commemorations, which on this occasion had been forbidden by the authorities. It was a spirited but nonviolent crowd, armed with nothing but song (the Czech national anthem and "We Shall Overcome") and jangling key rings (a sign of peaceful protest). They marched along the Vltava River, past Havel's house, shouting "Long live Havel!"

By the time the demonstration turned onto Národní Street past the Café Slavia, the crowd — students now joined by the general population — had swelled to 50,000. People seated in the Café Slavia, where Havel and his friends had sat thirty-five years ago, jumped up from their tables and ran out to join the throng. Across the street at the National Theater, a performance of the opera was just beginning. (When the curtain fell later that evening, the audience applauded the conductor and members of the orchestra who had signed a petition protesting Havel's recent imprisonment.)

Around 8 P.M., the crowd was suddenly surrounded by riot police. The police shouted commands to disperse through their megaphones, but were met with continued singing and chanting. Bolstered by the arrival of special antiterrorist troops, the police force acted; it tightened its flanks, squeezing the crowd into a breathless, hysterical mass, forcing people through a tunnel of club-wielding policeman. While the strains of the opera played in the National, the cries of Prague's students echoed down the blood-stained cobblestone streets.

Saturday, November 18: The next day, rumors abounded as to the events of the seventeenth and the extent of the violence. The officials downplayed it in the newspapers; word of mouth reported it as a massacre. One report was particularly shocking; it was rumored that a student named Martin Šmíd had been murdered by the police. This was untrue; the rumor was a ghoulish fabrication by a faction within the Soviet embassy together with a pro-Gorbachev faction within the Czech Communist Party. Its purpose was to inflame public opinion against the Husák leadership in favor of the moderates in the regime. Martin Šmíd never existed at all; he was simply the creation of a last-minute desperate attempt to maintain Communist control of some kind. But that was not known till later, and the rumor helped incite public anger further, although not as the plotters intended.[3]

For there was no doubt that the events of the day had unleashed a public outcry, one that had been trapped in the throats of a terrified, intimidated populace for decades. All day Saturday, as the rumors spread throughout the theaters and the universities and into the streets, the public's anger against the regime increased.

Havel came down from Hrádeček and began to join the action. That evening, representatives from various theaters met at the Realistické Theater and declared a strike. They planned to meet the next day at the Činoherní Klub.

The revolution had begun. Its epicenter: the theaters of Prague.

Sunday, November 19: The small auditorium of the Činoherní Klub was packed with representatives from student, theater, writer, human rights, and religious groups. Havel had made sure that as broad a spectrum of leadership as possible was invited. He sat on the podium, his eyes averted as he talked quietly into the microphone — hardly a dynamic public speaker. But his presence was riveting. After a short and passionate discussion, the meeting unanimously voted to declare itself the Civic Forum, a new citizens' consortium for change. They drafted a statement, demanding the immediate resignation of the government leadership, an investigation into the police brutality of November 17, and the release of imprisoned dissidents, writers, and artists.

Havel's first act of leadership had taken place. He had created a power base. He even had bodyguards assigned to him, organized by a young student admirer named John Bok. Now, just as he had drawn charts and diagrams of his plays, he began to mastermind and strategize. One of his first moves was to send students out into the countryside with video recordings of what happened in Prague and to send these videos to other European television stations. After a lifetime of working in the theater, Havel astutely realized that the theater community could lead but they could not "perform" the revolution without an audience. It needed a broader public.

Monday, November 20: The police and the army closed the bridges across the Vltava, but no matter. People milled through the streets; students set up strike committees and occupied their schools. University walls were plasters with posters of declarations, slogans, and the Czechoslovakian flag.

Tuesday, November 21: On day five of the revolution, a moment of comic relief was provided. A delegation from the Civic Forum was admitted to the Presidium to see Prime Minister Adamec, but Havel was refused entrance. While the other delegates met with Adamec, who droned on and on about perestroika, evidently in denial as to what was actually taking place, Havel sat in the lobby, posing as the porter, admitting various delegations and conversing with people.[4] Elsewhere, while police moved in to surround the building of the Central Committee of the Communist Party, technicians in Wenceslas Square prepared for Havel's first "entrance" on the political stage, rigging sound equipment to the balcony of the Melantrich publishing house, which had loaned its building to the Civic Forum for this occasion.

Wednesday, November 22: Enter Václav Havel, making his first public appearance during the revolution. He addressed an enormous crowd of over 200,000 from the balcony over Wenceslas Square, reporting on the Civic Forum. Television coverage of the event included the response of the crowd, which was wildly euphoric even on that bone-chilling afternoon. Despite rumors that 40,000 troops were closing in on the city to crush the movement for Czech democracy, the crowd cheered, shouting slogans of approval that reverberated through the loudspeakers, generating enough passion and heart to fracture the freezing air. Havel was now the indisputable leader of the opposition. Within hours, he was approached by an emissary of Adamec, suggesting a secret negotiation as to the future of the country.

On day six, Havel held his first press conference, and drafted letters to Presidents Bush and Gorbachev on behalf of the Civic Forum, informing them of the crisis in Czechoslovakia. On that day, Havel also chose the headquarters of the Civic Forum and, hence, of the revolution. It was to be at the Laterna Magika, the large theater next door to the National Theater, diagonally across from the Café Slavia, where our story of Havel's life in the theater began. It was a fitting stage for the unfolding drama.

Thursday, November 23: In the lower levels of the Laterna Magika, there was a maze of corridors that led past rows of dressing rooms and costume closets crammed with ballet tutus and masks. Guards, consisting of John Bok and his karate students, were posted at the doors. It was stifling. There were no windows, and everyone was smoking in nervousness and excitement. The ten-member core staff of Civic Forum crammed into the largest dressing room (ten by twelve feet), to begin their meetings, while ballet dancers made coffee and sandwiches. Every so often, a rumor circulated that a bomb had been placed in the basement. But people brushed it off; they had no time to worry about it. They were too engaged in performing political theater.

Friday, November 24: The end of week one of the revolution, and the beginning of a weekend of great successes. Crowds gathered daily in Wenceslas Square. Demonstrations were reported in Bratislava (100,000 people), in České Budějovice (25,000), and in Brno (120,000). The audience had expanded multifold. That evening, Miloš Jakeš, a key party leader, announced that he, his secretariat, and the politburo were resigning.

Saturday, November 25: The resignations were announced to a crowd of 750,000 on Letná Plain, north of the Old Town on the other side of the Vltava River. Again, there was the freezing weather and the passionate heat of the crowd. An editorial in *The Independent,* a London newspaper, featuring a caricature of Havel captioned "Mightier than the sword," concluded: "In 1989, the unbelievable seems routine in East Europe. Will we see Václav Havel, who this week has addressed cheering crowds on Wenceslas Square, as prime minister or president of a democratic Czechoslovakia? It still seems unthinkable."[5]

Sunday, November 26: A core group gathered in the dressing room of Laterna Magika to "rehearse" the upcoming meeting with Prime Minister Adamec. Once again, a demonstration was held on Letná Plain, this time with a throng of one million people. Havel appeared with Dubček and Adamec. After an attempt to apologize and explain himself to the crowd, Adamec was heckled and hissed into silence; ultimately, the Civic Forum marshals removed him from the podium for his own safety. With Adamec publicly disgraced, Havel's leadership became clear.

Tuesday, November 28: At the German embassy, Havel accepted the German Booksellers Peace Prize. His international status and recognition was growing daily.

Friday, December 1: Ivan Jirous, the organizer of the Plastic People of the Universe, was released from prison.

Sunday, December 3: Havel and Olga went for a walk in Prague for the first time in fourteen days. Except for select political meetings and appearances in Letná Plain, he had not left the underground labyrinth of the Laterna Magika, with its suffocating, smoke-filled air, artificial lights, dressing-room mirrors, and myriad of tiny nooks, crannies, and closets. It had been a dramatic scene: a phone with one line only, dozens of people crammed into rooms, meeting, talking, scurrying about with cups of coffee, dozing in their chairs. A bouncer stood by the door. Hectic press conferences were held nightly. There was tension, laughter, and disbelief. Was this really happening?

With the strength of the Civic Forum growing daily, and its activities overflowing in its current location, Havel requested a building from the authorities. In another touch of the absurd, they were moved to the building of the union of Czechslovak-Soviet Friendship on Wenceslas Square. Havel was given a room with a balcony overlooking the square.

Tuesday, December 5: At a crucial meeting of Civic Forum leaders, the issue of the future presidency was the topic of discussion. Havel sat quietly while different recommendations were discussed, and then confirmed, in his low voice, that if it were in the country's best interest for him to serve, he would. The issue then became Havel's recognition. Certainly, he was known in Prague, but outside the city, among the general working population, he was regarded simply as a dissident who was "opposing things."6

Thursday, December 7: Adamec resigned as prime minister. Around this time, Havel moved to an apartment at a secret location in Prague, where, high over the treetops, he could have moments of peace and concentrate on writing his television addresses.

Sunday, December 10: Jiří Bartoška, the actor, nominated Havel for the presidency in the name of the Civic Forum. This began a weeklong campaign by the Civic Forum to sharpen Havel's media profile. The group also addressed the issue of Dubček, the former president and the symbol of Prague Spring.

Friday, December 15: Havel and Dubček came to an understanding. Havel would be president at this time; and at the next free elections, he would support Dubček's candidacy.

Saturday, December 16: In his television appearance, Havel announced that he would accept the presidency on the conditions that he remain president only until free elections could be held, and that Dubček serve alongside him in some capacity.

Tuesday, December 19: Dubček asked parliament to elect Havel president by the end of the year.

Wednesday, December 20: Melantrich released *Disturbing the Peace*, the first *samizdat* book to be published legally in twenty years.

OPENING NIGHT

> Destiny had indeed played a strange joke on me . . .[1]
> — Havel, address at New York University, October 27, 1991

> I sometimes think God strikes back — as if I'd written an absurdist
> drama and put God in it . . . so God has put me here as president.[2]
> — Havel, in "Proč Havel?" (Why Havel?)

Friday, December 29, 1989: Havel was unanimously elected president
of Czechoslovak Republic by parliament. Thereafter, he and Olga proceeded to the majestic twelfth-century St. Vitus's Cathedral in the heart
of the Prague Castle complex, high above the Vltava River. The performance: Dvořák's *Te Deum*, the music written to be performed in celebration of a new sovereign. The cast: Olga and Havel, uncomfortable with
the pomp and circumstance. The costume: for him, a borrowed suit with
"high-water" trousers; for her, an outfit that included a borrowed blouse
(from the wife of the former American ambassador). The audience: millions of television viewers. The occasion: opening night of a new decade
and a new republic. The mood: euphoria, tinged with disbelief on the
part of the performers:

> When the idea first came up that I should let my name stand for
> president of Czechoslovakia, it seemed like an absurd joke. All my
> life I had opposed the powers that be. I had never held political of-
> fice, not even for a moment. I had always placed great store in my
> independence, and I had never liked anything too serious, too cer-
> emonial, too official. Suddenly, I was on the way to holding an of-
> ficial position and, moreover, the highest in the land.[3]

Monday, January 1, 1990: Havel addressed the nation for the first
time in the role of president. The tone of his speech: truth tinged with
hope. "Our country is not flourishing." "We live in a contaminated moral
environment." "We cannot blame the previous rulers for everything."
"We have to pay for our present freedom." "Self-confidence is not arro-
gance." And, significantly: "We were the spiritual crossroads of Europe. Is
there any reason why we could not become so again?"[4]

Olga and Havel, after his release from Pankrác Prison, 1989
(Ivan Kyncl, Prague Theatre Institute archive)

✣c PART V ɔ✣
The Nineties and Beyond
Politics and Theater as One

I haven't attended any schools for presidents. My only school was life itself.[1]

> — Havel, address to a joint session of the
> U.S. Congress, Washington, D.C., February 21, 1990

I am well aware that in the early months of my presidency, some of my ideas had more theatrical flair than political foresight."[2]

> — Havel, address to the
> Academy of Performing Arts, Prague, October 4, 1996

Now I won't have any more time to cook.[3]

> — Havel to Klaus Juncker

CURTAIN UP

Once a playwright, Havel was now playing the leading character in a drama written in his own hand.

The role: the "reluctant president," as the biographer Michael Simmons calls him. The drama: the birth of a new republic. The setting: Prague Castle.

The Cast: One by one, Havel cast his castle ensemble, drawing frequently from the theater community. For his chief cultural advisor, he chose Petr Oslzlý, the founder of Theater on a String, who had commissioned Havel's latest play *Tomorrow, We'll Start It Up* and spearheaded the theater movement against the regime. Together with Oslzlý, they redesigned the setting of Havel's new drama, the Prague Castle. They worked their way through the vast maze of rooms, eager to transform its cold, grim, dark décor. They restaged the ritual of the changing of the

Havel (center) during the Velvet Revolution, 1989
(Stanislav Slawicky, Prague Theatre Institute archive)

guard. Most important, they opened the castle grounds to the public. Stanislav Milota, a cameraman and husband of the actress Vlasta Chramostová, cofounder of *bytové divadlo* (living-room theater), became a political advisor to Havel. Later on, Havel appointed Anna Freimanová, his neighbor at Hrádeček and the wife of Andrej Krob, as his secretary in the Castle. Jiří Dienstbier, one of the authors of the Vaněk plays, became Foreign Minister of Czechoslovakia, and then head of a political party called the Civic Movement, a breakaway group from the Civic Forum. The list of "casting choices" from the theater community continued.

The Costumes: As Miloš Forman tells the story, President Havel drove himself to the castle on his first day at work. He arrived, parked his car, entered, and immediately called his friend Theodor Pištěk, the painter and costume designer for film and theater. "Doda," he said, "you have to come to the castle immediately and redesign the uniforms of the guards. The ones they're wearing at the castle are the same as the ones the prison guards wear, and I feel like I'm still in prison." Several weeks passed, and nothing changed. Once again Havel called Pištěk. "Doda, what happened?!" "It's difficult to deal with the army," Pištěk replied. "I just can't call them up and give orders." So Havel called the military liaison to the president into his office and, in his capacity as commander-in-chief, instructed him to name Pištěk a colonel. The next day, new uniforms were made. Then, as Forman remembers it, he and Pištěk went to the castle to bring President Havel his own new uniform and the sword that went with it. Havel put them on and said: "Good. Now let's go and scare the cooks." The three of them descended to the castle kitchen. "The two old ladies who had cooked for Husák saw us and simply froze," Forman said. A stack of raw potatoes were sitting on the kitchen table. "Don't be afraid," said President Havel, hand on his sword. "I just came to cut the potatoes."[1]

The Set: With the same theatrical flair, Havel addressed the cold and foreboding atmosphere of the castle. First, he surveyed it, riding a scooter through the castle halls, wearing jeans and a sweater. In an attempt to humanize it, he turned it into a theater:

> He threw a "festival of democracy" in the courtyards, with jugglers and mimes performing while he wandered around drinking Pilsner and greeting everyone. Later on, when he discovered that the chandeliers in the gilded Spanish Hall were outmoded, a couple of typ-

ical visitors, Mick Jagger and Keith Richards (of the Rolling Stones), paid for new fixtures. For weeks, he drove his staff crazy as he monkeyed around with the remote control, dimming the lights, then brightening them again.[2]

The stage was ready. And so the curtain rose on the next act of Havel's life in the theater and in politics — now as one.

1990–1992: HAVELMANIA

Havel is always about us.[1]
> — Vladimír Just, *Literární noviny*

The Garden Party is for everyone![2]
> — Havel, *The Garden Party*

While Havel was finding a new life on the national and world stage, his plays were finding a home in theaters in Prague and throughout the country. As the curtain went up on freedom during that first euphoric year, eager theaters scrambled to honor their playwright/president, performing work that had been banned for twenty-one years.

For the next two seasons, Prague became a festival of Havel's works. In jest, they called the phenomenon "Havelmania," and it spread like theatrical wildfire.

It began with the homecoming of Pavel Landovský. What better way to celebrate Havel's presidency and cultural liberation than in the theater, with a production of a Havel play starring Landovský, his dear friend, returning from exile after twelve years? The Činoherní Klub off Wenceslas Square, where Landovský had been part of the ensemble from 1967 to 1974, was only too ready to raise its curtain on a revival of the celebrated *Audience*, the play Havel and Landovský had read together thirteen years earlier in Andrej Krob's barn at Hrádeček.

As it became clear that the revolution would become a reality, Landovský's daughter, Andrea, traveled to Vienna in December to propose the idea to Landovský and to urge him to begin preparing his role of Sládek. Landovský was still performing at the Burgtheater in German; it was a terrible struggle for him. And to make matters worse, he hadn't performed in Czech for over a decade.

Traveling home to Prague on the train after his exile, Landovský felt his emotions running high. He was returning to a country he thought he would never see again, in circumstances that hardly seemed real. In all the excitement, his daughter remembers,[3] he could hardly concentrate. He tried to study his lines on the train ride, but somehow they didn't stick. Meanwhile, in Prague, anxiously awaiting Landovský, the director Jiří Menzel had rehearsed for five days with Josef Abrhám in the role of Vaněk.

Arriving at the theater in Prague in time for the evening performance of *Audience* on January 10, Landovský was frantic. He still didn't know his lines. Enlisting his daughter's assistance, they hurriedly taped pages of the script all over the brewmaster's desk on the set where he was to sit during the performance. They also taped pages to the door of the lavatory, where Landovský would make numerous exits. They diluted the beer Sládek was to drink on stage. And then the performance began.

With the country's favorite stage and film actor back onstage for the first time in sixteen years, the audience of the Činoherní Klub was filled to overflowing with theater artists and former dissidents. They packed the orchestra and balcony of the three-hundred-seat theater and went wild from the moment the curtain rose. Havel, of course, was there, and so was Pavel Kohout, back from Vienna after over a decade. The laughter crescendoed as Landovský downed beer after beer (the diluted brew was more powerful than they had imagined) while his daughter stood in the wings, desperately whispering his lines, in vain. The audience adored it. Wrote one of the critics in *Rudé právo*:

> The atmosphere was charged by Landovský, who obviously didn't know his lines . . . but that didn't matter because he has the ability and the heart to perform this role under any conditions. He didn't have to prepare; he's so alive and authentic in the role that he simply did it, and that's all.[4]

The videotape of that performance of *Audience* at the Činoherní Klub is one of the treasures of Czech theater archives. The camera captured Landovský swilling his beer while sneaking glances at the cribsheets on the desk. At one point, either drunk or expertly acting it, he lost his place and looped over his lines; the audience, many of whom knew the lines because they had listened for years to the *samizdat* record, burst into laughter and applause. Josef Abrhám, who played Vaněk, had to shield his face from the audience, while he shook with uncontrollable laughter.

As Landovský tells it: "The audience went crazy. They didn't know I was reading the lines." But of course they did, and so did Havel. As the actors took their bow, Havel called out from the audience over the applause: "You had fourteen years to learn your lines!" "I had other things to do in Vienna than learn your play," Landovský called back. "Anyway, Vaněk's part is so short, whereas Sládek's part is very long."[5] After the performance, Landovský opened a bottle of champagne and sprayed it into Havel's face.

"It was more a happening than a performance,"[6] wrote Vladimír Procháska in *Rudé právo*, one of the many critics present who were as emotional as the audience over such an extraordinary theatrical evening. Seated in the audience were some of the offstage characters whose names were mentioned in the script, among them Pavel Kohout, the exiled playwright, and Jiřina Bohdalová, the celebrated actress and object of Sládek's desire. Indeed, it was a happening, a historical event where one could witness both the beginnings of a new republic, the freeing of an imprisoned culture, the reunion of banned artists and dissidents, and the breakdown of the barriers between life and art.

The critics, who were reviewing the first Havel play to be performed publicly (and with an acknowledgment of authorship) in his country in twenty-one years, wrote about the emotion of the occasion as well as its significance. After all, *Audience* was a play written in 1975 by a playwright whose country forbade the productions of his plays. They had never officially reviewed this play before, nor any of his plays written in the 1970s and 1980s, for that matter. In fact, *Audience* had never been publicly performed in Czechoslovakia until now. And yet, thanks to the recording that had circulated throughout Czechoslovakia for the past ten years, it was widely known. For the critics, the occasion was unique. "People in Czechoslovakia have broken out of their prison,"[7] wrote Jan Reinisch in *Mladá fronta*. Others pointed out the universality of the play. "Havel's *Audience* presents a tragic misunderstanding between two different men which might happen anywhere in the civilized world,"[8] wrote Jan Foll in *Scéna* (Stage). Still others commented on the play's humanity. From Svobodné Slovo:

> *Audience* is probably the most famous of Havel's plays [referring to the *samizdat* recording]. The character of the brewery man, painted by Havel in all colors except black and white, is funny and dangerous,

stupid and smart, and understandably human in his effort to survive. This sort of man hides in each of us, somehow. And we can only hope that the polite and honorable Vaněk hides in us as well.[9]

After the broadcasting of this videotaped performance a year later, Petr Gabal of *Smena* wrote of the celebratory atmosphere of that night: "Havel doesn't need it. What we should celebrate is the truth of his plays."[10]

Actually, there were not one but two productions of *Audience* performed at the Činoherní Klub that week. The Actors' Studio production of *Audience*, produced in New York on November 17, 1989, directed by Václav Šimek, a Czech emigré director, was performed for two nights in January 1990 at the Činoherní Klub in Prague, starring Lou Brockway and Kevin O'Connor, directed by Frank Corsar, and filmed by PBS. It was intended as part of a documentary on the life of Havel, which included scenes shot in the brewery where he had worked and one of the prisons where he had been incarcerated, to show American audiences the realities of Czech life in the seventies. Lou Brockway, the actor playing Vaněk, commented on the play: "The power of this play lies in its universality. It speaks to many people in many different situations."[11]

In February 1990, Havel traveled to the United States. It was his first official visit abroad as president. On his way to New York, he and his official entourage stopped in Rejkjavik, Iceland, to attend a production of *Redevelopment* there at the Plodlejkhusid Theater. It was the first performance of one of his full-length plays that he was to attend after the revolution. He was very moved by the performance, and the production made a lasting impression on him. "It was really a special experience," recalls Dr. Alexandra Brabcová, the interpreter who traveled with him. "Not only because it was the first production he saw of a play after the Revolution, but also because it was in a language that Czechs couldn't understand at all. He was terribly excited, and appreciated it very much."[12]

In New York, he delivered a stirring speech in the Cathedral of St. John the Divine on February 22, 1990. Afterwards, a dinner was given in his honor at the Vivian Beaumont Theatre of Lincoln Center sponsored by the *New York Review of Books*. Guests included Saul Bellow, Elizabeth Hardwick, Norman Mailer, E. L. Doctorow, Susan Sontag, Arthur Miller, Edward Albee, Miloš Forman, Eli Wiesel, Ron Silver, Bernard Gersten, Joseph Papp, and Henry Kissinger. The critic Mel Gussow remembers the occasion well:

Henry Kissinger seemed to monopolize Havel. When I finally met him, he spoke to me in English and talked about the production of *Redevelopment* that he'd just seen in Iceland. I told him I had probably seen more of his plays than he had.[13]

After Havel returned to Prague, the Czech premiere of *Redevelopment* was waiting for him at the Realistické Theater. Opening night was on March 30, 1990, under the direction of Karel Kříž. The critics' remarks were mixed, citing other Havel plays as stronger. Sergej Machonin, writing in *Literární noviny*, found the play too heavy on philosophy, detracting from the characters' psychological development and substituting speech for action.[14] Others worried about the timing of producing the play just after the revolution, when everything Havel had written about was now about to change. For example, Jiří Hájek saw the play "as a unidimensional criticism of society, which suffers from too much thesis. And after the changes in society, it loses its theatrical effectiveness."[15] Actually, Havel himself had questioned the relevance of the production and had expressed his concerns to the artistic team at the Realistické Theater,[16] anticipating the kind of critical response that Zdeněk Tichý articulated in *Lidové noviny*, that "in the new political situation, the play has lost its aggressive spirit."[17]

But many put this production in a larger historical context and chose to write about the occasion of seeing a full-length play by Václav Havel after two decades of darkness. Despite his reservations, Zdeněk Tichý also praised the Realistické Theater because they decided to produce *Redevelopment* before the revolution was well underway, and were ready to face the consequences. "No matter how we perceive this production," he wrote, "it makes us think about ourselves, about our lives and our decisions which we've made over the past twenty-five years."[18] And in *Večerní Praha* (Evening Prague): "Havel's plays are not relaxing for the audience. They force us to think about what we could have done but didn't, about our apathy and intolerance. *Redevelopment* is a parallel of our history . . ."[19]

In his review of *Redevelopment*, Vladimír Just of *Literární noviny* also looked at the broader perspective, including the audience and its expectations. According to Just, that audience "has missed the milestones of absurdist world drama for the past twenty-five years. This is an audience that is even surprised by Woody Allen."[20] During that time, Just pointed out, they had not been challenged by the theater; rather, they were simply entertained. Furthermore, there was a new problem: Audiences knew Havel as a president, they knew his speeches, so when they came to the theater to see his plays, they were expecting to hear the voice of wisdom, rather than the voice of encoded absurdism. "The audience doesn't know the absurdist tradition," Just continued, "they forget that it has an irony which is meant to entertain." In other words, they were taking Havel's plays too seriously. He concluded by emphasizing their importance today:

> Havel is always about us, about our stereotypes, about our consumer oblivion, about our tendency to delegate our responsibility. . . . In the 1980s, we delegated our responsibility to Havel the dissident; in the 1990s, to Havel our president. . . . We should wake up and eventually understand that we all are acting in a theater without a curtain, that we're putting on a show for others and for ourselves as well.[21]

One of the most emotional theatrical moments during that first year of Havelmania came with his return to the Theatre on the Balustrade, his home in the golden 1960s. That return was coupled with the return of Jan Grossman, his director, collaborator, and mentor. During 1989, as the situation in the cultural community was softening, Vodička, the Balustrade's managing director, who had worked with Havel and Grossman in the 1960s and remained throughout the 1970s and 1980s, invited Grossman to serve as guest director for a production of *Don Juan*. Grossman had been banned from working in Prague for the past fourteen years, after the authorities had identified him in the audience at the performance of *The Beggar's Opera* in Horní Počernice in 1975. After the success of *Don Juan* in May 1989, Vodička offered Grossman a contract. He accepted, on the condition that he be able to direct a play by Havel. That was in the summer of 1989, and Vodička promised to try to get permission from the authorities. But then, the revolution happened, and the path was free and clear. Now Grossman was to direct the Czech premiere of *Largo Desolato*, starring Jiří Bartoška as Leopold Kopřiva.

On opening night, April 9, 1990, a thrilled audience packed the tiny Balustrade Theatre and, as the curtain rose, heard the recorded voice of Havel reading the stage directions. Knowing of Havel's postprison practice of recording his plays in his own voice, Grossman had asked him to make a new recording of the stage directions. After the performance, Havel took a bow with his cast, saying: "As soon as I heard the news that

Jan Grossman was coming to the Theatre on the Balustrade, it made me so happy that this guru of mine was returning. For eight long beautiful years we worked together here, side by side, like twins." Grossman replied: "Havel influences the theater, and the theater influences Havel. And in such an instance when the exchange is mutual, it's both fortuitous and unique."[22]

The critics were as excited as the audience about attending the first public performance of the first play Havel had written when he was released from prison six years earlier — and at the theater where he had been "born" as a playwright. The anticipation of seeing *Largo Desolato* was further heightened by the fact that some of the critics had read the play in *samizdat*. Přemysl Rut wrote in *Lidové noviny*:

> Five years ago, when I read the manuscript of Havel's *Largo Desolato*, it made me disgusted, angry, regretful, doubtful, fascinated, grateful, and frightened. And I laughed. That's what we call a strong artistic experience. It isn't that easy to affect me so much. Most forbidden literature was egocentric and defensive, and was written only to solve pseudo-problems. But *Largo Desolato* was completely different. Havel not only depicts himself, but also he reflects on the human condition. Meaning that he also reflects me. He doesn't comment on how he is — rather, he asks me how I am.[23]

Jiří Hájek of *Rudé právo* called *Largo Desolato* "a completely different chapter of Havel's work."

> [Leopold Kopřiva] is a man living under the constant threat of imprisonment to the extent that he begins to wish it would happen. The prison cell is perhaps the only place at that moment where he can become himself again.[24]

In an interview with *Rudé právo*, Havel echoed the sentiments of Leopold Kopřiva and reiterated that the issues he had written about six years earlier had not yet been resolved.

> In this play I try to analyze the state of mind called post-prison psychosis . . . and today the state of our society reminds me very much of this. It's the situation of a man who has just left prison where life has strict limits, where there is an order, a system — rough, difficult,

but known. A man can get used to it. And now suddenly he's free, and he starts to panic. He's frightened of the number of decision he has to make. Such a man feels so helpless, so defenseless, that sometimes he even wishes he could go back to prison, to the place he knows. It is exactly this frustration with freedom that is the current state of our society. And just as I didn't write directly about prison, I am not going to write directly about the presidency.[25]

For the audience, the production of *Largo Desolato* at the Theatre on the Balustrade was special for another reason. For the first time, the audience was given a vivid impression about dissidents and their private lives directly from a dissident. During the 1970s and 1980s, the broader public knew about dissidents only from official propaganda. While they had heard about Charter 77, they were not informed in depth of its contents. Instead, they were told about Havel's Mercedes, or Pavel Kohout's beautiful country home. The media depicted dissidents as disloyal Czechs, whose comforts represented illegal liaisons with the West. Now *Largo Desolato* was providing the broader public with firsthand information about the true life of a dissident, with its private struggles and crises.

A poignant aside to the scene above: One of the people who was not present on the opening night of *Largo Desolato* at the Balustrade was Jiřina Šiklová. "After the revolution, there were plenty of people who wanted to be visible. Why should I be at the opening night? That visibility was no importance to me. That's not why I did it," she said, referring to her dedication to the underground movement in the 1970s and 1980s to smuggle dissident literature out of the country, including a copy of *Largo Desolato*. After the revolution, Šiklová was "rehabilitated" as an assistant professor of sociology by the same people who had taken away her title of associate professor in 1969. "Why do you rehabilitate us? You should rehabilitate yourselves," she responded. "And that's why I'm proud that I'm only an assistant professor."[26]

Theaters also scrambled to produce *The Garden Party*, Havel's first full-length play, showing an intent to work their way through the entire Havel canon. In March 1990, while Petr Oslzlý was working with President Havel to humanize the decor of the castle, Oslzlý's Theater on a String was producing playwright Havel's *The Garden Party* in Brno.

During the same month, the curtain rose again on *The Garden Party* at the prestigious National Theater in Prague. By this time, the critics began to address the issue of the timeliness of Havel's plays. Zdeněk Tichý of *Lidové noviny* praised the play's relevance: "It hadn't aged at all." At the same time, he offered a strange admonition:

> At the opening night, during the performance, you could hear the voice of one woman in the audience: "Bejvalo" [that's the way it was]. This self-fulfilling prophesy seems to be premature. It's not so long ago that we'd all been listening to absurd speeches made by our politicians. How different are the Directors of the Inauguration and Liquidation Offices from our future politicians? *The Garden Party* raises contemporary questions — and that's why I consider *The Garden Party* very valuable and necessary today.[27]

Was the critic issuing a warning, lest the playwright/president find himself lost in a new bureaucracy like the one in his play, lest he find himself in danger of becoming a character entangled in a plot of his own making?

By May 1990, Havelmania was in full swing. Prague was like a Havel theater festival, with three productions running simultaneously: *The Garden Party* at the National Theater, *Largo Desolato* at the Balustrade, and *Redevelopment* at the Realistické Theater. After a hiatus of twenty-one years during which writing about Havel's plays in official publications was forbidden (performances of them were banned, so no one could see them, anyway), critics were now faced with no less than three productions of Havel's plays running simultaneously in Prague. In "Twice Havel" (about *Largo Desolato* and *Redevelopment*), Sergej Machonin praised *Largo Desolato* as the stronger play, calling it "a multi-dimensional tragicomedy" and calling Leopold Kopřiva the first of Havel's great and living characters.[28] Jiří Hájek, in "Thrice Václav Havel" (*Rudé právo*), noted that "these three plays were written over a period of twenty-five years but they are all united in human pathos. Each in its own way fights against dehumanizing mechanisms and repressive totalitarian deformations of the social system." He went on to say how deeply affected he was by *The Garden Party* when he first saw it in 1963:

> During the twenty-five years after the play was written, I myself have experienced the full horror of its prophecy, which became more and more real each day. That's why I appreciate this play and consider it to be so contemporary.[29]

Hájek went on to praise *Largo Desolato* as the "most relevant artistic act of the year." The production at the Balustrade was sold out every night for a year, when it was replaced in the repertoire by *Temptation*.

In June, Havelmania was augmented (ironically) by a production of *The Beggar's Opera* at the Činoherní Klub, the very theater that had originally commissioned it from Havel and then backed off in the early 1970s, fearing that the theater would be in jeopardy if it produced the play. The production featured Josef Abrhám in the role of Macheath, the same actor who had played Vaněk in *Audience* opposite Landovský a few months earlier. Again, Havel had expressed doubts as to the play's relevance. "'I like the play. And even my friends like it. But on the other hand, I have to confess that in this play I see no future," he told one critic from *Mladá fronta*. That critic disagreed.

> It's the 1990s; the play's message is relevant. In every society, even in a democratic one, there is some manipulation. *The Beggar's Opera* continues to warns us of this manipulation, which is somehow still present.[30]

The headline of the review in *Občanský deník* (Civic Daily) read: "Not to belong to yourself means not to exist," once again stressing the contemporary relevance of the play's themes.[31]

Others praised the entertaining aspects of Havel's *The Beggar's Opera*, seeing it as a palatable way of presenting a dark era of Czech history. From *Rovnost* (Equality):

> *The Beggar's Opera* is a universal satire, dealing with the common qualities in human nature — the desire to rule, to manipulate, to control, to own, and the basic desire of one man to have power over others.[32]

And so the merry-go-round of Havel plays continued in Prague throughout that euphoric year of 1990. While the new, freely elected Parliament of Czechoslovakia reelected Havel as president on July 5, productions proliferated throughout the countryside: *The Garden Party* in Zlín, Ostrava, and Brno; *The Memorandum* in Bratislava: *Audience* in Karlovy Vary; *Vernissage* in Brno; a dramatization of *Letters to Olga* in Brno; *Temptation* in Plzeň; *Redevelopment* in Brno and Liberec; *Mountain Hotel* in Trnava.

The world celebrated Václav Havel onstage, too. On December 27, 1989, critics had crowded into the lower depths of the Soho Poly Theatre in London to review an unprecedented theater event: the opening of the three Vaněk plays on the very night the Czech Communist Politburo was crumbling, making way for the overwhelming endorsement of the plays' author to lead his country. Throughout 1990, scores of productions of Havel plays were mounted all over Europe: in Paris, Jasna (Sweden), Tampere (Finland), Lodz (Poland), Oslo, Torino, Palermo, Marseilles, Toulouse, Lausanne, Sofia (Bulgaria), Jerusalem, Bucharest (Romania), Timosoara (Rumania), Istanbul, Ankara, Athens, Brussels, Krakow — and beyond, from Tunis to as far away as Hong Kong. German and Austrian stages were flooded with them. In Erfurt, Germany, from September 8 to 17, banners saying "Václav Havel Tag" (Václav Havel Day) announced a weeklong festival of his plays. At the Schauspielhaus theater in Zurich, on November 22, the director Achim Benning presented Havel with the Duttweiler Prize, a Swiss award in recognition of one who fights for liberty. At the ceremony, the playwright Friedrich Dürrenmatt made a speech, saying that today, thanks to Havel, things were more liberal in Czechoslovakia than in Switzerland.[33] When asked: "Where is a new play from Václav Havel?" the playwright/president, who was in attendance, replied: "Where is the time to write one?!"[34]

In America, the Vaněk plays appeared on the Arena Stage in Washington, D.C.; *Largo Desolato* in Washington at the American Showcase Theatre, in New Haven at the Yale Repertory Theater, and in Philadelphia at the Wilma Theater. A production called "By and for Havel" at the John Houseman Theater in New York included *Audience* (performed by Kevin O'Connor and Lou Brockway, who had performed it earlier that year at the Činoherní Klub in Prague) together with Samuel Beckett's *Catastrophe*. Mel Gussow commented in the *New York Times* that, despite some reservation he may have about the production itself, "one leaves the theater contemplating Mr. Havel. It is astonishing that in less than a year he has gone from confinement, as harrowingly pictured in *Audience* and *Catastrophe*, to the Presidency of his nation."[35]

There were lighter moments, too, during Havelmania. By 1991, there was still one theater that wanted to join in the fun, a nonconformist amateur company in Prague called Sklep Theater (Divadlo Sklep), known for its comedic sketches, skits, and montages of gags and jokes. Everyone was performing Havel, but Sklep wanted to make its own mark by doing something original. So the company decided to select a Havel play that no one had done. The result? An irreverent adaption of the one-act *The Life Ahead*, the very first play Havel wrote while in the army in 1958 and a play that had never been performed since. The production premiered on March 14, 1991, under the title of *Mlýny* (meaning "grist mills," suggesting a place where elements are ground up into dust, and hence a metaphor for the experience in the army). What the Sklep Theater performed was actually a spoof of Havel's original play, made much shorter and funnier for the occasion, also offering broader satirical statements about aspects of contemporary culture (such as television) under Communism. Most critics recognized the evening for what it was, a bunch of young amateur actors having fun, with low-level, satirical humor. Josef Holý of *Rudé právo* enjoyed the spirit of the evening, while at the same time finding its satire relevant and worthwhile:

> It's incredibly funny. And the audience understands perfectly what the fun in about. But perhaps it might be useful if the older generation came to see this performance, especially those who might have any nostalgia for the Communist era.[36]

RETURN TO THE THEATRE ON THE BALUSTRADE

> [When I write a play], in my mind I still imagine the stage of the Theatre on the Balustrade.[1]
> — Havel, "Daleko od divadla" (Far from the Theater)

During the dark decades of the 1970s and 1980s, after Havel and Grossman had left and normalization cast its shadow over the cultural community, the Balustrade kept producing a repertory season. But with the departure of Havel, Grossman, and later Andrej Krob, the spirit and the cutting edge were gone. Only Vladimír Vodička, the managing director, continued. During that era, the Balustrade was careful to produce a "safe" repertoire including Chekhov, Shakespeare, Gorky, Strindberg, Ibsen, Brecht, and Ostrovsky. The theater also became a haven for directors of the Czech New Wave films of the 1960s, such as Jiří Menzel, who later returned to the Činoherní Klub to direct *Audience* and *The Beggar's Opera* in 1990. Only toward the end did a flicker of the absurd and existentialism — the theater's hallmark of the 1960s — reappear, with a production of Albee's *Seascape* in 1983 and Camus' *Caligula* in 1987.

In 1990, with the ascent of its most famous playwright to the presidency, the return of Jan Grossman and the emotional premiere of *Largo Desolato*, there was the promise of a whole new era at the theater Havel had once called home. Still, they weren't all halcyon days at the Balustrade during the early 1990s. Discord between the acting ensemble and Grossman, who was appointed artistic director in 1991, resulted in an actors' strike and the departure of many actors at the beginning of that season, just after plans to produce Havel's *Temptation* were announced. Grossman was faced with establishing a whole new ensemble. He seized the opportunity to invite Pavel Landovský to play one of the directors in *Temptation*. After almost thirty years of hoping for such an opportunity, Landovský would perform in a play by Havel at the Balustrade. Grossman also issued invitations to new actors who would become the mainstay of the future company, including Jiří Ornest, a versatile leading man, and Leoš Suchařípa, an accomplished character actor with a tall, imposing frame and a deep, gravelly voice.

Grossman felt the pressure of having to redesign an entire new repertoire for the new company. But he kept *Temptation* on the schedule, although he worried that there would be only eight weeks of rehearsal (in the repertory schedule, a different play was performed every night, with multiple plays in rehearsal daily). Some critics observed that the production was a test, not only of Havel's new play, but also of the new ensemble.

Temptation opened on December 20, 1991. As with *Largo Desolato*, the critics were again reviewing the play for the first time. They were largely unanimous in their praise of the production, the new ensemble, and the direction. In particular, they were fascinated by the play's theme of temptation, made all the more compelling by the political changes brought about by the playwright himself.

The critics took up this theme and its relevance to Havel's political life with relish. For example, in a critique entitled "Devil's Tango" in *Lidové noviny*, Zdeněk Tichý was quick to discuss the letter of release from prison that Havel wrote in 1977, the humiliation he suffered because of its distortion, and its link with the play: "Dr. Foustka becomes a tragic victim of his own faith in his intellectual powers . . . He's convinced that he will be able to remain independent and unstained, but the Devil never buys half a soul."[2]

For Havel, Tichý points out, the devil was partly the secret police and also partly the good and the evil, the comfortable and the cynical, inside us all. If we don't know we're dealing with the devil, we're safe. But if we know we're dealing with him, that changes things. It doesn't matter what our intentions are — we only have one choice: to stand up and leave. No contact. Relating the moral of the play to the lesson Havel learned with that letter of release, Tichý notes that you can't give up half your soul or half your rights to save the other half, because the devil wants it all. Tichý also ties the play into Havel's political writings, saying: "The devil gives him [Foustka] an illusion of the power of the powerless; he tempts him by giving this illusion." As for the direction, he comments on Grossman's use of symbolism in his 1965 production of *The Memorandum* in which a steady dripping of water signifies both the flaws in the system and also the passage of time.

In *Mladá fronta dnes* (Young Front Today), critic Martin Nezval agrees with Tichý's interpretation about the devil within us. "When you start to flirt with the devil, he will grind you up as grist for his mill. Especially when one believes one can win this false game with the devil within."[3]

Of special note is the radical way in which Grossman changed the ending of *Temptation*. In the script, Havel calls for a frenzied scene in which the dancers are swallowed up in a cloud of smoke that blows into the audience. When it clears, the curtain has fallen and a lone fireman (a kind of absurdist deus ex machina) takes a solo curtain call. Grossman had another idea: to end the play according to an old Prague version of the Faust legend. As the version goes, there is a Faust house in Prague and, because Faust dealt with the devil, a hole appears in his roof and he flies up through it into hell. So in Grossman's production, the hole in the roof is revealed, with a ladder extending down to the stage. As Foustka stands at the base of the ladder, the smoke engulfs him; thus, the director leaves the ending up to our interpretation. Does he escape? Or does he hesitate? The audience never knows what decision he made at that critical moment.

This interpretation could well have expressed Grossman's concerns about Havel's presidency. In 1991, it was expected that Havel would be the dissident/president, the man of action whose door was open to anyone. But, according to some, he had already surrounded himself with advisors and was becoming less and less accessible. Is the presidency a new bargain that Havel has made with the devil? The production may have been asking this question.

THE COMING OF AGE OF THE THEATRE ON THE ROAD

> I founded a theater in Hrádeček with my friends, to put on my neighbor's forbidden plays. I couldn't understand why my polite neighbor is not allowed to earn money from what he knows best — writing for the theater.[1]
>
> — Andrej Krob, *Theatre on the Road 1975–1995*

> You mustn't take theater seriously. You must do it seriously.[2]
>
> — Jan Grossman, *Theatre on the Road 1975–1995*

If not the playwright, then the plays had found a home. While Václav Havel moved onto the world stage, his work finally found the theatrical home he had longed for those past twenty-one years.

Born in the countryside, the tiny troupe of Theatre on the Road remained hidden away in Hrádeček, far from the pressures of Prague. They had gathered for the first time in April 1975 at the invitation of Andrej Krob, a group of backstage workers, most of whom had never acted before. There they read Havel's new play, *The Beggar's Opera* in Krob's tiny cottage. It was the first time Havel had heard the play read, and it was by a group of amateurs whose goal it was to put on the play of Krob's neighbor, Havel, and thereby keep their lives in the theater going while their participation was being officially forbidden. Krob was so excited: "How could I ask for a rewrite! I didn't even understand the text!"[3] Later on that summer, they rehearsed outdoors, in preparation for the November performance at Horní Počernice.

The now-legendary performance of *The Beggar's Opera* at Horní Počernice established a sense of pride among the actors and Krob, as well as a sense of new identity. A tiny group of amateurs who had been behind the scenes all their careers had performed a play by a banned writer. Such an act of courage had ignited their imagination and instilled in them a new sense of purpose. As a result, there was a bond between them and a commitment to Havel's plays. That bond and that purpose had come to symbolize freedom.

The next summer (1976), they gathered once again in Krob's barn to read *Audience*, with Havel himself in the role of Vaněk. At Hrádeček, surrounded by nature, in the clean fresh mountain air, their agenda was simply to enjoy the freedom and pleasure brought by reading their friend's play.

When Havel went to prison, the company's activities slacked off. As Krob explains it:

> After the performance [of *The Beggar's Opera*] at U Čelikovských [the hotel/pub in Horní Počernice], the regime persecuted everyone who was present. They decided that this must never happen again. So the community isolated itself in self-protection, and it only gave performances every summer at Hrádeček in those so-called garden parties. And then it disbanded.[4]

They resumed their activities again in the late 1980s, a few years after Havel's release. After all, he was writing plays again, and there was a reason for being. At the time, the resourceful Krob had obtained some video equipment and with Olga's help had created a *samizdat* video production endeavor called *Originální videojournal* (Original Videojournal). Its purpose was to report on Czech cultural life by sending videotapes abroad, along the same route as *samizdat* literature was smuggled out of the country.

In April 1988, he arranged for a taping of Havel's play *Temptation*, performed by the Theatre on the Road. It would be the first staging of *Temptation* inside Czechoslovakia. For this production, Ivan Havel was enlisted to play the role of Foustka, and his wife, Dáša, played Houbová. The production was videotaped at both indoor and outdoor locations in and around Prague. Ivan Havel recalls:

> The outdoor scenes were taped in a friend of Krob's house south of Prague, next to a railroad station. A train was always passing by. So sometimes on the tape you can hear the sounds of the train. There were no rehearsals. The actors came in with their lines already learned; Andrej blocked the scenes and filmed it as he went along. I was making a "guest appearance" with Theatre on the Road — I'm not a member of the company, although there's really no such thing as membership in Theatre on the Road, is there? It took a lot of time; if I had more, perhaps I'd do it again. Although I couldn't remember my lines.[5]

Krob remembers especially the taping of the final scene:

Someone denounced us, saying that we were Satanists performing a Black Mass in the garden. It's because the last scene in *Temptation* is a costume party in the spirit of a Black Sabbath. Some frightened Praguer was watching our taping late in the night; it was two degrees below zero, and he saw these crazy people dressed up like devils and magicians and covered with smoke. So it was understandable that he called the police. Unfortunately, he placed the call in the morning, not at night, because it would have provided the best ending for the taping.[6]

The videotape was reviewed by Sergej Machonin in the *samizdat* journal *O divadle*. Machonin wrote, ironically, about the conditions that gave Theatre on the Road its raison d'être:

When the news spread about Havel and his new play on the theme of Faust, what a surprise it was that no directors chased after him for the new manuscript! No one called him on the telephone, because there was simply no one whose desire it was to produce good drama by a contemporary Czech playwright. Nor were there any actors who appeared at Andrej Krob's house, ringing the bell or trying to break down the door to get a role in this drama. For some serious reason they passed up the opportunity. And probably this is the reason for the resourceful and innovative approach of the director [Krob]. He couldn't recruit professionally trained actors to play the roles, because he couldn't find any who would do it. So instead, he decided to recruit people who — because of their natural temperament, look, and behavior, and especially because of their destiny, their souls, their unrealized talents, their sense of humor, their sense of music and rhythm, etc. — he thought might be able to perform his vision of Havel's play.[7]

Then the revolution happened, and the impossible became a reality. The company Krob had founded to put on his neighbor's plays now had a unique cultural mission — to present the dramatic oeuvre of the country's president.

Krob first turned his attention to Havel's plays that had still not received their premieres in his own country. In the summer of 1991, Theatre on the Road held an "open rehearsal" of *Mountain Hotel* at Hrádeček. Krob maintained the amateur quality of the company, which still consisted primarily of backstage theater workers. However, friends were encouraged to participate; in addition to the cameo appearance of Ivan Havel, a mathematician and philosopher, the troupe included other civilians in jobs ranging from psychologists to bartenders. Krob called it an "evolving ensemble." He then set about selecting a venue for his company's first official public performance.

One of the most moving chapters in the story of Havel's life in the theater is the coming together of Havel's two "homes": the Balustrade and the Theatre on the Road. In November, the Balustrade opened its doors to the official Czech premiere of *Mountain Hotel*. For the first time, Krob's amateur troupe would face a paying audience and critical scrutiny. For tradition's sake, he had chosen November 1, the date his company had performed *The Beggar's Opera* sixteen years earlier in their debut at Horní Počernice. For the troupe, it was a risk. For the critics, it was an adjustment.

But the critics saw past the troupe's amateur qualities to the heart of the artistic matter. In fact, they pointed out that some aspects of the production helped support Havel's theme of alienation between man and his world. In *Literární noviny*:

> Havel's plays are based on the matter of distancing between action and speech. When one speaks, it's not always he who speaks — sometimes it's his idea of what he should be saying, or what the listener wants to hear. In this process, he loses his own voice and ultimately his identity. All Havel's plays are based on this — above all, *Mountain Hotel* . . . which is so Havelian that it even sounds like self-parody. These peculiarities of Havel's poetics and Krob's amateur actors happily have found a union in this production. No professional company could play this more accurately and more surprisingly.[8]

Sergej Machonin, one of the leading Czech critics of the 1990s, also had to face an adjustment in expectations. But the freshness and clarity of Krob's approach won him over, too, and helped humanize Havel's cerebral style:

> I'm slowly getting used it, and am surprised to admit that I even like it. I like it that these nonactors put their true lives into their performances . . . It was more like watching a sad Chekhov play rather

than a demonstration of advanced absurd poetics . . . The whole evening seemed to me like something from a great distance, a distant memory or a sub-conscious act I couldn't catch. And then suddenly I realized what it was — an old photograph with faded edges. A snapshot of my entire class, my classmates staring out at the photographer, some seated, some standing, everyone frozen. Somewhere in the back there is a meadow and a mountain hotel in it. Do I recognize them? How many names do I remember? I only remember certain faces and random events, but years have passed and the stories become fragmented. Everybody has these pictures at home in their photo box — these pictures from schoolyards, from someone's wedding, someone's birthday party, someone's journey abroad with pigeons and cathedrals in the background. Andrej Krob did exactly this . . . a photo . . . like a souvenir. Into the photo box of memory it goes . . . [9]

Richard Erml of *Český deník* (Czech Daily) also placed the Theatre on the Road into a broader context. In his review of *Mountain Hotel*, he commented on the fact that the city's professional ensembles were not prepared artistically for the Velvet Revolution. The style of the nonpolitical plays of the 1970s and 1980s called for what he referred to as "TV civilism," a style completely inapplicable to playing Havel. By contrast, he felt that Krob understood Havel, since he had been directing his plays since 1975.

The ensemble of Andrej Krob succeeded in doing something almost impossible: to unite the qualities of amateur theater with professional discipline. Without this, you could never build the complicated construction of *Mountain Hotel*. . . . It's the image of a world in which everyone misunderstands everybody else. People just talk and talk to the point that they simply lose a connection to what they're saying.[10]

On the subject of their amateur status, Havel, the playwright president, had this comment: "I like the Theatre on the Road precisely because they are amateurs and have neither professional mannerisms nor pretentions."[11]

The "open rehearsal" of *Mountain Hotel* in Hrádeček that summer of 1991 proved such a success that thereafter it became an annual event for the Theatre on the Road, a kind of summer weekend theater festival.

Often these weekends were scheduled in conjunction with Olga's birthday on July 11, so in addition to a performance, there were exhibitions, readings, and a birthday celebration with everyone dressing up in costume. "It was always a mixture of culture and parties," recalls Anna Freimanová.[12] Krob adds: "Before the revolution, there would be 30 to 40 guests; after the revolution there would be 100 to 150."[13] All weekend, on the lawn sloping gently down from the Krob's house to the Havels, people milled around everywhere, reading scripts, rehearsing lines, strumming guitars, talking. Krob covered a part of the lawn with canvas, surrounded it with benches, and created an instant theater, where actors rehearsed in T-shirts and bathing suits. During those warm summer days, the clear mountain air at Hrádeček was filled with the sound of applause and laughter, while Krob scurried back and forth between directing the play and serving beer and goulash through the "refreshment window" of his little cottage to the actors and audience, who lined up on the porch. To this day, when he walks across the lawn or through the woods, Krob still finds rum bottles and other vestiges of the festivities that went on during those magical summers in the 1990s.

In the summer of 1992, the Theatre on the Road presented an open rehearsal of *The Conspirators*, the least favored play of its playwright-in-residence. After the production at Hrádeček, it followed the path of *Mountain Hotel* the year before and, on November 1, had its official Czech premiere at the Theatre on the Balustrade. Drama was occurring offstage as well that summer with the traumatic separation of the Czech and Slovak states. Deeply disturbed by the intrigue surrounding the event and at the same time realizing its inevitability, Havel resigned as president on July 20, rather than preside over the dissolution of the democratic republic he had founded only three years earlier. In his speech abdicating the presidency, Havel commented on the separation of the Czech states by quoting a speech from his own play, *The Garden Party*: "I'm not going to be the Liquidation Secretary." Then, in a dramatic reversal, the newly created Czech Republic reelected Havel as their president on January 26, 1993.

Once again, a formerly banned play by Václav Havel was reviewed for the first time. "The political types in *The Conspirators* were not only entertaining to the audience, but also scary, in the context of those days," wrote a critic in *Respekt*, looking back on the ironic timing of the production.[14] Once again, in a vivid example of art imitating life imitating art, Havel's plays both told and reflected his country's story. Josef Mlejnek wrote in *Český deník*:

> At the performance of *The Conspirators*, I had the suspicion that the playwright had been rewriting his text as recently as yesterday. That's how contemporary some aspects of his play are. It's a sad irony, after the fact, that the problems Mr. Havel was able to reconcile twenty years ago as a playwright, he is unable to reconcile today as a president. He still has the same idealistic barometer he had then. . . . Now he's in power, but he still maintains the philosophy that power is evil.[15]

For the third year in a row since the revolution, Krob rehearsed a Havel play in the summer (1993) at Hrádeček — this time, *The Memorandum*. Everyone gathered for the annual photo at the summer festival weekend; Havel, the playwright/president, was seated amongst the actors and his director Krob, who sported a top hat for the occasion. The production was performed once again at the Balustrade on November 1, the now-traditional anniversary date.

For this production, Krob added the ingenious touch of rotating the casting of a minor role on alternate evenings so a variety of theater artists could participate, including directors Petr Lébl and Jan Antonín Pitínský, two young rising stars in the Prague theater, as well as Ivan Jirous of the Plastic People, the photographer Bohdan Holomíček, and Andrej Krob himself. Once again, he united old friends from the 1970s with new artists in the 1990s, another Theatre on the Road tradition. As one critic put it, Theatre on the Road had its own unique identity: "a constantly transforming group of friends who meet to rehearse and perform Havel's plays for their pleasure."[16]

Critics still continued to adjust their expectations to the capabilities of this amateur ensemble. Still, they found the production noteworthy and the play lasting. "Ptydepe in better times" was the headline of a review in *Lidová demokracie* (People's Democracy) that said: "The meaning of the play is still contemporary, almost remarkably so. It is about a system we all know well, the concentric circles in which we always move and cannot escape."[17]

The charm and artlessness of the Theatre on the Road was beginning to take hold. Said a critic in *Denní telegraf* (Daily Telegraph): "Andrej

Krob's special approach doesn't destroy the irony of *The Memorandum*; on the contrary, it accentuates it."[18]

Above all, they commented on the lasting quality of the play: "A perfect description of the indestructible system," wrote the critic of *Lidová demokracie*, "Havel's *The Memorandum* remains a documentary of a period of our history . . . "[19] As yet another critic (who had seen *The Memorandum* in Ostrava the year before) concurred:

> *The Memorandum* gives us perfectly proven truths about ourselves, about our human weaknesses and imperfections. The way it does it is this: it makes us laugh, and suddenly our laughter transforms into embarrassment. Because we see we are laughing at ourselves. No wonder that these older plays like *The Memorandum* haven't lost their meaning at all. . . . The reaction of the audience shows that we haven't had enough of Havel yet.[20]

Krob was an anomaly, and so was his troupe. Here it was, a grassroots ensemble of nonactors, ever-changing in its ranks, but still devoted to the plays of its friend and neighbor, who now happened to be president. Actors came, actors went (some missed their lines, others missed their entrances). But there was something compelling about their fresh, unprepossessing, straightforward aesthetic. And slowly their appeal to the critics was taking hold.

Meanwhile, his confidence growing with each year, Krob branched out artistically. In May, 1994, he directed Beckett's *Krapp's Last Tape* at the Balustrade. At the summer festival in Hrádeček, members of the acting company of the Balustrade came out to join those of the Theatre on the Road in an open rehearsal of Chekhov's *The Three Sisters*. In January 1995, that production came to the stage of the Balustrade. The theater where Krob had once worked as an awestruck young carpenter building scenery welcomed him now as a director. A crossover was developing among the actors in the two theaters. Actors like Eva Holubová and Ladislav Klepal, for example, were now performing in both. Of the production of *The Three Sisters*, Havel himself commented:

> I adore the Theatre on the Road, but not only because they perform my plays. I also love their production of *The Three Sisters*. Just re-

cently, I was saying to Andrej Krob: "You had to perform Havel for twenty years in order to understand Chekhov."[21]

Then came 1995, a year in which the Theatre on the Road had something unique to celebrate. It was the twentieth anniversary of the performance of *The Beggar's Opera* at Horní Počernice. In July, the company presented an open rehearsal at the annual summer festival at Hrádeček. Krob tried to reassemble as many of the actors as he could who had performed in that historic production. Some of the actors from the 1975 production, like Jan Hraběta, for example who played Peachum, repeated their performances in 1995. But there was some recasting. The actress Lída Michalová, who played Polly the ingénue in 1975, played Diana the madam of the brothel in 1995. There were also special circumstances. The actor Jan Kašpar who had played Filch in 1975 was now in a wheelchair due to an accident. Krob dealt with this by creating the additional role of Filch's brother to navigate the wheelchair. There were new additions to the cast: Ladislav Smoljak, the artistic director of the popular Jára Cimrman Theater in Prague, played Macheath and brought other actors from his company to participate in the production. It was an occasion to celebrate.

Once again, the production followed the route of those before it, playing at the Balustrade on November 1. Once again, critics including Vladimír Just of *Literární noviny* commented on how, despite some amateurness, the actors provided "non-actorly authenticity." Just also cited the cleverness of Havel's Macheath, whom he called

a Czech Don Juan with the calm, concentrated logic, diction and story-telling skill of Josef Schweik. . . . The myth of seduction is perfectly deconstructed by the master of seduction himself. He observes love with the same passion as the scientist observes as rat.[22]

The critics also saw to the heart of the occasion. In *Respekt*:

The Theatre on the Road is inimitable. It's a community, and as such it's a part of life. Their private lives get caught up in their characters, and that doesn't happen in professional theater. This theater experience is about the meeting of old friends.[23]

Jiří Ornest, a leading actor at the Balustrade who was in the audience, said of the play:

> Havel's *The Beggar's Opera* is a small masterpiece. I've seen many versions of John Gay's play, but I think Havel found the "system" that is at the heart of it. It's the same situation we're in today. Everyone is paid off. Everyone is "on the list." In Havel's *The Beggar's Opera* you recognize, in the end, that there is almost no one who is not in the gang.[24]

To commemorate the occasion, Krob made a video documentary, entitled "Once Again, *The Beggar's Opera*," to chronicle this theatrical anniversary event. In it, Krob asks Havel: "Do you think life makes any sense?" Havel's reply: "The fact that I'm still here is proof that it does. If it didn't, I'd already have hung myself from one of these trees."[25]

By 1995, the Theatre on the Road festivals had become such a popular tradition that the "Wooden Andrej" was established, a mockery of the Oscar award. The statue itself was a comic likeness of Krob, fashioned out of wood. That summer at Hrádeček, with the celebration of the twentieth anniversary of *The Beggar's Opera*, the winners were Olga and Václav Havel.

On January 27, 1996, Olga died of cancer. The summer of 1996 was the last festival at Hrádeček. There were 450 people in attendance.

On November 1, for the sixth time that decade, Krob brought Theatre on the Road to the Theatre on the Balustrade. This time, it was a production of *The Garden Party* in honor of Havel's sixtieth birthday. While some critics found the play's political jargon anachronistic, others found it peculiarly relevant. "Still now, when I turn on my television, I don't have the impression that political jargon has disappeared from our lives," wrote a critic from *Mladá fronta dnes*.[26] In another review, a critic quoted Jaroslav Kořán, the mayor of Prague, as saying: "'Even contemporary politicians could sharpen their tongues by reading this wonderful play.'"[27]

By now, critics had acquired a respect for Krob's direction of Havel's work. Their recognition reflected the fact that by 1996, the Theatre on the Road had come of age. As critic Richard Erml wrote in *Mladá fronta dnes*:

> During the years of its existence, the Theatre on the Road has created its own acting style, which is different from that of amateurs

because the average amateur actors aspire to professional acting, whereas Krob's troupe doesn't do that at all. They have their own style. And it is the one that suits Havel's plays best. Furthermore, the playwright is usually satisfied with Krob's productions because Krob has the maximum respect for the text.[28]

To commemorate the theater's twentieth anniversary, Krob produced a book entitled *Theatre on the Road 1975–1995*. In it, he talks about Havel's plays and what they mean to him:

> I was always attracted by things I didn't understand. As a child, I deconstructed bicycles, clocks, electric shavers. The same thing happened with Havel's plays. I tried to deconstruct them but suddenly I'd become so confused that I got lost. So I stopped searching for allegories in Havel and started to search for stories. And through the story I also discovered the meaning. The most relevant thing Havel's plays have given me is the message that we may never get lost, whatever the conditions are; we may never forget the meaning of morality and immorality, politeness and impoliteness, courage and cowardice.[29]

Krob himself never had "professional pretentions," as he called them. He never masked the amateurism of his troupe, and he had no illusions as to the reasons for its popularity. "The main reason so many people came wasn't to see a performance of the Theatre on the Road, but rather the chance to meet the president every year," Krob says. According to Miloš Forman, that's why Havel loved the Theatre on the Road, for its truthfulness of spirit. "They were not burdened by professionalism," Forman said.[30]

In *Dear Václav . . . Yours Truly* (Milý Václave . . . Tvůj), a book of collected essays commemorating Havel's sixtieth birthday and presented to him weeks before Krob's *The Garden Party* performed at the Balustrade, there is a contribution by Luboš Pistorius, the director of the *Audience* recording in 1978. The essay, "On Václav Havel: Playwright," recalls his experience in the audience at Horní Počernice in 1975, when the Theatre on the Road performed *The Beggar's Opera* at such a great risk:

> I really loved Havel's lines about the Horní Počernice production: [he quotes Havel] "The will for freedom and the moral responsibility

of a group of young people gave this production a great theatrical-
ity, and because of this, many years later, I realize that I have felt
theater in its deepest of meanings. It was happiness, truth, freedom
and collective harmony." It wasn't an exhibition, it wasn't about the
art, it wasn't about the amateur theater, it was about the actors who
came there to present a remarkable play by an important playwright. They came to express how pleased and how happy and how
honored they were to be the first ones to perform it, and that they
had the courage not to worry about the reaction of the regime. This
element of nonprofessionalism belongs to Havel's aesthetics . . . the
sense of humor, the charm, the naïveté. . . . This is as it should be.[31]

What about the artistic home of the playwright/president? Why not
the National Theater, instead of the lawn at Hrádeček? "Of course Havel
would have been pleased to have his plays produced at a 'stone theater,'"
says Anna Freimanová, "but after the first night he'd have been unhappy
with the production."[32] As far as he was concerned, the true national theater and artistic home for Havel's plays lay in the spirit of his public, and
nowhere was that spirit better expressed than by a group of amateur actors on that grassy "stage" between his house and his neighbor's.

In *Theatre on the Road 1975–1995,* the book commemorating its
twentieth anniversary, Krob articulated his theater's mission simply and
clearly: "The Theatre on the Road is a changing community of people
who for twenty years have been meeting to rehearse and perform Václav
Havel's plays for their friends."[33]

Literary historians and critics are essentially in agreement that, in the
words of one critic: "The work of Andrej Krob and his company Theatre
on the Road is unique and essentially unequaled."[34]

For Krob's wife, Anna Freimanová, the key is the simplicity of the
theater's mission:

> The story of the Theatre on the Road is a phenomenon when we
> look back. . . . At the time it happened [in the 1970s and 1980s],
> the people involved in the theater were just friends, no one was
> thinking about it and no one thought it was anything special. . . .
> Those were the best of times.[35]

1993: AFTER HAVELMANIA

> The reaction of the audience shows that we haven't had enough of Havel yet.[1]
>
> — Jiří Gordon, *Listy pro Moravu a Slezsko-Svoboda*

No matter where, no matter when, the production of a Havel play during the 1990s resonated with the times. Often, that resonance was ironic.

For example, at the end of the 1992 televised production of Havel's play, *Tomorrow We'll Start It Up*, one hears the soaring strains from *Libuše*, an opera by Smetana, wherein the prophetess of the title dreams of the shining future of Prague and the Czech nation. Those were strains that could bring tears to Havel's eyes, as he once confessed to Olga in a letter from prison.[2]

But the realities in Czechoslovakia during 1992 were in sharp contrast to the idealism and romanticism that Smetana's music promised. It was a year of national strife and schism, and a crucible for Havel's presidency. By 1992, a rift between the Czech and Slovak politicians had emerged over the future organization of the state. Havel was a committed supporter of a common Federation of Czechs and Slovaks, but after the July 1992 parliamentary elections, the leading politicians could not agree on a federation model. The rift between Czech and Slovak political factions widened. Seeing that the federation was headed for dissolution, Havel resigned on July 20 rather than preside over an event that was against his conscience and his convictions.

After leaving office, Havel retired from public life for a while. In November, when it was clear that an independent Czech state was imminent, he confirmed that he would seek the presidency. In January 1993, four political parties of the ruling coalition government submitted his official nomination. On January 26, 1993, Havel was elected by the new Chamber of Deputies, giving him the unique distinction of being the last president of Czechoslovakia and the first president of the independent Czech Republic.

Against this dramatic backdrop, Czech television taped a performance of *Tomorrow We'll Start It Up*. It was the last play Havel wrote before leading his country through a revolution and into independence, and it is a play about a man who led that country through a revolution into independence seventy years earlier. Given the events of 1992, the play comes across as a prophesy. Life imitates art imitates life, once again, in the story of Havel's life in the theater.

In an interview with Petr Oslzlý made in conjunction with this taped performance, Havel talked about the rift between the Czechs and the Slovaks, and the play he had written (four years earlier) about his country's unification. In it, Havel talked about the accidents that change history. He pointed out that while the Czech and Slovakian republics are separating, it may be a historical necessity, as well as a challenge to create a new state again.[3] At one point in *Tomorrow We'll Start It Up*, Rašín, the protagonist reflects: "To found a state is not easy. But even more difficult is to assure that it will last."[4] Once again, another prophesy from a Havel play. The vision of *Tomorrow* had become the reality of today.

By the 1993 season, theaters had expressed their respect and admiration for their playwright/president. Havel's banned plays had all premiered in the Czech Republic and in the language in which they were originally written. Now, theaters in Prague went back to business as usual, focusing on the classics and the search for new voices. There was a lull in the production of Havel's plays. And as the world increasingly became his political stage, as his international leadership grew, Havel himself was once more drawn farther and farther away from the theater.

The Theatre on the Road remained the keeper of the Havel flame, with its appearances at the Balustrade during most of the 1990s. Meanwhile at the Balustrade, Grossman died in 1993. He was succeeded by an imaginative young artistic director named Petr Lébl, who began a vibrant new regime at the Balustrade with a brilliant theatrical vision. He built a solid ensemble, and his flair for innovative interpretations of Chekhov soon became the company's signature. In 1994, his production of *The Seagull* was awarded the coveted Alfred Radok Prize as Best Production of the Year, and his *Ivanov* won the prize again in 1997. It was one of the few productions Havel had attended during the 1990s, and it remains in his memory as one of his favorites.[5]

Havel's affection for *Ivanov* may have been due to its protagonist and his similarity to one of Havel's own creations. In 1997 at the Balustrade, Petr Lebl produced *The Increased Difficulty of Concentration*, whose central character, Eduard Huml, shares many qualities with Ivanov, Chekhov's version of the nineteenth-century "superfluous man" (*zbytečný člověk*, as the Czechs called him). Ivanov is a man who cannot connect thought with action, who is therefore misunderstood, who finds his soul numbed with ennui, who seeks refuge from a confusing and bruised existence in abstract philosophy. The same description applies to Huml, who finds himself "superfluous" in his own time and spends his days at home in his dressing gown, trying to compose a philosophical treatise on man's search for happiness.

For this production, the Balustrade invited Krob to make his debut directing a fully professional cast. By critical account, it was Krob's best direction to date. Using the talents of the Balustrade ensemble, Krob cast the versatile leading man Jiří Ornest in the role of Eduard Huml, as well as Eva Holubová as Dr. Balcar and Ladislav Klepal (once a stagehand at the Balustrade like himself, now a versatile character actor) as the surveyor. The scenic designer Jan Dušak provided a smartly dressed set on the tiny Balustrade stage, complete with four revolving doors through which the women in Huml's life entered and exited at a rapid rate. Under Krob's stylized direction, the scientists wheeled Puzuk, the talking machine, in and out of Huml's living room to the tune of lively Yiddish music, heightening the play's absurdist elements.

This high-spirited production opened on March 27, 1997, twenty-nine years after its premiere in the same theater. Profiting from Krob's familiarity with Havel's work, the play glowed with contemporary relevance, and showed how Havel's enduring portrait of a soul in existential crisis transcended political circumstances and resonates today, even in a democracy. Critics welcomed its revival and found it the most relevant of Havel's plays from the 1960s, thanks to Krob's interpretation. "Its contemporary stage interpretation proves that this play is even more topical today than in the 1960s," said one critic in *Rozhlas* (Broadcast).[6] The portrayal of an "empty and absurd human existence is not less grotesque than his pictures of the totalitarian social system," another wrote in *Denní telegraf*.[7] And in *Právo* (Law):

> *The Increased Difficulty of Concentration* is an almost forgotten play by Václav Havel. . . . It's good to have Havel back on our stages after the lull since Havelmania. And Andrej Krob's production is the production that Havel would want to have of this play.[8]

Jiří Ornest, the actor playing Huml, had been concerned.

Andrej Krob came to the first day of rehearsal and said that *The Increased Difficulty of Concentration* played for only a short time here in 1968, and was the first play by Havel in the 1960s at the Balustrade where no one in the audience laughed. I almost died. But in the end it was fine, because everyone perceived it as a situation comedy about a man with three women in his life. Krob understands the sense of the play — as a comedy with a surrealistic spin and a sense of paranoia. His production is one of the best and funniest of Havel's plays in a long time. It went over like a Neil Simon comedy. Havel's plays may have their roots in the 1960s, but it's fantastic that they still work. The second meaning of Havel's plays are always there — about one man and the system, establishment and corruption.[9]

As for Havel's response, Ornest remembers when he came to see a performance of *The Increased Difficulty of Concentration* in 1997. "Havel was the best member of the audience. He's the one who laughed the most. Havel's fear has been that his plays are over. But after all, he's a man of the theater, so when he heard the audience reaction, he was very pleased."

2000: IN SEARCH OF A NEW PLAY BY VÁCLAV HAVEL

Writing plays, in a sense, has remained with me to this day. . . . I don't think I've written myself out as a playwright. I have a lot of vague but therefore all the more exciting ideas about what I could and would still like to do on that territory, so I can still torment myself with that. . . . And so, in fact — though at a distance — I remain with the theater.[1]

— Havel, *Letters to Olga*

By the end of the decade that was synonymous with his presidency, Havel's plays had been performed throughout Prague — the full-length plays, the one-acts, even the ten-minute one-act called *Mistake*, which was given a satirical production by the young Experimental Studio Derniera. It was actually produced as a joke — the real occasion was a social event, to which Havel was invited, planned by two young actors trying to start a theater company (hence the double entendre of the title, *Mistake*, as well as a satire of Havelmania). All the full-length plays and the one-acts had received stage productions in Prague, except for *Vernissage*, which had been given a small production in Brno in 1990, a

1990 television production directed by Ivan Rajmont with Jiří Ornest in the role of Vaněk, and a reading at the Balustrade in 1997.

So in 2000, casting around for ideas for a new Havel production, the Czech director Jan Burian began discussing possibilities with the Vinohrady, one of Prague's stone theaters. The first thought was to do *Temptation*, but Burian had already directed it in Plzeň. So they came up with the idea of using the second stage at the Vinohrady to present *Vernissage*, which hadn't been performed in Prague since the revolution and which, according to Burian, appealed to the Vinohrady's taste for the psychological and realistic.[2] Havel's collected writings, the seven-volume *Spisy*, had just been published in 1999, and in it Burian discovered the one-act *An Evening with the Family*, Havel's very first play, which had been published for the first time and had never yet been performed. At the time, Havel told Burian that he had forgotten he had ever written it; once reminded of the fact, Havel confessed he had never even reread it.

To Burian, the idea of pairing *An Evening with the Family* with *Vernissage* seemed natural. Both are about the family unit. Both take place in living rooms; both deal with the life of the supposedly "average Czech." But one takes place before Prague Spring, and one after; hence, by pairing them, there was an opportunity to tell a story. By doublecasting the actors in the two plays, thought Burian, it could be an interesting theatrical experience, tracing the development of Czech society as reflected in family life and everyday existence over two decades. The early play constitutes "Act I," presenting a young couple during the 1950s; the later play constitutes "Act II," presenting the same couple, now successful, affluent and established during the 1970s. Is there progress over the passage of time? Is there growth? Enlightenment? In the earlier play, two actors play a young couple who come visit their parents in their old-fashioned apartment; the young couple are going to have a baby and make some money. They talk about the television (which is broken), what they'll do on the holidays, what new car they will buy. They are charmingly recognizable in their averageness. They speak in banalities and live a banal existence. As they talk, the grandmother plays solitaire; the canary in the cage dies; the young couple falls asleep. In the later play, those same actors play a more mature couple who now have a sleek and modern apartment, money, and a five-year-old child. They're upwardly mobile, they speak incessantly about their acquisitions, their antiques, their trips to Switzerland. They are exhibitionists, but inside they're insecure, they doubt themselves. Both plays are about material values that deaden the soul, that stifle identity and a sense of responsibility.

The evening of the two Havel one-acts — *An Evening with the Family* and *Vernissage* — premiered at the Vinohrady Theater on February 3, 2000. The critics were intrigued and stimulated by this combination. They praised the inspiration of the pairing. They saw the dramaturgical and thematic progression, from a twenty-year-old's first solo attempt at playwriting to a later work written by an established writer when he was almost forty. The pairing showed that Havel's writing had thematic continuity and a vision of his country's reality. The 1960s were a time of hope and a sense that the system might possibly, with provocation, be changed. The 1970s were a time of disillusionment. And the conformity of the couple in the second play was, as the critic Zdeněk Tichý said in *Mladá fronta dnes*, "a clever and ironic prediction of what is to come."[3]

Other critics agreed. In *Právo*: "For some, it's entertainment; for others, it's a chilling message of the emptiness of human existence."[4] As for the absurdity of the plays, in *Literární noviny*: "I think Mr. Burian is right: absurd drama actually doesn't exist. It's we who live an absurd life."[5]

In an interview about the production, Burian spoke about his vision of the plays:

> Question: In what time did *An Evening with the Family* happen?
>
> Answer: Thursday, January 7, 1960 at 5:30 P.M. That's what the author writes in the text about the time.
>
> Question: What is the connection between these two plays?
>
> Answer: The basic situation in both plays is a visit. Both happen in the context of the family, both are private occasions . . . They also have a theme in common: a portrayal of people who are so frightened of the world around them that they search for a substitution to make themselves happy. They search for it in family, in routine, in daily ritual, in conformity. It makes them feel secure. The playwright poses the question: is this fun, or is this the road to damnation? Of course, it's up to the audience to answer.
>
> Question: Did Havel have anything to say about casting, costumes, etc.?
>
> Answer: It was an absolutely normal collaboration, as with any other playwright. As for me, my only wish was to bring Havel back on the stage.[6]

Havel was also interviewed for the occasion by Zdeněk Tichý for *Mladá fronta dnes*:

> Question: Under what circumstances did you write *An Evening with the Family*, and why hasn't it ever been produced?
>
> Answer: I don't remember. The only thing I know is that I wrote it shortly after I returned from the military service, so it had to be 1959 or 1960, at a time when I was enchanted by Beckett and Ionesco. I simply tried to write an Ionesco-like play for myself. It was a sort of exercise in playwriting, if I may call it that. I don't remember if I offered it to Ivan Vyskočil [at the Theatre on the Balustrade] or not. Perhaps he read it. But we never talked about doing it. Later I decided to put it aside because it was too much influenced by Ionesco and Beckett. And after a while, I forgot about it.
>
> Question: Is there any other nonpublished text in your archives?
>
> Answer: As a matter of fact, I have no archive. I had to move from one place to another very frequently, and the drafts of my manuscripts were always very aesthetic (I made changes in colored pencil). But I don't have any of them anymore. I think I gave most of them away to my friends as gifts.
>
> Question: Why the Vinohrady Theater?
>
> Answer: Some might think that it is thanks to Dagmar [Dáša] Havlová. [In December 1996, Havel underwent an operation to remove a cancerous growth from his lung; in January 1997, he married the actress Dagmar Veškrnová of the Vinohrady Theater company, who had been a strong source of support through his illness.]
>
> Question: Did you have any doubts that *An Evening with the Family* should be published in your collected works?
>
> Answer: The publisher convinced me that I shouldn't underestimate my early works — the poems, essays, articles. So I agreed, but without them I probably never would have published the early works myself.[7]

Today, in Prague and elsewhere in the Czech Republic, one can always find a production of a Havel play. As Jan Burian says:

> In the early 1990s, it was a duty to do Havel. Then we stopped performing his plays, because we found that we were doing them because

they had been forbidden, rather than because of what they meant. Now we do his plays because we find that they are understandable, even amazing, and have something to say that touches us all.[8]

2004: HAVEL AND THE THEATER TODAY

Theatre, of all the artistic genres, is the most closely tied to a particular time and place.[1]

— Havel, Introduction to *Living in Truth*

After Havelmania, a void was created in the Czech theater.

As Andrej Krob said in a BBC interview during 2000: "We expected utopia."[2] That's what Krob and Havel and all their friends dreamed of.

But utopia has not arrived. Foreign plays still dominate the Prague stage, just as foreign powers dominated the nation's past. It's the great paradox of Czech theater. Today at the great so-called stone theaters in Prague — the National, the Estates, the Vinohrady — there is Shakespeare, Schiller, Goldoni, Feydeau. At the small independent theaters like the Balustrade and the Činoherní Klub, there is Pinter, Chekhov, Genet, and Thomas Bernhard.

In terms of new writing for the Czech theater, as Jiří Pehe, political analyst and one of Havel's closest advisors, says: "There is no trend, no school, no coherent vision."[3] After the first flush of freedom, the theater community felt a void, a lack of definition. Havel himself likens it to "a sensation of the absurd. What Sisyphus might have felt if one fine day his boulder stopped, rested on the hilltop, and failed to roll back down."[4]

For the past three decades, dissident writers, Havel being the most dramatic example, had defined themselves in opposition. As Pehe says: "Now they find themselves lost, unfocused, without a theme. So they're looking to their past and to the West, taking eagerly, without the structure of a unifying idea."

For the new generation of Czech playwrights, there is also the question of identity. The playwright Ivan Klíma says:

You can't compare the experience of writing under a totalitarian system with that of writing in a free system. It was once a mission to be a writer. The Czech writer was once the conscience of the nation. Today, it's just a profession like any other.[5]

There is nostalgia for the dramatic days of late 1989, when theaters were the gathering places for a revolution. The dressing rooms of the Laterna Magika were headquarters for the leaders of the Civic Forum, and the auditoriums of the Balustrade and others were scenes of urgent dialogue between actors and the audience. Havel expressed it at a roundtable discussion he organized in the late spring of 1994. He gathered twelve Czech writers, critics, directors, and dramaturgs to talk about the state of Czech theater and the sense of a void now that oppression had ended. "Wasn't I in fact happier under Communism because I constantly had a certain horizon, a certain perspective, something to struggle with, something to fight for?"[6]

What world are playwrights writing for today? In the last months of his presidency, Havel expressed his own theories:

> My impression is that the world now is a very different from my time . . . Theatres come and go, the theater community is not really structured, it's a fluid situation, and it's hard to follow what's going on. There are probably certain values that are enshrined in that environment, but for me, with the limited time in which I have to follow it, it's rather difficult to identify them properly. As for the responsibility of young writers, again it seems to me that they have a different role than the one we had when we lived in a totalitarian regime, when, whether we liked it or not, any work of art inevitably had to relate to the times. Today, everything is different. Probably the most relevant themes today are the existential ones, themes related to the state of the world and the destruction of values in general. So it doesn't matter any more if life goes on in a country with censorship or without. It's a different world, and I'm not sure that I understand it at all.[7]

In 2003, new voices in Czech theater are emerging, among them Jan Antonín Pitínský (the playwright/director), Petr Zelenka, and Egon Tobiáš. But it is too early to identify a strong new school or trend. And at the Balustrade, after Petr Lébl's tragic death in 2000, a search for new artistic leadership and vision — both in directors and playwrights — continues.

So in the meantime, Václav Havel remains his country's greatest living playwright. And while he did not write any new plays during his presidency, he did not lose his sense of the theater. Far from it. His theatrical sensibilities were simply put to use on a broader stage.

In fact, during the first two seasons of the millennium in Prague, the most compelling new theater has been not in a theater, but in a castle, Havel's castle, where his sense of drama has been transferred to political theater of the nation and of the world. And spectacular theater it has been, with Havel displaying not only his conceptual playwriting abilities but also his directorial skills.

The example cited here is called Forum 2000, a five-year program wherein every October Havel transformed the historic Prague Castle into the setting for his newest production, of which he was also producer and director. Forum 2000 consisted of a three-day annual international symposium on globalization, whose purpose it was to consider the major issues facing a diverse world as it moves into the twenty-first century — including health, environment, science, technology, spiritual values, human rights, education, arts, culture — and their interrelation. The international cast was all-star, including Nobel Laureates, heads of state, religious leaders, writers, artists, philosophers, former dissidents; participants included the Dalai Lama, Shimon Peres (former prime minster of Israel), F. W. de Klerk (former president of South Africa), Wole Soyinka (Nigerian writer), Peter Gabriel (British rock singer), Bill Clinton (former U.S. president), and Elie Wiesel (writer, humanitarian, and Holocaust survivor). The multisetting set was stunning: Act I, in the majestic sixteenth-century Spanish Hall, illuminated by fourteen huge chandeliers; Act II, in the Gothic St. Vitus Cathedral; act 3, in the castle ballroom.

Havel views the world in theatrical terms. So his life in the theater has a broad and dual sense. Catapulted as he was, almost overnight, from a life in the theater onto the world stage, he has put the theater to use in politics, mindful always of the interconnections between the art of writing plays and the phenomenon of making history.

> We playwrights, who have to cram a lifetime or an entire historical era into a two-hour play, can scarcely understand this rapidity ourselves. And if it gives us trouble, think of the trouble it must give to political scientists, who spend their whole lives studying the realm of the probable and have even less experience with the realm of the improbable than playwrights do.[8]

KING LEAR

> The paradoxes will continue. I'll go on, as I've always done, sitting down in front of a blank piece of paper with distaste; I will try everything to avoid writing, always terrified of those first words on the page. I will continue to find artificial ways of giving myself the courage to write. I will despair that it's not coming, yet I'll always manage to write a new play. The mysterious inner furies who have invented these torments will probably not leave me in peace and will have their own way in the end.[1]
>
> — Havel, *Disturbing the Peace*

> Just as I didn't write directly about prison, I am not going to write directly about the presidency.[2]
>
> — Havel, interview with *Rudé právo*, March 25, 1992

In 2003, Havel ended a thirteen-year term as president, first of Czechoslovakia and then of the Czech Republic. He has led his country politically, historically, morally and spiritually. These have been years full of drama. Now, what about Václav Havel, playwright? Will he write plays again?

Vladimír Just, critic of *Literární noviny*, offers an opinion:

> As President, Václav Havel is like a character in his own play. He's too close to have perspective. He'll need to step back to write again. Could Tartuffe have written *Tartuffe*?[3]

Michael Billington, critic of the *Guardian* (Manchester), offers another perspective:

> Václav Havel never had to confront the crisis that western writers have had to face: what do I write next? They are trapped in their celebrity status. Václav Havel had a different crisis. He was prevented from writing. But he never ran out of life. He always had something to say, because of his engagement with the world.[4]

Actually, Havel started a new play, just before the revolution. It was early in 1989, and Havel and Petr Oslzlý, fresh from the success of "Rozrazil I" (in which Havel's play *Tomorrow We'll Start it Up* was included) were talking about the idea Havel's writing a new play for the

Theater on a String. Today, they can't remember who came up with the theme of King Lear, but in any case Havel eagerly set about writing it. In fact, he completed almost two-thirds of the manuscript. As he explains it:

> But then the revolution came, and I later threw that manuscript away, only to remember it several years later, when I realized that the main idea of that play (a man who identifies with power to the extent that, when he loses it, his world starts disintegrating and he goes mad) had gradually gained a special meaning for me, as someone in a high political position. Because I observed many people of that sort around me, people who tied their lives so extensively to their position of power. So I keep coming back to this theme in my mind, and I can't exclude the possibility that when I have time to write plays again, I will be able to revive that theme.[5]

King Lear is not the only idea Havel has for a new play. In February, 2003, a symposium on Havel's plays was held at the Orange Tree Theatre in London, in conjunction with a production of *The Beggar's Opera*. One of the panelists, Pavel Seifter, the former Czech ambassador to the United Kingdom, and a longtime friend and colleague, recalls Havel speaking of an image that he'd like to capture on the stage. The image was that of a nation's leader seated at his desk in his office. A top aide enters and whispers something in his ear. Perhaps he might explore how that moment could be expanded into a dramatic study about power, Havel told Seifter.[6]

There is no doubt that the Velvet Revolution, the founding of a new nation, and the turbulent thirteen-year presidency would provide rich material for plays to come.

The question is: Will Václav Havel write these plays? Says Miloš Forman: "He'll be asked to give speeches and write articles every day. I don't know if this will tempt him. The world will not leave him alone."[7]

Says British critic Michael Billington: "It doesn't matter. It was a sacrifice worth making for Czechoslovakia to have given up a playwright. Freedom is more important than art. The world is full of playwrights, the world is full of artists, but not of Václav Havels."[8]

Inauguration, December 1989
(Viktor Krombauer, Prague Theatre Institute archive)

Epilogue

We are each other's continuation . . . and so we hold your space
open for you, dear friend . . . [1]
    — Arthur Miller, *I think about you a great deal*

By the time this book is published, Václav Havel will have yet a new identity: citizen.

Havel's presidency may be over, but that is not necessarily the case
with Havel's playwriting. How, then, do we measure the impact of the
playwright and the legacy of his work?

First, consider the unprecedented commitment given to him by colleagues and theaters around the world.

I THINK ABOUT YOU A GREAT DEAL:
ALBEE, BECKETT, MILLER, PINTER, STOPPARD

A man crouches on a black box, stage center, his head bowed, his body
hunched over like a clenched fist, his arms hugging his twisted, shivering
frame. Strands of scraggly hair hang in his eyes; the rest is gathered in a
stringy ponytail. His gray pajamas fall limply over his limbs. Around him
circles a woman in a white coat. (Is she a doctor? A scientist?) She orders
him to stand up, whereupon she drapes his shabbily clad frame in a velvet cloak. She loosens his ponytail and places a felt hat on his head. Then
she peers into the audience for approval, as if to ask: Is he presentable for
public viewing?

A director dressed in a fur coat enters from the audience, surveying
the subject. The two begin to talk:

Assistant: . . . Like the look of him?
Director: So so . . . Light . . . How's the skull . . .
Assistant: Moulting. A few tufts.

above Havel and Achim Benning, Prague, 1986

below Joseph Papp and Havel at Hrádeček, 1984 (Papp estate)

Director: Colour?
Assistant: Ash . . .
Director: The hands, how are the hands? . . .
Assistant: Crippled. Fibrous degeneration.
Director: Clawlike?
Assistant: If you like . . . Like that cranium?
Director: Needs whitening . . .
Assistant: He's shivering.
Director: Bless his heart. *(Pause.)*
Assistant: *(Timidly.)* What about a little . . . a little . . . gag? . . . Sure
    he won't utter?
Director: Not a squeak . . . [1]

The director instructs the assistant to make further corrections. They
continue to adjust the body, dressing and undressing it. Bare the neck, the
legs, the shins, whiten them — the director commands. The assistant
obeys. Raise his head to show his face. Finally, the director has the effect
he wants:

Director: Good. There's our catastrophe. In the bag. Once more
    and I'm off.
Assistant: . . . Once more and he's off.
    *(Fade-up of light on Protagonist's body. Pause. Fade-up of general
    light.)*
Director: Stop! *(Pause.)* Now . . . let 'em have it. *(Fade-out of gen-
    eral light. Pause. Fade-out of light on body. Light on head alone.
    Long pause.)* Terrific! He'll have them on their feet. I can hear it
    from here. *(Pause. Distant storm of applause. Protagonist raises his
    head, fixes the audience. The applause falters, dies. Long pause. Fade
    out of light on face.)* [2]

The play is called *Catastrophe,* the dedication reads "for Václav Havel,"
and the profound compassion for his fellow playwright's torture is expressed by Samuel Beckett.

Beckett wrote *Catastrophe* for the evening of short plays produced by
the Avignon Festival in 1982. They were commissioned in honor of
Havel, who was serving the third of his four-year prison term. The six-
hour-long evening, called "A Night for Václav Havel," was performed on
July 21, 1982.

Catastrophe was performed the following year at the John Houseman
Theater in New York, in an evening directed by Alan Schneider, together

with two other new Beckett plays, *Impromptu* and *What Where*. In his review, Mel Gussow wrote:

> Even without knowing the provenance of the play, there is no mistaking the message. It offers testimony in resolute opposition to tyranny . . . The protagonist becomes the ultimate victim. The director is so confident about the man's dehumanization that he does not allow for the possibility that he might suddenly find his voice and utter a final plea . . . We are left, finally, with a spectral tableau: a martyr, raising his head, fixing his audience in his gaze and staring in abject supplication.[3]

The subsequent contact between the two playwrights, ending with Havel's presidency and Beckett's death in the same month (December 1989) is little known, fascinating, and prophetic in the way that the theater of the absurd can be prophetic.

In response to *Catastrophe*, Havel dedicated the first play written after his release from prison to Beckett. "It was not only an expression of gratitude for the solidarity shown in Avignon, but also of Havel's deference to the supreme master of the genre," wrote Karel Kyncl, an editor of *Index on Censorship*, the London-based emigre magazine that published the works of banned writers.[4] The play was called *Mistake*, written in 1983 just months after his release. It was Havel's homage to a playwright, thirty years his senior, whom he had admired all his life, as well as an expression of heartfelt appreciation for his support.

A correspondence ensued between the two writers. It has never been published, although a copy of a letter from Beckett to Havel (in English, written on May 29, 1983) in response to Havel's letter thanking Beckett for having written *Catastrophe*, has been furnished by Klaus Juncker from his private archives. It reads as follows:

> Dear Václav Havel:
> Thank you for your most moving letter. To have helped you, however little, and saluted you and all you stand for, was a moment in my writing life that I cherish. It is I who stand in your debt. I have read and admired your plays in French translation. I send you my heartfelt wishes for better days.
>
> Samuel Beckett[5]

Although they corresponded all through the 1980s, Havel and Beckett never actually met. But according to Karel Kyncl in an article written on December 30, 1989 (the day after Havel became president) in London's *The Independent,* there is a telling story that speaks to the nature and depth of their friendship. In 1985, uncharacteristically, the reclusive Beckett permitted a picture of him taken with a gag in his mouth to be used on a poster to promote the English monthly *Index on Censorship,* which describes itself as "the only publication in the world striving to expose the evil of censorship in all its manifestations."[6] The poster carried the slogan: "If Samuel Beckett had been born in Czechoslovakia, we'd still be waiting for Godot" (referring to a play that, of course, was banned there at the time). In early November 1989, the *Index on Censorship* decided to copy the poster onto T-shirts as a publicity effort for its cause. Two weeks later, on November 17, a sweeping historical change was set in motion on Wenceslas Square. As Kyncl puts it in his article, "Godot arrived in Prague." By December, it seemed clear that Havel would soon be president of a new, democratic Czechoslovakia. So Kyncl sent fifty T-shirts to the Civic Forum for Christmas, asking Havel if he would kindly allow himself to be photographed in one, "and thus to reimburse the *Index on Censorship* for the financial loss suffered as a result of the wonderful recent developments in Czechoslovakia."[7]

Then the truth was revealed. Havel, who would have been glad to have done so, was one of the few people in the world who knew, because of their special and confidential correspondence, that Samuel Beckett was dying in a private hospital. Under these circumstances, he understandably felt that his photograph in the Beckett T-shirt would have been inappropriate. Kyncl wrote:

> I can't help thinking that Samuel Beckett, the high priest of absurdity, would be very amused by the choice Havel was facing and by his solution of the problem: he refused to cooperate not because of the possibly endangered dignity of his future office but because of the possible lese-majesty of Death. As for Havel's own sense of the absurd, in one of the television interviews he granted at the time when he had that T-shirt problem, he said: "I am constantly conscious of the ridiculousness and absurdity of my situation."[8]

Beckett was not the only writer who was thinking about Havel during his darkest time. The image of Havel was a vivid one in the minds and hearts of so many writers and artists. One was Arthur Miller, who had met Havel in Prague in 1963, while he was visiting the Theatre on the Balustrade. At the time, Havel was preparing his very first full-length play, *The Garden Party*, for production, and his eagerness and energy made a lasting impression on the visiting American playwright. Subsequently, during the 1970s, Miller followed the news of Havel's dissidence and ultimate imprisonment with deep concern. So in 1982, when the Avignon Festival asked Miller to write an original play for the "A Night for Václav Havel," he did so with the image of that vital young writer in mind. He called the play, appropriately, *I think about you a great deal*. It depicts a writer seated at his desk, while another character, called the Imprisoned One, sits silently nearby. The writer sorts though his mail, overburdened with solicitations from various international causes. At the same time, he speaks to the Imprisoned One (the play, in effect, is a monologue), saying that all this mail makes the writer think of him.

> I must say, though — it does remind me of you. Your situation seems worse than all the others. . . . That people who even call themselves Socialist should imprison the imagination . . . That's really what it is, isn't it — the war on the imagination. And maybe, too, because your prison is probably further west than Vienna. You are almost within range of the sound of our voices. You can almost hear us. I suppose. In effect. Whatever the reason, I really do think about you a great deal. . . . In fact, it joins us together, in a way. In some indescribable way we are each other's continuation . . . you in that darkness where they claw and pound at your imagination, and I out here in this space where I think about you . . . a great deal. There will be another clump (of mail appeals) tomorrow. And the next day and the next. Imagine . . . if they stopped! Is that possible? Of course not. As long as mornings continue to arrive, the mail will bring these acts of goodness demanding to be done. And they will be done. Somehow. And so we hold your space open for you, dear friend.[9]

As published in the collection of writings under the title *Living in Truth*, the play ends with this note:

> This monologue was written as expression of solidarity with Václav Havel, for performance at the International Theatre Festival in Avignon on 21 July, 1982.[10]

Solidarity. A word that expresses the collective and profound feelings of commitment by so many writers during those dark decades when Havel's writings were banned in his own country, when his name was eradicated from libraries and the state publishing house, when the doors of his theater were locked to him, when he in essence was told that as a writer he had ceased to exist.

No writer in the twentieth century has received the expression of solidarity that Havel has, as evidenced in the number of plays dedicated to him and the depth of feeling and commitment of the playwrights who wrote them. Consider the following: A play by dedicated to Havel by Samuel Beckett, who understood the existential meaning and value of freedom. A play dedicated to Havel by Arthur Miller, who had experienced the blacklisting of the McCarthy era. The shared understanding of the meaning of a signature, dramatized in Havel's *The Beggar's Opera* where Macheath is forced to sign, in Havel's *Protest* where Staněk won't sign for fear of taking sides, and in Miller's *The Crucible* where John Proctor goes to his death rather than sign his name falsely to a document.

> Proctor: What others say and what I sign to is not the same!
> Danforth: Why? Do you mean to deny this confession when you are free?
> Proctor: I mean to deny nothing!
> Danforth: Then explain to me, Mr. Proctor, why you will not let —
> Proctor: *(With a cry of his whole soul.)* Because it is my name! Because I cannot have another in my life! Because I lie and sign myself to lies! Because I am not worth the dust on the feet of them that hang! How may I live without my name? I have given you my soul; leave me my name![11]

John Proctor's cry could have been Havel's cry, too.

"We are each other's continuation . . ." — these words of Arthur Miller apply also to Havel and British playwright Tom Stoppard. "Mirror images" is another way of describing them, as the British critic Kenneth Tynan did.[12] A little known fact is that Stoppard was born in Czechoslovakia, less than a year after Havel.[13] Had Stoppard's family not emigrated when he was only two years old, perhaps he might have been sitting in the Café Slavia in the 1950s with Havel and the other 36ers, or at least at the next table (Stoppard was born in 1937). But destiny had other designs.

Kenneth Tynan speaks of a "convergence" between the lives and careers of Stoppard and Havel that later developed into friendship and collegiality. A citizen of Britain and an esteemed playwright by the mid-seventies, Stoppard had been planning to write a teleplay for the BBC to mark Amnesty International's "Prisoner of Conscience Year" (1977). His deadline (December 31, 1976) arrived, and he had nothing to show for it. And then, as he describes it:

> On January 6 in Prague three men, a playwright, an actor and a journalist, were arrested in the act of attempting to deliver a document to their own government. This document turned out to be a request that the government should implement its own laws . . . I had had ill-formed and unformed thoughts of writing about Czechoslovakia for a year or two. Moreover, I had been strongly drawn to the work and personality of the arrested playwright.[14]

Stoppard was in California at the time of Havel's arrest on January 7, 1977. He subsequently went to Moscow and St. Petersburg in February with a representative of Amnesty International. But meanwhile, the Charter 77 arrests had ignited his dramatic imagination. "The charter seemed to me to be not a political document but a moral one,"[15] he thought. So in March, he sat down and began work on a new play for the BBC. He called it *Professional Foul*, and he dedicated it to Havel. As he was writing the introduction to the play (quoted above and below), Havel was on trial in their common country of origin.

> He would be the first to object that in mentioning his name only, I am putting undue emphasis on his part in the Czechoslovakian human rights movement. Others have gone to gaol, and many more have been victimized. This is true. But I have in mind not just the Chartist but the author of *The Garden Party, The Memorandum, Audience,* and other plays. It is to a fellow writer that I dedicated *Professional Foul* in admiration.[16]

Set in the late 1970s, Professional Foul tells the story of McKendrick and Anderson, two Oxbridge professors who are attending a colloquium in Communist Prague. Anderson, a professor of ethics, is presenting a paper on "Ethical Fictions as Ethical Foundations"; McKendrick, a professor of philosophy, is presenting one on "Philosophy and the Catastrophe

Theory." Anderson is approached in his hotel room by a former student, Pavel Hollar, a reticent Vaněk-type, who has fallen victim to normalization and is cleaning lavatories in the bus station. Nervously, Hollar leads Anderson into the corridor (the hotel room might be bugged), where he entreats his former professor to smuggle a copy of his unpublished Ph.D. dissertation, on a topic related to human rights, out of the country.

Anderson balks, saying that he is a guest of the Czech government and such an act would be unethical. Still, Hollar persists in leaving his only copy of the dissertation with Anderson, who tries to return it the next day, only to find Hollar's wife hysterical and his apartment occupied by a swarm of StB agents who are ransacking it for Western books. Hollar has been arrested on criminal charges (the secret police has planted a wad of American dollars in the floorboards). Hollar's small son confides in Anderson, saying that his father has been arrested for signing "something" (like Havel), that he is being sent to Ruzyně prison (like Havel), and that he wants his father's manuscript taken out of the country by someone other than Anderson, who is now under suspicion by the police. All this occurs against the background sound of a British/Czech soccer match (hence, the play's title, which means "an intentional foul committed in football to prevent a score"[17]), as well as the righteous indignation of Anderson, who promises to appeal the arrest all the way to the Queen.

As Anderson gives his speech on human rights at the colloquium, the police are searching his hotel room.

> Anderson: . . . There is a sense of right and wrong which precedes utterance. It is individually experienced and it concerns one person's dealings with another person. From this experience we have built a system of ethics which is the sum of individual acts of recognition of individual right . . . If this is so, the implications are serious for a collective or state ethic which finds itself in conflict with individual rights, and seeks, in the name of the people, to impose its values on the very individuals who comprise the state. The illogic of this manoeuvre is an embarrassment to totalitarian systems . . . [18]

In the end, knowing that he will be searched thoroughly as he leaves the country, Anderson places Hollar's manuscript in McKendrick 's briefcase, a fact he tells McKendrick after they have successfully cleared customs and are once more airborne to London.

Anderson: . . . I'm afraid I reversed a principle . . .

McKendrick: You utter bastard.

Anderson: I thought you would approve.

McKendrick: Don't get clever with me . . . Jesus. It's not quite playing the game is it?

Anderson: No, I suppose not. But they were very unlikely to
search you.

McKendrick: That's not the bloody point.

Anderson: I thought it was. But you could be right. Ethics is a very
complicated business. That's why they have these congresses.[19]

Though the Czechs defeat the British in the soccer match, Anderson
balances this by successfully smuggling Hollar's thesis out of the country.
It is a moral and ethical victory, and yet Anderson has deceived a colleague in doing so, using McKendrick's cynical positions on morality
("there aren't any principles in your sense. There are only a lot of princi-
pled people trying to behave as if there were"[20]) as justification to act un-
ethically himself.

Anderson: You make your points altogether too easily, McKendrick.
What need have you of moral courage when your principles reverse themselves so conveniently?"[21]

Through *Professional Foul*, Stoppard is able to "meet" Havel on common ground, to fight Havel's fight, and to articulate Havel's issues, philo-
sophically and ethically. Indeed, in *Professional Foul*, one might say that
Stoppard has written his own version of a Vaněk play. The moral and ethical issues that Anderson faces — in upholding a former student's human
rights by smuggling his manuscript out of the country in the hands of an
unsuspecting colleague, even while Anderson is the guest of the country
whose laws he is breaking — present the same kind of complexities that
Vaněk faces in *Audience* and *Protest*. Like Havel, Stoppard is saying that
under the system, nothing is clear any more — least of all, right and
wrong. And if that is the case, what about the most precious of rights,
"human rights"? Who will define them? Who will uphold them? And at
what price? How can one help one's fellow man? And what means will be
used to do so? Will they be ethical ones? Does it really matter?[22]

Deeply focused in his commitment, Stoppard spent much of 1977
engaged in activities of vigorous protest against the imprisonment of

Havel and the treatment of the other Chartists. As the first response of solidarity with Havel, Stoppard wrote a letter to the *Times* (London), cosigned by thirteen playwrights and actors, including Howard Brenton, Arnold Wesker, and Donald Pleasence:

Sir:

Connoisseurs of totalitarian double-think will have noted that Charter 77 — the Czech document which calls attention to the absence in that country of various human rights beginning with the right of free expression — has been denied expression in the Czech newspapers on the grounds that it is a wicked slander.

The subsequent news from Prague that the main signatories of the Charter are "in the pay of Western reactionary circles" comes less like a bolt form the blue than the thud of the second shoe dropping on to the floor above.

So far, so familiar. However, the arrest of four people, including Václav Havel, the Czech playwright who is one of the three nominated spokesmen for the Charter, is an ominous sign of hardline influence in a regime where President Husák counts as a "moderate." . . .

In calling for the release of those arrested, we are especially concerned for Václav Havel, who was clearly the main target. His charge carries a maximum of ten years' imprisonment, this after a history of harassment and persecution.

Mr. Havel's personal integrity, his courageous dedication to the upholding of human rights, and his art are known and admired by his many friends in the British theater. The undersigned include fellow playwrights as well as some of the actors who have had the privilege of performing Mr. Havel's plays in Britain, and I also have the honor to address you as one of the four British members (the others being Graham Greene, Iris Murdoch and Stephen Spender) of the International Committee for the Support of the Principles of Charter 77. We want to assure Mr. Havel and his colleagues of our solidarity in their support.

Buckinghamshire, February 1, 1977[23]

Next, Stoppard wrote an article about Charter 77 in the *New York Times*, entitled "Dirty Linen in Prague" (February 11, 1977). Named after his play *Dirty Linen*, which was running on Broadway at the time, Stoppard expressed outrage about the arrest of Havel, Patočka, Jiří Hájek, and Kohout, calling it a real test of international commitment to human rights, as well as "an occasion which should push that commitment through the barrier of 'foreign interference in internal affairs.'" Urgently, Stoppard wrote:

> And, in truth, the Charter was indeed more the occasion for, rather than the root cause of, the deeper and more terrible vengeance that can be observed in the charge made against the fourth prisoner [Havel] . . . Clearly the regime had decided finally and after years of persecution and harassment to put the lid on Václav Havel . . . For Havel's sake and a great deal more, isn't it really time we told them that a human right is not an "internal affair,' that signing a petition is not a "serious crime" against any state which claims to be civilized, that a weasel is not a bloody whale? And went on telling them at the highest level?[24]

On May 20, 1977, Havel was released from prison. On June 18, after a thirty-eight-year absence (and two weeks before his fortieth birthday), Stoppard returned to his native land of Czechoslovakia. He drove to Hrádeček, where, in the words of Kenneth Tynan, "he meets his Doppelgänger for the first time."[25] The two playwrights spent hours together, talking in English. When Stoppard returned to England, he said to Tynan, "He is a very brave man."

In August, after Stoppard's visit to Havel, he wrote "Prague: The Story of the Chartists" in the *New York Review of Books*, where in describing Havel's plight in Czechoslovakia, he captured the absurdities in his land of birth, calling it

> a weird, upside-down country where you can find boilers stoked by economists, streets swept by men reading Henry James in English; where filing clerks rise early to write articles for learned journals abroad, and third-rate time-servers are chauffeured around in black, bulbous, chrome-trimmed Tatra 603s straight out of a Fifties' spy film; where millions of crowns per month are spent on maintaining little cordons of policemen in vehicles to disarm a handful of dangerous men whose only weapon is free conversation. Corruption is everywhere and bribes are part of the common currency. You bribe the butcher for meat, the mechanic for a spare part. In the upper reaches of his corruption — say, to get a better flat — you bribe the bureaucrat to tell you whom to bribe. To keep this ramshackle,

profoundly flawed edifice upright requires one apparatchik for every twenty Czechoslovaks.[26]

In September, *Professional Foul* was produced by the BBC.

Clearly, Havel's activism had a great impact on Stoppard. "With only slight exaggeration," writes Ira Nadel, Stoppard's biographer, "Havel may be said to have become Stoppard's political conscience."[27] After Havel was arrested again and sentenced in October 1979, Stoppard intensified his efforts, writing letters of protest to foreign governments, making public statements to the press, drafting petitions, and participating in marches to the Czech embassy in London. In February 1980, he joined together with other supporters to reenact Havel's trial for a television documentary filmed in Munich. Stoppard played the part of Havel's defense lawyer, Pavel Kohout played Havel; Simone Signoret played Otta Bednářová, a journalist who was arrested along with Havel; Volker Schlöndorff, the German film director, played another defense lawyer; and Yves Montand played a silenced supporter.[28]

In 1981, following Havel's example, Stoppard wrote his own letter to President Husák, in this case requesting a visa to revisit Prague. He was refused. In the letter, he had added, sardonically: "Frankly, Havel's prison sentence has been a great nuisance to me. Every week or so I have to ask myself what I can do to help him instead of being able to get on with my life and work . . ."[29]

In 1981, Stoppard also wrote the introduction to a new edition of Havel's *The Memorandum*. On February 17, 1982, he gave an address in Paris where Havel was awarded, in absentia, the Jan Palach Prize. On May 14, 1984, Stoppard represented Havel when he was awarded an honorary doctorate, again in absentia, at the University of Toulouse-La Mirail; on that occasion, he gave a reading of Havel's essay "Politics and Conscience." According to Stoppard, after the ceremony, he dreamed that he himself was sent to prison for three years, without reason. The dream focused on the first day of his sentence, and he was filled with despair. As he described it afterwards, in a letter to Havel:

> Then one of my children woke me up when he was going to school and after the first moment of relief that I wasn't in jail but merely in bed I immediately thought of you and how frightful it must have been when there was no possibility of waking up and finding yourself at home. So here I am on a sunny day, half way through adapt-

ing a Molnar comedy for the National Theatre . . . dozens of silly jokes and no politics. (May 29, 1984)[30]

That feeling of identification with Havel would remain. "If I had not left the country [Czechoslovakia]," Stoppard has said," my life would likely be like his, alternating between prison and menial work."[31] That same year, to show his reciprocal appreciation, Havel dedicated *Largo Desolato* to Stoppard. Stoppard in turn adapted the play, and his English version was premiered in 1986 at the Bristol Old Vic.

After Havel became president, their connection continued. In March, 1990, Havel traveled to London to open an East European forum at the Institute of Contemporary Arts. Afterwards, Havel dined with Stoppard at 10 Downing Street with the prime minister, John Major. Then in 1991, Stoppard went to Prague to see a production of his *Travesties* at the Realistické Theater. The day following the performance, Stoppard was invited to watch the changing of the guard at the Prague Castle. Stoppard felt as if he were in a play "and all you had to do was write it. Except that I would be writing his [Havel's] play, instead of mine."[32] In 1994, Stoppard and Arthur Miller joined Havel for a panel discussion chaired by Ronald Harwood on "Not Only About Theatre," held at the International Theatre Festival in Plzeň. Then in February 1998, Stoppard went to Prague to see his play *Arcadia* performed at the Comedy Theater (Divadlo Komedie), where he met with Havel. That October, when Havel went to England, he was invited to "an improvised literary party" in Stoppard's apartment.

Inspired by Tynan's metaphor, Klára Hůrková has written a scholarly study entitled *Mirror Images,* subtitled: "A comparison of the early plays of Václav Havel and Tom Stoppard with special references to their political aspects." In it, she cites some striking similarities between the writers: Czech origins, a lack of university education, a delight in language games, a fascination with science and systems, an original sense of the absurd, an acute political awareness, a love of playing with time, and a deeply humanistic sensibility.[33]

As for the work itself, Havel felt a strong affinity for Stoppard's plays. We know that from one of his letters to Olga from prison, in which he devotes half of his precious four-page weekly allotment to an intense discussion of Stoppard's *Rosencrantz and Guildenstern Are Dead* (written in 1967), a play Havel greatly admired. At one point, as he explained in his letter, he had wanted the Balustrade to produce it in repertoire with *Waiting for Godot* (introduced at the Balustrade in 1964), and cross-cast the roles of Vladimir and Estragon with Rosencrantz and Guildenstern.

I felt that Stoppard's play was close to our theater not only in its intellectual sophistication and its clever multilayered meaning, but also because it pointed (more than Beckett the metaphysician did, of course) to the moral and social dimension of human existence (the theme of betrayal). After all, my plays, too, gave our theater that general direction — and it's no accident that in the Czech intellectual context, this comes up again and again. Later, I saw *Rosencrantz and Guildenstern* in a large theater on Broadway [in 1968]; it was marvelously acted and the audience was lively and responsive, yet I still think that the play belongs more properly in a small, "high profile" theater and that a touch of nightclub or cabaret atmosphere in the performance setting would not hurt it a bit. Everything in that play is properly turned on its head, everything is paradoxical, and so I think that its "high" meanings would resonate well in a somewhat obscure "low" setting, the kind of atmosphere that the Balustrade worked with (mainly before the renovations) and the kind that probably best serves the plays of Ionesco and Beckett as well.[34]

Stoppard, in turn, expressed similar feelings about Havel's plays. He first read Havel's plays in the late 1960s. The character of George Moore, a philosophy professor in Stoppard's *Jumpers* (1972) who is preparing a lecture, was in part inspired by the character of Eduard Huml, the professor in *The Increased Difficulty of Concentration* (1968) who is dictating a treatise on the nature of happiness. At the playwrights' panel at Plzeň in 1994, Stoppard said:

When I was starting to write plays there were two or three which at that time meant something very, very acute . . . two were called *The Garden Party* and *The Memorandum*. In the case of these plays I had a completely unique reaction to them — I thought "Damn, somebody wrote my play!"[35]

While Beckett, Miller, and Stoppard wrote plays in Havel's honor with characters who represented him, Harold Pinter expressed his solidarity and admiration in another way. He actually played Havel, or rather, Vaněk, the character of Havel's creation closest to his own persona. In 1977, as an expression of solidarity with Havel and Charter 77, the BBC produced the two Vaněk plays, *Audience* and *Vernissage*, translated into English by Vera Blackwell, performed under the joint title of "Private View." Pinter played the role of Ferdinand Vaněk in both. They were broadcast on April 3 and again on October 2, 1977. "Playing Vaněk was great," says Pinter today. "I felt very close to the author while doing it."[36]

Like Stoppard, Pinter showed his solidarity with Havel during his years of imprisonment. On Pinter's fiftieth birthday (October 10, 1980), the Royal National Theatre presented his play *Landscape* for one night, and the proceeds went to Havel's family. About that event, he said, in 1981:

> On my 50th birthday last year [10 October 1980] the National Theatre were kind enough to put on a play of mine [*Landscape*] for one night and the proceeds from that were for Havel's family. The awful thing is that now, a year later, nothing has changed for him.[37]

Determined to show his support, Pinter and his wife, Lady Antonia Fraser, helped to organize a benefit in 1982 called "The Night of the Day of the Imprisoned Writer."

Pinter's sense of solidarity with Havel continued. In 1988, he went to Czechoslovakia, where he met Havel and spent the night at Hrádeček. Two years later, in February 1990, Pinter and his wife visited Havel to celebrate his presidency. He saw Havel later in the 1990s on several occasions: once, when they were shooting Pinter's screenplay of the *The Trial* in Prague, another time at a state lunch at Buckingham Palace. "He is the most sympathetic, intelligent and generous of men," Pinter says of his fellow playwright.[38]

Like Miller, Edward Albee thinks a great deal about Havel, too. He had heard of Havel when he first visited Prague in the 1960s (at the invitation of John Steinbeck, who was on a cultural exchange program to Russian, Poland, and Czechoslovakia). Subsequently, Albee visited Prague on several occasions during the 1980s, once to attend a performance of his play *Seascape* at the Balustrade in 1983 and again in 1985 at the invitation of the American embassy. Albee recounts his first secret meeting with Havel on that second visit:

> The first time I met Havel, somebody arranged a meeting between us. It was a very private meeting; I'm not exactly sure of the date. I had to be picked up by a taxi, which dropped me off in front of a

building. I was instructed to walk through the building to an exit, where another car was waiting for me, which took me to yet another building. I went to an apartment. Havel was there. (I don't think it was his.) He was under "house arrest" at the time. He asked me to deliver a letter from him to Samuel Beckett.[39]

There was more drama during that visit in 1985. William Luers, who was the U.S. ambassador at the time, had encouraged Albee to bring to Prague his production of *Hawk Moon*, an adaptation of a Sam Shepard play, which Albee had previously presented at the English Theatre in Vienna. Luers arranged for the production to be presented at the Czech Theatre Institute in Celetná Street near the Old Town Square, a white, multistory building set back off the street in a courtyard with a great wrought-iron gate before it. Hoping to circumvent the restrictions placed on the dissident community, Luers had also unofficially invited a group of dissident theater artists to attend the performance. Havel was among them. As Mel Gussow describes the occasion:

> These artists gathered in the courtyard leading to the theater, hoping to elude the guards posted at the doors and sneak inside. Albee went out into the courtyard to talk to Havel, whom he had met secretly that afternoon. Luers was supposed to introduce Albee, who would then introduce the play. When the performance was about to begin, the institute chairman locked the gate to the theater, leaving Albee, Havel and others outside. Albee shouted to the chairman: "You're going to have a hard time keeping your crowd happy if you don't let me in." His words were translated and the official reluctantly unlocked the gate. Albee entered, leading more than fifteen dissidents into the theater. Havel, though, waited outside, and according to Glyn O'Malley [Albee's assistant], finally slipped in at the end of the performance, shielded from view by his compatriots. "Everyone knew he was in the room," said O'Malley, "but no one could see him. The tension and energy were electric."[40]

Wendy Luers, the ambassador's wife, who was inside the building with the other guests when this incident occurred, remembers the look on the theater institute chairman's face when her husband announced: "Mr. Chairman, you have locked Mr. Albee out!" She also remembers the dinner that evening at the American embassy, which followed the performance. "The theater officials sat at one end of the table, and Albee and

Havel sat at the other."[41] It was an unprecedented occasion, wherein the two polarized groups dined together in the same room.

Albee and Havel were not to see each other again for twelve years, when they met at a lunch in honor of President Havel at the Metropolitan Museum of Art, given by William Luers, who was now the museum's president. At the time, Havel was recovering from an operation (he suffered from lung cancer) and was accompanied by his new wife, Dáša. "When I knew him early on, he was vibrant, communicative," Albee recalls. "Then after he became president, there was a formality, a distance."[42] But that earlier visit of 1985 had left a lasting impact on Albee, who today feels keenly an abiding kinship with Havel, as well as a particular admiration for his ability to have endured the years of imprisonment. "Not being able to write —" says Albee, "that's probably crueler than taking you away and shooting you."[43]

The theatrical lives of Pinter, Stoppard, Albee, and Havel in the theater paralleled each other. All came of age in the 1960s — their formative playwriting years — and their independent spirits and sensibilities were born in those turbulent times.[44] All acknowledge an admiration for Beckett. All have been linked, more or less, to the movement known as the theater of the absurd. All share what scholar Susan Hollis Merritt calls an outsider's perspective.[45] All share a common humanity, a sense of morality, and a passionate commitment to freedom of thought and expression.

And what drew them together was solidarity with their fellow playwright, Václav Havel. More than a character in his own plays, more than a character in the plays of his Czech playwright friends, Havel has become a character in the plays of other international writers. A playwright's playwright, he has become the symbol of the twentieth-century writer — in his struggle for the right to write.

HOMES AWAY FROM HOME

> You can put Havel in prison, but you can't put Vaněk in prison.[1]
> — Achim Benning, Burgtheater, Vienna

For so many years, Havel was deprived of a theatrical home in his own country. Yet, although he did not realize it at the time, no less than five theaters have been steadfastly dedicated to his work.

The Theatre on the Balustrade, of course, was his place of "birth," where his first three full-length plays were premiered. Tragically, it was forced to close its doors to him in the 1970s and 1980s, but reopened them with gratitude in 1990. And of course there was the Theatre on the Road, born of ingenuity, resourcefulness, and friendship, which dedicated itself to keeping Havel's voice alive in his country during the years when they tried to silence him.

Attention must also be paid to three theaters outside Czechoslovakia that provided a home away from home for Havel during the decades when the curtains in his own country fell on his plays. The Public Theater (New York Shakespeare Festival) and the abiding commitment of its artistic director, Joseph Papp, have been cited throughout the story of Havel's life in the theater. There are also two other theaters that, like the Public, had the courage and the commitment to give their stages to Havel's plays. And like that of his fellow playwrights, the solidarity expressed by these theaters and their artistic directors is unprecedented.

The Burgtheater in Vienna

Achim Benning, artistic director of the Burgtheater, began producing Havel's plays in 1976, during his very first season. Like Papp, he made his commitment clear from the very beginning.

Benning, a tall, warm, affable German-born actor/director, tells the story of how the Burgtheater became Havel's home away from home. During the 1960s, Klaus Juncker, Havel's dedicated agent, worked vigorously to place *The Garden Party* and *The Memorandum* in theaters throughout West Germany. Notable among them was the prestigious Schillertheater in Berlin, which produced *The Garden Party* in 1964, *The Memorandum* in 1965, and *The Increased Difficulty of Concentration* in 1968. After 1968, however, with the departure of its artistic director, Boleslav Barlog, the one responsible for the Havel productions, it became more difficult for Juncker to find West German theaters to present Havel. According to Benning, "in Germany, there was a prejudice against Eastern European countries at the time because they were Communist, and furthermore there was no interest in dissident issues. It was so silly. Except for the writers Heinrich Böll or Günther Grass who had connections with the dissidents, others weren't really interested in Havel."[2]

So in 1976, when Benning became artistic director of the Burgtheater, Juncker sent him the two one-act plays Havel had just written, *Audience* and *Vernissage*, which Juncker had smuggled out of the country himself. "I care about Havel; let's do Havel," Benning said, seizing the opportunity. In his first season, he produced both works along with the Polish writer Slawomir Mrozek's play *Polizei* under the banner title "Polizei," providing Havel's plays with their professional world premieres. The opening night was October 8, 1976, on the Akademietheater stage, the second largest in the Burgtheater complex. According to Benning, the audiences were enthusiastic:

> The plays were more in the tradition of Schweik, and therefore were popular, because they seemed to be more realistic than literary. In Vienna they like popular theater, not intellectual theater, and they know the types (in *Audience*) because half of the Viennese population is Czech. Just look in the telephone book, and you'll see. They came here, they settled here. So they knew the characters, they liked the humor. They knew the type of Sládek, the brewmaster, for example; he's a person they could meet on the street. They understood Havel's characters, they had empathy for them. Vaněk is unpretentious, he's not an intellectual with airs. They want to be like Vaněk, to have the moral standards that he has. Vaněk is a kind of hero, because there are no heroes today. A definition of a hero? Somebody who is able to do things that you are not able to do.[3]

As for the Austrian audience's response to *Vernissage*, said Benning: "They understood the materialism."[4]

That year, Havel had received the prestigious Austrian State Prize for European Literature. "Of course we invited him to come to the opening night," said Benning "But he couldn't. Thereafter, on every first night of a Havel play, a tradition developed at the Burgtheater. After the play and the applause, there was moment where the stage was empty and a sign would come flying down with the name Václav Havel. It was in place of Václav Havel in person."[5]

After Havel went to prison, Benning's commitment intensified. On November 17, 1979, he produced Havel's new play *Protest*, along with Kohout's *Permit*. According to Benning, the audiences understood the character of Staněk, the successful writer, too:

Opportunism is the most universal political quality. All dictator-
ships profit from opportunism. As such, it's a universal problem,
not one special to Czechoslovakia alone. Moreover, Havel shows it
in a comical, and not a didactic, way. The Viennese public enjoyed
it very much.[6]

Two of Havel's theatrical colleagues also found a home at the Burgtheater. Kohout had been working there as a dramaturg, and when he was
prevented from returning to Czechoslovakia, Benning gave him a home
there, too. That same year (1979), Pavel Landovský was also denied reentry into Czechoslovakia, and he too came to Benning.

Landovský came to the Burgtheater because he had no place else to
go. He knew this theater would be sympathetic. And of course the
problem was that Landovský was an actor. He spoke only Czech
and Russian, so he'd have been lost without the Burgtheater as a
home. We hired him without speaking a word of German. The first
role he played here was in *The Inspector General.* He played the German doctor, who also didn't speak a word of Russian.[7]

Landovský remained at the Burgtheater till 1989. During that time,
Benning's commitment to Landovský, as well as to Havel's plays, remained steadfast. In 1981, for example, the Burgtheater's production of
Gorky's *Summerfolk* was chosen to play in Moscow, Leningrad, and Talin,
as part of a theater exchange between Russia and Austria. Landovský was
playing a role in it — albeit a small one, since he was still having difficulty with the German language. The day the exchange was to take place,
the Burgtheater company gathered in the theater lobby and boarded the
buses that were to take them to the airport for their flight to Moscow. The
buses never left the theater. Word had come that the Russian government,
responding to pressure from the Czech authorities, had denied Landovský's visa. Benning announced: "Either we all go, or none of us goes."
So the Austrian government cancelled the exchange. "All the Moscow theaters were sold out, so it was a terrible scandal," explained Benning. "This
only could have happened because of the strong stand of the Austrian
government. Under the leadership of Bruno Kreisky, Chancellor of
Austria, there was a liberal policy of cultural friendship and support of
Eastern European artists. The Russians, in the end, didn't want this. Lan-

dovský didn't interest them. So the exchange happened one year later. Havel is not isolated; he's part of a whole. He was the catalyst."[8] By the end of the 1970s, Juncker recognized Benning's abiding commitment to Havel, and thereafter sent Havel's plays to Benning as soon as he received them. Because of Benning, there was never a time between 1979 and 1989 that a Havel play was not in the repertory of the Akademietheater. As Benning explains:

Havel was permanent in our repertory for years and years, just like Gorky. We'd keep a Havel play in the repertory for two years and then a new one would come along, so he was always present. Meanwhile, at the time we had many connections with theaters in other countries. Officials from these theaters would come to select plays from our repertoire for an exchange. For example, a Russian delegation came once; they were here for a while, and they'd come into the theater bar at night and they'd whisper, "Can we get a ticket to see the Havel play at the Akademietheater?" You see, many officials of Eastern bloc countries knew that Havel plays were banned in their own countries, so they always ordered their tickets with a whisper. And that's political theater! Political theater does not mean putting on a play about politics; it means putting on a play by Václav Havel. That is a deliberate act. That is a political act. You can put Havel in prison, but you can't put Vaněk in prison.[9]

After Havel went to prison, Benning went a step further.

There was a special event wherein officials from the Austrian government were invited to attend a performance of a Havel play at the Akademietheater. We'd then call in the Austrian television cameras. At the performance, the officials from the Austrian government would sign Amnesty International protest notes, and that was broadcast on television. This put pressure on the Czech government. Also, actors from the theater would go to the Czech embassy in Vienna with petitions, and that was on television too. Since this would be broadcast in Czechoslovakia, that was the way that the Czech people saw it and got to know what was happening to Havel, because it wasn't in their newspapers. The Czech people didn't even know that Václav Havel was in prison! So it was thanks to Austrian television that the Czech people knew. So one can say that, in a way, without the Burgtheater, Václav Havel wouldn't be president![10]

The commitment to Havel continued at the Burgtheater. In 1981, Benning produced *Mountain Hotel*; in 1983, *The Memorandum*; in 1985, *Largo Desolato*; and in 1986, *Temptation*. All were world premieres, and at the end of each, the sign flew down onto the stage, honoring the play's absent author. After every opening night, Benning called Havel, who eagerly asked him for a report on the audience response. "Those were long phone conferences," recalls Benning.

Then in 1986, Benning went to Prague to meet Havel for the first time. To hide the true purpose of his visit, he participated in an official cultural exchange, which included a visit to the Balustrade to meet Fialka, the mime, who was still directing his productions there. Havel met Benning and accompanied him to the Balustrade door.

> It was like a bad spy film. I went to the Balustrade, and of course Fialka [the director of the resident mime troupe] wanted to meet me, because I was the director of the Burgtheater. But Havel was with me. Havel went up to the bar in the theater lobby and asked to speak with Fialka. Fialka came out and said we should wait at the door during intermission, because Havel wasn't allowed into the theater, and someone would come and get us. We waited and waited, and the door never opened. So we stood out on the sidewalk, talking. Havel looked exhausted.[11]

By 1989, Benning had moved from the Burgtheater to the Schauspielhaus in Zurich.

> The first thing I did there was to arrange for the world premiere of *Redevelopment*. When we picked the play, Havel was in prison. When we rehearsed it, he was still in prison. [Opening night was September 26.] While it was playing, the revolution was happening. No one imagined it.[12]

Joachim Bissmeyer, the actor who had played Vaněk and Leopold Kopřiva (in *Largo Desolato*) at the Burgtheater, directed the production in Zurich. That year, the Duttweiler Prize was awarded to Havel, who was not allowed to come to Switzerland to receive it. A celebration was held at the Schauspielhaus in his honor. After the revolution, on November 22, 1990, Havel finally came to Switzerland to accept the prize.

In the early 1990s, Benning visited the playwright/president Havel in

Lani Castle outside Prague. He was escorted there privately by the police. When Benning arrived at the castle, Havel greeted him and his police escort. "You see," he said to Benning, "nothing has changed."

Looking back on those Burgtheater years, Benning says:

> Theatre is more than an aesthetic institution. It's a human one; sometimes it's art, but not always. It's also important when it is not art. The Burgtheater commitment was unique. It's not about putting on a play about politics, it's about putting on the plays of Václav Havel.[13]

The Orange Tree Theatre in Richmond (London)

Another theater that has dedicated itself with equal determination to Havel and his plays was — and still is — the tenacious and spirited Orange Tree Theatre.

It all began in 1977, when the theater was located in a tiny, 102-seat room above the Orange Tree pub on the pleasant main street of Richmond, on the outskirts of London. The dynamic Sam Walters, who founded the theater in 1971 and serves as its artistic director, was already acquainted with Havel's work, having read *The Memorandum* when it was published in England in the 1960s. In 1976, a colleague called to his attention *Audience* and *Vernissage*, which had just been published in the *Index on Censorship*. Walters in turn called Peggy Ramsey, the British agent to whom Klaus Juncker had sent the plays. Ramsey mentioned that Vera Blackwell, a Czech translator of Havel's plays and also a childhood friend, was doing a translation for radio in which Pinter was performing, and she gave the rights to Walters for a February, 1977 production at the Orange Tree.

As rehearsals were about to begin, Walters remembers:

> Charter 77 burst upon the world, and as one of its first designated spokesmen, Václav Havel was consistently on the front page of the newspapers. The Czech Charter was the big political news of the moment, and our author suddenly became the best known playwright in the world."[14]

So Walters decided to add *The Memorandum* to his theater's season schedule; although it had been presented on BBC radio and television, it had yet to have its British stage premiere. "The plays interested me," Walters explained. "One got caught up in what was happening in Czechoslovakia and it seemed like the sensible thing to do. In our own little way, we became supporters and champions. So we had three months worth of Havel."[15]

Audience and *Private View* (as *Vernissage* was called in this translation) opened on February 18. The plays were directed by Anthony Cornish, with Gordon Reid as Vaněk in both, and Bill Wallis first as Sládek and then as the husband. The critical response was strong. In the *Morning Star:*

> To take a moral stand over Václav Havel, the imprisoned Czech writer, is so easy and so inevitable that the excellence of his short plays *Audience* and *Private View* (Orange Tree) seem almost suspect. But it has to be said: he makes most, not all, of our political plays look shabby . . . for his ability to see a situation humanistically and ironically, in the round.[16]

A month later, the *The Memorandum* opened on March 20, directed by Walters, with Roger Swaine as Gross, John Challis as Baláš, John Baddely as the Ptydepe teacher, and Paddy Ward as Mr. P. As one critic described it, the tiny theater found itself "as tightly packed as fire regulations and the need for the actors to have some space in which to perform permit; there is also nightly a disappointed trail of would-be patrons all the way down the stairs to the bar."[17] As another critic described it:

> Opening night of *The Memorandum* at the Orange Tree . . . looked like a critics' convention. No less than twenty seats had been reserved for critics, including such august figures as Bernard Levin and Kenneth Tynan. A terrifying ordeal for the cast, who must have been deafened by the sound of critical brains ticking over. . . . If you can get in . . . I strongly advise you to see this important and enjoyable piece while you can. But be prepared to queue — close on 100 people were turned away for the first night![18]

Walters remembers this night vividly.

> The critics came en masse on opening night to that tiny pub theater. I thought: this is unfair, we haven't even had a preview, I hadn't even organized any music for the production. So I rushed around and chose some music by Eric Sati. The critics were kind, although on

the first night things went so wrong that I sat by the door with my nails digging into my wife's arm and I thought: I can't watch the second half. So I didn't. I was so upset. An actor forgot to carry his fire extinguisher, another actress forgot the bag of food — things like that — and the actor delivering the lecture "dried" on something [forgot his lines] and I felt more responsible than one feels ordinarily because of Havel's situation and because the audience and critics didn't know this play . . . and meanwhile, everyone loved it.[19]

If possible, the reviews for *The Memorandum* were even more enthusiastic. Said Irving Wardle in the *Times* (London):

The prophetic quality of this satire, once labelled absurdist but long overtaken by the nonsensical iniquities of Czech life, is one mark of the classic. . . . Applying equally to the bureaucratic inhumanities of East and West, everything is implicit in the fable of a managing director's struggle with a synthetic new language. . . . The story is very much the work of a compatriot of Kafka, and one can imagine how he might have begun it: "Someone must have been telling lies about Joseph G, for one fine morning he found himself out of his job." But it is Kafka plus marvelous jokes, plus a mastery of mathematical design. A satire on mechanistic thinking, it is itself a beautiful machine, containing nothing but essential working parts.[20]

During this "three months of Havel," Walters added yet another element — a lunchtime docudrama titled "A Faraway Country" (drawn from Chamberlain's 1938 phrase about Czechoslovakia: "We can't go to war over Czechoslovakia; it's a faraway country of which we know little"). Compiled by the translator Vera Blackwell together with actress Veronica Hyks and playwright Jeremy Paul, the program provided background information on Prague Spring and the Russian invasion in August 1968. It also sought to explain why Havel's works were banned and described events leading up to his imprisonment as the leading signer of Charter 77.

During the run of the first two plays, over 1,200 names were collected from the audience on a petition calling for Havel's release, representing over 75 percent of the audience. Among the signers were critics Kenneth Tynan, Bernard Levin, Michael Billington, and Irving Wardle. A delegation from the theater including Walters and Tom Stoppard attempted to deliver the petition to the Czech embassy in Kensington Palace Gardens on April 14, 1977. As Walters described the event to a reporter:

"We rang the embassy's door bell, but the man who answered it held his arms high above his head, so we couldn't put the petition into his hand." Nothing daunted, the demonstrators went to the visa office entrance instead. There they were able to walk in, but did not get far. "The moment we were inside a woman barred the way, crying 'Out! Out! The office is closed.'" Said Mr. Walters: "We pointed out that closing time was one o'clock, and it was now only 12:45, but she refused to let us see anyone."[21]

They solved the problem by putting the petition through the letterbox. "Meanwhile," Walters recalls, "back at the Orange Tree, along the stairway going up to the theater in the pub, we lined the walls with clippings about what was going on in Czechoslovakia. We became a sort of center for the Czechs; by then a lot of well-known people had left the country, and they all came to the theater."[22]

Like Benning, Walters remained steadfast in his commitment to Havel. In 1978, he produced *The Increased Difficulty of Concentration*, directed by Christie Dickason, with Rio Fanning as Eduard Huml. The opening night was October 27, 1978. Michael Billington wrote in the *Guardian* (Manchester):

It emerges as a sprightly, humanist attack on anything that reduces man's infinite variety to carefully catalogued data. Tynan in *The New Yorker* recently described the play as an antecedent to Stoppard's *Jumpers*. . . . But I was reminded much more of an unholy alliance between two other wildly dissimilar writers, Kafka and Ayckbourn.[23]

The *Richmond Herald* commented:

Bureaucracy in the West is the subject of much humorous disparagement, most of it relaxed, because we can afford it to be. In the police states of eastern Europe it can be a nightmare. So it's hardly surprising that the plays of the dissident Czech playwright, Václav Havel, much given as they are to knocking the stuffing out of that particular bureaucratic regime, themselves take on a nightmarish quality. . . . The message, finally delivered by Huml, is clear: when it comes to analysing man, "love, friendship, compassion are the only tools." The mindless machine, be it bureaucratic or mechanical, is useless. Havel himself might well take comfort from this production, locked up as he is in the faraway country about which he's succeeded in telling us quite a bit.

As with the previous production, Walters supplemented the mainstage program with a lunchtime reading of *Guardian Angel*, Havel's radio play.

In 1980, Walters received a copy of *Protest* and produced it together with Kohout's *Permit*, directed by Geoffrey Beevers. The opening night was on September 19, 1980. Critic Michael Billington described both plays in the *Guardian* (Manchester) as "largely about the burden of cowardice."

> Havel, currently serving a four and a half year prison sentence, knows whereof he speaks. But what is striking about this bracing satire is that there is no easy condemnation of the wriggling Staněk. Robert McBain as Staněk gives a splendid display of moral contortionism posing as liberalism while Frank Moorey's Vaněk looks on in silent pity . . . Havel's play is a classic statement about cowardice that could be applied to any society. Kohout's is a more obvious, localised swipe at a timorous bureaucracy.[25]

Havel's imprisonment was on the minds of audience and critics alike. In his article "Just another name on the Czech-list," Alan Franks commented on the Orange Tree Theatre's efforts in the *Times* (London):

> The irony of it all would not have been lost on Václav Havel. In the upstairs room of a pub in a middle-class suburb of London the audience files out and signs a petition at the cash desk complaining to the Czech embassy about the playwright's detention. . . . They have nothing to lose by scribbling their names on the sheet, except possibly a sense of their own political inertia. The man in the play had everything to lose, the liberty and the livelihood which he managed to retain by toeing the party line for the years since the Russian invasion of 1968. . . . Another irony that Havel would have enjoyed was the presence of the Czech philosopher Julius Tomin at a performance. . . . The two are prominent mentors of the Charter 77 movement, and had it not been for the authorities' continuous harassment of his seminars in Prague he would probably not now be freshly cloistered in Oxford, just an hour's drive from this bitter reminder of conditions at home. . . . Quite what effect our freely

given signatures will have is uncertain. But as Stephen Lukes said in this paper last week, it is better to live in a world in which futile gestures take place than one in which they do not. As an essay on conscience Havel's play (*Protest*) is anything but futile.[26]

Once again, Walters created a lunchtime documentary to complement Havel's play, this time, an edited dramatization of the VONS trial (the Committee for the Defense of the Unjustly Prosecuted). The actress Peggy Ashcroft, the critic Bernard Levin, the playwright James Saunders, and Tom Stoppard took turns reading from excerpts from Havel's essay "The Power of the Powerless." Looking back on these events, Walters remembers:

> Someone said: "Wait a minute, Sam, it's a bit of overkill. They'll get fed up with Havel." But after all, he was in prison, so it only seemed right to do his work. I think his plays are good, and furthermore I believe he's undervalued as a playwright. Because he's a dissident, people don't pay enough attention to him as a playwright.[27]

Walters pressed on. Once again, he collected over eight hundred signatures on a petition in protest of Havel's imprisonment, this time calling for the release of both Havel and Kohout, whose works were being performed at the Orange Tree. The petition read:

> We, the undersigned, appeal to you on behalf of the distinguished playwright Václav Havel and his associates, imprisoned since October 1979. We ask you to intercede in obtaining their release, thereby abiding by the Helsinki Agreement and the Czechoslovak Constitution. It would be a positive step by the Czech authorities if the release of these prisoners could be effected before the follow-up to the Helsinki Conference which will be held in Madrid during November.[28]

Walters and a delegation attempted to deliver the petition to the Czech embassy on Monday, October 13, 1980. Once again, they stood outside the embassy gate ringing the bell, petition in hand. Through the intercom, they were told to send it by mail.

The Orange Tree's next production of a Havel play came in 1987. It was *Largo Desolato* in the English version by Tom Stoppard, directed by

Walters, with Geoffrey Beevers as Leopold Kopřiva. Once again, critics acknowledged the Orange Tree Theatre's commitment to the plight of its playwright of choice. *Largo Desolato*, in its London premiere, opened on February 6, and the fact that Havel had just been released, once again, from jail called critical attention to the significance of the production. In the *Daily Telegraph*:

> The Czechs arguably know more about tyranny than any other civilised people. Long familiar with the small-minded superintendence of the Habsburg Austrians who produced a first draft of totalitarianism, their twenty-year indigenous democracy was succeeded first by the Nazis — Austrians in spades — and then by the Russians employing repulsive local functionaries. This is knock-on-the-door country. Secret policemen grow like buttercups. Václav Havel, himself familiar as a long-term prisoner with the regime's prisons (which he refers to as "there"), is in the tradition of Hašek . . . and of Kafka himself. . . . Havel, whose *Largo Desolato* appears at the small but mighty Orange Tree Theatre in a version by that other sardonic Czech, Tom Stoppard, has written a major work which it hurts the mouth to bite on. . . . This is totalitarianism in sonata form, an immensely provocative play beautifully acted throughout, and directed with great sensibility by Sam Walters. Not easy? Too sad . . . ? This is how a great many of the finest spirits live (and not just in Eastern Europe). It is unlikely that we shall see a better play this year. Inconceivable that we shall see one which is more important.[29]

And in *Time Out:*

> It is not difficult to see what attracted adaptor Tom Stoppard to Václav Havel's work — in addition to both being Czech they share a delight in the ludic that in no way undermines the seriousnesss of intent. Time and again phrases are recited, the words of one character repeated by another, and movements reiterated so that an intense nightmare world is created in which even the act of nondenial is enough to condemn a man.[30]

Then, in 1989, an unanticipated opportunity presented itself. Walters was awarded a Winston Churchill Travelling Fellowship, part of which he spent traveling to Prague. At last, he would meet the playwright to whom he provided a home for twelve years. Once again, Walters's timing was uncanny. He arrived on November 21, right in the middle of the Velvet Revolution.

Once again, Václav Havel led me into heady times. I gatecrashed press conferences, was introduced in debates at theaters, rattled my keys in Wenceslas Square and when my wife arrived to join me, we got to meet with him in his apartment. He apologised that he was so busy, but said "we are in the middle of a revolution and we are amateurs."[31]

Upon his return, Walters scheduled a reading of *Redevelopment*. He was worried that it might not be relevant any more, now that the revolution had come; still, he was determined to produce the play, and at the same time fearful that, given Havel's increasing international celebrity status, another theater might seize the opportunity to do so. So the Orange Tree produced the English-language premiere of *Redevelopment* on September 18, 1990, in a version by James Saunders, directed by Walters, with Tim Hardy as Bergman, Timothy Watson as Albert, and Janet Key as Luisa. It was to be the last production of a play at the pub theater, before it moved to new quarters.

Critics assuaged Walters's concerns (as well as Havel's) about the play's relevance; indeed, the production gave them an opportunity to place in the play in its unexpected historical context. "Much has happened in Czechoslovakia in the last two years, but nothing to invalidate the meaning to be extrapolated from Havel's allegory," said the *Daily Telegraph*.[32] The *Times* (London) added:

No playwright will ever have been better placed to understand authority. Even Nero, whose works have not survived, was never imprisoned by Caligula. He (Walters) adds a final knock on the castle door (absent in the text) but this is a permissable nod to the latest, marvelous change in Czech history.[33]

Others praised the quality of the play. From the *Times Literary Supplement*:

James Saunder's English version (based on a literal translation by Marie Winn) fluently captures the vital linguistic nuances, while the Hamlet-like network of personal relationships . . . is not merely another reminder of the tragic human consequences of an immoral seizure of power, but evidence of theater's universality and hence, as Havel's career shows, its marvelously sustaining power.[34]

In 1991, the year after Havel became president, the Orange Tree moved from its location above the pub to a new home across the street. But Walters' commitment for Havel did not wane. In 1995, he produced *The Memorandum* for a second time. He explained:

> I wanted to do it again in the new theater because it's a wonderful play, and even though the political allegory wasn't relevant any more, it still works as a piece of theater. It's funny and satirical and when I reread it, I thought: there are plays that miss their time and move past their time, but not this one.[35]

Walters's second production of *The Memorandum* opened on March 28, 1995, this time with David Allister as Gross, John Baddeley once again as the Ptydepe teacher, and Victoria Hamilton as Maria. The critics echoed Walters's conviction that *The Memorandum* was lasting — and in fact offered fresh insights into Havel's interconnected life in politics and the theater. Michael Billington of the *Guardian* (Manchester) wrote:

> Václav Havel's most durable play, *The Memorandum*, from 1965, gets a welcome revival at the Orange Tree Theatre, Richmond, which for two decades has treated him almost as a house author. . . . It is, among many other things, a sharp-toothed attack on office politics written by a man who himself now seems trapped in the deadening politics of presidential office.[36]

Jeremy Kingston of the *Times* (London) shared this perspective:

> Written and produced in 1965 when its author, Václav Havel, was a relatively free man; first staged in this country twelve years later, when he had been placed under house arrest, this famous play is being revived at a time when he appears to become incarcerated again, although now as his country's President. The Velvet Revolution gives a special significance to the words spoken by the typist

Maria:, the only decent character in the play . . . : "I believe that if one doesn't give way, truth must always come out in the end.[37]

In 2003, to honor the culmination of Havel's presidency, Walters produced *The Beggar's Opera*, directed by Geoffrey Beevers, with a cast including Bruce Alexander as Lockit, Howard Saddler as Macheath, and David Timson as Peachum. The play premiered on January 19, just weeks before Havel stepped down from the presidency.

Appropriately, the critics praised the Orange Tree's commitment to the playwright as much as they attended to the play. In a comment echoed by others, Michael Billington of the *Guardian* (Manchester) said: "This theater's loyalty to the playwright Václav Havel is beyond praise."[38] Other critics joined him in reminding the public of the Orange Tree's — and Sam Walter's — twenty-five year commitment, which included the production of ten of his plays.

As for *The Beggar's Opera* itself, the critics recognized its value as a record of those treacherous times. Benedict Nightingale of the *Times* (London) cracks the code of Havel's parable, citing how the playwright

> turned Gay's tale of small grubby thieves and big respectable thieves into one about deception, double-dealing, entrapment, compromise, treachery, and universal surveillance. The programme aptly reprints a joke from Havel's Czechoslovakia: "Under capitalism, man exploits man, while under Communism it's the other way around." . . . For thief, read dissident. For underworld, read a resistance movement that has been penetrated by the police and is being manipulated until man is set against man, trust eroded, and even Macheath compromised. But Gay's pickpocket Filch improbably resists the tide. . . . [I]t's a reminder of bad times, a warning of future dangers and yet more proof that the Czech Republic's retiring president was and is a man to treasure.[39]

Michael Billington of the *Guardian* (Manchester) also commented on the value of a play that reminds us of the reality in which Havel wrote, showing us

> a world of spiralling mistrust in which nothing is what you think it is. . . . Havel works out his idea with a mathematical brilliance that puts you in mind of his fellow Czech playwright, Stoppard . . . you can understand why [Havel] regards this [play] as a favourite:

it is his most elaborate statement of the destructiveness of a world in which everyone is a potential informer.[40]

Charles Spencer of the *Daily Telegraph* praised the subtlety of Havel's satirical humor:

> What's remarkable about the play, however, considering Havel's constant harassment by the authorities, is the piece's tone. It is mockingly ironic rather than strident, full of delightful wit rather than bitterness. Havel is superb, too, on the way his characters attempt to justify their corrupt behaviour, as intent on deceiving themselves as well as others, while the increasingly complex plot is resolved with real élan.[41]

Reflecting on this period and the solidarity with Havel expressed by so many writers, Walters says: "All those plays were dedicated to Havel because he was beleaguered. Those writers felt an affinity for him, because he was not free and they were. It's worse than for a poet. Havel's plays were done, but he couldn't see them."[42] As for his theater's role, Walters adds:

> It was an exciting time. Not only were we introducing terrific new plays to the British public, but also we were involved in the politics of the moment and making a positive contribution. This was important. . . . We might not be able to change the world, but we can sometimes offer succour and hope and get inspiration in return. Not often does it fall to theater to feel so much a part of history.[43]

Critic Michael Billington acknowledges Walters's commitment: "If it weren't for Sam Walters, Havel's plays would have languished."[44] That can be said for Achim Benning and Joseph Papp, as well.

The commitment of the Public Theater, the Burgtheater, and the Orange Tree would not have been forthcoming without the deep affinity for Havel and his work felt by their artistic directors, all of whom have played significant roles in Václav Havel's life in the theater. They had convictions, both artistic and ethical ones; they had loyalty; they took risks. The dedication of the Public Theater to Havel's plays has already been documented. But there is a postscript.

While Joe Papp was dying in a New York hospital in 1991, Havel, who was in America at the time, made an attempt to visit him. But, according to Papp's widow, Gail, because of various reasons pertaining to security, the visit could not be arranged. On October 27, three days before Papp died, Havel talked with him on the telephone. Helen Epstein, Papp's biographer, quotes Havel's sentiments about their long-term friendship, which began on his first visit to New York in 1968:

> I was eternally grateful to Joe Papp, because it was my first and for a long time last visit to America, which I fell in love with. It was the time of the hippies, the student strikes and a thoroughly interesting election campaign. Thanks to him I saw *Hair* . . . Thanks to him I caught a glimpse of the atmosphere of those days. After that, I didn't see him for many years until he appeared in Czechoslovakia sometime in 1984 just in order to visit me.
>
> Despite the fact that we hadn't seen one another for so long, it seemed like we just started up where we had left off in our last conversation. We talked about many things — politics, spiritual things, cultural matters, theater. Then we met again when I was in America as a president on a state visit. He was a man who belonged to the same blood group as my own.[45]

Blood group. The sense of kinship, of being connected. As Miller put it: being "each other's continuation." Playwrights writing plays expressly for a fellow playwright. Artistic directors making steadfast commitments. No less than five theaters in four different countries devoted to one writer's work, putting themselves at risk, to sustain Havel's life in the theater.

Few, if any, playwrights in the twentieth century have had such solidarity expressed on their behalf. But then again, few have had the kind of life in the theater that Václav Havel has had.

above Havel and Edward Albee, Prague, 1986 (Jaroslav Kořan)

below Sam Walters, on the streets of Prague,
during the Velvet Revolution, 1989

❖❖ PART VII ❖❖
Curtain Call

I am just beginning to understand how everything has, in fact, been a diabolical trap set for me by destiny. Because I was really catapulted overnight into a world of fairy tales, and then, in the years that followed, had to return to earth, the better to realize that fairy tales are merely a projection of human archetypes and that the world is not at all structured like a fairy tale.[1]

— Havel, "A Farewell to Politics"

ENCORE

In September 2002, Václav Havel made his last official visit to America in his capacity as president of the Czech Republic.

At an award ceremony at CUNY, he gave a moving farewell speech to an audience of admirers and friends. In it, he spoke ironically about the fairy-tale quality that has sometimes been ascribed to his life in politics.

His life in the theater can hardly be called a fairy tale, either. It has a storylike quality, though, as has already been noted. Once more, in summary . . .

A while ago, there was an era called the 1960s. A new playwright of promise comes of age in a country under a severe Socialist rule, a country that is now experiencing a brief and precious period of cultural liberation. A small theater invites him to call it his home. Emboldened by the scent of freedom in the air throughout his stifled society, he writes three new full-length plays (*The Garden Party, The Memorandum, The Increased Difficulty of Concentration*). For the first time, these plays hold "the mirror up to nature" (*Hamlet*, III, ii) and show people the truth of how they were living. He soon becomes the most celebrated playwright in the land. But then hostile foreign tanks invade, rolling right past his little

Curtain call at the Balustrade, after the Czech premiere of *Temptation*, 1991
(Alan Pajer)

theater into the square of his town and taking away the freedoms that he and his culture were celebrating. His life in the theater goes dark; a curtain of silence descends.

Then come the 1970s. A young playwright is ostracized from his society. Once the toast of his town, his works are forbidden. The doors to the theater he once called home are locked to him. Alone, in isolation, he finds himself "at a crossroads," not knowing what direction to take. He experiments with form (*The Conspirators* and *Mountain Hotel*), but this exploration gives him little satisfaction. As a diversion, he adapts an existing classic (*The Beggar's Opera*), but the theater for whom he wrote it is afraid to produce it. Just for the fun of it, he dashes off a series of small one-act plays (*Audience, Vernissage, Protest*), which he reads for his friends in the safety of his own home. Gradually, unexpectedly, something happens. His friends rejoice over the one-act plays, and a whole new genre of short works (the Vaněk plays) is born. His neighbor gathers together a group of amateur actors who risk their lives and well-being to perform his adaptation (*The Beggar's Opera*). Without trying, without realizing it, he's found his "second wind." Yes, he lost one theater, but somehow he's found other ones — in the garden of his country house, or in a pub outside Prague where a company of dedicated amateurs just want to "put on their neighbor's play" and experience one moment of freedom. Inspired by that one forbidden moment, he speaks out for human rights. But then he is betrayed by his own country. He is arrested, tried, and imprisoned.

The 1980s follow. A playwright, confined to prison, is denied the right to write for three years and nine months. He is finally released, traumatized, exhausted. In a desperate state of crisis, he feverishly writes two plays (*Largo Desolato, Temptation*) directly affected by this experience, to express his bankrupt spiritual state. He hides the plays from the authorities, and they are smuggled out the country and performed in foreign lands in theaters he is forbidden to attend and in languages he does not understand. He is harassed by the police, and arrested again and again. Meanwhile, he senses that his country is on the threshold of change. He consolidates past themes with the present state of spiritual crisis (*Redevelopment*). Standing at this threshold, he reaches back into his country's past in order to predict its future (*Tomorrow, We'll Start It Up*). Then, unbelievably, the impossible happens. A political and theatrical miracle.

The theaters in his country become the rehearsal rooms for a revolution. And he is cast as his country's leading man.

Then come the 1990s. A playwright, now president, finds that all the world is his stage — including once more at home. The curtain rises on his plays all over the land. Soon, however, all his plays have been performed, and the number of their productions dwindle. The theaters in his land gradually loses their dynamism. Meanwhile, he has no time to write new plays to revitalize them. He is too busy performing a role in a larger theater.

It's now the first decade of the new millennium. The playwright is no longer president. Meanwhile, what about his plays? Will they last? What is their value as an oeuvre? And will he write new ones?

Seldom — if ever — has there been a playwright whose work has been so shaped by his time, and whose time in turn has been so shaped by his work. But that does not mean that Václav Havel's plays can be enjoyed by his countrymen alone, or that they will last only as long as the conditions under which they were written.

So the question remains. What about his plays? Will they live on?

A LEGACY

That, in fact, is the very question Havel was asking, with deep and poignant uncertainty, during that same speech in September 2002:

> The time is inexorably approaching when . . . the world . . . will start asking me what I have actually achieved . . . what I would like my legacy to be, and what kind of world I would like to leave behind me. And suddenly I feel that the very same spiritual and intellectual unease that once compelled me to stand up against the totalitarian regime and go to jail for it is now causing me to have such deep doubts about the value of my own work.[1]

A legacy. The same question may well apply to his life in the theater, too. Until now so much focus has been placed on Havel's contribution to his nation's history and to world politics that there has been little consideration of his body of dramatic work — what it has meant and what it will mean in the future.

As Anna Freimanová, Andrej Krob's wife, points out in her introduction to *Dear Václav . . . Yours Truly* (Milý Václave . . . Tvůj, 1997), a
collection of essays from theater friends and others on the occasion of
Havel's sixtieth birthday:

> One cannot be satisfied with what has been written and published
> about Havel and his [dramatic] work so far. One obvious reason for
> this is the fact that Havel's works could not be openly discussed in
> his home country for so many years. . . . And the interest abroad in
> Havel as a human rights activist was stronger than the interest in his
> dramatic work.[2]

Freimanová is accurate in her observation. Until the Velvet Revolution, official critical writings of Havel's plays were nonexistent in his country. After all, his works were banned. Meanwhile, Western writers were
focusing on the political rather than the literary drama. Thanks to a few
dedicated scholars, however, most notably Marketa Goetz-Stankiewicz, a
Czech emigré (now professor emerita of Germanic studies and comparative literature at the University of British Columbia), attention was paid to
Havel's evolving dramaturgy outside Czechoslovakia throughout the
1980s. There is a chapter devoted to Havel's plays in her study *The Silenced Theatre: Czech Playwrights Without a Stage* (1979), and an illuminating and comprehensive introduction to her collection *The Vaněk Plays:
Four Authors, One Character* (1985). There is also her introduction to
Drama Contemporary: Czechoslovakia (1985), a collection of plays by
banned Czech playwrights of the 1970s. Translators Vera Blackwell, Jan
Novák, James Saunders, George Theiner, Marie Winn, and others, including adaptor Tom Stoppard, have brought Havel's plays to a grateful
English-speaking audience. Paul Wilson's fine translations of the autobiographical *Disturbing the Peace, Letters to Olga*, and selected essays have illuminated a significant portion of Havel's writings about the theater.

After the revolution and during the 1990s, the drama of his ascent to
the presidency once again eclipsed the drama on the page. But by the end
of the decade, perhaps in anticipation of the end of Havel's presidency,
scholarship has slowly been mobilizing to address the question of his dramatic legacy. In 1999, Marketa Goetz-Stankiewicz compiled a collection
entitled *Critical Essays on Václav Havel*, containing twenty-three essays on
various aspects of Havel's political life and writings, including seven in-

sightful ones on his plays. In 1998, an international conference on the subject of Havel's plays was held in Brno, in recognition of Havel's receipt of the Compostela Prize the year before for his contribution as a dramatist. The main contributions to this conference — fifteen critical papers by European scholars — were published in 2001 in a collection entitled *Václav Havel as a Dramatist.* Havel was more than delighted; he was surprised. In the preface, he wrote:

> By means of my plays I have been thinking aloud about the world and myself. . . . Of course, I wanted to provoke a bit, too, and disturb the "circles" of the then totalitarian structures; yet, first of all, I have wished to entertain my audience, friends and myself. If these plays after fifteen, twenty, or even thirty years of their existence and nonexistence on the stage still inspire so many analyses and literary-critical contemplations, it is my great pleasure.[3]

Then in 2001, a new translation by Paul Wilson of *The Beggar's Opera* was published, with an informative foreword by Peter Steiner.

So now his plays are beginning to be discussed in the context of his complete dramatic oeuvre and will be increasingly, now that the curtain has fallen on his presidency. Some critics say that Havel's exit might even spark a revival of Havelmania. After all, politically, Havel has been center stage in his country for decades. If he cannot be on the stage any more himself, perhaps his plays can.

What, then, is Havel's legacy to the theater and to dramatic literature? And what is its meaning, its value?

Havel's legacy is a significant body of dramatic work: ten full-length plays and five one-acts plays, plus one teleplay, one radio play, and four coauthored cabaret plays. It is an arresting dramatic oeuvre for a number of reasons.

One: it tells an evolving story of man's struggle to survive under totalitarianism in a society that happened to be Socialist and also happened to be Czech, but could indeed be any society in which there is repression and inhumanity. As such, its unifying themes transcend the time and place in which the plays are set. Indeed, they are universal to human existence in a social context.

Two: it has its own original and distinctive system of "poetics," as Havel is fond of calling it.

Three: it gives us a number of remarkable character portrayals, especially one who lives on, uniquely, outside his creator's work.

Four: it the work of a writer who had an innate sense of his country's destiny and his place in it. As a result, the dramatic oeuvre has played a unique role in shaping that country's destiny.

A Theme

> All my plays, as I have said several times already, deal in one way or another with the theme of human identity and the state of crisis in which it finds itself.[4]
>
> — Havel, *Letters to Olga*

Over and over, in his essays, his letters, and his articles about the theater, Havel declares that his unifying theme of his plays is that of human identity.

In the 1960s, Havel wrote of "man in the system," and the resulting identity crisis. The system? Bureaucracy, the institution, the nameless, faceless organization that slowly erases a man's identity to the point where he no longer recognizes himself, where even his own parents don't recognize him (*The Garden Party*). In the bureaucratic prison, all aspects of life are dehumanizing, like the irrational language he is forced to speak (*The Memorandum*), like the mechanical private life he leads and the meaningless, repetitive cycle of relationships he maintains (*The Increased Difficulty of Concentration*). The dehumanization escalates to the point where a machine is installed in his private life in order to define his identity (*The Increased Difficulty of Concentration*).

In the 1970s, Havel wrote of "man in the system" and the resulting moral crisis. The system? Power structures. One example is in government (*The Conspirators*), where leaders destroy a democracy in the name of saving it, just to preserve their own positions of power. The individual is afraid to take responsibility for living in a democracy, which might mean relinquishing an illusive sense of power that to him is more precious than freedom. Another example is on "the street" (*The Beggar's Opera*), where a balance of power between commerce, law enforcement, and crime is maintained through an elaborate system of informing, collaboration, and betrayal. Yet another example is the relationship between a man in the system and a man outside it (the insider and the outsider), or the powerful and the powerless. The only way to maintain a semblance of morality is to live outside the system, in truth. But what happens when an attempt is made to draw a man back into the system (*Audience, Vernissage, Protest*)? Herein lies the conflict: Should a man collaborate, should a man conform, should a man inform, if it means saving his fellow man? What is his moral responsibility? To help his fellow man in the system, or to live in truth outside it? With the individual outside the system, in isolation, struggling to survive, these moral dilemmas are irreconcilable. How can he maintain his identity?

In the 1980s, Havel wrote of "man in the system" and the resulting spiritual crisis. The system? Prison — the threat of it, the reality of it — and its effect on the human soul. Fear of imprisonment drives a man to a state of paranoia and dysfunction (*Largo Desolato*), to the point that he begs for prison as a release from the spiritual void in which he finds himself confined. Indeed, any attempt to avoid imprisonment by bargaining with the powers that be (*Temptation*) only damages man's soul worse than prison itself. Meanwhile, fear and mistrust of the future in the hands of those who control the system (*Redevelopment*) causes man to lose hope altogether and drives him into the dungeon (prison, again) or to suicide. The choice? To live with the devil you know, or not to live at all.

Decade by decade, paralleling his country's political evolution, Havel's plays tell the story of the human condition under totalitarianism. Whether set in a faceless institution, an organization, a nameless country, a scientific institute, or a castle, Havel's characters are caught up in a mechanized, dehumanized system where their identity is at stake. To survive in the system, they play both sides, like Hugo Pludek in *The Garden Party*, the man who plays chess against himself. That's safe because one side always wins. On the other hand, one side always loses. Like Gross in *The Memorandum*, who keeps his job as director of the institute, he survives only by instituting yet another indecipherable, inhuman anti-language that he himself cannot speak. And when they refuse, like Vaněk, they live on the outside, isolated and static like Beckett characters in a spiritual void. Yes, they are moral, yes, they live in truth, but what is that truth worth?

Havel shares the theme of identity with his fellow playwrights in solidarity, Beckett, Stoppard, and Pinter. As critic Kenneth Tynan observed about them all, when he first saw a play by Havel in the 1960s:

The new playwrights share one grand theme that recurs throughout modern drama: How much of a man belongs to external authority, and how much to himself? Where do the legitimate demands of society begin to encroach intolerable on his selfhood? At what point must the individual say no?[5]

But Havel does not show compassion for man's dilemma. When it comes to human identity, he is uncompromising in his expectations. Speaking about his play *The Beggar's Opera* and its central theme, he said: "What is human identity? It is that you have the responsibility for what you did yesterday, what you do today, what you will do tomorrow. In modern times, man must struggle to earn his identity."[6]

Beyond the reality of Czechoslovakia under totalitarian rule, the themes of Václav Havel's plays will resonate on and on, to any audience in any culture that values its freedom. And the plays will remain as a reminder of just how precious these freedoms are, and what the price is of shirking one's responsibility to safeguard one's identity.

A Poetics

Secondly, Havel's body of work distinguishes itself by a distinct and original approach to the art and practice of playwriting. It's what he calls a system of poetics.

Havel is a playwright who sees the world of the theater with a sense of order. His is a systematized approach to dramatic writing, a ritualized one, if you will. This manifests itself in so many elements of his work. Multiple drafts for *The Garden Party* and *The Memorandum*. Charts and collages for *The Increased Difficulty of Concentration*. Commentaries for *The Increased Difficulty of Concentration*, *The Conspirators*, and *Mountain Hotel*. And essays like "The Power and the Powerless" and "Politics and Conscience," which serve as an *explication du texte* for many of them. As he himself describes his approach to playwriting:

> Before I start to write a play, I draw it. I make such drawings in which I decide the entire composition, the size of the scenes, and how the characters come and go. It is all in very strict order. I believe in architecture like that very much, because theater as a genre is based on rhythm and gradation.[7]

Havel's passion for order expressed itself in his repetitions — of scenes, dialogue, and phrases. He experimented with the collage technique he learned at the poet Kolář's table at the Café Slavia, cutting *The Increased Difficulty of Concentration* into thirty-three pieces and pasting them together in nonchronological order to reflect the fragmentation and illogic of Eduard Huml's life. He experimented with the repetition of scenes and dialogue in *Mountain Hotel*; he changed the characters' personae, too, to express the loss of identity and the meaningless of existence. He ended his plays just as he began them, with the repetition of their first scenes (*The Increased Difficulty of Concentration, Audience, Vernissage*) to show the absence of forward motion in the static society in which he found himself trapped. As he explained it: "The principle of repetition has enormous value, in my opinion, because it uncovers yet more meanings. I think that if you repeat sentences in the right combinations you can send a message to the world."[8]

The most distinctive feature of Havel's poetics is his use of dramatic language. To use Jan Grossman's phrase about *The Garden Party*, language is a "main character" in Havel's plays. Whether the distorted proverbs that Hugo's parents speak and the garbled clichés of *The Garden Party*, the indecipherable language of Ptydepe in *The Memorandum*, the inane phrases that changing characters in *Mountain Hotel* hurl at each other, the political jargon in *The Conspirators,* or the meaningless repetitions in *The Increased Difficulty of Concentration*, language in Havel's plays is not language. It loses its basic purpose, communication. After all, if language is nonsensical, there is nothing to communicate, because people will neither say anything nor understand one another. Furthermore, since language is the vessel of tradition and wisdom, when it is distorted to the point of nonsense, so are the traditional values of a culture.[9] Hence, the culture loses its identity, too.

The epitome of Havel's use of language as a main character is in *The Memorandum*, where a made-up language takes over the entire reality of the play. Based on a rational set of laws, it becomes an antilanguage, an irrational force. No one speaks it, no one understands it, and yet it rules. And when it is phased out, because no human can speak it, it is simply replaced by another incomprehensible language.

What, then, has language become, in the world of Havel's plays? It is a system in and of itself, a dehumanizing power, a weapon, a controlling force, a lie. People do not control language; language controls people.

"We live in an age of deformity," Edward Albee wrote in his play *The American Dream* (1959),[10] just a few years before Havel wrote *The Garden Party* and *The Memorandum*. In Havel's plays, the deformation of language dramatizes just that.

Havel's system of poetics is highly individualistic. A philosopher, essayist, poet, and humanist as well as a dramatist, he brings together all those sensibilities and ways of viewing the world when he writes a play. The result is an original, quirky combination of the visual, the theoretical, the intellectual, the philosophical — and the heartfelt. As he said recently in an address to the Academy of Performing Arts in Prague:

> The world as the experience of a structured environment has an inherent dramatic dimension, and theater is actually an expression of our desire for a concise way of seizing this dramatic element. A play of no more than two hours always presents, or is meant to present, a picture of the whole world and attempts to say something about it.[11]

But a system of poetics must have a higher purpose than itself, Havel observes. Quite simply, it helped him say what he wanted to say, in theatrical terms. In a letter to Olga, he wrote:

> If, for example, conventions and structures are characteristic of my plays (e.g., the mechanical and geometric patterns that occur in the dialogue), then this was only because I was attempting, through them and against the backdrop they provided, to give dramatic shape to a particular question, surprise, mystery or shock — either by developing those patterns ad absurdum or, on the contrary, by gradually breaking them down. In any case, I've often said that where everything is permitted, nothing can surprise, that conventions can only be challenged or broken down when they already exist. . . . I don't suppose I'm explaining this very well, though perhaps what I'm trying to say is clear: that there's simply no order like order."[12]

Perhaps this need for a system of poetics reflects Havel's sense of urgency about the crisis of human identity and a conviction that a solution can be found if a kind of order (as he calls it) is imposed upon the "two hours' traffic" on the stage. At the same time, Havel counterbalances this dramaturgical order with a spontaneous element — an original wit and humor, which are so fresh and so surprising that the effect is ultimately liberating. It is as if Havel is showing us, in the theater, that humor and satire are man's weapons against a dehumanizing system, and that somehow they will set him free.

A Hero

Thirdly, Havel's dramatic oeuvre further distinguishes itself by presenting us with a number of remarkable character portrayals, including one who is unique.

About the world of his plays, Havel has said: "I have always tried to inhabit it simply by humans."[13] By that, he means that his characters are ordinary people. At the same time, he insists, they are not heroes. On that point he is clear.

Recently, in a conversation with Havel, the word *hero* was used in reference to Vaněk, the silent protagonist of three of his plays of the 1970s (*Audience*, *Vernissage*, and *Protest*). The playwright winced. "Vaněk, a hero?" he replied. "I suppose that, in contrast to all the 'low lifes' around him, one might think so."[14]

His harsh choice of words may have been a reflection of the playwright's own frustration and disappointment. After all, how could Vaněk, a dissident, be called a hero? According to the classical definition, a hero is a man of action. How could a bunch of dissidents — banned, silenced, resorting to driving trains, stoking furnaces, hauling garbage, or rolling barrels of beer — be perceived as men of action? All they could have done, all they did do, was to write.

So if Vaněk, in Havel's opinion, does not qualify as a hero, who are his nonheroes? What is their identity? Take Hugo Pludek of *The Garden Party*, for example. Critics have commonly referred to him as an "everyman," although in his case, "any man" might be more apt. Pludek is a nonperson, an anonym, a fellow who lacks an identity to the extent that he plays chess against himself, a fellow whose answer to the question "Who are you?" is "I don't like that one-sided question." Why should he commit himself? He can be anyone — and prefers to be, for that is how he adapts to his surroundings and survives. And not only does he survive, he also succeeds. He climbs up the organizational ladder, not necessarily because he wanted to, but because his parents threw him out of the house. Then he adapts; he shows them he can succeed at what they want him to become, which is absolutely unrecognizable to himself as well as to them.

Gross of *The Memorandum* could be "any man," too, since he sacrifices language — the crucial expression of one's identity — to maintain his position in the system. Yes, he fights Ptydepe, but he will institute Chorukor in the end if he must, in order to survive. In other words, he is a man who (literally) speaks out of both sides of his mouth, a man who will say anything in any language, even an incomprehensible one, to keep his position. Macheath, like Gross, plays both sides (actually three sides, Peachum's, Lockit's, and his own) to maintain his position of power. The ironic implication of all three men's choices — Pludek's, Gross's, and Macheath's — is: given the circumstances, well, wouldn't any man?

Then there is Eduard Huml, the social scientist in *The Increased Difficulty of Concentration*, and Leopold Kopřiva, the professor of philosophy in *Largo Desolato*. Both appear to be contemporary spin-offs of the "superfluous man,"[15] that nineteenth-century Russian antihero who, while educated, intellectual, articulate and sensitive, is unable to act, partly because of personal weakness, partly because of political and social constraints. The main characteristic that Huml and Kopřiva, both men of intellect, share is that they do not act, although Kopřiva actually does act, at the end, when he begs to be dragged off to prison. They are agoraphobics, never leaving their living rooms, clad always in their dressing gowns; they maintain multiple love relationships; they live in continual spiritual crisis. Above all, they do not act; they simply repeat the cyclical patterns of their meaningless existence.

"Some hero . . . some hero . . . some hero . . . some hero . . ."[16] So goes the choric chant, ironic and accusatory, in Tom Stoppard's version of *Largo Desolato*. Clearly, Kopřiva's creator thinks he is not. No, anonyms and superfluous men hardly qualify as heroes.

Speaking of heroes, let us once more return then to Vaněk, and what Havel said recently about him in that conversation provoked by the mention of the word:

> That fellow Vaněk, in my view, is such a muddler, that if indeed he appears to some to be a hero, then that just says something about his surroundings and the people in them, who are so hopelessly narrow minded and unenlightened.[17]

What are Vaněk's qualities? He is modest, polite, deferential, non-confrontational, undemanding, apologetic, self-effacing, self-deprecating. Above all, he is silent—an irony, since he is a playwright. While others— the brewmaster Sládek, the upwardly mobile couple Věra and Michael, the establishment writer Staněk — drone on and on about their lives, their passions and their personal crises, Vaněk simply remains silent. When he does reply, his answers are monosyllabic, elliptical, inarticulate, sotto voce.

It's a challenging role. As Jiří Ornest of the Balustrade, who played Vaněk in *Vernissage*, describes him: "For me, Vaněk is the one unplayable part of Havel's plays. He's always honest, he has no good jokes, he's modest, shy, and he speaks in one-word sentences. For any normal actor, Vaněk is just too good. Now Sládek, the brewmaster, that's a fantastic part."[18]

Although Vaněk does not act, his inaction defines him. In *Audience*, he refuses to inform on himself or anyone else, thereby forfeiting his promotion. In *Vernissage*, he refuses to sacrifice his principles for personal gain, thereby maintaining his impoverished lifestyle. In *Protest*, he refuses to impose his views on Staněk or to press him to sign his petition, thereby weakening his own cause. No, Vaněk cannot act, Vaněk can only remain silent. He can only "be."

Silence and inaction. These qualities may have disqualified the categorization of Vaněk as a hero by classical standards — hence Havel's protestations. But under those circumstances, aren't these qualities heroic? While Havel may dismiss Vaněk as a hero, still, he regards him as not just an ordinary character. He's something more. Havel explored Vaněk's identity in his essay "Light on a Landscape:"

> Vaněk is really not so much a concrete person as something of a dramatic principle: he does not usually do or say much, but his presence on stage and his being what he is make his environment expose itself one way or another. He does not admonish anyone in particular; indeed, he demands hardly anything of anyone. And in spite of this, his environment perceives him as an invocation somehow to declare and justify itself. He is, then, a kind of "key," opening certain — always different — vistas onto the world in which he lives: a kind of catalyst, a gleam if you will, in whose light we view a landscape. And although without it we should scarcely be able to see anything at all, it is not the gleam that matters, but the landscape.

The Vaněk plays, therefore, are essentially not plays about Vaněk, but plays about the world as it reveals itself when confronted with Vaněk.[19]

If Vaněk is "a light on a landscape," as Havel calls him, then he is also remarkable in another way. He could not be confined to his creator's oeuvre alone. Vaněk came alive, traveling as if at will from the play of one author to the next. In this regard, the borrowing of Vaněk by other authors is, as Goetz-Stankiewicz calls it, "truly an uncommon, if not a unique, occurrence in modern theater."[20]

As such, Vaněk is an enduring representation of the so-called dissident, a man Havel defines in the essay "The Power of the Powerless" as one who lives within the truth, a thinking individual who writes and/or speaks out publicly against injustices in his society to the extent that he is identified as a threat to the establishment and who ultimately becomes engaged in political activism whether he likes it or not. While the role of the activist is one that the dissident has not sought out initially, he plays it nonetheless — and, ironically, he soon is regarded by his compatriots, by the public, and by the press abroad more as an activist as a writer.[21]

For Havel, dissidence is ultimately a state of being, which motivates an individual to live in truth, to speak out and to write according to his conscience and his inner convictions, regardless of the consequences. How fortunate we are to have Vaněk as his dramatic personification.

Perhaps the need for a Vaněk is gone, at least for now, in our part of the world, but he lives on as a vital reminder that a writer must never be silenced. If that would ever occur again — who knows? — Vaněk could potentially walk the stage once more, as a warning. When asked today if he'd write another Vaněk play again, Havel replied, briefly, in Vaněk-like fashion: "Well, of course, it's possible."[22]

There is a final point on which the playwright is clear — indeed, emphatic: Vaněk is not Havel. As he states in his essay, "Light on a Landscape":

> It might, above all, be appropriate to emphasize that Vaněk is not Havel. Of course, I have transferred into this character certain of my own experiences, and I have done so more distinctly than is usual among writers. Undoubtedly, I have also implanted in him a number of my personal traits or, more precisely, presented a num-

ber of perspectives from which I see myself in various situations. But all of this does not mean that Vaněk is intended as a self-portrait. A real person and a dramatic character are entirely different things. The dramatic character is more or less always a fiction, an invention, a trick, an abbreviation consisting only of a limited number of utterances, and subordinated to the concrete "world of the play" and its meaning. In comparison with any living persons, even the most enigmatic and psychologically most rounded character is hopelessly inadequate and simplistic. On the other hand, however, he should also exude something a real person cannot possibly possess: the ability always to say something perspicuous and essential about "the world as it is" — all within the context of a few lines of dialogue and the few situations that make up his entire being.[23]

Or, as Havel said in an interview:

The character of Vaněk is a medium or a mirror through which we obeserve the world, who makes people around him reveal themselves. He's not a certain type of personality — he's an element of a principle, like Schweik, although Schweik is of course a completely different character from Vaněk. But he too serves as a medium through whom we observe the world. Although Vaněk is not an autobiographical character, a part of my personal experience is reflected there because — and it's happened to me a million times — people of whom I asked no questions at all felt compelled to explain things to me — for example, why they signed the Anti-Charter or why they informed on me.[24]

Some would disagree on this issue, however. Havel's fellow playwright Pavel Kohout, for one, does so, and forcefully: "What is the essence of Vaněk? Havel. And the essence of Havel?"[25] That essence, says Kohout, is hard to describe:

Omnipotent authority is faced with a shy, polite, even obliging intellectual of a visibly nonathletic cast. . . . But when authority enters, this man does not rant and rave: he neither quarrels nor exchanges blows: he does not even lie. At the most, he is silent, if truth might hurt someone other than himself. When authority displays its candies of all flavours and whips of all sizes, it at first misses his quiet "No," and when it finally hears it, it does not believe. It shows him its instruments; it uses them. . . . Ferdinand Vaněk has inherited his disposition.[26]

A dramatic device, a light on a landscape, a medium, a mirror. "Some hero," indeed. Could this leitmotif throughout Havel's writing reflect some deep disappointment not only in his characters, but in himself? Despite his protestations, despite his circumspection, there seems to be a profoundly felt hope, a great expectation on Havel's part that someone, somehow, might have saved the day. How ironic it is that Havel didn't see that, for those who attended his farewell in New York in 2003, the person who has saved the day is the one they came to honor.

It will be difficult for anyone ever to call Vaněk a hero unless his creator will one day tolerate being called one, too.

A "Bioliterary" Sense

Havel also leaves us a body of work deeply connected to his times.

They say it over and over again, the Czechs who lived through those decades and saw Havel's plays — whether they saw them in theaters, in living rooms, in gardens of neighbor's houses, or heard them on cassette recordings smuggled from house to house, hand to hand. It's the same remark as Hamlet's to the Players about the theater, "whose purpose is, as 'twere, to hold a mirror up to nature."[27]

Andrej Krob puts it succinctly: "Havel's plays are full of wisdom. They are connected to the reality we live in and to those things we experience every day but cannot articulate. These plays do it for us and help us understand the world around us."[28]

So does Miloš Forman: "Václav Havel's plays are the most significant mirror of the times we have. They reflect both its tragedy and its absurdities with wit and humor."[29]

It is Havel's sense of his country and his place in it that makes his body of work so valuable a legacy. For Havel's plays have both reflected his country's reality and prophesized its future. Moreover, they have served as a catalyst for change. Indeed, they have helped to shape his nation's destiny.

Such an innate sense of the history and destiny of one's country is rare; so is the passion and the feeling of responsibility to express it. Havel calls it his "bioliterary" sense. As he said in his essay "Second Wind," written in 1976:

> The fortunate way in which my own "bioliterary" time meshed with the historical time gave me another tremendous advantage: my early beginnings as a playwright coincided with the 1960s, a remarkable and relatively favorable era in which my plays, despite being so different from what had been permitted until then, could actually reach the stage, something that would have been impossible both before and after that. It was not just the formal fact that my plays were permitted; there was something deeper and more essential here: that society was capable of accepting them, that they resonated with the general state of mind, that the intellectual and social climate of the time, open to new self-knowledge and hungry for it, not only tolerated them, but — if I may say so — actually wanted them. And of course every such act of social self-awareness — that is, every genuine and profound acceptance of a new work, identification with it, and the integration of it into the spiritual reality of the time — immediately and inevitably opens the way for even more radical acts. With each new work, the possibilities of the repressive system were weakened; the more we were able to do, the more we did, and the more we did, the more we were able to do. It was a state of accelerated metabolism between art and its time, and it is always inspiring and productive for phenomena as social as theater.[30]

Havel was both with his times and ahead of them. Just as his country felt itself becoming freer in the 1960s, so did Havel feel he could write without inhibition. Just as his country found itself at a political crossroads in 1970, so did Havel find himself at a crossroads as a playwright where he got a "second wind" that provoked a storm and changed his country's course. Just as his country dragged itself through the 1980s in a spiritual void, so was Havel able to endure and to write. Just as the tides began to turn in the late 1980s, so did Havel prophesize the future, from the stage.

A playwright — his life, his plays, his theater, his country, his times. One can't speak of one without referring to the other. There are few playwrights whose private, public, and artistic lives were so deeply intertwined. As Helena Albertová, curator of the Theatre Institute's international literary exhibition on Havel's work, has written:

It seems as if the age in which Václav Havel was born shaped his artistic and human paths. Rare are those who succeeded, like Václav Havel, to mark their time with their lives and with their dramatic and literary creativity.[31]

A PLACE IN TWENTIETH-CENTURY DRAMA

Influences, comparison, categorizations, literary traditions, trends. When it comes to placing Havel's oeuvre in twentieth-century drama, once again, it's a question of identity. What should we call Havel's plays? That's almost as complex a question as asking what should we call Václav Havel.

Influences

From the moment they first saw a Havel play onstage that unforgettable December night in 1963 when *The Garden Party* opened at the Balustrade, they knew, audience and critics alike, that here was something new. Then in 1965 when *The Memorandum* opened, there was no question. Here was a unique voice. The question was: how to place it?

Enter the Western critics, who at first tried to discuss the plays in the context of the Czech tradition. Kenneth Tynan, who visited Prague in 1967 and saw those two plays at the Balustrade, wrote about the strong tradition of Czech writers from which Havel emerged, acknowledging that it has some striking characteristics that set it apart from the Western tradition:

> In one sense he was a traditional Czech writer. Using a technique that derived from Kafka, Čapek, and countless Central European authors before them, he expressed his view of the world in nonrealistic parables. His plays were distorting mirrors in which one recognized the truth. . . . Stoppard belongs in precisely the same tradition, of which there is no Anglo-Saxon equivalent.[1]

American critic Harold Clurman, who saw *The Memorandum* at the Public in 1968, was also struck by Havel's Czech influences.

> His play *The Memorandum* is to some extent in the vein of Franz Kafka's novels and short stories. To most of us Kafka represents the

key figure in the literature of latter-day alienation. We associate him
with a certain horror. But Kafka thought his work funny and it
makes the Czechs laugh. *The Memorandum* [is] a comedy which
tickles the Czechs as farce . . . [2]

Martin Esslin, whose definitive study *The Theatre of the Absurd* was
originally published in 1961, agreed. In fact, he updated the second edition (1968) to include mention of Havel's plays and their Czech influences, describing *The Garden Party* as a "mixture of hard-hitting political
satire, Schweikian humour and Kafkaesque depths which are highly characteristic of Havel's work."[3] A few years later, in his introduction to *Three
Eastern European Plays*, Esslin commented in the same vein: "Franz Kafka
and Jaroslav Hašek, two seemingly irreconcilable worlds of brooding,
metaphysical anguish on the one hand and of genial low-life clowning on
the other, seem strangely fused in Havel's plays."[4]

Havel readily acknowledges his Czech influences, including the playwright Čapek and the novelist Hašek. In the instance of Čapek, his
themes of bureaucracy and technology versus humanism are clear precur-
sors to Havel's own. The robot in Čapek's play *RUR* (1921) comes readily to mind when one meets Puzuk, the talking computer in *The Increased
Difficulty of Concentration*. As for Hašek's novel *The Good Soldier Schweik*
(1922), his protagonist of the same name is considered an archetype of
Czech literature, a resourceful rogue who fools the authorities into thinking he is cooperating, a cunning survivor as well as a subversive. Havel's
Vaněk, a new Czech archetype, offers another form of protest, this time
in the persona of the dissident, who, unlike Schweik, works from the outside rather than from within. While Schweik and Vaněk are markedly different in their tactics, as Havel himself puts it, both are "a medium
through whom we observe the world."[5]

Yes, Čapek's robot and Hašek's Schweik were part of Havel's cultural
heritage. In fact, they have made an international contribution; the Czech
words *robot* and *Schweikian* are part of our vocabulary today. But for
Havel, the fundamental Czech influence is Kafka, whose works he read
eagerly in unpublished translation around the table at the Café Slavia in
the 1950s. Havel acknowledges Kafka's influence throughout his writings,
but nowhere as personally and pointedly as in an address given at the Hebrew University in Jerusalem on April 26, 1990, four months after he

became president. There, he offered a tribute to Kafka and to the kinship he feels for Kafka's work.

I'm not an expert on Kafka, and I'm not eager to read the secondary literature on him. I can't even say that I've read everything Kafka has written. I do, however, have a rather special reason for my indifference to Kafka studies: I sometimes feel that I'm the only one who really understands Kafka, and that no one else has any business trying to make his work more accessible to me. And my somewhat desultory attitude to studying his works comes from my vague feeling that I don't need to read and reread everything Kafka has written because I already know what's there. I'm even secretly persuaded that, if Kafka did not exist, and if I were a better writer than I am, I would have written his works myself.

What I've just said may sound odd, but I'm sure you understand what I mean. All I'm really saying is that in Kafka I have found a large portion of my own experience of the world, of myself, and of my way of being in the world. I will try, briefly and in broad terms, to name some of the more easily defined forms of this experience.

One of them is a profound, banal, and therefore utterly vague sensation of culpability, as though my very existence were a kind of sin. Then there is a powerful feeling of general alienation, both my own and one that relates to everything around me that helps to create such feelings; an experience of unbearable oppressivenesss, a need constantly to explain myself to someone, to defend myself, a longing for an unattainable order of things. . . .

I can already hear your objections — that I style myself in these Kafkaesque outlines only because in reality I'm entirely different: someone who quietly and persistently fights for something, someone whose idealism has carried him to the head of his nation. . . .

I would only that add that, in my opinion, the hidden motor driving all my dogged efforts is precisely this innermost feeling of being excluded, of belonging nowhere, a state of disinheritance, of fundamental nonbelonging.[6]

What is the source of this keen sense of kinship with Kafka? In his speech, Havel indicates that he and Kafka are soulmates in at least three respects.

One, they share a feeling of being "outsiders" — Kafka, the frail, ascetic Jew writing in German in the Czech culture; Havel, the chubby, pampered bourgeois youth in a Communist society. Both felt themselves alien in their cultures, even in their own skins. To the "outsider" like Kafka and Havel, the world is a menacing place. This is reflected in both their writings, wherein even the ordinary is pervaded with a sense of the unknown: the nameless Institution, the faceless Man at the Door, the anonymous One in Charge (behind whom there is always Another). Whether the story takes place in an office or in a castle (as it does in both Kafka and Havel) or in an institute, there is a sense of being watched, of being in some kind of undefined peril.

Two, as outsiders, they share a preoccupation with identity. As Havel has said over and over, human identity is the unifying theme of all his plays. It is of primary concern to Kafka, too, who once wrote about his Jewish heritage: "What have I in common with Jews? I have hardly anything in common with myself and should stand very quietly in a corner, content that I can breathe."[7] Where is there a more vivid expression of anguish over one's identity than in the case of Gregor Samsa, who awakens one morning in Kafka's short story "Metamorphosis" to find that he has become a cockroach? The idea of metamorphosis is also dramatized by Havel; consider the character of Hugo Pludek in *The Garden Party*, the man who can morph into being any man to anyone. The threat of alienation from oneself, so acute in Kafka's writings, is also felt by Leopold Kopřiva in *Largo Desolato*, the paranoid dissident who protests: "If I understand you correctly, you want me to declare that I am no longer me . . ."[8]

Three, Havel and Kafka share a vague and profoundly unsettling sense of guilt, a sense of being to blame, of being responsible for everything around them. They even shared the sense of being "on trial" for it. As Havel told a surprised audience in Jerusalem, six months after he became president:

> I would even venture to say that everything worthwhile I've ever accomplished has been done to conceal my almost metaphysical feeling of guilt. The real reason I am always creating something, organizing something, it would seem, is to defend my permanently questionable right to exist. . . .
>
> I am the kind of person who would not be in the least surprised if, in the very middle of my presidency, I were summoned and led off to stand trial before some shadowy tribunal, or taken straight to

a quarry to break rocks. Nor would I be surprised if I were suddenly to hear the reveille and wake up in my prison cell, and then, with great bemusement, proceed to tell my fellow prisoners everything that I had dreamed had happened to me in the past six months. The lower I am, the more proper my place seems, and the higher I am, the stronger my suspicion is that there has ben some mistake.[9]

That undefinable feeling of culpability, so insidious in Kafka's *The Trial* and *The Castle*, is keenly felt by Havel's dissident characters Vaněk and Leopold Kopřiva, too. Like Kafka, Havel was haunted by this pervasive, personal sense of guilt throughout his life. It was a great burden to him, and his plays provided an outlet in which to express it. These critical assessments of Czech influences were readily confirmed by the playwright himself. But even in the early days, both Tynan and Esslin already sensed that there was something more in Havel's work — an exotic hybrid of influences. And indeed, there were. From his earliest days of playwriting, Havel has indicated that the writers who affected him most were Beckett and Ionesco. As he wrote in a letter to Olga:

> It was also by accident that . . . I had discovered the dramatic world of Samuel Beckett, Eugene Ionesco and other more or less "absurd" playwrights. I was tremendously excited, inspired and drawn to them, or rather I found them extremely close to my own temperament and sensibility, and it was they who stimulated me to try to communicate everything I wanted to say through drama.[10]

In Havel's fascination with dramatic structure, one can see the influences of Beckett, whose notion of dramaturgy was so revolutionary in the 1950s. "Form is content, content is form. Writing is not about something, it is something," Beckett wrote.[11] In Havel's system of poetics, with its meaningless repetitions, nonsensical dialogues, and cyclical patterns in which endings are beginnings, one sees a demonstration of Beckett's principle. And in Havel's questioning of human identity, one finds a personal expression of existential anguish that was akin to Beckett's own. Like Vladimir and Estragon in *Waiting for Godot*, Havel's Leopold Kopřiva and Vaněk live in uncertainty. And they wait.

With respect to Ionesco, Milan Kundera wrote about his special impact on young Czech writers, including Havel and himself, in the late 1950s:

No contemporary foreign writer had for us at that time such a liberating sense as Ionesco. We were suffocating under art conceived as educational, moral or political. *The Bald Soprano, The Chairs, L'avenir est dans les oeufs* — all these plays fascinated us by their radically anti-ideological nature. They returned autonomy to art and beckoned it to take again the path of freedom and creativity.[12]

Havel confirms that it was not a matter of imitation, but rather an awakening of his own aesthetic: "I was struck by Ionesco — reading him, there was a sudden touch of something that I found very close to my heart."[13]

Havel was delighted by Ionesco's devilish use of language. He also saw what an effective a dramatic device it was. As Ionesco demonstrated, it can provide supreme entertainment and at the same time a warning that language, like power, in the hands (or mouths) of those who abuse it, can become dangerous. This notion of language struck a strong chord in Havel, who set out to illustrate it his own plays. Language can be used to distort the truth, like the perverted proverbs in Ionesco's *The Bald Soprano* and Havel's *The Garden Party*. Language can be used as a weapon, in the hands of those like the murderous Professor in Ionesco's *The Lesson* or the menacing Professor of Ptydepe in Havel's *The Memorandum*. When the principles of language become irrational, as they do in the case of the mythical language "neo-Spanishe" in *The Lesson* or the nonsensical language Ptydepe in *The Memorandum*, then those principles reflect the irrational tyranny of who are imposing it. When language spins out of control, as in the ending of *The Bald Soprano* and *The Memorandum*, so does reality. Finally, when language fails altogether, as it does in the gibberish of the inarticulate Orator at the end of *The Chairs*, or in the classroom of *The Memorandum* where one language that no one can speak (Ptydepe) is simply replaced by another that is equally useless (Chorukor), the vision is apocalyptic. Language becomes antilanguage, and the systems in which it is used become antihuman.

Speaking again of the influence of Ionesco, Kundera is quick to emphasize:

> One cannot conceive of Havel without the example of Ionesco, yet he is not an epigone (meaning a disciple or an imitator). His plays are an original and irreplaceable development within what is called the "Theatre of the Absurd."[14]

Through this wonderful and colorful concoction of influences — predominantly Kafka's and Ionesco's — Havel speaks in his own distinct dramatist's voice. It is utterly fresh and original. How to describe it? Try "tragical-comical-historical-pastoral," then add "satirical-philosophical." It is hilarious and harrowing, entertaining and unsettling, quirky and cunning, with an absurdity and a truth all its own. One might also call it Havelian.

Categories and Comparisons

In her introduction to *Critical Essays on Václav Havel*, Professor Goetz-Stankewiez points out that Havel's plays have been most frequently described as either theater of the absurd or political theater. She and other scholars agree, however, that to attempt to categorize Havel is to miss the point of his work.[15]

In this regard, the playwright himself can help us. Havel has words of insight to offer on the theater of the absurd and political theater, words that challenge existing usage of these terms, illuminate the pitfalls of categorization, and at the same time enlighten us on the terms themselves and their applicability to his work.

Theater of the Absurd

If you ask Václav Havel, he would be the first to point out that the theater of the absurd is the tradition most frequently mentioned in association with his plays. He himself sees a connection between his outsider identity and an absurd view of the world.

> What else but a profound feeling of being excluded can enable a person better to see the absurdity of the world and his own existence or, to put it more soberly, the absurd dimensions of the world and his own existence? My plays have been described as a Czech version of the theater of the absurd. It's not up to me to decide to what extent I learned from or was instructed by absurd theater as an artistic trend (probably quite a bit, even though I think that Kafka had a greater impact); still, I would scarcely have been so alive to the absurd outlines of the world without those early existential experiences I've mentioned here. So I should be thankful for my bourgeois origins.[16]

Since his early days in the Café Slavia, Havel read the absurdist play-wrights from the West avidly and mentioned them frequently in his writings. Even after he became president, he commented on them:

> I was probably very much influenced by Beckett and Ionesco, and the theater of the absurd, which I began to discover at the end of the fifties and the beginning of the sixties. Perhaps all the members of my generation must in some way have experienced this. . . . Naturally, from my youth, I loved the plays of Arthur Miller, Tennessee Williams, Eugene O'Neill — I admired them, but they didn't provoke me to write plays because I knew that I could never write such good ones. What first provoked me to write plays was the Theatre of the Absurd. I suddenly had the feeling that I might be able to do it.[17]

For Havel — and this is crucial to understanding his work — it was not so much that the theater of the absurd was an influence or a literary tradition or a "tendency" (his term) that he sought to emulate. Rather, as he put it, absurdity was "something that was in the air."[18] He meant this in a dual sense, referring both to the influences of Western writings that were passed around the table at the Café Slavia in the late 1950s, and to the reality of life in Czechoslovakia. As Havel wrote in *Disturbing the Peace*:

> Personally, I think it's the most significant theatrical phenomenon of the twentieth century, because it demonstrates modern humanity in a "state of crisis," as it were. That is, it shows man having lost his fundamental metaphysical certainty, the experience of the absolute, his relationship to eternity, the sensation of meaning — in other words, having lost the ground under his feet. This is a man for whom everything is coming apart, whose world is collapsing, who senses that he has irrevocably lost something but is unable to admit this to himself and therefore hides from it. He waits, unable to understand that he is waiting in vain: *Waiting for Godot*. He is plagued by the need to communicate the main thing, but he has nothing to communicate: Ionesco's *The Chairs*. He seeks a firm point in recollection, not knowing that there is nothing to recollect: Beckett's *Happy Days*. He lies to himself and those around him by saying that he's going somewhere to find something that will give him back his identity: Pinter's *The Caretaker*. He thinks he knows those closest to him and himself, and it turns out that he doesn't know anyone: Pinter's *The*

Homecoming. Obviously these are model situations of man in de-
cline. These plays are often inspired by quite trivial everyday situations, such as a visit to friends (Ionesco's *The Bald Soprano*),
pedagogical tyranny (*The Lesson*), a woman burying herself in sand
at the beach (*Happy Days*). . . . The plays are not — and this is important — nihilistic. They are merely a warning. . . . I should perhaps say, though, that absurd theater as such — that is, as a tendency
in dramatic literature — was not an explicit part of the artistic program of any of the small theaters in Prague in the 1960s, not even in
the Theatre on the Balustrade, which came the closest to it of any.
And yet the experience of absurdity did exist somewhere in the bow-
els of all those theaters. It was not merely transmitted through particular artistic influences; it was, above all, something that was "in
the air." That's what I value most in absurd theater: it was able to
capture what was "in the air."[19]

Secondly, as Havel put it: "And I can't resist a provocative quip here:
I have the feeling that, if absurd theater had not existed before me, I
would have had to invent it."[20] It is indeed a provocative statement, when
first we hear it. Yet, the proof of it lies in his first two plays. Both the writing of *The Garden Party* and the first draft of *The Memorandum* predated
the Balustrade's celebrated absurdist season of 1964.

The British critic Michael Billington sees the distinction between
Havel's brand of absurdism and that of Ionesco and Beckett. Billington
observes:

The absurdists write that life is without meaning, purpose and definition, and that therefore action is meaningless and futile. But
Havel's plays assume that there is a better society that is achievable,
wherein people can be allowed to live better lives. So he's not an absurdist entirely, because in Havel's plays there is hope. For example,
Havel is saying in his plays that a despotic society can corrupt language to its own ends, but a better society can restore it to us. In
other words, Havel draws from absurdism but not from its philoph-
ical pessimism.[21]

With two new generations of writers provoked, as Havel was, by the
original absurdists (Beckett and Ionesco, among others) since the writing
of Martin Esslin's definitive book in 1961, scholars will be revisiting the

theater of the absurd as a literary tradition. In the meantime, let us consider some of the absurdities of Havel's life in the theater, in that country that journalists and historians once called "Absurdistan." The list is seemingly endless:

(1) Havel's plays were written in a language understood by only fifteen million people living in one country, and by few outside it. And yet: (2) He wrote the majority of his plays for an audience who was forbidden to see them for two decades. (3) Six out of his ten full-lengths were premiered in theaters outside his own country. (4) They were not premiered in the language in which he wrote them. Instead, they were premiered in German, once the official literary language of Czechoslovakia and a language that his countrymen struggled three centuries to eliminate from their theaters in order to instate their own. (5) Havel was forbidden to attend the premieres of those six plays. (6) The theater where Havel was "born" and that he called home for a decade was forced to lock its doors to him for twenty years. If you telephoned that theater during the time and asked for Havel, the reply was, "Who?" (7) Havel invited his chief collaborator, Jan Grossman, to the performance of his banned play *The Beggar's Opera* at Horní Počernice in 1975. Grossman was arrested for having directed it. But he had not directed it; he was seated in the audience. As a result of this arrest, Grossman was not allowed to direct in Prague for fourteen years thereafter, and also was locked out of the Theatre on the Balustrade that he and Havel had once led. (8) No professional actors were allowed to perform in *The Beggar's Opera*. And yet, professional actors were punished anyway just because the performance took place — that is, unless they denounced Havel. Hundreds attended a meeting at the National Theater to do so, publicly. They did it to keep their jobs. Then, after the revolution, after Havel became president, they rallied once more in the National Theater — this time, to applaud him. (9) Havel wrote a play, *Audience*, in which the protagonist (Vaněk) refused to inform on himself. However, after he wrote that play, Havel was sent in prison, where he found himself doing exactly what Vaněk refused to do. As Havel revealed in March 2002:

> There is one thing I remember which I've never told anyone before.
> In the first Vaněk play, *Audience*, Vaněk refuses to inform on himself. This theme returned to me later when I was in prison, where

frequently I would write reports about myself for my fellow prisoners, because they were asked to report on Havel, just like Sládek (who was asked to report on Vaněk). Everyone who was in a cell with me was questioned each week: what did Havel say? What did he think? They were probably like Sládek. They didn't know what to write. So they asked me to help. It had to be done secretly, and that was extremely difficult to do in prison, because there is no privacy. For example, I remember in Kovice where I would stand next to some noisy machinery and whisper the report to a fellow prisoner about myself, because he didn't know what to write about me. At the same time, by doing this I thought I could confuse the secret police. So in some paradoxical way, this theme came back to me full circle. Vaněk, in the end, says that he has his principles and that he refuses to participate in the practice which he doesn't agree with. But I myself participated. And in fact my very well-written reports helped some of my prisoners to be released early.[22]

Havel was right. The absurd was "something that was in the air." And he captured it in his plays in a manner that was so provocative, so compelling, that it only seems appropriate to find a fresh way to describe his plays and the times in which they were set. Here are three varied articulations:

Tom Stoppard described Havel's plays as "absurdities pushed to absurdity compounded by absurdity and yet saved from mere nonsense by their internal logic."[23]

Friedrich Dürrenmatt, the Swiss playwright (as quoted in Michael Simmon's *The Reluctant President*) called Havel's plays "'tragic grotesques,' where everything that man touched, he turned upon its head."[24]

Miloš Forman, the Czech/American film director, said: "I wouldn't call Havel an absurdist. The times were absurd, not Havel."[25]

Political Theater

Then there is the category of political theater. In his introduction to *Three Eastern European Plays* written in 1970, Martin Esslin wrote that "the non-political Theatre of the Absurd [in Western Europe] turned out to be the ideal form of political theater in Eastern Europe."[26] In a single sentence, the critic Martin Esslin illustrates the problem. Political theater or nonpolitical theater — it depends on who defines it.

Ask a Czech writer. Ivan Klíma, the esteemed novelist/playwright and friend of Havel, commented on this subject in conversation with fellow writer Philip Roth:

> As a dramatist Havel is placed by world critics in the stream of the theater of the absurd. But back when it was still permissible to present Havel's plays in our theaters, the Czech public understood them primarily as political plays. I used to say, half-jokingly, that Havel became a dramatist simply because at that time the theater was the only platform from which political opinions could be expressed.[27]

Ask a Czech theater critic. Zdeněk Hořínek says:

> There is no easy answer to this question. In the 1960s, politics meant something different than it does to an English readership today. In the 1960s, Havel wasn't writing about politics exclusively, he was criticizing the entire society in general. After all, at that time, a man had to live in society with which he did not agree. So everything in the 1960s had a political context and meaning, intentionally or unintentionally. And the view that everything was political worked both ways — not only from the authorities' point of view, but also from the audience's. In the 1960s, everything was interpreted politically.[28]

Ask a Western writer. Speaking today of both Havel's plays and his own, playwright Edward Albee says: "All art is political in one way or another because we make people think differently and respond differently. That's why we write."[29]

Ask a Western journalist. As Michael Simmons, British journalist and Havel's political biographer, puts it: "Political theater? Definitely. Everything in those times was political, and everyone in Czechoslovakia was living a political life. Every shrug of the shoulder was a political act."[30]

Ask one who is both Czech and Western. Film director Miloš Forman says: "They can call it 'political theater,' if they like. I wouldn't. Everything that rings true is political, in one way or another."[31]

Meanwhile, Havel has his own thoughts to contribute on the subject of political theater. Here are two — one written early in his life in the theater, and one at its culmination. Both cut to the heart of the question of political theater — its definition and application. In 1967, as a young playwright, Havel wrote an essay entitled "Politics and the Theatre" for the *Times Literary Supplement*. In it, he challenged the existing notion of political theater and called upon his readers to rethink it:

> Indeed, all I know about the history of the theater and everything that my modest experiences as a dramatic author have taught me confirm for me that the best theater is and always has been, naturally, political. Political, I repeat, in the broadest and truly serious sense of the term: in other words, in no way as an instrument of propaganda for this or that political ideology, conception, power, party or group but as something which has the innate characteristic that it is not indifferent to the fate of the human polis, that it has a live, committed and penetrative relationship with the social reality of its country and its time and that it attains its "timeless" and "universal" understanding through its concrete knowledge of its place and its time. . . . Theatre can be political because it has no political purpose. For this reason it seems to me that all ideas of "political theater" are erroneous.[32]

In 1994, twenty-seven years later, at a symposium in Plzeň with fellow playwrights Arthur Miller and Tom Stoppard, the now-president Havel replied in much the same way to the question about being a political playwright:

> This might surprise you, but it was never my ambition to write a political play. . . . I simply wanted to write about people, about social mechanisms, about the mechanisms which crush people and how people let themselves be crushed, about the inhibiting role which language can play, and things like that. When I wrote [a play], they always said that it was political. In our conditions, everything was political. A play which, under the conditions of Communism, was not said to be political I would have found suspicious, because it probably wouldn't be about people.[33]

At that symposium, the British playwright Ronald Harwood, who served as moderator, asked Havel a question about the relationship between politics and art. It is the kind of philosophical question that Havel relishes. He replied:

I think the reason that everything that was good here became something explosive, something that was regarded as politically dangerous — the reason lay in the very explosive nature of freedom. A free artistic act, a free display, began because of its freedom, to be perceived by those in power as something potentially dangerous, something subversive. I know of many cases in which people who did not have the slightest ambition to protest against the regime, who for example, only made the kind of music they liked and sang the kind of songs they liked, and did it completely freely, began because of this to be regarded as some kind of subversive element. This says something about politics being about life and all the problems of life having this political dimensions, that these two things cannot be divided from one another.[34]

So how can the term *political theater* be applied to Havel's life and work, if it is not, as Havel says, about the content of his plays? Quite simply, as Achim Benning of the Burgtheater in Vienna suggests: "Political theater does not mean putting on a play about politics; it means putting on a play by Václav Havel. That is a deliberate act. That is a political act."[35]

Examples: The premiere of Havel's banned play *The Beggar's Opera* at Horní Počernice. The reading of *Audience* by Havel and friends in his living room at Hrádeček. The recording of *Audience* in Vladimír Merta's kitchen that was made into a record in Sweden, smuggled back into Czechoslovakia, circulated among the population, and recited in pubs. The sign with Havel's face lowered on the stage after every performance of his plays at the Burgtheater. The borrowing of a character (Vaněk) from the play of a silenced author by fellow playwrights so that his voice could be heard in other plays. The taping of Havel's readings of his own plays himself. The removal of all playwrights' names from the program at the Theater on a String production of "Rozrazil I" because one name (Havel, author of *Tomorrow We'll Start It Up*) was forbidden.

So — a definition of "political theater" from Václav Havel's example? It is the exercising of a human right. It is a freedom.

MORE THAN A BODY OF DRAMATIC WORK

What, then, is Havel's legacy to the theater? It is more than a body of dramatic work. Václav Havel gives us an idea of the theater — a sense of what it is and what it can be. And an idea of the playwright in the theater and in the world.

An Idea of the Theater

Over the years—in his letters to Olga, in scores of articles, in interviews—Havel has talked about an idea of the theater. It has several aspects. One is the idea of theater as a catalyst:

> What should theater do, actually? According to my opinion, it should awaken in man his authenticity; it should help him to become aware of himself in the full span of his problems, to understand the situation in which he lives, to provoke him to think about himself. . . . At most, I can only help the spectator to formulate problems, which he must solve himself.[1]

Another is of theater as a community:

> Another thing which attracted me to the theater was the sense of community — the theater as some sort of event which affects a group of people, and they can't leave. It lasts two hours, they can't skip a section, they can't go back. If I wrote novels, it would bother me a lot that they would perhaps read one chapter, and then another a month later. In the theater they're forced to experience it continuously and in that community, in that limited time and space, and these are all things which, for me, personally, given my character, make drama uncommonly attractive.[2]

> Every theatre is automatically a social phenomenon. . . . The first embryonic appearance of genuine socialness happens the moment those participating in the theater cease to be a mere group of people and become a community. It is that special moment when their mutual presence becomes mutual participation; when their encounter in a single space and time becomes an existential encounter; when their common existence in this world is suddenly enveloped

by a very specific and unrepeateable atmosphere; when a shared experience, mutually understood, evokes the wonderful elation that makes all the sacrifices worthwhile.[3]

A third is of theater as the "spirit of the nation":

> Theatre as an institution (that is, the kind of theater I believe in, love, and have had the good fortune to work in) is never just an institution: it is a focus (or more precisely one of the focuses) of social life and social thought, an irreplaceable component of the "spirit of the nation," a small organism, bound by thousands of threads to the great organism of society, and playing an irreplacable and actual social role within it.[4]

A fourth is of theater as an agent of change:

> Since Karl Marx wrote that the task of the philosopher is not to explain the world but to change it, the phrase "change the world" has had a bad reputation. But it depends what you mean. If we mean a rational project for a better world into which we then stuff the world by force, then of course in that sense I am not in favour of any changing of the world. But changing the world can mean, indirectly, everything good that we do, and people do, including theater. Theatre can function as a mechanism to help society, to help people to get to know themselves — it need have no other ambition — and still with this it changes the world.[5]

All these ideas were put to practice by Havel's life in the theater and by his plays. Plays and performances that changed the course of the lives of so many people, and, through them, the course of a nation.

An Identity for the Playwright

Like Chekhov's, Havel's plays are written by a man who is far more than a playwright. Chekhov was also a doctor, a humanitarian, a conservationist, a short-story writer, a correspondent, and a humorist. His multi-faceted identity has informed the depth and vision of his plays. So too with Havel.

While in prison, Havel had a lot of time to think about many issues, one of which was his identity. In Letter 102 to Olga, Havel makes an interesting distinction: "I am definitely not what we call a 'divadelník' — a professional theater person, someone for whom theater is the only imaginable vocation."[6] In that letter, he adds that his life in the theater was a result of a "series of coincidences" and that luck had to do with it. However, he concludes the letter by saying:

> But writing plays, in a sense, has remained with me to this day. If I ask why, I realize that it is not just because of the events that shaped my destiny, nor is it (I hope) the outcome of complacency or inertia on my part. . . . I don't think I've written myself out as a playwright.[7]

How interesting it is that Havel, a writer whose key theme is human identity, is a man who himself has had so many different ones: apprentice carpenter, engineering student, laboratory technician, poet, editor, critic, essayist, stagehand, dramaturg, "hippie,"[8] brewery worker, human rights activist, dissident, petitioner, prisoner, ethicist, philosopher, humanist, politician, statesman, visionary, president, globalist. How interesting it is, too, that the identity of playwright is the one that has stayed with him throughout his life. Havel offers more than an idea of theater. He also gives us an idea of a playwright — who he can be, in the theater and in the world. He can be a playwright of conscience:

> The idea that a writer is the conscience of his nation has its own logic and tradition here. For years, writers have stood in for politicians; they were renewers of the national community, maintainers of the national language, awakeners of the national conscience, interpreters of the national will. This tradition has continued under totalitarian conditions, where it gains its own special coloring; the written word seems to have acquired a kind of heightened radioactivity — otherwise they wouldn't lock us up for it![9]

He can be a playwright of responsibility:

> The warning voices of poets must be carefully listened to and taken very seriously, perhaps even more seriously than the voices of bankers or stock brokers. But at the same time, we cannot expect

that the world — in the hands of poets — will suddenly be transformed into a poem.[10]

He can be a playwright of prophesy:

> One day you'll go back and hobnob with the stars and brag about
> your martyrdom and romantic past in the brewery[11]
> — Sládek to Vaněk, in Havel's *Audience*

We stand before a historic challenge, and we must have the courage to face it, though we don't know for certain — indeed, we can't know — that we can fulfill it. Not without sacrifice.[12]
— Rašín, in Havel's *Tomorrow We'll Start It Up*

He can be a playwright of morality:

> Question: Who is Václav Havel?
> Answer: *(From the Czech critic and literary historian Zdeněk Hořínek.)* A moralist.[13]

Whoever Václav Havel is — the man, the playwright — he is profoundly connected to the world around him.

A Life in the Theater, the Theater in a Life

> All the world's a stage,
> And all the men and women merely players.
> They have their exits and their entrances;
> And one man in his time plays many parts."[14]
> — Shakespeare, *As You Like It*, Act II, scene vii

Philosopher, politician, prisoner, president . . . playwright. The question of identity again. Havel is a man who has played many parts in his life. "He is a renaissance man," his friend Miloš Forman says. "He is everything and nothing at the same time."[15]

Whatever roles he has played, whatever his identity, he is a man with a sense of theater in life. He sees the world in theatrical terms. Call him a "metatheatrical" playwright, if you will, he is a man for all seasons and all stages.

No wonder his life — in the theater and in politics — has inspired so many metatheatrical epithets. One among countless, from the scholar Susan Hollis Merrit: "When first elected, [he] was revered by university students as a 'Godot' who had finally arrived."[16] No wonder the British biographer John Keane titled his biography: "*Václav Havel: A Political Tragedy in Six Acts.*"

No wonder, too, that Havel sees the world in terms of theatrical metaphor, and himself as a character in it. As a playwright, he said (through his character Leopold Kopřiva): "I sometimes have the feeling that I'm acting the part of myself instead of being myself."[17]

No wonder, when he became president, he remarked: "I sometimes think that God strikes back: as if I wrote an absurdist drama and put God in it, so God has put me here as president."[18]

As a playwright, Havel sees the infinite possibilities of the theater. He sees that the theater is a place where one can say what is forbidden to be said elsewhere and be heard by the audience (the 1960s). That a play can be presented anywhere — in a living room, a garden, a kitchen — and be an expression of freedom (the 1970s). And when the theater is forbidden, or physically inaccessible, when one is far from it, one can still remain "in" the theater (the 1980s). And when one plays a new role (president), one is simply playing on a larger stage (the 1990s). And at the end, one can stand on an empty stage (the millennium), and create a role in a whole new life.

As president, Havel said he played his role with "a sense of dramatic structures in politics."[19] Moreover, he has seen the possibilites of the world as a stage — where all his ideals and hopes might be enacted, including the principles of morality and ethics to which he had dedicated his writings and his political and private life. The stage is a world. The world is a stage. That is how he sees it.

FINAL BOW

> I cannot help feeling that at the end of my long fall from a fairy-tale
> world onto the hard earth, I suddenly find myself once more inside
> a fairy tale.[1]
>
> — Havel, "A Farewell to Politics"

In his farewell speech at CUNY in September 2002, Havel talked with
great emotion about the conclusion of his presidency. Once again, he expressed himself in theatrical terms:

> And I've discovered an astonishing thing: although it might be ex-
> pected that this wealth of experience would have given me more
> and more self-assurance, confidence, and polish, the exact opposite
> is true. In that time, I have become a good deal less sure of myself,
> a good deal more humble. You may not believe this, but every day
> I suffer more and more from stage fright; every day, I am more
> afraid that I won't be up to the job, or that I'll make a hash of it. It's
> harder and harder for me to write my speeches, and when I do write
> them, I am more fearful than ever that I will hopelessly repeat my-
> self, over and over again. More and more often, I am afraid that I
> will fall woefully short of expectations, that I will somehow reveal
> my own lack of qualifications for the job, that despite my good faith
> I will make even greater mistakes, that I will cease to be trustwor-
> thy and therefore lose the right to do what I do. . . . And the more
> enemies I have, the more I side with them in my own mind, and so
> I become my own worst enemy.[2]

Stage fright. It's an act of courage, to admit to it on the world political stage while taking one's final bow.

The ovation from an audience of admirers and the adulation of colleagues and friends assured him otherwise.

After that speech, the moderator posed a question to once a president, always a playwright, Václav Havel.

Question: What will your next play be about?
Answer: Freedom . . . [3]

Curtain call at Hrádeček, Andrej Krob, foreground;
Havel, background, 1991 (Hana Rysová)

PRODUCTION PHOTOS

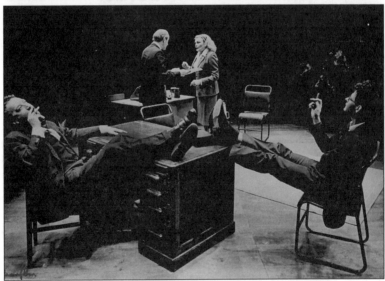

above *The Garden Party,* 1963, Theatre on the Balustrade
(Lubomír Rohan, Balustrade archive)

below *The Memorandum,* Orange Tree Theatre, 1980
(Orange Tree Theatre archive)

above Puzuk, in *The Increased Difficulty of Concentration,* 1968,
Theatre on the Balustrade (Jovan Dezort, Balustrade archive)

below Mountain Hotel, Theatre on the Road at Hrádeček, 1991
(Hana Rysová)

Josef Abrhám and Pavel Landovský in *Audience,* Činoherní Klub, 1990
(Činoherní Klub archive)

above Protest, at the Burgtheater, Vienna, 1979
(with permission of Achim Benning)

below Vernissage, at the Vinohrady Theatre, 2000
(Martin Poš, Vinohrady Theatre archive)

above Jiří Bartoška in *Largo Desolato,* Theatre on the Balustrade, 1990
(Josef Ptáček, Balustrade archive)

below An Evening with the Family, at the Vinohrady Theater, 2000
(Martin Poš, Vinohrady archive)

Temptation, Theatre of the Balustrade 1991
(Viktor Krombauer, Prague Theater Institute archive)

Redevelopment, at the Realistické Theater, 1990
(with permission of Vlasta Gallerová and Karel Kříž)

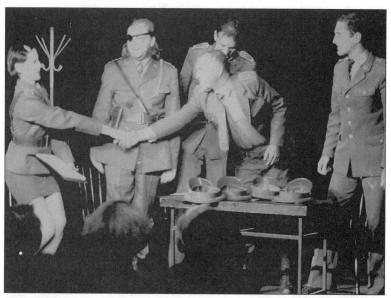

above *Mlýny* (a version of *The Life Ahead*), Sklep Theater, 1991
(Prague Theater Institute archive)

below Theatre on the Road, rehearsing *The Beggar's Opera,* 1995.
Andrej Krob, second row, fourth from left; Havel, top row, third from left.
(Hana Rysová)

APPENDIX A

Chronology of Plays

The following is a list of the plays written by Václav Havel. One of the primary sources of information for production dates is "A List of Theatrical Productions of the Plays of Václav Havel," compiled by Helena Albertová in *Václav Havel: A Citizen and a Playwright* (Prague: Theatre Institute, 1999).

The Life Ahead (Život před sebou).* Written: 1957–1958 (in collaboration with Karel Brynda). Amateur production: 1958, Czech army theater festival; premiere: March 14, 1991, Sklep Theater (under the title *Mlýny* [The Mills]).

An Evening with the Family (Rodinný večer). Written: 1959. Premiere: February 3, 2000, Vinohrady Theater, Prague (with *Vernissage*), directed by Jan Burian.

Hitchhiking (Autostop).* Written: 1960 (in collaboration with Ivan Vyskočil). Premiere: March 19, 1961, Theatre on the Balustrade, directed by Václav Hudecek.

The Best Rock Years of Mrs. Hermanová (Nejlepší roky paní Hermanové).* Written: 1962 (in collaboration with Miloš Macourek). Premiere: November 1, 1962, Theatre on the Balustrade, directed by Jan Grossman and Václav Havel.

The Demented Dove (Vyšinutá hrdlička).* Written: 1962 (in collaboration with others, set to music by Radim Vašinka). Premiere: February 8, 1963, Theatre on the Balustrade, directed by Jan Grossman.

The Garden Party (Zahradní slavnost). Written: 1962–1963. Premiere: December 3, 1963, Theatre on the Balustrade, directed by Otomar Krejča.

The Memorandum (Vyrozumění). Written: 1960–1965. Premiere: July 26, 1965, Theatre on the Balustrade, directed by Jan Grossman); English language premiere: April 23, 1968, Public Theater (New York Shakespeare Festival), directed by Joseph Papp.

The Increased Difficulty of Concentration (Ztížená možnost soustředění). Written: 1966–1968. Premiere: April 11, 1968, Theatre on the Balustrade, directed by Václav Hudecek; English language premiere:

---

*Havel did not include these plays in *Spisy* (Writings), his seven-volume collected works published by Torst in 1999.

October 27, 1978, Orange Tree Theatre, Richmond (England), directed by Christie Dickason.

Guardian Angel (Anděl strážný) (radio play). Written: 1968 (shorter version first written in 1963). Premiere (airing): 1968, Czechoslovak Radio.

A Butterfly on the Antenna (Motýl na anténě) (teleplay). Written: 1968. Premiere: (as a radio play) February 25, 1975, by Norddeutscher Rundfunkt, Federal Republic of Germany. Czech premiere: December 28, 1991, Ceskoslovenska televize.

The Conspirators (Spiklenci). Written: 1970–1971. Premiere: February 8, 1974, Theater der Stadt, Baden-Baden (Federal Republic of Germany); Czech premiere: summer 1992, Theatre on the Road, Hrádeček, directed by Andrej Krob; and again on November 1, 1992, at the Theatre on the Balustrade.

The Beggar's Opera (Žebrácká opera). Written: 1972. Premiere: November 1, 1975, Theatre on the Road at U Čelikovských, Horní Počernice, Prague; British premiere: January 19, 2003, Orange Tree Theatre, Richmond, directed by Geoffrey Beevers.

Audience (Audience). Written: 1975. Premiere: summer 1976, Theatre on the Road in the Krob barn at Hrádeček, directed by Andrej Krob, with Havel as Vaněk; English language premiere: February 18, 1977, Orange Tree Theatre, Richmond, directed by Anthony Cornish; official Czech premiere: January 11, 1990, Činoherní Klub, directed by Jiří Menzel.

Unveiling or *Private View* (Vernissage). Written: 1975. Premiere: summer, 1976, Theatre on the Road in the Krob barn at Hrádeček, directed by Andrej Krob; English language premiere: February 18, 1977, Orange Tree Theatre, Richmond, directed by Anthony Cornish.

Mountain Hotel (Horský hotel). Written: 1970–1976. Premiere: May 23, 1981, Burgtheater (on the Akademietheater stage), Vienna, directed by Peter Palitsch; Czech language premiere: October 17, 1991, Theatre on the Road, directed by Andrej Krob, at Theatre on the Balustrade.

Protest (Protest). Written: 1978. Premiere: November 17, 1979, Burgtheater (on the Akademietheater stage), Vienna, directed by Leopold Lindtberg; English language premiere: September 19, 1980, Orange Tree Theatre, Richmond, directed by Geoffrey Beevers.

Mistake (Chyba). Written: 1983. Premiere: November 29, 1983, Stadsteater, Stockholm (evening of solidarity with Charter 77); English language premiere: spring 1984, Royal Shakespeare Company at the Barbican, staged jointly with Beckett's *Catastrophe*, under the title "Thought Crimes"; Czech language premiere: October 25, 1992, Divadelní spolek Kašpar, Prague, directed by Petr Hruška.

Largo Desolato (Largo Desolato). Written: July 1984. Premiere: April 13, 1985, Burgtheater (on the Akademietheater stage), directed by Jürgen Bosse; English language premiere: March 25, 1986, New York Shakespeare Festival, directed by Richard Foreman; British premiere: October 9, 1986, Bristol/New Vic (Stoppard version), directed by Claude Whatham; Czech language premiere: April 9, 1990, Theatre on the Balustrade, Prague, directed by Jan Grossman.

Temptation (Pokoušení). Written: October 1985. Premiere: May 23, 1986, Burgtheater (on the Akademietheater stage), directed by Hans Kleber; English language premiere: April 22, 1987, Royal Shakespeare Company, Stratford, in The Other Place Theatre, directed by Roger Michell; Czech language premiere: December 20, 1991, Theatre on the Balustrade, directed by Jan Grossman.

Redevelopment (Asanace). Written: 1987. Premiere: September 26, 1989, Schauspielhaus, Zurich, Switzerland, directed by Joachim Bissmeier; Czech language premiere: March 30, 1990, Realistické divadlo, Prague, directed by Karel Kříž; English Language premiere: September 18, 1990, Orange Tree Theatre, directed by Sam Walters.

Tomorrow We'll Start It Up (Zítra to spustíme). Written: 1988. Premiere: October 21, 1988, Theater on a String, Brno, Czechoslovakia.

APPENDIX B

Dramatis Personae
and Other Names

Below is a list of the key dramatis personae and settings of Václav Havel's life in the theater, as well as other references. You will find these names and places throughout this book.

DRAMATIS PERSONAE

Jiří Bartoška

(1947–) Actor at the Theatre on the Balustrade from 1978 to 1991. Bartoška played the leading role of Leopold Kopřiva in *Largo Desolato*, the first production of a Havel play performed at the Balustrade since his plays were banned in 1969.

Samuel Beckett

(1906–1989) Celebrated Irish playwright, poet, and novelist (living in Paris and writing in both English and French), and one of the greatest influences on Havel's dramatic work. During Havel's imprisonment, Beckett wrote a play in honor of Havel entitled *Catastrophe*, which was performed in "A Night for Václav Havel" at the Avignon Festival in 1982. While they never met, the two writers maintained a private correspondence until Beckett's death in 1989, just days after the Velvet Revolution was underway.

Achim Benning

(1935–) Artistic director of the Burgtheater in Vienna from 1976 to 1989. Benning was one of the three artistic directors outside Czechoslovakia who provided Havel with a "home away from home" during the dark decades of the 1970s and 1980s when his plays were banned in his own country. From 1976 to 1988, Benning produced seven plays by Havel at the Burgtheater and made certain that there was always a Havel play in the repertory of his second stage, the Akademietheater.

Vlasta Chramostová

(1926–) Czech actress. Chramostová founded *bytové divadlo* (living-room theater) in the 1970s for banned theater artists who could not find work because they were not members of the Communist Party. Havel and other playwrights attended these gatherings, and read their work.

Jiří Dienstbier

(1937–) Czech journalist, political writer and playwright. A key signer of Charter 77 and founding member of VONS (Committee to Defend the Unjustly Prosecuted), Dienstbier was sentenced to prison together with Havel in 1979. He was one of three Czech playwrights who adopted Havel's character Vaněk for his own work (*Reception*). After the Velvet Revolution, Dienstbier became foreign minister of Czechoslovakia.

Libor Fára

(1925–1988) Set and costume designer at Theatre on the Balustrade in the 1960s. Fára and his wife, along with Jan Grossman, were the only witnesses at Havel and Olga's wedding in 1964. Fára was a frequent visitor to Hrádeček, Havel's country home, in the 1970s and 1980s, and his sculpture was featured in the garden there.

Miloš Forman

(1932–) Eminent Czech-born film director. Forman was a schoolmate and close friend of Václav Havel from their days at Poděbrady. He emigrated to the United States in the late 1960s, and tried to arrange to have Havel released from prison in the late 1970s and join him there. Forman is the recipient of several Oscars (including for the direction of *Amadeus*, which was filmed in Prague).

Anna Freimanová

(1951–) Neighbor of Václav Havel at Hrádeček and wife of Andrej Krob. Freimanová was a great supporter of Havel's work and of Theater of the Road, founded by her husband. She was instrumental in founding *O Divadle*, a theater magazine in the 1980s, along with Olga Havlová. After Havel became president, he appointed her his cultural secretary at the castle.

Jan Grossman

(1925–1993) Celebrated Czech theater director, critic, and scholar. Grossman served as artistic director at the Theatre on the Balustrade from 1962 to

1968, Havel's formative years as a playwright. During that period, he was the dramaturg for *The Garden Party* and director of *The Memorandum*. He became Havel's most important artistic mentor, and they formed a lifelong collegiality in the theater. (Havel dedicated *The Garden Party* to him.) After the Velvet Revolution, Grossman was invited back to the Balustrade, where he served as artistic director from 1990 until his death in 1993. During that period, he directed the Czech premieres of *Largo Desolato* and *Temptation*.

Ivan Havel

(1938–) Philosopher, mathematician, scientist, and Havel's younger brother and only sibling. Ivan has played a variety of important roles in his brother's life in the theater, including the creation of Pytdepe, the fictitious language *in The Memorandum*.

Dagmar (Dáša) Havlová

(1953–) A leading actress with the Vinohrady Theater in Prague (Dagmar Veškrnová). Havel married her in 1997, following the death of his first wife, Olga.

Olga Havlová

(1933–1996) Born in Žižkov, a working-class neighborhood of Prague, and trained as a factory worker, young Olga Šplíchalová shared Havel's passion for the theater. They met at the Café Slavia in 1950s, worked together at the Theatre on the Balustrade throughout the 1960s, and were married in 1964. A strong woman who was very much "her own person," Olga was Havel's bedrock of support, spiritually, emotionally and dramaturgically (she was first reader on all his plays, and together they founded a *samizdat* press, Edice Expedice). She stood by him steadfastly through the dissident days and during his imprisonments; she was by his side when he was inaugurated president of Czechoslovakia in 1989. She died in 1996 of cancer. They had no children.

Klaus Juncker

(1922–) Internationally known literary agent from the Rowohlt Verlag publishing house in Reinbek, Germany. Juncker "discovered" Havel at the Balustrade in 1964 and remained his dedicated and indefatigable supporter for over three decades. In addition to publishing his plays, Juncker was responsible for placing them in dozens of European theaters (and beyond) and for fostering and developing his international reputation during the dark decades when his plays were banned.

Ivan Klíma

(1931–) Czech novelist, short story writer, and playwright. Klíma started a literary circle for banned writers in the 1970s, in which Havel was a participant. Klíma cofounded the first *samizdat* press (Edice Petlice) together with writer Ludvík Vaculík. Selected prose works: *Love and Garbage; Lovers for a Day; My Golden Trades.*

Pavel Kohout

(1928–) Czech playwright, prose writer, poet, and close friend of Havel. Havel, Kohout, and Klíma met frequently in the 1970s as part of a circle of banned writers. After a year's stay in Vienna in 1978, Kohout was denied reentry into Czechoslovakia and worked at the Burgtheater until the Velvet Revolution in 1989. Kohout is one of the three Czech playwrights who adopted Havel's character Vaněk for his own work (*Permit, Morass, Safari*). Selected plays: *August, August, august; Play Macbeth* (performed in livingroom theater throughout the 1970s).

Jiří Kolář

(1914–2002) Czech poet, visual artist and creator of collages. Kolář founded a literary circle called Group 42 of banned writers who gathered at the Café Slavia, where Havel first met him in the 1950s. Havel admired Kolář's avantgarde aethestic, and it inspired him in his writing of poetry. The Kolář aesthetic influenced an aspect of his playwriting technique, as well.

Otomar Krejča

(1921–) Czech theater director at the National Theater and the Theater Beyond the Gate (Divadlo za branou), among others. Krejča directed Havel's first full-length play, *The Garden Party*, at the Theatre on the Balustrade in 1963.

Andrej Krob

(1938–) Havel's neighbor at Hrádeček in the Czech countryside. Krob has played a major role throughout Havel's life in the theater. Krob began as production manager at the Balustrade during the 1960s, where Havel served as dramaturg and playwright. Then in the mid-1970s, Krob founded an amateur company called Theatre on the Road, dedicated to performing the banned plays of his neighbor. In 1975, Krob courageously staged *The Beggar's Opera* on the outskirts of Prague for an invited audience; it was to be the only performance of a play by Havel in Czechoslovakia over a twenty-one-year period. Since the revolution, Krob's Theatre on the Road has continued its mission and is still active today.

Pavel Landovský

(1936–) Celebrated Czech actor of stage and screen, playwright, and lifelong friend of Václav Havel. Landovský was a member of the acting ensemble of Činoherní Klub from 1968 to 1976. He was one of the key participants in the Charter 77 movement; thereafter, he lived in exile in Vienna from 1979 to 1989, working as a member of the Burgtheater ensemble. He is one of three Czech playwrights who adopted Havel's character Vaněk for his own work (*Arrest*). Days after Havel became president, Landovský returned to Prague to appear in Havel's play *Audience* at the Činoherní Klub to celebrate his friend. The performance marked the first official public production of a play by Václav Havel in his own country in twenty-one years.

Arthur Miller

(1915–) Eminent Amercian playwright who first met Havel at the Theatre on the Balustrade in the 1960s. Miller wrote a play in Havel's honor during his imprisonment, entitled *I think about you a great deal*, which was performed in "A Night for Václav Havel" at the 1982 Avignon Festival.

Jiří Ornest

(1946–) Czech actor and director at the Theatre on the Balustrade who was the leading man in a number of productions of Havel's plays in the 1990s. Ornest served as a coartistic director of the Theatre on the Balustrade from 2000 to 2002.

Petr Oslzlý

(1945–) Artistic director of the Theater on a String (Divadlo na Provázku) in Brno. An unswerving champion of Havel's plays and of new Czech drama, Oslzlý commissioned a new play from Havel in 1988 (*Tomorrow We'll Start It Up*), which in effect became the only one of Havel's new plays produced at a theater for an audience in his own country from 1968 to 1989, although his name could not be publicly ascribed to it. Oslzlý was active in organizing the theater community in the late 1980s and in helping to galvanize it into a driving force during the Velvet Revolution. After he became president, Havel acknowledged Oslzlý's support by appointing him chief cultural advisor at the castle.

Joseph Papp

(1921–1991) Artistic director of the New York Shakespeare Festival (the Public Theater). Papp chose to produce and direct Havel's play *The Memorandum* for his inaugural season (1968) and continued to provide a home for Havel's work during the next two decades when his plays were banned in Czechoslovakia, producing three full-length and three one-acts by Havel. Papp visited Havel in Hrádeček in the 1980s, and they maintainted a close friendship until Papp's death in 1991.

Jan Patočka

(1907–1977) One of the most significant Czech philosophers of the twentieth century, and a student of Heidegger. Patočka served as one of the first three spokesmen of Charter 77 and died from a heart attack while being interrogated by the police for his involvement. Havel revered the philosopher's writings and teachings, and Patočka's concept of "living in truth" became Havel's watchword.

Harold Pinter

(1930–) Esteemed British playwright. During the difficult years of Havel's trial and imprisonment, Pinter expressed his support by performing the role of Vaněk in Havel's *Audience* on the BBC (1977) and by remaining his public advocate thereafter. The two writers maintain a friendship today.

Alfred Radok

(1914–1976) A leading Czech stage and screen director of the 1950s and 1960s. Havel's first job in the theater was as Radok's assistant at the ABC Theater in Prague (1960). Havel dedicated his one-act play *Audience* to Radok's memory.

Jiřina Šiklová

(1935–) Esteemed Czech professor of Sociology. Šiklová lost her academic position at Charles University in the 1970s. She subsequently organized a smuggling network to get manuscripts from the dissident community out of Czechoslovakia. Imprisoned for her activities in 1980, she was released and continued her dedication to the cause.

Tom Stoppard

(1937–) Eminent English playwright, who championed Havel and his fellow dissidents in the Charter 77 movement. Like Beckett and Miller, Stoppard wrote a play that he dedicated to Havel, entitled *Professional Foul* (1977). Stoppard also wrote an English language version of *Largo Desolato*, which Havel had dedicated to him. Stoppard was an outspoken champion of Havel's cause abroad throughout the late 1970s and 1980s.

Jan Tříska
(1936–) Actor, close friend of Václav Havel, and one of the founders of Theater Beyond the Gate in Prague. Tříska and Havel were together on the night of August 21, 1968, when the Russian tanks rolled into Prague. Tříska was fired from the National Theater for attending the performance of Havel's *The Beggar's Opera* at Horní Počernice in November, 1975. He emigrated to the United States in 1977. In 1986, he read Havel's acceptance speech of the Erasmus Prize in Rotterdam.

Zdeněk Urbánek
(1917–) Czech essayist, scholar, translator of Shakespeare's plays, and close friend of Havel. Urbánek remained very close to Havel and Olga during their Hrádeček years (1970s), when his work was banned, and was a mainstay of support. After Havel was released from prison, Urbánek supplied books for Havel's research on *Temptation*, a play that Havel in turn dedicated to Urbánek.

Ludvík Vaculík
(1926–) Czech writer, journalist, and close friend of Havel. In the early 1970s, Vaculík helped cofound Edic Petlice (Padlock Press), the first *samizdat* press, together with Ivan Klíma.

Ivan Vyskočil
(1929–) Czech actor, director, and writer. Vyskočil was cofounder and artistic director of the Theatre on the Balustrade from 1959 to 1962. He invited Havel to work at the theater as a stagehand in 1960, where he fostered Havel's playwriting talent, and they collaborated on a number of projects. Vyskočil's "text appeals," with their eccentric brand of humor and the absurd, had a strong influence on Havel's work. Vyskočil helped to inspire Havel's first produced full-length play, *The Garden Party*.

Sam Walters
(1939–) Founding artistic director of the Orange Tree Theatre in Richmond (Surrey) outside London. Walters provided a home away from home for

Havel's plays beginning in 1977 and worked vigorously to call attention to Havel's cause throughout the late 1970s and 1980s. To date, he remains dedicated to Havel's work and has produced ten of Havel's full-length and one-act plays at his theater.

Jan Werich
(1905–1980) Cofounder of the Liberated Theater in Prague in the late 1920s and member of the celebrated Voskovec-Werich comedy team. Werich became artistic director of the ABC Theater in Prague and gave Havel his first job in the theater (as a general assistant and dramaturg) in 1959 to 1960.

SETTINGS
In order of chronology in Havel's life in the theater:

Havlov
The family country estate of the Havel family, on the Bobrůvka River in the Moravian forests. It featured a grand home, a swimming pool, and was surrounded by gardens, woods, and fields. It provided the family with an idyllic retreat during the second World War, where Božena and Václav Havel's two young sons, Václav and Ivan, could go to school in safety. The family spent most of the war and the early postwar period in the beauty and protection of their rural retreat. The family eventually lost the estate to the government in the late 1950s.

Rašínovo nábřeží
The site of Havel's family five-story Prague mansion, built in 1905 by his grandfather. Václav Havel lived there with his family from his birth in 1936 (except for their retreat to Havlov during World War II), till after his marriage in 1964. During that period, the family was forced to moved to the top floor, which became their apartment. After the Russian invasion, Havel and Olga returned to live there sporadically; Havel's brother Ivan, also lived in the apartment with his family. (see note 2 on page 438).

Café Slavia
Located on the corner of Národní and the embankment of the Vlata River in Prague's old town section. This bright, airy, high-ceilinged, Art Nouveau café was the vibrant center of Prague's intellectual life throughout the 1950s and 1960s. It was there that Havel received his "education" in the 1950s, and met so many writers, artists, and intellectuals who are close personal friends today.

ABC Theater

One of the many small, dynamic Prague theaters proliferating in the late 1950s to early 1960s. Its artistic director, the famed Alfred Radok, gave Havel his first job in the theater, as his assistant at the ABC Theater for the 1959–1960 season.

Theatre on the Balustrade (Divadlo na zábradlí)

Cofounded in 1959 by Ivan Vyskočil and Jiří Suchý in an abandoned dormitory building on the Annenské námĕsti (square) in Prague's old town section, just steps from the Charles bridge. There, Vyskočil staged his "text appeals" (a eclectic genre of "stand-up" intellectual comedy/satire), and the mime Fialka staged performances of his troupe. In 1960, Vysckocil hired Havel as a stagehand and nurtured his playwriting talent as well. The Balustrade became the leader of the Prague theater renaissance of the 1960s, and Havel became its dramaturg and playwright-in-residence, with three new, groundbreaking plays during that decade. After the Russian invasion in 1968, the doors of the theater were shut to Havel for twenty-one years. They were reopened in 1989 with the Velvet Revolution, and the theater reaffirmed its commitment to its playwright-now-president.

Hrádeček

A site, whose name means "little castle," in the Northern Bohemian mountains a few hours northeast of Prague, near the Polish border. Named for the ruins of an old castle perched high on a hill-top, there are a few surrounding structures, including a charming old stucco farmhouse on the slope just below. In 1967, Havel and Olga bought the farmhouse, which also happened to be situated next door to a cottage owned by Andrej Krob, the production manager of the Balustrade at the time. After the Russian invasion in 1968, Havel and Olga retreated to Hrádeček, and it became their primary residence for the next twenty-one years (except for when Havel was in prison). During that period of the 1970s and 1980s, Hrádeček became the cultural center of Czech writers, artists and intellectuals, and the site of many gatherings where banned works were read. It also became the home of the Theatre on the Road, and thus, Havel's artistic home.

Theatre on the Road (Divadlo na tahu)

An amateur theater company founded in the early 1970s by Andrej Krob, for the purpose of putting on the banned plays of his neighbor, Václav Havel. In 1975, the troupe gave its first performance — of Havel's play, *The Beggar's*

Opera — before a private audience at Horní Počernice, on the outskirts of Prague, for one night only. It was a performance of great risk, and of great consequence, too. Every summer thereafter, the troupe performed on the lawn between Krob and Havel's houses (or in the barn) at Hrádeček. After the revolution, the Theatre on the Road continued its mission (and its amateur membership), performing the plays of its playwright-in-residence who was now his country's president. Throughout the 1990s, in addition to their annual performances at Hrádeček, the Theatre on the Road now also performed at the Theatre on the Balustrade.

Theater on a String (Divadlo na provazku)

Founded by Petr Oslzlý in Brno in the 1970s, this theater was the first to "commission" a play by the playwright Havel (in 1988) during the twenty-one period when his plays were banned. When Havel offered that his name not be listed in the program, for fear of putting the theater at serious risk with the authorities, Oslzlý decided that none of the other authors on that evening's program would be listed, either.

OTHER NAMES

AMU

(Akademie Muzických Umění: meaning The Academy of Arts). From the mid-fifties on, Havel applied repeatedly for acceptance in both DAMU, the theater program, and in the film program as well. He was repeatedly rejected. Finally, in 1966, he was admitted and completed a course of external study in dramaturgy at the theater department.

Bytové divaldo

"Living-room theater" founded in the 1970s by Vlasta Chramostová, a Czech actress. Her Prague apartment became a gathering place for banned theater artists, where they would read new work aloud.

Charter 77

The name of the human rights document written by a group of Czech writers and intellectuals, including Václav Havel. Alarmed that the basic human rights guaranteeed by signator states in the Helsinki Agreement were not being upheld in Czechoslovakia, the authors of Charter 77 collected 243 signatures and attempted to deliver the document to Gustáv Husák, general secretary of the Czechoslovak Communist Party, on January 7, 1977. Havel and others involved were arrested, interrogated, imprisoned, and prosecuted. Despite an international outcry against these injustices, a long-term, brutal era of persecution of the dissidents in Czechoslovakia was launched, one that would last twelve years.

Group 42
The name of a distinguished group of avant-garde writers, intellectuals, poets and artists, founded in 1942. Their work was subsequently banned and they, like the 36ers, had their own table at the Café Slavia. Jiří Kolář, the poet, was one of its members, as was Zdeněk Urbánek and Josef Hiršal.

Samizdat
While growing up in the 1950s, Havel and others eagerly read Western literature that was unofficially translated and reproduced in various *samizdat* publications in Czechoslovakia — as well as banned literature and literary criticism of their own country. (*Samizdat* means the unofficial reproduction of unpublished manuscripts.) Later, in the 1970s, Havel and his circle of friends established their own *samizdat* presses, called Edice Petlice (Padlock Press) and Edice Expedice (Expedition Press). These "presses" produced carbon copies of the founders' typed manuscripts and those of their friends, colleagues, and other banned Czech writers — as well as forbidden literature from abroad, which was smuggled into the country and translated. Today, the Libri prohibiti (Forbidden Books) museum in Prague houses thousands of *samizdat* publication.

36ers
A so-called group of sixteen-year-old aspiring writers, poets, and artists, founded by Václav Havel (with his mother's encouragement) in 1952 for his friends who, like he, were born in 1936 and who, like he, were denied formal higher education under Communism because of their parents' class status. The group (which had a Prague and a Brno contingent) met every Saturday at the Café Slavia in Prague over a period of three years. It boasted its own publications and yearly reports, all produced by Havel.

VONS (Výbor na obranu nespravedlivě stíhaných)
An acronym for the Committee to Defend the Unjustly Persecuted. Formed in 1978 to follow and support cases of those who were indicted in their involvement in Charter 77, the key members of the committee, Havel included, were nonetheless eventually tried and imprisoned in 1979.

NAMES OF CZECH THEATERS

Činoherní Klub
Divadlo ABC (ABC Theater)
Divadlo na provázku (Theater on a String)
Divadlo na tahu (Theatre on the Road)
Divaldo na zábradlí (Theatre on the Balustrade)
Národní divadlo (National Theater)
Realistické divadlo (Realistic Theater)
Vinohradské divadlo (Vinohrady Theater)

NAMES OF CZECH PUBLICATIONS

The following is a list of Czech publishing houses and publications (magazines, newspapers, journals), both official and *samizdat*, cited in this book. (*Note:* Some of these publications no longer exist.)

Český deník (Czech Daily)
Denní telegraf (Daily Telegraph)
Divadlo (Theater)
Edice Expedice (Expedition Press)
Edice Petlice (Padlock Press)
Hospodářské noviny (Economic News)
Host do domu (A Guest of the House)
Lidová demokracie (People's Democracy)
Lidové noviny (People's News)
Listy (Letters)
Literární listy (Literary Letters)
Literární noviny (Literary News)
Mladá fronta (Young Front)
Mladá fronta dnes (Young Front Today)
Mladý svět (Young World)

Občanský deník (Civic Daily)
O divadle (About Theater)
Podoby (Forms)
Práce (Labor)
Právo (Truth)
Rovnost (Equality)
Rozhlas (Broadcast)
Rudé právo (Red Truth)
Scéna (Stage)
Smena (Exchange)
Svědectví (Witness)
Svět a divadlo (World and the Theater)
Světová literatura (World Literature)
Svobodné slovo (Free Word)
Večerní Praha (Evening Prague)

APPENDIX C

Czech Pronunciation

Czech is a Slavic language, written in the Latin alphabet. It is a phonetic language, meaning that, in general, words are pronounced as they are written. The accent is always on the first syllable. Here is an abbreviated guide for the reader:

VOWELS

a	as in *far*
á	elongated *a* as in *aah*
e	as in *bet*
é	as in *say*
ě	as in *yet*
i, y	as in *wit*
í, ý	as in *meet*
o	as in *dog*
u	as in *book*
ů	as in *rule*

CERTAIN CONSONANTS

c	as in *hats* (for example, Václav is pronounced vats-lav)
č	as in *check* (for example, Český is pronounced chess-kee)
ch	as in *Bach* (for example, Machonin is pronounced ma-khon-in)
j	like the *y* in *yes* (for example, Jiří is pronounced yir-zhee)
ř	as in *rzh* (for example, Jiří is pronounced yir-zhee)
š	as in *sh* (for example, Hašek is pronounced ha-shek)
ž	like the *s* in *measure* (for example, the Czech word for *life*, *Život,* is pronounced zhee-vot)

Selected Bibliography

WORKS BY VÁCLAV HAVEL

Plays and Collected Essays

In English

Havel, Václav. *Audience*, Jan Novak, trans.; *Unveiling*, Jan Novalk, trans.; *Protest*, Vera Blackwell, trans. In *The Vaněk Plays: Four Authors, One Character*, Marketa Goetz-Stankiewicz, ed. Vancouver: The University of British Columbia Press, 1987.

———. *The Art of the Impossible: Politics as Morality in Practice*. Speeches and writings, 1990–1996, Paul Wilson and others, trans. New York: Fromm International, 1998.

———. *The Beggar's Opera*, Paul Wilson, trans. Ithaca: Cornell University Press, 2001.

———. *Disturbing the Peace: A Conversation with Karel Hvížďala*, Paul Wilson, trans. New York: Vintage Books, 1991.

———. *Letters to Olga*, Paul Wilson, trans. New York: Henry Holt, 1989.

———. *Open Letters: Selected Writings, 1956–1990*, Paul Wilson, ed. New York: Alfred A. Knopf, 1991.

———. *Selected Plays 1963–1983*. *The Garden Party*, Vera Blackwell, trans.; *The Memorandum*, Vera Blackwell, trans.; *The Increased Difficulty of Concentration*, Vera Blackwell, trans.; *Audience*, George Theiner, trans.; *Unveiling*, Jan Novák, trans.; *Protest*, Vera Blackwell, trans.; *Mistake*, George Theiner, trans. London: Faber & Faber, 1992.

———. *Selected Plays 1984–1987*. *Largo Desolato*, Tom Stoppard, trans.; *Temptation*, George Theiner, trans.; *Redevelopment*, James Saunders, trans. London: Faber & Faber, 1994.

———. *Summer Meditations*, Paul Wilson, trans. New York: Vintage Books, 1993.

Havel, Václav et al. *The Power of the Powerless*, John Keane, ed. Armonk, New York: Palach Press/M. E. Sharpe, Inc., 1985.

Vladislav, Jan, ed. *Václav Havel or Living in Truth*. London: Faber & Faber, 1986. (Part One: Six Texts by Václav Havel; Part Two: Sixteen Texts for Václav Havel.)

In Czech

Havel, Václav. *Spisy*/1–7. (Writings, volumes 1–7). Praha: Torst, 1999. 1: Básně, Antikódy (Poems, Anticodes). 2: Hry (Plays). 3: Eseje a jiné texty z let 1953–1969 (Essays and other texts from 1953–1969). 4: Eseje a jiné texty z let 1970–1989 (Essays and other texts from 1970–1989). 5: Dopisy Olze (Letters to Olga). 6: Projevy z let 1990–1992; Letní přemítání (Speeches from 1990–1992; Summer Meditations). 7: Projevy a jiné texty z let 1992–1999 (Speeches and other texts from 1992–1999).

Selected Essays and Articles About the Theater

In English

Havel, Václav. "A Farewell to Politics," Paul Wilson, trans., in *New York Review of Books*, October 24, 2002.

———. "Last Conversations," Milan Pomichalek and Anna Mozga, trans., in *Good-bye, Samizdat: Twenty Years of Czechoslovak Underground Writing*, Marketa Goetz-Stankiewicz, ed. Evanston: Northwestern University Press, 1992.

———. "Light on a Landscape," by Milan Pomichalek and Anna Mozga, trans., in *The Vaněk Plays: Four Authors, One Character*, Marketa Goetz-Stankiewicz, ed. Vancouver: University of British Columbia Press, 1987.

———. "Politics and the Theatre," *Times Literary Supplement*, September 28, 1967.

———. "Second Wind," Paul Wilson, trans., in *Good-bye, Samizdat. Twenty Years of Czechoslovak Underground Writing*, Marketa Goetz-Stankiewicz, ed. Evanston: Northwestern University Press, 1992.

"Not Only About Theatre," a discussion between playwrights Václav Havel, Arthur Miller, and Tom Stoppard; Ronald Harwood, chairman, in *Théâter tchéque* (Czech Theater), vol. 12, September 1995.

In Czech

Havel, Václav. "Anatomie gagu" (The Anatomy of the Gag), *Spisy*/3. Praha: Torst, 1999.

———. "Daleko od divadla" (Far from the Theater), *Spisy*/4. Praha: Torst, 1999.

———. "Dovětek autora ke knize *Hry 1970–1976*" (Afterword to Plays 1970–1976). Toronto: Sixty-Eight Publishers Corporation, 1977. (Also in *Spisy*/4.)

————. "Fakta o představení *Žebrácká opery*" (Facts About the Performance of *The Beggar's Opera*), *Spisy*/4. Praha: Torst, 1999.

————. "Ještě jednou obrození?" (Yet Another National Revival?), *Divadlo* (Theater), vol. 20, no. 1, January 1969.

————. "Komentář ke hře *Eduard*" (Commentary on the Play *Eduard*), *Spisy*/3. Praha: Torst, 1999.

————. "Komentář ke hře *Spiklenci*," (Commentary on the Play *The Conspirators*), *Spisy*/4, Praha: Torst, 1999.

————. "Několik poznámek ze *Švédské zápalky*" (Some Notes on *The Swedish Match*), *Spisy*/3. Praha: Torst, 1999.

————. "Z poznámek Václava Havla, psaných pro inscenátory hry *Largo Desolato*" (Annotations by Václav Havel for the Production of *Largo Desolato*), *O divadle* (About Theater), 1986.

Unpublished

Correspondence between Václav Havel and Joseph Papp, January 26, 1967–July 28, 1968 (with the permission of Gail Papp, from her private archive).

Letter from Václav Havel to Andrej Krob regarding *The Beggar's Opera*, April 24, 1975 (with the permission of Andrej Krob, from his private archive).

Letter from Václav Havel to Andrej Krob and Anna Freimanová regarding *Temptation*, October 1986 (with the permission of Andrej Krob, from his private archive).

Letter from Václav Havel to Miloš Forman regarding Joseph Papp's invitation to America in 1979 (no date; probably 1983) (with the permission of Miloš Forman, from his private archive).

Letter from Samuel Beckett to Václav Havel, May 29, 1983 (with the permission of Klaus Juncker, from his private archive).

Havel, Václav. Stage Manager notes, from the Theatre on the Balustrade, February–November 1965 (with the permission of the Theatre on the Balustrade).

OTHER BOOKS

In English

Albertová, Helena, ed. *Václav Havel: A Citizen and a Playwright*. Prague: Theatre Institute, 1999.

Burian, Jarko. *Modern Czech Theatre*. Iowa City: University of Iowa Press, 2000.

Epstein, Helen. *Joe Papp: An American Life*. New York: Da Capo Press, 1996.

Esslin, Martin. *The Theatre of the Absurd*. London: Penguin, 1980 (3rd edition).

————. *Three East European Plays*. London: Penguin, 1970.

Fukač, Jiří, Zdenka Pospíšilová, and Alena Mizerová, eds. *Václav Havel as a Dramatist*. Brno: Compostela Group of Universities/VUTIUM Press, 2001.

Goetz-Stankiewicz, Marketa, ed. *Good-bye, Samizdat: Twenty Years of Czechoslovak Underground Writing*. Evanston: Northwestern University Press, 1992.

————. *The Silenced Theatre: Czech Playwrights Without a Stage*. Toronto: University of Toronto Press, 1979.

————. *The Vaněk Plays: Four Authors, One Character*. Vancouver: University of British Columbia Press, 1987.

Goetz-Stankiewicz, Marketa, and Phyllis Carey, eds. *Critical Essays on Václav Havel*. New York: G. K. Hall & Co., 1999.

Gussow, Mel. *Edward Albee: A Singular Journey*. New York: Simon & Schuster, 1999.

Hůrková , Klára. *Mirror Images: A Comparison of the Early Plays of Václav Havel and Tom Stoppard*. Frankfurt, Peter Lang: Europaischer Verlag der Wissenschaften, 2000.

Keane, John. *Václav Havel: A Political Tragedy in Six Acts*. New York: Basic Books (Perseus Books Group), 2000.

Klíma, Ivan. *My Golden Trades*, Paul Wilson, trans. London: Granta Books, 1992.

Kriseová, Edá. *Václav Havel, The Authorized Biography*. Caleb Crain, trans. New York: St. Martin's Press, 1993.

Kyncl, Karel. *After the Spring Came Winter*. Sweden: Askelin & Hagglund, 1985.

Loggia, Marjoria and Glenn Young, eds. *The Collected Works of Harold Clurman*. New York: Applause Books, 1994.

Merritt, Susan Hollis. *Pinter in Play*. Durham: Duke University Press, 1990.

Nadel, Ira. *Double Act: A Life of Tom Stoppard*. London: Methuen, 2002.

Roth, Philip. *Shop Talk*. New York: Houghton Mifflin Company, 2001.

Simmons, Michael. *The Reluctant President*. London: Methuen, 1991.

Tynan, Kenneth. *Show People: Profiles in Entertainment*. New York: Simon & Schuster, 1979.

In Czech

Kosatík, Pavel. *Člověk má dělat to, nač má sílu, Život Olgy Havlové.* (One Does What One Can: The Life of Olga Havlová). Praha: Mladá Fronta, 1997.

———. *Fenomén Kohout* (The Phenomenon Kohout). Praha: Paseka, 2001.

Krob, Andrej. *Divadlo na tahu: 1975–1995.* Praha: Originální Videojournal, 1995.

Milý Václave . . . Tvůj: Přemýšlení o Václavu Havlovi (Dear Václav . . . Yours Truly; Reminiscences of Václav Havel). Praha: Divadelní Ústav a NLN, Nakladatelství Lidové noviny, 1997.

SELECTED ARTICLES

In English

Bernstein, Richard. "Exit Havel to Muted Applause from Czechs," *New York Times,* January 25, 2003.

Dienstbier, Jiří. "On Reception," in *The Vaněk Plays: Four Authors, One Character,* Marketa Goetz-Stankiewicz, ed. Vancouver: University of British Columbia Press, 1987.

Kohout, Pavel. "The Chaste Centaur (Havel's Vaněk and Vaněk's Havel)," in *The Vaněk Plays: Four Authors, One Character,* Marketa Goetz-Stankiewicz, ed. Vancouver: University of British Columbia Press, 1987.

Landovský, Pavel. "Ferdinand Havel and Václav Vaněk," in *The Vaněk Plays: Four Authors, One Character,* Marketa Goetz-Stankiewicz, ed. Vancouver: University of British Columbia Press, 1987.

Merritt, Susan Hollis. "The Outsider in Pinter and Havel," in *Pinter at Sixty,* Katherine H. Burkman and John L Kundert-Gibbs, eds. Bloomington: Indiana University Press, 1993.

Oslzlý, Petr. "On Stage with the Velvet Revolution," *The Drama Review* 34, no. 3 (T127), fall 1990.

Reslová, Marie. "The Theatre Divadlo na tahu," in *Théâter tchéque* (Czech Theater), vol. 12, 1996.

Stoppard, Tom. "Dirty Linen in Prague," *New York Times,* February 11, 1977.

———. "Prague: The Story of the Chartists," *New York Review of Books,* August 4, 1977.

Tynan, Kenneth. "The Theatre Abroad: Prague," *The New Yorker,* April 1, 1967.

Wilson, Paul. "Havel's Victory," *New York Review of Books.* vol. I, no. 6, April 10, 2003.

In Czech

Grossman, Jan. "Uvedení Zahradní slavnosti" (introduction to *The Garden Party*) in *Spisy*/2. Praha: Torst, 1999.

Kantůrková, Eva. "Je něco jisté?" (Is Nothing Certain?) in "Sešly jsme v této knize" (We Met in This Book), *Index Koln*, BDR, 1980.

Landovský, Pavel. "Jmenoval jsem se hercem" (I Declare Myself an Actor), a six-part series in *Divadelní noviny*:
I: "Jak jsem dobýval uhlí" (How I Dug Coal), No. 10/May 15, 2001.
II: "Jak jsem dobýval Divadlo na zábradlí" (How I Got to the Theatre on the Balustrade), no. 11, May 29, 2001.
III: "Jak jsem dobyl Činoherní Klub" (How I Conquered the Činoherní Klub), no. 12, June 12, 2001.
IV: "Jak mě vybyli z Činoherní Klub" (How I Was Excommunicated from the Činoherní Klub), no. 13, June 26, 2001.
V: "Jak mě bili, ale nezabili" (How They Beat me, but Didn't Kill Me), no. 14, September 6, 2001.
VI: "Jak jsem dobýval Vídeň" (How I Conquered Vienna), no. 15, September 18, 2001.

VIDEOTAPES

"Charta 77: Proměny" (Change). Česká televize, January 9, 1997.
"Charta 77: Začátky" (Beginning). Česká televize, January 7, 1997.
"Czechmate: Inside the Revolution." BBC, May 30, 1990.
"From Playwright to President." 20/20, ABC News, February 2, 1990.
Kisil, Alex. "Jan Grossman: Žít svůj osud" (Jan Grossman: To Live Your Fate). Česká televize, 1997.
Krob, Andrej. "A znovu *Žebrácká Opera*" (Once Again, *The Beggar's Opera*). Česká televize, 1995.
———. "Chyba aneb muž ze seznamu" (Mistake, or Man from the List). Originální videožurnál. Česká televize, 1995.
———. "Divadlo na tahu." Česká televize. 1995.
"Proč Havel?" (Why Havel?). Praha: Les Productions La Fete, 1990.

PLAYS CITED (other than Havel's)

Albee, Edward. *The American Dream* in *Two Plays* by Edward Albee. New York: Signet, 1961.

Beckett, Samuel. *Catastrophe* in *Collected Shorter Plays*. New York: Grove Press, 1984.

Dienstbier, Jiří`. *Reception* in *The Vaněk Plays: Four Authors, One Character*, Marketa Goetz-Stankiewicz, ed. Vancouver: University of British Columbia Press, 1987.

Kohout, Pavel. *Permit. Morass. Safari.* in *The Vaněk Plays: Four Authors, One Character*, Marketa Goetz-Stankiewicz, ed. Vancouver: University of British Columbia Press, 1987.

Landovský, Pavel. *Arrest* in *The Vaněk Plays: Four Authors, One Character*, Marketa Goetz-Stankiewicz, ed. Vancouver: University of British Columbia Press, 1987.

Miller, Arthur. *The Crucible.* New York: Penguin Books, 1976.

————. *I think about you a great deal*, in *Václav Havel or Living in Truth*, Jan Vladislav, ed. London: Faber & Faber, 1986.

Stoppard, Tom. *Professional Foul*, in *Plays 3*. London: Faber and Faber, 1993 (c. 1978).

Notes

Note: In the case of the Czech references, quotations from those works where a translator's name is not indicated have been translated by Tomáš Rychetský.

PROLOGUE

1. Richard Bernstein, "Exit Havel, to Muted Applause from Czechs," *New York Times*, January 25, 2003.

2. Václav Havel, "A Farewell to Politics," *New York Review of Books*, October 24, 2002, p. 4.

PART I: THE FIFTIES: THE EDUCATION OF A WRITER

Biographical information for this part has been obtained from the following sources, among others: Václav Havel, *Disturbing the Peace*; John Keane, *Václav Havel: A Political Tragedy in Six Acts*; Pavel Kosatík, *Člověk má dělat to, nač má sílu, Život Olgy Havlové* (One Should Do What One Can: The Life of Olga Havlová); Edá Kriseová, *Václav Havel: The Authorized Biography*. Information has also been obtained from interviews with Ivan Havel, Miloš Forman, and Edá Kriseová.

1. Václav Havel, *Disturbing the Peace: A Conversation with Karel Hvížďala*, Paul Wilson, trans. (New York: Vintage Books, 1991), p. 23.

Scene One

1. Božena Havlová. In Czech, "Havlová" is the feminine surname for "Havel." It will be used, where appropriate, throughout this study.

2. According to Havel's brother, Ivan, the name of the street on which their family house stood changed many times, reflecting the country's political shifts. Before World War II, it was called Palackého nábřeží (Palacky's embankment), named after the nineteenth-century poet who wrote the first Czech-German dictionary. During the war, it was called Vltavské nábřeží, after the Vltava River, upon whose embankment it sat. After the war, the name reverted briefly to Palackého nábřeží; after the advent of Communism in 1948, it was called Engelsovo nábřeží (after Karl Engels). Since the Velvet Revolution, it became Rašínovo nábřeží (Rašín's embankment) after one of the leading politicians who helped create the Czechoslovak nation in 1918. And so it went with names and places, during the decades of revolving foreign rule throughout the twentieth century.

1951–1955: The Education of an Outsider

1. Havel, *Disturbing the Peace*, p. 6.
2. Kenneth Tynan, *Show People* (New York: Simon & Schuster, 1979), p. 74.
3. Interview with Ivan Havel, October 7, 2002.
4. Václav Havel, Letter 74 (April 4, 1981) in *Letters to Olga*, Paul Wilson, trans. (New York: Henry Holt, 1989), p. 179.
5. Havel, *Disturbing the Peace*, p. 5.
6. Havel, Letter 74 (April 4, 1981) in *Letters to Olga*, p. 180.
7. Interview with Miloš Forman, January 31, 2003.
8. John Keane, *Václav Havel: A Political Tragedy in Six Acts* (London: Basic Books, 2000), p. 114.
9. Edá Kriseová, *Václav Havel: The Authorized Biography* (New York: St. Martin's Press, 1993), pp. 83–87.
10. Interview with Miloš Forman, January 31, 2003.
11. Keane, *Václav Havel*, p. 107. The title character of Jaroslav Hašek's famous novel, *The Good Soldier Schweik* (1921), is a soldier who drives his superior officers to distraction by practicing passive resistance beneath a mask of conformity. Schweik (Svejk, in Czech) is the archetypical little man who beats the system and survives through resourcefulness and cunning, while fooling the authorities into thinking he is cooperating. There are various spellings of Schweik's name (Svejk, Schweyk); for the sake of consistency, Schweik is used here.
12. Pavel Kosatík, *Člověk má dělat to, nač má sílu, Život Olgy Havlové* (One Should Do What One Can: The Life of Olga Havlová) (Prague: Mladá Fronta [Young Front], 1997), p. 49.
13. Ibid., p. 50.
14. Interview with Aleš Kisil, May 20, 2002.
15. Havel, *Disturbing the Peace*, p. 27.
16. Ibid.
17. Ibid.
18. Ibid., p. 6.
19. The National Theater in Prague was built in the nineteenth century under the Habsburg rule. As the first theater built expressly for performances in the Czech language, it is a symbol of national identity, and the story of its construction is now legendary. When its foundation was laid in May 1868, a three-day national festival was held to celebrate the occasion. The cornerstone was imported from (the supposedly magical) Mount Rip in Bohemia, a significant site in Czech mythology. The theater had its grand opening on June 11, 1881; then, two months later, it burned to the ground. Remarkably, it was rebuilt in only two years. The second opening on November 18, 1883, is considered its official one. According to theater historian Jarka Burian, the

theater is "a symbol of national identity fused with the concept of theater as a moral and educational force." (Jarka M. Burian, *Modern Czech Drama* [Iowa City: University of Iowa Press, 2000], p. 15).

1956: A Young Writer Makes his Debut

1. Havel, *Disturbing the Peace*, p. 32.
2. Václav Havel, "Second Wind," Paul Wilson, trans., in *Good-bye, Samizdat*, Marketa Goetz-Stankiewicz, ed. (Evanston: Northwestern University Press, 1992), p. 206.
3. Havel, *Disturbing the Peace*, p. 32.
4. Pavel Kosatík, *Člověk má dělat to, nač má sílu*, pp. 50–51.
5. Havel, "Tvá duše je předměstí (Your Soul Is on the Outskirts), in "Na okraji Jara" (On the Edge of Spring), in Václav Havel, *Spisy*/1 (Writings, vol. 1), Básně (Poems), (Praha: Torst, 1999), p. 183.
6. Kosatík, *Člověk má dělat to, nač má sílu*, pp. 50–51.

1957–1959: A Soldier Plays (pages 21–23)

1. Pavel Landovský, in Kriseová, *Václav Havel*, p. 20.
2. Havel, *Disturbing the Peace*, p. 40.
3. Keane, *Václav Havel*, p. 145.

PART II: THE SIXTIES: ENTER VÁCLAV HAVEL

Background information for this part has been obtained from the following sources, among others: Václav Havel, *Disturbing the Peace*; Jarko Burian, *Modern Czech Drama*; John Keane, *Václav Havel: A Political Tragedy in Six Acts*; Edá Kriseová, *Václav Havel: The Authorized Biography*. Information has also been obtained from interviews with Václav Havel, Ivan Havel, Miloš Forman, Zdeněk Hořínek, Klaus Juncker, Aleš Kisil, Andrej Krob, Jiří Paukert/Kuběna, Pavel Landovský, Marie Málková, Jiří Ornest, Vladimír Vodička, and Ivan Vyskočil.

1. Havel, "Second Wind," p. 208.

1960: Learning the ABCs

1. Havel, *Disturbing the Peace*, p. 40.
2. Ibid.
3. Havel, "Několik poznámek ze Švédské zápalky" (Some Notes on *The Swedish Match*, 1962) in *Spisy*/3 (Writings, vol. 3), Eseje a jiné texty z let 1953–1969 (Essays and various texts from 1953–1969), p. 418.
4. Havel, *Disturbing the Peace*, p. 40.
5. Ibid.

1960: The Playwright Finds a Home

1. Havel, *Disturbing the Peace*, p. 45.
2. Ibid., p. 43.
3. Ibid., p. 77.
4. Interview with President Václav Havel, Prague Castle, March 13, 2002.
5. Jan Grossman, *Divadelní noviny* (Theater News), vol. 4, 1960, p. 170.
6. Ibid.
7. Havel, *Disturbing the Peace*, p. 47.
8. Ibid, p. 46.
9. Interview with Václav Havel, March 13, 2002.
10. Interview with Zdeněk Hořínek, March 12, 2002.
11. Interview with Marie Málková, May 16, 2001.
12. Havel, *Disturbing the Peace*, p. 61.
13. Ibid., p. 48.
14. Ibid., p. 45.

1963: *The Garden Party*

1. Director, in Václav Havel, *The Garden Party*, Vera Blackwell, trans., in *Selected Plays 1963–1983* (London: Faber & Faber, 1992), p. 31.
2. Kriseová, *Václav Havel*, p. 51.
3. Interview with Andrej Krob, May 17, 2001.
4. Andrej Krob, *Theatre on the Road* (Divadlo na tahu) (Praha: Original Videojournal [Originální Videojournal], 1995), p. 36.
5. Havel, *Mladý svět* (Young World), August 7, 1969.
6. Havel, *The Garden Party*, p. 7.
7. Ibid., p. 15.
8. Ibid., p. 23.
9. Ibid., p. 20.
10. Ibid., pp. 35–36.
11. Ibid., p. 50.
12. Shakespeare, *Hamlet*, II, ii.
13. Havel, *The Garden Party*, pp. 4–6.
14. Ibid., p. 20.
15. Ibid., p. 37.
16. Interview with Jiří Paukert/Kuběna, June 1, 2001.
17. Interview with Miloš Forman, January 31, 2003.
18. Interview with Ivan Havel, May 23, 2002.
19. Interview with Vladimír Vodička, October 18, 2001.
20. Interview with Jiří Ornest, May 12, 2001.
21. Jan Kopecký, in *Rudé právo* (Red Law), December 14, 1963.
22. Sergei Machonin, in *Literární noviny* (Literary News), December 7, 1963.

23. Jaroslava Suchomelová in *Mladá fronta*, April 28, 1964.
24. Eva Uhlířová, in *Divadelní noviny*, June 17, 1964.
25. *Smena* (Exchange), January 21, 1964.
26. Kenneth Tynan, "The Theatre Abroad: Prague," in *The New Yorker*, April 1967, p. 112.
27. Grossman, "Uvedení Zahradní slavnosti" (introduction to *The Garden Party*), in *Spisy/2* (Writings, vol. 2), Hry (Plays), p. 1001.
28. Paul Trensky, "*The Garden Party* Revisited," in *Critical Essays on Václav Havel*, Marketa Goetz-Stankiewicz and Phyllis Carey, eds. (New York: G. K. Hall & Co., 1999), p. 159.

1963–1964 in Prague: A Cultural Awakening

1. Kosatík, *Člověk má dělat to, nač má sílu*, p. 84.
2. Interview with Ivan Havel, October 7, 2002.
3. Jarka M. Burian, *Modern Czech Theatre*, p. 101.
4. Havel, *Disturbing the Peace*, pp. 50–51.
5. Kosatík, *Člověk má dělat to, nač má sílu*, p. 84
6. Martin Esslin, in *Ira Nadel, Double Act: A Life of Tom Stoppard* (London: Methuen, 2002), p. 276.

1964: A Season of the Absurd at the Theatre on the Balustrade

1. Havel, *Disturbing the Peace*, 54.
2. Aleš Kisil, "Jan Grossman: Žít svůj osud" (To Live Your Fate) (video documentary), Ćeská televize, 1997
3. Havel, *Disturbing the Peace*, p. 54.
4. Interview with Václav Havel, March 13, 2002.
5. Ibid.
6. Havel, "Anatomie gagu" (The Anatomy of the Gag), in *Spisy/3* (Writing, vol. 3), p. 589.
7. Interview with Klaus Juncker, October 27, 2002.
8. Zuzana Jánská, "Muž, který objevil Václava Havla světu" (The Man Who Discovered Václav Havel for the World), *Hospodářské noviny-víkend* (Economic News), 41st ed., 2002, p. 14.
9. Interview with Klaus Juncker, October 27, 2002.
10. Jánská, "Muž, který objevil Václava Havel světu," p. 14.

1964: Marriage

1. Václav Havel, introduction to *Letters to Olga*, p. 10.
2. Keane, *Václav Havel*, p. 158.
3. Pavel Landovský, "Jak jsem dobýval Divadlo na zábradlí" (How I conquered the Theatre on the Balustrade), in *Divadelní noviny*, May 15, 2001.

4. Eva Kantůrková, "Je něco jisté?" (Is nothing certain?), interview with Olga Havlová; published under the title "Sešly jsme se v této knize" (We Met in this Book) in *Index Koln*, BDR, 1980, p. 7.

5. Havel, Letter 74 in *Letters to Olga*, pp. 181-82.

6. Kantůrková, "Je něco jisté?," p. 7.

1964: Anticodes

1. Havel, *Disturbing the Peace*, p. 24.

2. Josef Hiršal, "Předmluva," "Antikódy" (preface to Anticodes) in *Spisy*/1, p. 393.

3. Havel, "Vpřed" (Ahead) in ibid., p. 272.

4. Havel, "Filosof" (Philosopher) in ibid., p. 276.

5. Hiršal, "Předmluva" (Preface) in *Spisy*/1, p. 393.

1965: The Memorandum

1. Kubš, in Václav Havel, *The Memorandum*, Vera Blackwell, trans., in *Selected Plays 1963-1983*, p. 122. Note: In this translation, the character's name is Pillar.

2. Interview with Ivan Havel, May 23, 2002

3. Kantůrková, "Je něco jisté?," p. 7.

4. Interview with Andrej Krob, May 17, 1901.

5. Havel, *The Memorandum*, p. 58.

6. Ibid., pp. 63-64. Blackwell's versions of Havel's character names are quoted here.

7. Ibid., p. 102.

8. Ibid., p. 94.

9. Ibid., pp. 74-76

10. Ibid., p. 79.

11. Ibid., pp. 125-26.

12. Ibid., p. 123.

13. Ibid., pp. 128-29.

14. Interview with Miloš Forman, January 31, 2003.

15. Pavel Bryn in *Lidová demokracie* (People's Democracy), July 18, 1965.

16. Jaroslav Opavsky, *Rudé právo*, September 29, 1965.

17. D. K., *Svobodné slovo* (Free Word), July 29, 1965.

18. Tibor Ferko, *Pravda* (Truth), Bratislava, August 5, 1965.

19. Zdeněk Hořínek, *Host do domu* (Guest of the House) September 1965.

20. Sergej Machonin, *Literární noviny*, August 8, 1965.

21. Stage manager notes handwritten by Havel, from the Theatre on the Balustrade archives, February–November 1965 (unpublished; quoted with the permission of the Theatre on the Balustrade).

22. Kriseová, *Václav Havel*, p. 47.

23. Ibid., p. 48.

1965–1968: From the Balustrade to the Theater of Politics
1. Havel, *Disturbing the Peace*, p. 77.
2. Ibid.
3. Ibid.
4. Ibid., p. 89.

1965–1968: *The Increased Difficulty of Concentration*
1. Kenneth Tynan, *The New Yorker*, April 1, 1967, p. 99.
2. Ibid.
3. Tynan, *Show People*, p. 74.
4. Tynan, *The New Yorker*, p. 112.
5. Tynan, *Morning Star* (London), May 6, 1967.
6. "Komentář ke hře *Eduard*" (Commentary on the play *Eduard*), 1966, in *Spisy/3*, p. 710.
7. Interview with Václav Havel, March 13, 2002.
8. Václav Havel, *The Increased Difficulty of Concentration*, Vera Blackwell, trans., in *Selected Plays 1963–1983*, p. 156.
9. Ibid., p. 175.
10. Ibid., pp. 176–77.
11. Ibid., pp. 179–80.
12. Vlasta Gallerová, in *Práce* (Labor), April 23, 1968.
13. Sergej Machonin, *Literární listy* (Literary Letters), May 9, 1968.
14. Zdeněk Hořínek, *Divadlo* (Theater), October 1968.
15. Alena Stránská, *Svobodné slovo*, April 17, 1968
16. Josef Šafařík, in "Program Divadla Na zábradlí psáno k premiéře hry *Ztížená možnost soustředění*" (Program notes for the production of *The Increased Difficulty of Concentration*, Theatre on the Balustrade), April 1968.
17. Harold Clurman, *The Nation*, December 22, 1969, in Harold, Clurman, *The Collected Works* (New York: Applause Theatre Books, 1994), p. 732.

1968: *Guardian Angel* and *A Butterfly on the Antenna*
1. Marie, in Václav Havel, *Motýl na anténě* (A Butterfly on the Antenna), in *Spisy/2*, p. 240, Tomaš Rychetsky and Carol Rocamora, trans.
2. The first version of *Guardian Angel* was published in *Divadelní noviny*, 1963–1964, vol. 10–11, p. 10.
3. *Guardian Angel*, quoted from an unpublished translation by Vera Blackwell, courtesy of the Orange Tree Theatre.
4. Havel, *Motýl na anténě* (A Butterfly on the Antenna), p. 254.
5. "They," meaning the censors.
6. Havel, *Motýl na anténě* (A Butterfly on the Antenna), pp. 225–26.

7. Ibid, p. 252.

8. Ibid., pp. 247–48.

9. Ibid., pp. 242–43. References in this speech are to Czech writers, and are erudite and intentionally arcane. Shalda was a literary critic of the 1930s; Sramek was a poet of the 1930s; Ludvík Kundera was a Brno novelist of the 1950s.

1968: Prague Spring

1. Havel, *Disturbing the Peace*, pp. 93–94.

2. Ibid, p. 94.

1968: New York Spring

1. Letter from Havel to Joseph Papp, July 28, 1969 (unpublished; quoted with the permission of Gail Papp).

2. Interview with Gail Papp, September 30, 2002.

3. Helen Epstein, *Joe Papp: An American Life* (New York: Da Capo Press, 1996), pp. 224–25.

4. Letter from Joseph Papp to Václav Havel, January 26, 1967 (unpublished; quoted with the permission of Gail Papp).

5. Letter from Havel to Papp, February 5, 1967.

6. Letter from Papp to Havel, December 8, 1967.

7. Letter from Havel to Papp, January 14, 1968.

8. Letter from Papp to Havel, March 25, 1968.

9. Keane, *Václav Havel*, p. 186.

10. Epstein, Joe Papp, p. 207.

11. Clive Barnes, *New York Times*, May 6, 1968.

12. Ibid.

13. Interview with Olympia Dukakis, March 6, 2003.

14. Interview with Miloš Forman, January 31, 2003. Forman would emigrate to America a year later, in 1969. He became a U.S. citizen in 1977.

15. Janska, "Muž, který objevil Václava Havla světu," p. 15.

16. Letter from Havel to Papp, July 28, 1968.

1968: Summer

1. Tynan, *The New Yorker*, p. 99.

2. Kosatík, *Člověk má dělat to, nač má sílu*, p. 102.

3. Jan Tříska, in *Milý Václave . . . Tvůj: Přemýšlení o Václavu Havlovi* (Dear Václav . . . Yours Truly: Reminiscences of Václav Havel) (Praha: Divadelní Ústav, 1997), p. 67.

4. Ibid., pp. 68–72.

1968–1969: The Aftermath

1. Staněk, in Václav Havel, *Protest*, Vera Blackwell, trans., in *The Vaněk Plays: Four Authors, One Character*, Marketa Goetz-Stankiewicz, ed. (Vancouver: University of British Columbia Press, 1987), p. 57.
2. Václav Havel, in *Mladý svět* (Young World), August 7, 1969.
3. Havel, "Second Wind," in *Good-bye, Samizdat*, p. 210.
4. Keane, *Václav Havel*, p. 224.
5. Václav Havel, "Letter to Alexander Dubček," in *Open Letters: Selected Writings 1965–1990*, Paul Wilson, ed. (New York: Alfred A. Knopf, 1991), pp. 36–37.
6. Ibid., pp. 48–49.

The 1960s: Conclusion

1. Václav Havel, "Second Wind," p. 207.
2. Kosatík, *Člověk má dělat to, nač má sílu*, p. 84.
3. Václav Havel, "Generace 21 sprna," in *Spisy*/1, p. 334.
4. Havel, *Disturbing the Peace*, pp. 51–52.
5. Havel, "Second Wind," p. 205.
6. Ibid., p. 208.
7. Ibid., pp. 206–7.

PART III: THE SEVENTIES

Background information for this part has been obtained from the following sources, among others: Václav Havel, *Disturbing the Peace*; Václav Havel, *Letters to Olga*; John Keane, *Václav Havel: A Political Tragedy in Six Acts*; Edá Kriseová, *Václav Havel: The Authorized Biography*; Peter Steiner's introduction to Václav Havel's *The Beggar's Opera*; Pavel Kosatík, *Fenomén Kohout* (The Phenomenon Kohout); Pavel Landovský's six-part series of articles "Jmenoval jsem se hercem" (I Declare Myself an Actor), in *Divadelní noviny*, May 15–September 18, 2001; *The Vaněk Plays: Four Authors, One Character*, Marketa Goetz-Stankiewicz, ed. Information has also been obtained from interviews with Václav Havel, Ivan Havel, Vlasta Chramostová, Anna Freimanová, Bohumil Holomíček, Jan Kačer, Ivan Klíma, Andrej Krob, Pavel Landovský, Jiřina Šiklová, and Tomáš Vrba.

1. Havel, *Disturbing the Peace*, p. 119.

1970: A Dark Decade Begins

1. Havel, "Second Wind," pp. 209–210.
2. Ibid.
3. Keane, *Václav Havel*, p. 232.
4. Havel, "Second Wind," p. 208.
5. Ibid., p. 210.

1970–1971: *The Conspirators*

1. Havel, *Spiklenci* (The Conspirators), in *Spisy*/2, p. 223.
2. Havel, *Disturbing the Peace*, p. 120.
3. Interview with Václav Havel, March 13, 2002.
4. Havel, "Dovětek autora ke knize *Hry 1970–1976*" (Afterword to Plays 1970–1976) in *Spisy*/4, p. 153.

1970–1976: *Mountain Hotel*

1. Václav Havel, "It Always Makes Sense to Tell the Truth: An Interview with Jiří Lederer," Paul Wilson, trans., in *Open Letters*, p. 93.
2. Havel, Letter 71 (March 13, 1981) in *Letters to Olga*, pp. 170–71.
3. Havel, "Dovětek autora," p. 156.
4. Václav Havel, *Horský hotel* (Mountain Hotel), in *Spisy*/2, p. 615.
5. Havel, Letter 19 (January 27, 1980) in *Letters to Olga*, p. 85.
6. Ibid., Letter 71 (March 3, 1981), p. 171.
7. Havel, "Dovětek autora," p. 156.
8. Havel, "Second Wind," p. 209.
9. Ibid.
10. Havel, "Dovětek autora," p. 153.

1971–1974: Writers in Search of a Home

1. Havel, *Disturbing the Peace*, pp. 119–20.
2. Ibid., 121.
3. Kantůrková, "Je něco jisté?," p. 8.
4. No Czech playwright in the 1960s, 1970s, or 1980s could contract Western agencies directly; every agreement had to go through Dilia, the state agency for writers.
5. Janska, "Muž, který objevil Václava Havla světu," p. 16.
6. Interview with Ivan Klíma, June 25, 2001.
7. Today in Prague, there is a museum called Libri prohibiti (Forbidden Books) on Senovážné náměstí, housing the treasures of *samizdat*, including thousands of typewritten manuscripts self-published during the 1970s and 1980s. It is open to the public for reading and research.
8. Pavel Kosatík, *Fenomén Kohout* (The Phenomenon Kohout), (Paseka, 2001), p. 340.
9. Interview with Vlasta Chramostová, September 27, 2001.
10. Kosatík, *Fenomén Kohout*, p. 343.
11. Ibid.
12. Karel Kyncl, *After the Spring Came Winter* (Sweden: Askkelin & Hagglund, 1985), p. 63.
13. Ibid., p. 65.

14. Klára Hůrková, *Mirror Images: A comparison of the early plays of Václav Havel and Tom Stoppard with special reference to their political aspects* (Frankfurt am Main: Peter Lang, Europaischer Verlag der Wissenschaften, 2000), p. 197.
15. Interview with Jiřina Šiklová, October 28, 2002.
16. Ibid.

1972–1975: *The Beggar's Opera*

1. Interview with Andrej Krob, May 17, 2001.
2. Havel, *Disturbing the Peace*, p. 120.
3. Havel, "Dovětek Autora," p. 154.
4. Interview with Jan Kačer, May 22, 2002. There is an ironic footnote to the story of the Činoherní Klub's commissioning of *The Beggar's Opera* from Havel. According to Vladimír Procháska in *Rudé právo*, at the outset, they had invited Havel to write it with the notion that Havel would make an anticapitalist adaptation of Brecht's play that would not be offensive to the new communist leadership. In that way, they could get the adaptation approved by the officials. But Havel's script was too anti-Communist, and too true a representation of normalization, where everyone was in partnership with everyone else, and everyone informs on everyone else. After the theater rejected Havel's manuscript, they commissioned another version, which was ultimately not produced. (Reported by Vladimír Procháska, *Rudé právo*, June 23, 1990.)
5. Interview with Andrej Krob, May 17, 2001. This quote and the following ones in this part are taken from two lengthy interviews with Andrej Krob: May 17, 2001 and March 10, 2002.
6. The phrase *na tahu* has several other meanings including the name of a chess move and "making the rounds," as in pub crawling.
7. Letter from Václav Havel to Andrej Krob, April 24, 1975 (unpublished; quoted with the permission of Andrej Krob).
8. Ibid.
9. Ibid.
10. Ibid.
11. Ibid.
12. Ibid.
13. Peter Steiner, introduction to Václav Havel's *The Beggar's Opera*, Paul Wilson, trans. (Ithaca: Cornell University Press, 2001), p. xvii. Before Communism, the hotel pub in Horní Počernice called U Čelikovských had belonged to the Čelikovský family; once it was nationalized, it wasn't used for twenty years till the late 1960s. Then it was called the Hospoda u Bastily (Hotel Bastille).
14. Ibid.

15. Kriseová, *Václav Havel*, p. 92.
16. Olga Sommerová, "A znovu *Žebrácká opera*" (Once Again, *The Beggar's Opera*), objekt videopořadu (video documentary), 1995.
17. Havel, *Disturbing the Peace*, pp. 124–25.
18. Sommerová, "A znovu *Žebrácká opera*."
19. Interview with Ivan Klíma, June 25, 2001.
20. Sommerová, "A znovu *Žebrácká opera*."
21. Havel, *Disturbing the Peace*, p. 125.
22. Interview with Vlasta Chramostová, September 27, 2001.
23. Havel, "Dovětek autora," p. 154.
24. Havel, in Sommerová, "A znovu *Žebrácká opera*."
25. Ibid.
26. Steiner, introduction to *The Beggar's Opera*, p. xxi.
27. Václav Havel, "Fakta o představení *Žebrácká opery*," (Facts About *The Beggar's Opera*), in *Spisy/*4, Eseje a jiné texty z let 1970–1989 (Essays and Other Texts from 1970–1989), p. 114.
28. Aleš Kisil, "Jan Grossman: Žít svůj osud" (To Live Your Fate) (video documentary), Česká televize, 1997.
29. Havel, *Disturbing the Peace*, 125.
30. Sommerová, "A znovu *Žebrácká opera*."
31. Havel, "Fakta o představeni *Žebrácká opery*," pp. 115–16.
32. Ibid.
33. Ibid.
34. Havel, *The Beggar's Opera*, p. 84.
35. Ibid., pp. 42–43.
36. Ibid., p. 62.
37. Ibid., p. 63.
38. "*Někdo tu práci dělat musí*" (Someone has to do the job) was also a slogan in Czechoslovakia in the 1970s.
39. Havel, *The Beggar's Opera*, p. 71.
40. Ibid., p. 81.
41. Ibid., p. 84.
42. Havel, "The Power of the Powerless," Paul Wilson, trans., in *Václav Havel, or Living in Truth*, Jan Vladislav, ed. (London: Faber & Faber, 1986), p. 45.
43. Havel, *The Beggar's Opera*, p. 74.
44. Ibid., p. 66.
45. Kriseová, *Václav Havel*, pp. 92–93.
46. Sommerová, "A znovu *Žebrácká opera*."
47. Havel, *Disturbing the Peace*, p. 125.

1974–1975: "Second Wind"

1. Havel, "Second Wind," p. 208.
2. According to Klaus Juncker, Havel's agent, who had sent him the royalties: "Havel's father had said to his son: 'Our family once had a Mercedes; you should buy one. They're the best.' So Havel bought a used one." (From interview with Klaus Juncker, October 27, 2002.)
3. Interview with Tomáš Vrba, October 18, 2001.
4. Ivan Klíma, *My Golden Trades*, Paul Wilson, trans. (London: Granta Books, 1992), p. 283.
5. Ibid., p. 284.
6. Havel, "It Always Makes Sense to Tell the Truth," p. 90.
7. Kriseová, *Václav Havel*, pp. 91–92.
8. Havel, *Disturbing the Peace*, p. 122.
9. Ibid.
10. Václav Havel, "Letter to Dr. Gustáv Husák," Paul Wilson, trans., in *Living in Truth*, pp. 34–35.
11. Havel, *Disturbing the Peace*, p. 123.

1975: *Audience* and *Vernissage*

1. Sládek in Havel, *Audience*, in *The Vaněk Plays*, pp. 9–10.
2. Havel, "Light on a Landscape," Milan Pomichalek and Anna Mozga, trans., in *The Vaněk Plays*, p. 237.
3. Havel, *Audience*, Jan Novák, trans., in *The Vaněk Plays*, p. 6.
4. Ibid., p. 6.
5. Ibid., p. 9.
6. Ibid., pp. 19–20.
7. Ibid., pp. 22–23.
8. Ibid., p. 25.
9. Ibid., p. 23.
10. Havel, *Disturbing the Peace*, p. 123.
11. *Vernissage*, the title that Havel gave his play in Czech, means "the day before an exhibition opens reserved for artists to put finishing touches to their paintings," or "private showing or preview of an art exhibition." Since its translation varies — *Private View, Unveiling*, etc. — the original title given by Havel, *Vernissage*, has been used throughout this study. As for the character names: with respect to Michal, the husband, the translator quoted in this study uses the anglicized Michael; however, in this context, the original Michal has been preserved.
12. Havel, *Vernissage*, Jan Novák, trans., (as *Unveiling*), in *The Vaněk Plays*, p. 41.
13. Ibid., pp. 47–48.
14. Interview with Klaus Juncker, October 27, 2002.

NOTES TO PAGES 158–173   451

15. Janska, "Muž, který objevil Václava Havla světu," p. 16.

16. Havel, *Disturbing the Peace*, pp. 123–24.

17. Vilém Prečan, "A Short Bio-Bibliography of Václav Havel," in *Living in Truth*, p. 303.

18. Havel, "Dovětek autora," p. 157.

1976: A New Theatrical Home

1. Havel, "It Always Makes Sense to Tell the Truth," pp. 100–101.

2. "Na zbořenci": A further playful dimension to the street sign is its multiple meaning; namely: (1) on the site of the ruins of a house that has fallen down; (2) on the site where a person, who has had too much to drink, has fallen down.

3. Kantůrková, "Je něco jisté," p. 7.

1976–1979: *Living in Truth*

1. Havel, "The Power of the Powerless," in *Living in Truth*, pp. 59–60.

2. Havel, *Disturbing the Peace*, pp. 126–27.

3. Ibid., p. 128.

4. Ibid., p. 132.

5. Tom Stoppard, "Prague: The Story of the Chartists," *New York Review of Books*, August 4, 1977.

Charter 77

1. Jan Patočka, "What Charter 77 Is and What It Is Not," in *Good-bye, Samizdat*, p. 143.

2. Havel, *Disturbing the Peace*, p. 132.

3. Ibid., p. 134.

4. Ibid., p. 138.

5. Pavel Landovský, "Jak mě bili, ale nezabili" (How They Beat Me, but Didn't Kill Me), in *Divadelní noviny*, September 6, 2001, p. 16.

6. Havel, *Disturbing the Peace*, p. 140.

7. Václav Havel, "Last Conversation," Milan Pomichalek and Anna Mozga, trans., in *Good-bye, Samizdat*, p. 212.

8. Ibid., p. 213–14.

9. Havel, *Disturbing the Peace*, p. 143.

10. Ibid.

11. Ibid.

12. Krob, *Divadlo na zábradlí 1975–1995* (Theatre on the Road 1975–1995) (Prague: Originální videojournal, 1995), p. 6.

13. Havel, *Disturbing the Peace*, p. 143.

14. Interview with Pavel Landovský, June 22, 2001.

15. Havel, *Disturbing the Peace*, 145.
16. Ibid., p. 155.
17. Interview with Miloš Forman, January 31, 2003.
18. Helen Epstein, Joe Papp, p. 226.
19. Eva Kantůrková, "Je něco jisté?," pp. 5–7.
20. Ibid.
21. Kriseová, *Václav Havel*, p. 137.
22. Havel, Letter 138 (July 25, 1982) in *Letters to Olga*, p. 348.
23. Ibid., Letter 139 (July 31, 1982), p. 353.

1978: *Protest*
1. Staněk, Havel, *Protest*, p. 68.
2. Ibid., p. 61.
3. Ibid., pp. 67–68.
4. Ibid., p. 69.
5. Ibid., p. 71–72.
6. Ibid., p. 73.
7. Ibid., p. 74.
8. Ibid., p. 75.

The Vaněk Plays: A "Light on a Landscape"
1. Havel, "Light on a Landscape," p. 238.
2. Marketa Goetz-Stankiewicz, introduction to *The Vaněk Plays*, p. xviii.
3. Pavel Kohout, "The Chaste Centaur (Havel's Vaněk and Vaněk's Havel)," in *The Vaněk Plays*, p. 241.
4. Kosatik, *Fenomén Kohout,* p. 303.
5. Kohout, *Permit*, in ibid., p. 95.
6. Kohout, *Morass*, in ibid., p. 109.
7. Ibid., p. 125.
8. Ibid., p. 127.
9. Ibid., p. 130.
10. Ibid., p. 128.
11. Ibid., p. 142.
12. Landovský, in "Jak jsem dobýval Vídeň" (How I Conquered Vienna), in *Divadelní noviny*, Sept. 18, 2001, p. 16.)
13. Kohout, "The Chaste Centaur," p. 242.
14. Goetz-Stankewiecz, introduction to *The Vaněk Plays*, p. xviii.
15. Jiří Dienstbier, "On Reception," in *The Vaněk Plays*, p. 248.
16. Jiří Dienstbier, *Reception*, in *The Vaněk Plays*, p. 179.
17. Ibid., p. 196.
18. Dienstbier, "On Reception," p. 248.

19. Kohout, "The Chaste Centaur," p. 242.
20. Pavel Kohout, *Safari*, in *The Vaněk Plays*, p. 211.
21. Ibid., pp. 215–16.
22. Ibid., p. 236.
23. Kohout, "The Chaste Centaur," p. 244.
24. Ibid.
25. Pavel Landovský, "Ferdinand Havel and Václav Vaněk," in *The Vaněk Plays*, pp. 245–46.
26. Havel, "Light on a Landscape," p. 239.

PART IV: THE EIGHTIES: FAR FROM THE THEATER

Background material for this part has been obtained from the following sources, among others: Václav Havel, *Disturbing the Peace*; Václav Havel, *Letters to Olga*; John Keane, *Václav Havel: A Political Tragedy in Six Acts*; Edá Kriseová, *Václav Havel: The Authorized Biography*; Pavel Kosatík, *Člověk má dělat to, nač má sílu*; *Život Olga Havlová*. Information has also been obtained from interviews with Václav Havel, Ivan Havel, Miloš Forman, Andrej Krob, Vilém Prečan, Petr Oslzlý, Gail Papp, and Jiřina Šiklová and from the BBC documentary *Czechmate*, aired May 30, 1990.

1. "Václav Havel, "Daleko od divadla" ("Far from the Theater"), in *Spisy/4*, p. 636.

May 29, 1979–January 23, 1983: Serving the Sentence

1. Havel, *Disturbing the Peace*, p. 72.
2. Paul Wilson, introduction to *Letters to Olga*.
3. Kantůrková, "Je něco jisté?," pp. 5–7.
4. Havel, Letter 19 (January 27, 1980) in *Letters to Olga*, p. 69.
5. Ibid., Letter 17 (New Year's Eve, 1979), p. 63.
6. Ibid.
7. Ibid., Letter 126 (May 1, 1982), p. 310.
8. Kriseová, *Václav Havel*, p. 189.
9. Havel, Letter 81 (May 23, 1981) in *Letters to Olga*, p. 200.
10. Havel, *Disturbing the Peace*, p. 158–59.
11. Ibid., p. 161.

1979–1983: Letters to Olga from "the Convicted Václav Havel"

1. Havel, *Disturbing the Peace*, p. 152.
2. Wilson, introduction to *Letters to Olga*, p. 8.
3. Havel, *Disturbing the Peace*, p. 149.

4. Ibid., p. 148.
5. Wilson, introduction to *Letters to Olga*, p. 7.
6. Havel, *Disturbing the Peace*, p. 150.
7. Havel, Letter 44 (August 31, 1980) in *Letters to Olga*, p. 103.
8. Havel, author's preface to *Letters to Olga*.
9. Havel, *Disturbing the Peace*, p. 150.
10. Havel, author's preface to *Letters to Olga*.
11. Havel, Letter 13 (November 3, 1979), p. 44.
12. Ibid., Letter 5 (July 21, 1979), p. 29.
13. Ibid., Letter 14 (November 17, 1979), pp. 49–50.
14. Ibid., Letter 17 (New Year's Eve, 1979), pp. 61–62.
15. Ibid., Letter 31 (April 27, 1980), p. 85.
16. Ibid., Letter 45 (September 6, 1980), pp. 107–8.
17. Ibid., Letter 71 (March 13, 1981), p. 172.
18. Ibid., Letter 47 (September 21, 1980), p. 112.
19. Ibid., Letter 62 (January 2–6, 1981), p. 144–45.
20. Ibid., Letter 69 (February 22, 1981), p. 165.
21. Havel, Letter 102 (November 14, 1981), p. 249.
22. Ibid., Letter 89 (August 15, 1981), p. 215.
23. Ibid.
24. Ibid., Letter 90 (August 23, 1981), p. 218.
25. Ibid., Letter 91 (August 29, 1981), p. 223.
26. Ibid, Letter 102 (November 14, 1981), pp. 247–48.
27. Ibid., Letter 102 (November 14, 1981), pp. 248–49.
28. Ibid., Letter 116 (February 20, 1982), p. 289.
29. Ibid., Letter 103 (November 21, 1981), p. 250.
30. Ibid., Letter 107 (December 19, 1981), p. 261.
31. Ibid., Letter 112 (January 23, 1982), pp. 275–76.
32. Ibid., Letter 114 (February 6, 1982), p. 282.
33. Ibid., Letter 115 (February 13, 1982), p. 285.
34. Ibid.
35. Ibid., Letter 115 (February 13, 1982), p. 286.
36. Ibid., Letter 116 (February 20, 1982), p. 289.
37. Ibid., Letter 117 (February 27, 1982), p. 291.
38. Ibid., Letter 92 (September 6, 1981), p. 226.
39. *Libuše* and *The Bartered Bride* are operas by the Czech composer Bedřich Smetana.
40. Havel, Letter 115 (February 13, 1982) in *Letters to Olga*, pp. 286–87.
41. Havel, introduction to *Letters to Olga*, p. 10.
42. Havel, Letter 46 (September 12, 1998) in *Letters to Olga*, p. 109.

43. Ibid., Letter 13 (November 3, 1979), p. 46.

44. Kosatík, *Člověk má dělat to, nač má sílu*, p. 154.

45. Ibid., pp. 156–58.

46. Interview with Miloš Forman, January 31, 2003.

47. Kantůrková, "Je něco jisté?," pp. 5–7.

48. Havel, Letter 17 (New Year's Eve 1979) in *Letters to Olga*, p. 59.

1983: Mistake

1. Leopold in Václav Havel, *Largo Desolato*, Tom Stoppard, trans., in *Selected Plays 1884–1987* (London: Faber and Faber, 1994), p. 27.

2. Havel, *Disturbing the Peace*, pp. 161–62.

3. "I Take the Side of Truth," an interview with Antoine Spire, in *Le Monde*, April 10–11, 1983, George Theiner, trans., in *Václav Havel, Open Letters*, p. 237.

4. *Maryáš*: an old Czech card game, similar to bridge.

5. When Pavel Kohout left for Vienna in the late 1970s, for example, he still had his Czech citizenship. But while he was at the Burgtheater working as a consultant and director, the state held a mock trial in Czechoslovakia wherein Kohout's activities in Austria were declared to be against the interests of the Czech state. For this reason, his citizenship was revoked in absentia.

6. *Monstrák* (monster trial): a political trial conducted against a group such as the one in November 1952 during the Stalinist era, wherein Rudolf Slánský, general secretary of the Czech Communist Party, and thirteen high-ranking Communist codefendents were publicly tried. Slánský and ten others were hanged and cremated.

7. Letter from Václav Havel to Miloš Forman, 1983 (unpublished; quoted with the permission of Miloš Forman).

8. Václav Havel, *Chyba* (Mistake), in *Spisy/2*, p. 684. The last line of the play *Mistake*, is "Jeho chyba," meaning "that's (or it's) his mistake." There are other translations of this last line. George Theiner, for example, offers: "Well, that's his bloody funeral . . ." in Václav Havel, *Mistake*, in *Selected Plays 1963–1983*, p. 273. Here, I have used Tomáš Rychetský's translation: "Well, that's his mistake . . ."

9. Andrej Krob, "Chyba aneb muž ze seznamu" (Mistake or The Man from the List), Olga Sommerová, dramaturgie; Originální videožurnál, Česká televize, 1995.

10. Ibid.

11. Havel, Letter 13 (November 3, 1979) in *Letters to Olga*, p. 43.

12. Havel, *Disturbing the Peace*, p. 145.

13. Ibid., p. 146.

1984: *Largo Desolato*

1. Leopold, in Havel, *Largo Desolato*, p. 33.
2. Ibid., p. 26.
3. Interview with Andrej Krob, May 17, 2001.
4. Kriseová, *Václav Havel*, p. 202.
5. Ibid., p. 204.
6. Ibid.
7. Mel Gussow, *New York Times*, November 21, 1983.
8. Keane, *Václav Havel*, pp. 311–15.
9. Havel, *Disturbing the Peace*, p. 64.
10. *Hra o sedmi obrazech* (a play in seven scenes): the word *obrazech* means "frames, images, pictures."
11. Havel, *Largo Desolato*, p. 56.
12. Ibid., p. 59.
13. Ibid., p. 59–60. In Tom Stoppard's version of *Largo Desolato*, he uses anglicized names for the characters. For the purpose of consistency, their original Czech names are used here when quoting from Stoppard's version.
14. Havel, *Disturbing the Peace*, p. 63.
15. Havel, *Largo Desolato*, pp. 46–47.
16. Ibid., p. 24.
17. Ibid., p. 41. "Nichols" is the translator's (Tom Stoppard's) anglicized substitution for "Urbánek," the Czech name Havel used in this speech.
18. Havel, *Disturbing the Peace*, p. 63.
19. Ibid., p. 64.
20. Jánská, "Muž, který objevil Václava Havla světu," p. 16.
21. Havel, *Disturbing the Peace*, p. 64.
22. Interview with Klaus Juncker by Bernd Michael Kraske, Hamburger Radio Sendung, May 25, 2000.
23. Jánská, "Muž, který objevil Václava Havla světu," p. 16.
24. Havel, "Z poznámek Václava Havla, psaných pro inscenátory hry *Largo Desolato*" (Annotations by Václav Havel for the producer of *Largo Desolato*), *O divadle* (About Theater), (1986) pp. 93–98.
25. Kisil, "Jan Grossman: Žít svůj osud."
26. Havel, *Disturbing the Peace*, p. 65.
27. Ibid.
28. Havel, *Largo Desolato*, p. 48.
29. Ibid., p. 56.
30. Interview with Gail Papp, September 30, 2002.
31. Ibid.
32. Interview with Jiřina Šiklová, October 28, 2002.
33. Interview with Vilém Prečan, October 30, 2002.

1985: *Temptation*

1. Director, in Václav Havel, *Temptation*, George Theiner, trans., in *Selected Plays 1984–1987*, p. 133.
2. Ivan Jirous, *Temptation*, from the Theatre on the Balustrade program of *Temptation*, December 1991.
3. Havel, *Disturbing the Peace*, p. 67.
4. Ibid.
5. Havel, Letter 17 (New Year's Eve, 1979) in *Letters to Olga*, p. 61.
6. Ibid., Letter 138 (July 25, 1982), p. 348.
7. Letter from Havel to Pavel Landovský, March 16, 1986, from the Theatre on the Balustrade program of *Temptation*, 1991.
8. Letter from Havel to Andrej Krob and Anna Freimanová, October 1986 (unpublished; included with the permission of Andrej Krob). Krob has this letter framed, and today it hangs on the wall of the living room in his dacha. "Andulko" is the dimunitive of Anna.
9. Ibid., p. 88.
10. Ibid., p. 92.
11. Ibid., p. 104.
12. Ibid.
13. Ibid., p. 133.
14. Ibid.
15. Ibid., p. 134.
16. Ibid., p. 85.
17. Havel, *Disturbing the Peace*, pp. 68–69.
18. Václav Havel, in "Dramatici o dramatu" (Dramatists About Drama), in *samizdat O divadle*, reprinted in *Almanach o divadle*, pp. 86–89, *Nakadatelství lidové noviny* 1990, pp. 58–59.
19. Letter from Havel to Pavel Landovský, March 16, 1986.
20. Interview with Anna Freimanová, June 25, 2001.
21. Ivan Jirous, "*Temptation*."
22. Ibid.
23. Interview with Jiřina Šiklová, October 28, 2002.

1986: "Far from the Theater"

1. Havel, "Daleko od divadla," p. 635.
2. Ibid., p. 636.
3. Irving Wardle, *Times* (London), October 14, 1986.
4. Jon Peter, *Sunday Times* (London), October 19, 1986.
5. Interview with Roger Michell, December 10, 2000.
6. Irving Wardle, *Times* (London), May 1, 1987.
7. Jon Peter, *Sunday Times* (London), May 3, 1987.

8. Jane Edwards, *Time Out*, May 4, 1988.

9. Milton Shulman, *Evening Standard* (London), April 28, 1988.

10. Keane, *Václav Havel*, p. 327.

11. Kriseová, *Václav Havel*, pp. 213–14.

12. Timothy Garten Ash, "Prague — a poem, not disappearing," in *Living in Truth*, p. 218.

13. Kriseová, *Václav Havel*, p. 208.

14. Foreword, *Living in Truth*, p. ix.

15. Havel, Letter 102 (November 14, 1981) in *Letters to Olga*, p. 248.

16. Zdeněk Urbánek, "Letter to a Prisoner" in *Living in Truth*, p. 286.

1987: *Redevelopment*

1. Second Inspector in Václav Havel, *Redevelopment*, James Saunders, trans., in *Selected Plays, 1984–1987*, p. 200.

2. Michael Simmons, *The Reluctant President* (London: Methuen, 1991), p. 157.

3. Václav Havel, *Redevelopment*, p. 147.

4. Ibid., p. 158.

5. Ibid., p. 168.

6. Ibid., p. 187.

7. Ibid., p. 189.

8. Ibid., p. 201–2.

9. Ibid., p. 206.

10. Kohout, *Morass*, in *The Vaněk Plays*, p. 120.

11. Ibid., p. 185.

12. Interview with Vilém Prečan, October 30, 2003.

13. Interview with Vlasta Gallerová and Karel Kříž, June 23, 2001.

1988: *Tomorrow We'll Start It Up*

1. Václav Havel, *Zítra to spustíme* (Tomorrow We'll Start It Up), *Spisy*/2, Tomaš Rychetsky, trans., p. 955.

2. Kriseová, *Václav Havel*, pp. 225–28.

3. Burian, *Modern Czech Drama*, p. 182.

4. Petr Oslzlý, "On Stage with the Velvet Revolution," *The Drama Review*, vol. 34, no. 3 (T127), fall 1990.

5. Havel, *Zítra to spustíme* (Tomorrow We'll Start It Up), p. 946.

6. Ibid., pp. 950–51.

7. One can't help but recall the greengrocer in "The Power of the Powerless," whom Havel had selected as the everyman of the essay.

8. Havel, *Zítra to spustíme* (Tomorrow We'll Start It Up), pp. 968–69.

9. Ibid., pp. 975–76.

10. It was the widely held view that the revolution was a natural outcome of historical inevitability. Woodrow Wilson saw that the Austro-Hungarian empire was collapsing; he already championed the idea of self-determination of the small central European nations, and of course Masaryk was fighting for this. The Czechoslovak Republic was already recognized by the Western countries before October 28, 1918 in the Washington declaration, so it was just a question of how to conduct the revolution within the Czechoslovakian governmental structure itself.

11. Havel, *Zítra to spustíme* (Tomorrow We'll Start It Up), pp. 954–55.

12. Interview with Václav Havel, March 13, 2002.

1988–1989: Prologue for a Revolution

1. Havel, *Zítra to spustíme* (Tomorrow We'll Start It Up), p. 958.

2. Interview with Petr Oslzlý, June 21, 2001.

3. Interview with Václav Havel, March 13, 2002.

4. Kriseová, *Václav Havel,* pp. 228–29.

5. D. K., review of *Tomorrow We'll Start It Up* in *Rovnost* (Equality), October 25, 1988.

6. Interview with Petr Oslzlý, June 21, 2001.

7. Petr Oslzlý, "On Stage with the Velvet Revolution," p. 103.

8. Kriseová, *Václav Havel,* p. 241.

9. Oslzlý, "On Stage with the Velvet Revolution," p. 103.

10. Interview with Petr Oslzlý, June 21, 2001.

November–December 1989: Writing and Staging a Revolution

1. Havel, foreword to *The Art of the Impossible: Politics as Morality and Practice,* Paul Wilson, trans., (New York: Fromm International, 1994), p. xi.

2. Havel, in "Not Only About Theatre," a discussion between playwright Václav Havel, Arthur Miller, and Tom Stoppard; Ronald Harwood Chairman, published in *Czech Theatre,* vol. 9, 1995, p. 48.

3. For an in-depth view of this plot, see the BBC documentary "Czechmate: Inside the Revolution," aired May 30, 1990.

4. Kriseová, *Václav Havel,* p. 249.

5. "Profile: Václav Havel, Czechoslovakia's Inspiration," *The Independent,* Saturday, November 25, 1989.

6. Keane, *Václav Havel,* p. 366.

Opening Night

1. Havel, address at New York University, October 27, 1991, in *The Art of the Impossible,* p. 83.

2. "Proč Havel?" (Why Havel?), video documentary narrated by Miloš Forman (Praha: Les Productions La Fete Inc., 1990).
3. Václav Havel, introduction to *Summer Meditations*, Paul Wilson, trans. (New York: Vintage Books, 1993), p. xv.
4. Havel, "New Year's Address to the Nation," Prague, January 1, 1990, in *The Art of the Impossible*, pp. 3–9.

PART V: THE NINETIES AND BEYOND: POLITICS AND THEATER AS ONE

Background information has been obtained from the following sources, among others: Helena Albertová, *Václav Havel: A Citizen and a Playwright* (Prague: Theatre Institute, 1999); and interviews with Václav Havel, Ivan Havel, Jan Burian, Miloš Forman, Anna Freimanová, Vladimír Just, Andrej Krob, Andrea Landovská, and Jiří Ornest.

1. Václav Havel, address to a Joint Session of the U.S. Congress, Washington, D.C., February 21, 1990, in *The Art of the Impossible*, p. 17.
2. Václav Havel, address to the Academy of Performing Arts, Prague, October 4, 1996, in ibid., p. 249.
3. Havel to Klaus Juncker, from interview with Klaus Juncker.

Curtain Up

1. Interview with Miloš Forman, January 31, 2003.
2. David Remnick, "Exit Havel," *The New Yorker*, February 17 and 24, 2003, p. 92.

1990–1992: Havelmania

1. Vladimír Just, *Literární noviny* (Literary News), May 17, 1990.
2. Plzák in Havel, *The Garden Party*, p. 13. Note: In this translation, the character's name is Falk.
3. Interview with Andrea Landovská, May 22, 2002.
4. Vladimír Procháska, *Rudé právo*, January 16, 1990.
5. Interview with Pavel Landovský, June 22 and 24, 2001.
6. Vladimír Procháska, *Rudé právo*.
7. Jan Reinisch, *Mladá fronta*, January 13, 1990.
8. Jan Foll, *Scéna* (Stage), February 7, 1990.
9. J. S., *Svobodné slovo*, January 17, 1991.
10. Petr Gabal, *Smena*, January 13, 1990.
11. Lou Brockway, from an interview with Martina Hublová, *Expres Magazine*, March 9, 1990.

12. Interview with Dr. Alexandra Brabcová, October 30, 2002.

13. Interview with Mel Gussow, March 27, 2003.

14. Sergej Machonin, "Václav Havel podruhé" (Twice Havel), *Literární noviny*, May 17, 1990.

15. Jiří Hájek, *Rudé právo*, May 15, 1990.

16. Interview with Vlasta Gallerová and Karel Kříž, June 23, 2001.

17. Zdeněk Tichý, *Lidové noviny* (People's News), April 2, 1900.

18. Ibid.

19. Z. Pšenicová, *Večerní Praha* (Evening Prague), April 9, 1990.

20. Vladimír Just, *Literární noviny*, May 17, 1990.

21. Ibid.

22. Kisil, "Jan Grossman: Žít svůj osud."

23. Přemysl Rut, *Lidové Noviny*, May 17, 1990.

24. Jiří Hájek, in "Třikrát Václav Havel" (Thrice Havel), *Rudé právo*, May 15, 1990.

25. Václav Havel, interview with Josef Holý in *Rudé právo*, March 25, 1992.

26. Interview with Jiřina Šiklová, October 28, 2002.

27. Zdeněk Tichý, *Lidové noviny*, May 4, 1990.

28. Sergej Machonin, "Václav Havel podruhé."

29. Jiří Hájek, "Třikrát Václav Havel."

30. Pavla Matějů, *Mladá fronta*, June 19, 1990.

31. Miroslav Sára, *Občanský deník*, June 23, 1990.

32. Pavel Doležel, *Rovnost* (Equality), March 23, 1991.

33. Interview with Achim Benning.

34. Interview with Klaus Juncker, October 27, 2002.

35. Mel Gussow, *New York Times*, March 9, 1990.

36. Josef Holý, *Rudé právo*, January 27, 1992.

Return to the Theatre on the Balustrade

1. Havel, "Daleko od divadla," p. 637.

2. Zdeněk Tichý, *Lidové noviny*, December 28, 1991.

3. Martin Nezval, *Mladá fronta dnes*, December 20, 1991.

The Coming of Age of Theatre on the Road

1. Andrej Krob, *Divadlo na tahu 1975–1995* (Praha: Originální videojournal, 1995), p. 6.

2. Ibid., p. 4.

3. Interview with Andrej Krob, May 17, 2001.

4. Krob, *Divadlo na tahu*, p. 2.

5. Interview with Ivan Havel, May 23, 2002.

6. Krob, *Divadlo na tahu*, p. 35.

7. Sergej Machonin, *O divadle*, vol. 2, April 1988.

8. Přemysl Rut, *Literární noviny*, November 7, 1991.

9. Sergej Machonin, *Literární noviny*, November 7, 1991.

10. Richard Erml, *Český deník* (Czech Daily), October 16, 1991.

11. Sommerová, "A znovu Žebrácká opera."

12. Interview with Anna Freimanová, June 25, 2001.

13. Interview with Andrej Krob, May 17, 2001.

14. Marie Reslová, *Respekt*, February 12, 1996

15. Josef Mlejnek, *Česky deník*, December 3, 1992.

16. Blanka Kubičková, *Denní telegraf* (Daily Telegraph), November 13, 1993.

17. Jana Machalická, *Lidová demokracie*, November 5, 1993.

18. Kubičková, *Denní telegraf.*

19. Jana Machalická, *Lidová demokracie.*

20. Jiří Gordon, *Listy pro Moravu a Slezsko-Svoboda* (newspapers for Moravia and Slezsko-Svoboda), December 17, 1992.

21. Havel, in Sommerová, "A znovu Žebrácká opera."

22. Vladimír Just, *Literární noviny*, November 16, 1995.

23. Marie Reslová, *Respekt*, February 12, 1996.

24. Interview with Jiří Ornest, October 29, 2002.

25. Sommerová, "A znovu Žebrácká opera."

26. Martina Klapalová, *Mladá fronta dnes*, October 30, 1996.

27. Josef Mlejnek, *Lidové noviny*, November 5, 1996.

28. Richard Erml, *Mladá fronta dnes*, May 11, 1996.

29. Krob, *Divadlo na tahu*, p. 67.

30. Interview with Miloš Forman, January 31, 2003.

31. Luboš Pistorius, "O Václavu Havlovi divadelníkovi" (On Václav Havel, Playwright), in *Milý Václave . . . Tvůj*, pp. 106–7.

32. Interview with Anna Freimanová, June 25, 2001.

33. Krob, *Divadlo na tahu*, p. 1.

34. Marie Reslová, "Divadlo na tahu" (Theatre on the Road), *Divadlo*, vol. 12, 1996, p. 26.

35. Interview with Anna Freimanová, June 25, 2001.

1993: After Havelmania

1. Gordon, *Listy pro Moravu a Slezsko-Svoboda.*

2. Havel, Letter 115 (February 13, 1982) in *Letters to Olga.*

3. Havel, in interview for the taping of *Zítra to spustíme* (Tomorrow We'll Start It Up), director: Viktor Polesný, dramaturg: Petr Oslzlý; Ćeská televize 92, Televizní studio, Brno.

4. Havel, *Zítra to spustíme* (Tomorrow We'll Start It Up), p. 971.

5. Rocamora, "A Glimmer of Satire Amidst Freedom's Obscurities," *New York Times*, arts and leisure section, December 17, 2000.

6. Bronislav Pražan, *Rozhlas* (Broadcast), vol. 21, 1997.

7. Vladimír Mikulka, *Denní telegraf*, April 9, 1997.

8. Jiří Kříž, *Právo* (Law), April 1, 1997.

9. Interview with Jiří Ornest, October 29, 2002.

2000: In Search of a New Play by Václav Havel

1. Havel, Letter 102 (November 14, 1981) in *Letters to Olga*, p. 249.

2. Interview with Jan Burian, June 20, 2001.

3. Zdeněk Tichý, *Mladá fronta dnes*, February 12, 2000.

4. Radmila Hrdinová, *Právo*, February 14, 2000.

5. Irina Svobodová, *Literární noviny*, March 1, 2000.

6. Eva Jeníková for *Zemědělské noviny*, February 3, 2000.

7. Interview with Zdeněk Tichý in *Mladá fronta dnes*, Feburary 1, 2000.

8. Interview with Jan Burian, June 20, 2001.

2003: Havel and the Theater Today

1. Havel, introduction to *Living in Truth*, p. xiv.

2. Rocamora, "A Glimmer of Satire."

3. Ibid.

4. Ibid.

5. Ibid.

6. Burian, *Modern Czech Theatre*, pp. 225–26.

7. Interview with Václav Havel, March 13, 2002.

8. Václav Havel, address to a Joint Session of the U.S. Congress, Washington, D.C., February 21, 1990, in *The Art of the Impossible*, p. 11.

King Lear

1. Havel, *Disturbing the Peace*, p. 205.

2. Havel, in an interview with Josef Holý, *Rudé právo*, March 25, 1992.

3. Rocamora, "A Glimmer of Satire."

4. Interview with Michael Billington, June 20, 2003.

5. Rocamora, "A Glimmer of Satire."

6. Pavel Seifter, at a symposium on Václav Havel, Orange Tree Theatre, February 9, 2003.

7. Interview with Miloš Forman, January 31, 2003.

8. Interview with Michael Billington, June 20, 2003.

PART VI: EPILOGUE

Background information for this part has been obtained from the following sources, among others: interviews with Edward Albee, Achim Benning, and Sam Walters and correspondence with Harold Pinter and Tom Stoppard.

1. Arthur Miller, *I think about you a great deal*, in *Living in Truth*, p. 265.

I Think About You a Great Deal: Albee, Beckett, Miller, Pinter, Stoppard

1. Samuel Beckett, *Catastrophe*, in *Collected Shorter Plays* (New York: Grove Press, 1984), pp. 297–99.
2. Ibid., pp. 300–301.
3. Mel Gussow, *New York Times*, June 19, 1983.
4. Karel Kyncl, "Havel, Beckett: The Intolerable Shirt of Fame," *The Independent*, December 30, 1989.
5. Letter from Samuel Beckett to Havel, May 29, 1983 (unpublished; quoted with the permission of Klaus Juncker).
6. Kyncl, "Havel, Beckett."
7. Ibid.
8. Ibid.
9. Arthur Miller, *I think about you a great deal*, pp. 263–65.
10. Ibid.
11. Arthur Miller, *The Crucible* (New York: Penguin Books, 1952), p. 133.
12. Tynan, *Show People*, p. 120.
13. Tom Stoppard, né Tom Straussler, was born on July 3, 1937, in Zlin, Czechoslovakia. While Havel's family remained in the country, Stoppard's family moved to Singapore in 1939 to escape the Nazis. Shortly before the Japanese invasion of Singapore in 1941, young Tom fled to Darjeeling, India, with his mother and brother. His father, Eugene Straussler, remained behind and was killed during the invasion. In 1946, the family emigrated to England after Tom's mother married Kenneth Stoppard, a major in the British army.
14. Tom Stoppard, introduction to *Professional Foul*, in *Two Plays* by Tom Stoppard (New York: Grove Press, 1978), p. 8.
15. Nadel, *Double Life*, p. 277.
16. Stoppard, introduction to *Professional Foul*, p. 9.
17. Nadel, *Double Life*, p. 278.
18. Stoppard, *Professional Foul*, p.p. 90–91.
19. Ibid., p. 93.
20. Ibid., p. 78.
21. Ibid.
22. Stoppard wrote other plays dealing with the dissidents' dilemma, too, including *Cahoot's Macbeth*, a minitravesty of Pavel Kohout's *Play Macbeth*,

which Kohout had written for *bytové divadlo* (living-room theater) in the 1970s and performed at Vlasta Chramostova's apartment.

23. Stoppard, "Letter to the Editor," in *Times* (London), February 7, 1977.

24. Tom Stoppard, "Dirty Linen in Prague," *New York Times*, February 11, 1977. The reference — "a weasel is not a bloody whale" — is to Polonius's speech in *Hamlet*, act 3, scene ii.

25. Kenneth Tynan, *Show People*, p. 120.

26. Tom Stoppard, "Prague: The Story of the Chartists," *New York Review of Books,* August 4, 1977, p. 15.

27. Nadel, *Double Life*, p. 287.

28. Ibid.

29. Ibid.

30. Ibid., p. 284.

31. Ibid, p. 287.

32. Ibid., p. 410.

33. Klára Hůrková, *Mirror Images*, p. 25.

34. Havel, Letter 58 (December 6, 1980) in *Letters to Olga*, pp. 136–37.

35. "Not Only About Theater," p. 42.

36. Letter from Harold Pinter to Carol Rocamora, December 22, 2002.

37. Susan Hollis Merritt, *Pinter in Play* (Durham: Duke University Press, 1990), pp. 176–77.

38. Letter from Harold Pinter.

39. Interview with Edward Albee, November 7, 2002.

40. Mel Gussow, *Edward Albee: A Singular Journey* (New York: Simon & Schuster, 1999), p. 333.

41. Interview with Wendy Luers, November 22, 2002.

42. Interview with Edward Albee, November 7, 2002.

43. Ibid.

44. The 1960s was a prolific decade for Pinter, Stoppard, and Albee, during which their early dramatic works paralleled Havel's. In 1963, there were premieres of both Havel's and Stoppard's very first full-length plays: Havel's *The Garden Party* in Prague, and Stoppard's *A Walk on the Water* in Bristol (later rewritten and retitled *Enter a Free Man*). Stoppard's second play, *Rosencrantz and Guildenstern Are Dead*, premiered at the Royal Shakespeare Company in 1967 — between Havel's second and third plays, *The Memorandum* (1965) and *The Increased Difficulty of Concentration* (1968). Pinter's *The Dumb Waiter* and *The Caretaker* (his first full-length play) were both written in 1960. *The Collection* (1962) and *The Homecoming* (1965) followed. Albee's earliest plays were *The Zoo Story* (1958), *The Sandbox* (1959), and *The American Dream* (1960), followed by *Who's Afraid of Virginia Woolf* (1962) and *A Delicate Balance* (1966).

45. Susan Hollis Merritt, "The Outsider in Pinter and Havel," in *Pinter at Sixty*, eds. Katherine H. Burkman and John L. Kundert-Gibbs (Bloomington: Indiana University Press, 1993), pp. 64–72.

Homes Away from Home

1–13. Interview with Achim Benning, October 9, 2002. Quotes are from this interview.

14. Sam Walters, program notes, *The Memorandum*, Orange Tree Theatre (March 23–April 29, 1995).

15. Interview with Sam Walters, October 25, 2002.

16. *Morning Star* (London), March 4, 1977.

17. Anne Morley-Priestman, *Entertainment Scene*, March 23, 1979.

18. *Richmond & Twickenham Times*, March 25, 1977.

19. Interview with Sam Walters, October 25, 2002.

20. Irving Wardle, *Times* (London), March 21, 1977.

21. *Richmond Herald*, April 21, 1977.

22. Interview with Sam Walters, October 25, 2002.

23. Michael Billington, *Guardian* (Manchester), October 30, 1978.

24. J. M., *Richmond Herald*, November 2, 1978.

25. Michael Billington, *Guardian* (Manchester), September 20, 1980.

26. Alan Franks, *Times* (London), October 3, 1980.

27. Interview with Sam Walters, October 25, 2002.

28. *Richmond & Twickenham Times*, October 10, 1980.

29. Edward Pearce, *Daily Telegraph* (London), February 9, 1987.

30. Mark Sanderson, *Time Out*, February 11, 1987.

31. Sam Walters, program notes, *The Memorandum*.

32. Charles Osborne, *Daily Telegraph* (London), September 24, 1990.

33. Jeremy Kingston, *Times* (London), September 20, 1990.

34. Peter Sherwood, *Times Literary Supplement*, no. 1034, September 28–October 4, 1990.

35. Interview with Sam Walters, October 25, 2002.

36. Billington, *Guardian* (Manchester), March 30, 1995.

37. Jeremy Kingston, *Times* (London), March 29, 1995.

38. Michael Billington, *Guardian* (Manchester), January 20, 2003.

39. Benedict Nightingale, *Times* (London), January 18, 2003.

40. Michael Billington, *Guardian* (Manchester), January 20, 2003.

41. Charles Spencer, *The Telegraph*, January 22, 2003.

42. Interview with Sam Walters, October 25, 2002.

43. Sam Walters, program notes, production of *The Beggar's Opera*, January–February 2003, Orange Tree Theatre.

44. Interview with Michael Billington, June 20, 2003.

45. Epstein, *Joe Papp*, p. 6.

PART VII: CURTAIN CALL
Encore
1. Havel, "A Farewell to Politics," *New York Review of Books*, p. 44.

A Legacy
1. Havel, "A Farewell to Politics," p. 4.
2. Anna Freimanová, introduction to *Milý Václave . . . Tvůj*, pp. 8–9.
3. Havel, introduction to *Václav Havel as a Dramatist*, Jiří Fukač, ed., Zdenka Pospíšilová, and Alena Mizerová (Prague: Compostela Group of Universities, 2001), p. 21.
4. Havel, Letter 37 (June 22, 1980) in *Letters to Olga*, p. 92.
5. Kenneth Tynan, "The Theatre Abroad: Prague," p. 105.
6. Sommerová, "A znovu *Žebrácká opera*."
7. Havel, interview with Josef Holý in *Rudé právo*.
8. Ibid.
9. Paul Trensky, "*The Garden Party* Revisited," *Critical Essays*, p. 161.
10. Edward Albee, *The American Dream*, in *Two Plays by Edward Albee* (New York: Signet, 1961), p. 86.
11. Havel, address to the Academy of Performing Arts, in *The Art of the Impossible*, p. 251.
12. Havel, Letter 80 (May 16, 1981) in *Letters to Olga*, p. 198.
13. Havel, introduction to *Václav Havel as a Dramatist*, p. 21.
14. Interview with Václav Havel.
15. The term *superfluous man* was first used by Pushkin to describe his hero, Eugene Onegin, and was popularized by Turgenev in the title of his novel, *Diary of a Superfluous Man*. The prototype is considered to be Byron's Childe Harold. Lermontov's Pechorin from *A Hero of Our Times* falls into this literary category, as does Turgenev's Rudin. Chekhov's Ivanov also shares some of these characteristics.
16. In Czech, the line is *Jsi bačkora*, literally translated as "You are a coward." In his version, "Some hero . . . ," Tom Stoppard captures the essence of Havel's intent.
17. Interview with Václav Havel.
18. Interview with Jiří Ornest, May 12, 2001.
19. Havel, "Light on a Landscape, in *The Vaněk Plays*, pp. 238–39.
20. Introduction to *The Vaněk Plays*, p. xviii.
21. A reading of the essay "The Power of the Powerless" is essential for an appreciation of Havel's profile of a dissident. In it, Havel debunks the elitist notion that is widely held by many and takes an ordinary greengrocer as an example of an everyman, who, by living in truth, can become a dissident.

From her own reading of Havel's essay, Professor Goetz-Stankiewicz offers a succinct summary of Havel's definition of a dissident:

> Havel's main points are the following: Firstly, such persons make their critical opinions known publicly, albeit within the severely limited possibilities at their disposal. Secondly, they have reached a stage in which they are taken more or less seriously by their government, and even their persecution causes certain complications for this government. Thirdly, their critical engagement extends beyond a narrow circle and has therefore taken on a political character. Fourthly, these people are for the most part intellectuals (Havel calls them "men of the pen") whose only political means is their writing; the attempts of others, namely, nonwriters, to "live in truth" rarely penetrate beyond their country's borders and are by and large unknown in the West. Fifthly, Westerners refer more frequently to the political engagement of these people than to their activity as writers. Havel himself knows from personal experience that at some point — and he did not realize exactly when this came about — people in the West began to regard him less as a writer than as a "dissident" who in his spare time also wrote some plays. (Marketa Goetz-Stankiewicz, introduction to *The Vaněk Plays*, p. xxiv.)

22. Interview with Václav Havel.
23. Havel, "Light on a Landscape," in *The Vaněk Plays*, p. 238.
24. Interview with Václav Havel.
25. Kohout, "The Chaste Centaur," in *The Vaněk Plays*, p. 242.
26. Ibid., p. 243.
27. Shakespeare, *Hamlet*, III, ii.
28. Krob, in Sommerová, "A znovu *Žebrácká opera*."
29. Interview with Miloš Forman, January 31, 2003.
30. Havel, "Second Wind," in *Good-bye, Samizdat*, p. 207.
31. Helena Albertová, "Exhibition," in *Václav Havel: A Citizen and a Playwright* (Prague: Theatre Institute, 1999), p. 32.

A Place in Twentieth-Century Drama

1. Tynan, *Show People*, p. 75.
2. Harold Clurman, in *New York Magazine,* June 3, 1968, *The Collected Works of Harold Clurman* (Applause Theatre Books, 1994), p. 697.
3. Martin Esslin, *The Theatre of the Absurd* (Penguin, 1980), p. 324.
4. Esslin, introduction to *Three East European Plays* (Harmondsworth, U.K.: Penguin, 1970), p. 16.
5. Interview with Václav Havel.
6. Havel, address at the Hebrew University, Jerusalem, April 26, 1990, in *The Art of the Impossible*, pp. 29–30
7. Franz Kafka, entry on January 8, 1914, in *Diaries 1910–1923* (New York: Schocken Books, 1988), p. 252.

8. Havel, *Largo Desolato*, p. 29.

9. Havel, address at The Hebrew University, in *The Art of the Impossible*, p. 31.

10. Havel, Letter 102 (November 14, 1981) in *Letters to Olga*, p. 248.

11. Samuel Beckett, "Dante . . . Bruno . . . Vico . . . Joyce," (1929) in *Disjecta: Miscellaneous Writings and a Dramatic Fragment*, Ruby Cohn, ed. (London: John Calder Publishers, Ltd., 1983), p. 27.

12. Milan Kundera, "Candide Had to Be Destroyed," in *Living in Truth*, pp. 259–60.

13. Interview with Václav Havel.

14. Kundera, "Candide Had to be Destroyed," pp. 259–60.

15. Marketa Goetz-Stankiewicz, introduction to *Critical Essays*, p. 6.

16. Havel, *Disturbing the Peace*, p. 6.

17. Havel, in "Not Only About Theater," *Czech Theatre*, vol. 9, 1995, p. 41.

18. Havel, *Disturbing the Peace*, p. 54.

19. Ibid., pp. 53–54.

20. Ibid.

21. Interview with Michael Billington, June 20, 2003,

22. Interview with Václav Havel.

23. Tom Stoppard, introduction to *The Memorandum*, in *Living in Truth*, p. 278.

24. Simmons, *The Reluctant President*, p. 217.

25. Interview with Miloš Forman, January 31, 2003.

26. Esslin, introduction to *Three East European Plays*, p. 13.

27. Philip Roth, *Shop Talk* (New York: Houghton Mifflin Company, 2001), p. 71.

28. Interview with Zdeněk Hořínek, March 12, 2002.

29. Interview with Edward Albee, November 7, 2002.

30. Interview with Michael Simmons, February 6, 2003.

31. Interview with Miloš Forman, January 31, 2003.

32. Václav Havel, "Politics and the Theatre," *Times Literary Supplement*, September 28, 1967.

33. Havel, in "Not Only About Theater," p. 43.

34. Ibid.

35. Interview with Achim Benning, October 9, 2002.

More Than a Body of Dramatic Work

1. Havel, in "Ještě jednou obrození?" (Yet Another National Revival?) in *Divadlo*, vol. 20, no. 1, January, 1969, p. 110.

2. Havel, in "Not Only About Theater," p. 40.

3. Havel, Letter 103 (November 21, 1981) in *Letters to Olga*.

4. Ibid., Letter 107 (December 19, 1981), pp. 260–61.

5. Havel in "Not Only About Theater," p. 46.

6. Havel, Letter 102 (November 14, 1981) in *Letters to Olga*, pp. 247–48.

7. Ibid., p. 249.

8. Interview with Roger Michell, December 10, 2000. (British director Michell described Havel as "a hippie in aspic.")

9. Havel, *Disturbing the Peace*, p. 72.

10. Václav Havel, "A Farewell to Politics," p. 4. Here, "poet" can be interpreted in the classical meaning, i.e., also referring to playwrights.

11. Havel, *Audience*, p. 209.

12. Havel, *Zítra to spustíme* (Tomorrow We'll Start It Up), p. 955.

13. Interview with Zdeněk Hořínek, October 29, 2002.

14. Shakespeare, *As You Like It*, II, vii.

15. Interview with Miloš Forman, January 31, 2003.

16. Merrit, *Pinter at Sixty*, p. 66.

17. Havel, *Largo Desolato*, p. 23.

18. "Proč Havel?"

19. Roth, *Shop Talk*, p. 70.

Final Bow

1. Havel, "A Farewell to Politics," p. 4.

2. Ibid.

3. Václav Havel, remarks after delivery of the speech "A Farewell to Politics," Graduate Center of the City University of New York, September 19, 2002.

Index

The Author

Dr. Carol Rocamora is a translator, playwright, and teacher. Her three volumes of the complete translated dramatic works of Anton Chekhov have been published by Smith and Kraus (1996–1999). Her new play, *"I take your hand in mine … ,"* based on the correspondence between Chekhov and Olga Knipper, also published by Smith and Kraus, premiered in September 2001 at the Almeida Theatre in London and opened in Paris in October 2003 at Peter Brook's Theatre des Bouffes du Nord under his direction.

Dr. Rocamora is the recipient of the David Payne Carter Award for Teaching Excellence at New York University's Tisch School of the Arts, where she is currently a faculty member in the Department of Dramatic Writing. She is also the founder of the Philadelphia Festival Theatre for New Plays at Annenberg Center, an independent, nonprofit professional theater. She has written about theater for *The Nation* and the *New York Times.* She is a graduate of Bryn Mawr College and received her M.A. and Ph.D. degrees from the University of Pennsylvania.